# D E S I G N   W I T H   C L I M A T E

## bioclimatic approach to architectural regionalism

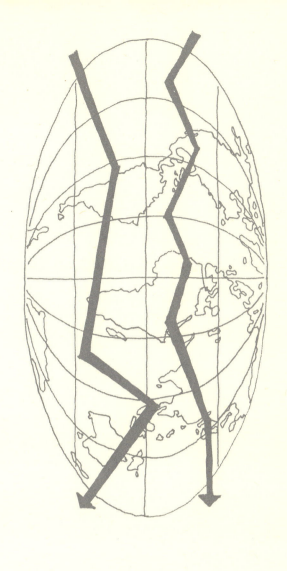

# DESIGN WITH CLIMATE

## BIOCLIMATIC APPROACH TO ARCHITECTURAL REGIONALISM

### VICTOR OLGYAY

some chapters based on cooperative
research with ALADAR OLGYAY

PRINCETON UNIVERSITY PRESS
PRINCETON, NEW JERSEY

# PREFACE AND ACKNOWLEDGMENTS

THE problem of controlling his environment and creating conditions favorable to his aims and activities is as old as man himself. Through the ages men have sought, in the building of shelter, to fulfill two basic human needs—protection from the elements and provision of an atmosphere favorable to spiritual endeavor. House design has reflected, throughout its history, the different solutions advanced by each period to the continuing problem of securing a small controlled environment within a large-scale natural setting—too often beset by adverse forces of cold, heat, wind, water, and sun.

Each epoch seems to have had its own philosophy of house design; the past thus provides us with a rich fabric of experience, symbolized in man's dwellings. This is delightfully documented wherever the architectural crystallization of a period is a faithful mirror of its especial thought and feeling.

The architectural patterns familiar to Western civilization, however, have not often considered the problems and solutions inherent in buildings of distant regions and climates. With the widening spread of communications and populations, a new principle of architecture is called for, to blend past solutions of the problems of shelter with new technologies and insights into the effects of climate on human environment.

This book will endeavor to show the influence of climate on building principles. In this respect, architecture so far has been in a subjective trial-and-error stage; it must adopt the techniques of analytical reasoning to mature properly.

To meet the problem of climate control in an orderly and systematic way requires a pooling of effort by several sciences. The first step is to define the measure and aim of requirements for comfort. For this, the answer lies in the field of biology. The next is to review the existing climatic conditions, and this depends on the science of meteorology. Finally, for the attainment of a rational solution, the engineering sciences must be drawn upon. With such help, the results may then be synthesized and adapted to architectural expression.

Some architects may find this book too detailed for their immediate use in design. Some scientists will rightly find their own fields of research inadequately represented. But it is my hope that, in bridging these different fields, this study will combine both creative and analytical approaches to develop a unifying architectural concept.

My own interest in environmental effects stems from my work as an architect in preparing experimental building designs. The framework presented in this book is the result of my research over the past eight years. This research was aided by financial assistance from the federal Housing and Home Finance Agency, by a later grant from the Simon Guggenheim Foundation, and by support from Princeton University's Research Fund. The research was completed in the Architectural Laboratory of Princeton University's School of Architecture.

Here, first of all, tribute should be paid to my brother Aladar Olgyay, who shared in many of these investigations. The years spent together on the research problems were fruitful and productive. His work was concerned mainly with the subject of solar control, but many of the thoughts that he furthered, and graphs and drawings that he developed, appear in several chapters of this book. I record with regret that his interest later was drawn away to other architectural problems. With his continuing participation, the approach here presented would have been more complete in many respects.

As the work proceeded, papers on its different phases were published. The first article outlining the method was "The Temperate House" (1951),[1] which was followed by papers on "Bioclimatic Approach to Architecture"[2] and "Solar Control and Orientation to Meet Bioclimatical Requirements" (1952);[3] a more comprehensive edition treated the "Application of Climate Data to House Design" (1954).[4] Subsequently articles appeared on "Sol-Air Orientation"[5] and on "Environment and Building Shape" (1954),[6] and in 1957 the book *Solar Control and Shading Devices* was published.[7] This last, in abbreviated form, constitutes a chapter of this work, just as the previous discourses were molded into the general context of the present publication.

This work was inspired, sometimes by the interest of the unsolved problems themselves, sometimes by the stimulus of controversial opinions. I owe much directly or indirectly to many sources and authors: the initial encouragement of Dr. Paul Siple, the discussions with Dr. Maria Telkes, the advice of C. P. Yaglou, the comments of Dr. Douglass H. K. Lee, the sessions with the members of the Advisory Committee of M.I.T., James M. Fitch's book, *American Building: the Forces That Shape It*,[8] the approach of Ernst Egli in his book, *Climate* and Town Districts, Consequences and Demands,[9] the method of the experiments at Texas A. and M. College, the climate charts published by the American Institute of Architects, and the data and procedure of the American Society of Heating and Ventilating Engineers. All these gave impetus to the direction described here. However, those mentioned are only some of many who contributed help, criticism, and data that helped to shape and organize the material into a concept.

Although all debts can not be acknowledged, I wish to express my thanks to Robert W. McLaughlin, Director of Princeton's School of Architecture, who made it possible to bring this publication to its present form by his friendly understanding and encouragement. My gratitude for the benefit of their suggestions and aid is also due Francis A. Comstock, Associate Director of the School of Architecture, who took the burden of correcting the manuscript; Donlyn Lyndon for his help in arranging and organizing the material; and many students and visiting Fellows of the University who were engaged in various phases of the research proceedings, especially Peter Kovalski, Robert W. Heck, Philemon Sturges, Charles Hilgenhurst, Lutfi Zeren, and Dominique Gampert.

It is hoped that the thesis here presented— although only an exploratory step—will open new insights into the relationship of the climatic environment to housing, and will contribute to architecture by shedding light on some long-debated principles.

VICTOR OLGYAY

Princeton, 1962

# CONTENTS

PART **1** CLIMATIC APPROACH

1. Urner Boden, Central Switzerland.

# 1. GENERAL INTRODUCTION

## THE EARTH AND LIFE

The full spectrum of earth's arena ranges from the rigor of the cold blues to the oppression of the torrid reds, and only the restful hues near green are associated with life. The bluish-white of icecaps in the polar regions blends into a brownish-green where vegetation makes its first stand in the tundra. This gives way to the dark green coniferous belt of the cold zone, which merges southward with the broad-leaved deciduous trees of the fertile temperate region. Further down, the warm middle latitudes are marked with the sparsely inhabited yellowish-reds of the desert areas, and the tones finally deepen into the lush green of the permanent verdure around the equatorial belt.

Surrounded by oceans, the great land masses are relieved by heights and depths of mountains, plains, and plateaus, and enlivened by veins of rivers and networks of streams and lakes. On and beneath the surface lie the meager or abundant soils and minerals which make life prosperous or infertile.[1]

There is a discipline, however, imposed on this complexity. The revolution of the globe gives the heartbeat of day and night which regulates the activities and reposes of natural life. The tilted rotation of the earth around the sun sets the rhythm of the seasons, which call to life the dormant vegetation and donate the bounty of harvests. Whether each locale is cool or warm is largely determined by its relative distance from the equator; but the imperative regularity of the sun also sets the pace for the patterns of humidity and wind that sweep across the earth.

The features of the physical environment are blanketed by a vast ocean of air, whose tides carry climatic elements to all parts of the earth and are in turn modulated by them. Climate not only plays a great part in the composition of soils, but strongly affects the character of plants and animals in different regions and—most important from our point of view—man's energy.[2]

As life has arisen through the hidden aspects of natural laws, so for better or worse the rules of nature command that life make a close adjustment to natural background. The setting is impartial; it can be kind or cruel, but all living species must either adapt their physiology, through selection or mutation, or find other defenses against the impacts of environment.

## ANIMAL LIFE AND SHELTER

Mankind's physical flexibility and capacity for adaptation are relatively feeble compared to those of many animals, who possess natural defenses against a large range of unfavorable climates. Against the danger of dryness animals have a number of weapons, and to relive the impacts of excessive heat they use heightened transpiration. The bear, in cold weather, can reduce his metabolism through slumber. The bat can survive a change of its body temperature of 60 degrees. The elephant can cool its blood by moving its honeycombed ear. As cold arrives the mink grows a new fur coat. In the hostile territory of the desert many animals reverse their life rhythm, live by night, and tuck away underground at dawn. Some rabbit breeds place their burrows with efficient foresight in relation to water and wind.

Birds can regulate their body insulation by trapping minute air bubbles with their adjustable feathers. When hardship becomes excessive, they seek to change to an environment where food and warmth are more favorable for existence. Birds during their stay do not rely entirely on their ability to adapt, but enlarge this ability with their building habits,

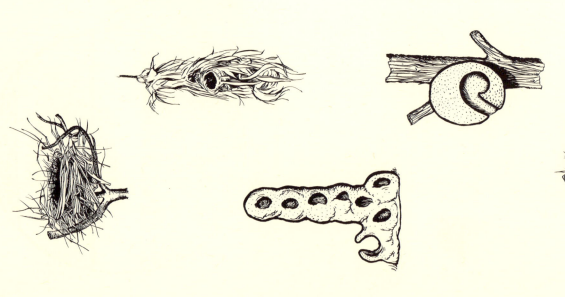

3. East (left) and south views of termites' nests.

with an innate instinct to cope with their environment. The varied forms and delicate patterns thus produced provide enlightening examples of the intuitive reconciliation of natural forces.

The open nest secures insulating qualities; the hanging nest utilizes the tensile strength of fibers, or grasses, and, pendulum-like, avoids the wind forces. The nest which is massively built from clay and straw prevents the intrusion of the direct sun and rain by its steep entrance. The vertical mud and straw nest is similar to apartment dwellings, where each opening is an individual nest comprised of two chambers. The first serves as an entrance foyer, the second an egg laying and hatching area. This very special form successfully avoids the nearly vertical sun rays, and minimizes the effect of precipitation. The mass of the earth can effectively relieve extreme temperature differences

and secures more stable heat conditions. Each solution is an effort, with a different approach, to cope with some main element of the climatic surroundings.[3]

These individual efforts for shelter are surpassed by the collective building of the insect world. Anthills vary with their surroundings; in temperate regions they are often found on southeast slopes, and elongated on a northeast-southwest axis to catch early morning warmth.[4] But in the tropics, the immense buildings of Hamitermes meridionalis ("compass termites") are blade-shaped and point due north. The east and west exposures help to secure an equable temperature; but, as with most mound-buildings, the large mass of earth stabilizes the caloric range.[5] Their towers are immense, reaching 400 times their body-length (10 mm), which translated into human terms would equal 2400 feet.

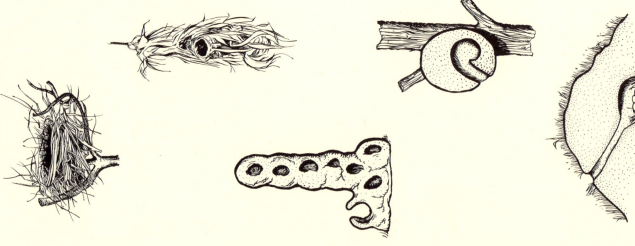

2. Bird nests to react against climatic impacts.

2

## HUMAN LIFE AND SHELTER

Mankind in the same environments encounters the same stresses as other fauna. From Aristotle to Montesquieu, many scholars believed that climate had pronounced effects on human physiology and temperament. More recently interest has centered on human energy in relation to environment. Ellsworth Huntington has hypothesized that climate ranks with racial inheritance and cultural development as one of the three great factors in determining the conditions of civilization.[6]

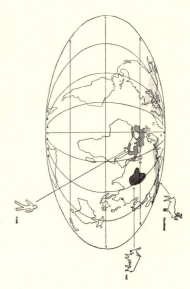

4. Early history habitat of man and animals.

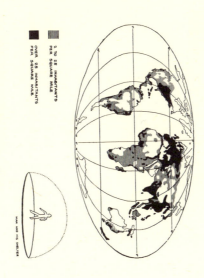

5. Present density of world population.

1 TO 25 INHABITANTS PER SQUARE MILE

OVER 25 INHABITANTS PER SQUARE MILE

MAN AND HIS SHELTER

6. Macrobius's climate zones.

According to him, man, who can apparently live in any region where he can obtain food, has strictly limited conditions under which his physical and mental energy (and even his moral character) can reach their highest development. He postulates optimum climate conditions for human progress:

1. average temperature ranges from somewhat below 40° F in the coldest months to nearly 70° F in the warmest months;

2. frequent storms or winds, to keep the relative humidity quite high except in hot weather, and provide rain at all seasons;

3. a constant succession of cyclonic storms which bring frequent moderate changes in temperature but are not severe enough to be harmful.

Another contemporary, Julian Huxley, relates human history to climate by comparing the incidence of early civilizations with that of dry and wet epochs.[7] He speculates that the biological and economic effects of the shifts in climatic belts hold the balance for populations.

## ADAPTATION OF SHELTER TO CLIMATE

Virgil wrote: "Five zones possess the sky, of which one is ever/red from blazing sun and ever burnt by fire."[8] Sacrobosco, in his *Sphaera Mundi*, projected these five celestial zones on the earth, and agreed that the central one was

Man's inventiveness enabled him to defy the rigors of his environment with fire for warmth and with furs for clothing. When the weakling among animals substituted Promethean inventiveness for the physical adaptation of other species, the shelter became his most elaborate defense against hostile climates. It enlarged the space of biological equilibrium and secured a favorable milieu for productivity. As the shelter evolved, accumulated experience and ingenuity diversified it to meet the challenges of widely varying climates.

When the belts shift, migrations are caused, which in turn bring not only wars but the fertilizing exchange of ideas necessary for the rapid advance of civilization.

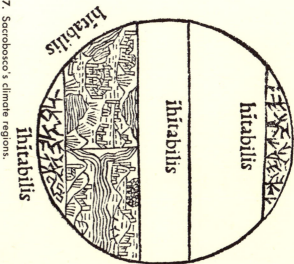

ihitabilis

hitabilis

ihitabilis

hitabilis

ihitabilis

7. Sacrobosco's climate regions.

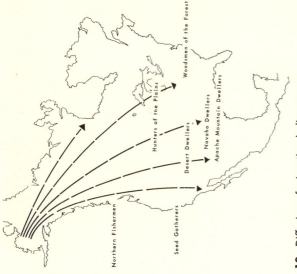

10. Diffusion of migrating Indian groups.

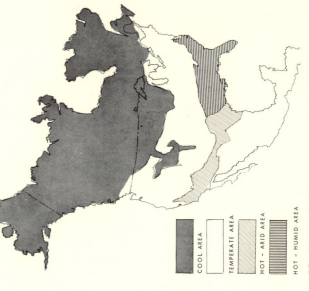

COOL AREA
TEMPERATE AREA
HOT - ARID AREA
HOT - HUMID AREA

11. Regional climate zones of the North American continent.

uninhabitable "because of the fervor of the sun. . . . But those two zones . . . about the poles of the world are uninhabitable because of too great cold, since the sun is far removed from them."[9] Hence, he concluded, only the temperate zones were fit for civilized habitation, and most of the classical world agreed with him.

Nevertheless, the ancients recognized that regional adaptation was an essential principle of architecture. Vitruvius said in *De Architectura*.[10] "For the style of buildings ought manifestly to be different in Egypt and Spain, in Pontus and Rome, and in countries and regions of various characters. For in one part the earth is oppressed by the sun in its course; in another part the earth is far removed from it; in another it is affected by it at a moderate distance."

In contemporary architectural thinking there are many approaches to man's physiological, as well as aesthetic, well-being. To treat climate as a primary factor is justifiable only if the thermal environment proves to be one of the influential factors on the architectural expression. Dr. Walter B. Cannon maintained that it is: "The development of a nearly thermostable state in our buildings should be regarded as one of the most valuable advances in the evolution of buildings."

One corroboration of this thesis is apparent when one considers the diverse housing forms developed by groups of similar ethnic background when they encountered widely varying climatic regions. It is generally agreed that the American Indians stemmed from Asia and that the waves of their migration across the Bering Strait established their populations from end to end of North and South America. As they spread throughout North America, the Indians entered into a broad variation of climatic environments, from the cold-cool northern territories to the warm-hot areas of the south, from the dry western areas to the humid parts of the southeast.

The tribes entering the cold zone encountered extreme cold and relatively scarce fuel. Under these circumstances, the conservation of heat became essential, so their shelters were compact, with a minimum of surface exposure. The Eskimo igloo is a well-known solution to the problem of survival in extreme cold. These low hemispherical shelters deflect the winds and take advantage of the insulating value of the snow that surrounds them. The smooth ice lining which forms on their interior surface is an effective seal against air seepage, and their tunnel exits are oriented away from

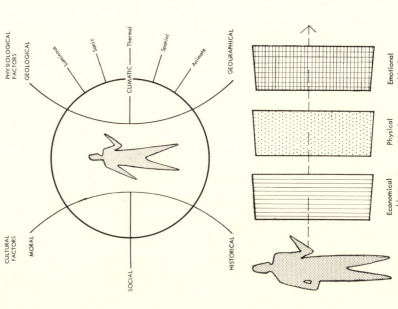

8-9. Factors influencing architectural expression.

the prevailing winds to reduce drafts and prevent the escape of warmed air. The heat retention of this type of structure makes it possible to maintain a temperature of 60° F inside when the exterior temperature is −50° F. Such structures may be heated by a small lamp supplemented by body heat.

The Pacific Coast tribes of British Columbia encountered a less extreme climate, although the need for heat conservation remained acute. To meet this demand these Indians adopted a form of communal living, as shown by the structure of the habitations of the Kwakiutl Indians. The homes of these tribes were joined together to reduce the exposed surfaces. The large plank-and-timber shelters were built as double shells, an arrangement that produced an insulating air space and provided an enclosed ambulatory between family units for the snowy winter months. In the summer the outer shell could be removed for ventilation. Further mutual benefit was achieved by the placing of fire pits within individual apartments along a center aisle, thus creating a concentrated heat source. In the Mackenzie Basin, shelters were constructed of bark and timber,

covered by low-pitched roofs with long poles anchored to the covering to retain the snow as an insulating blanket.

The temperate area, offering a naturally favorable climate, made fewer thermal demands on its inhabitants, and there is a corresponding diversity and freedom in the structures of these peoples. Unlike the communal groupings of the Pacific Coast, the villages of the eastern woodsmen and plains dwellers were freely organized and spread out, with peripheral units merging into the surrounding landscape. The typical dwelling unit of these tribes was the wigwam, a conical structure of poles covered by skin, which effectively shed wind and rain and was easily heated from a central source. It could be readily transported, an essential to migration.

In contrast, the hot-arid zone made extreme demands on the constructors of tribal dwellings. Characterized by excessive heat and glaring sun, this area requires that the shelter be designed to reduce heat impacts and provide shade. The southwestern tribes, like those far north of them, often built communal structures for mutual protection—in this case from

the heat. Structures such as the pueblo of San Juan were constructed of massive adobe roofs and walls, which have good insulative value and the capacity to delay heat impacts for long hours, thus reducing the daily heat peaks. They also used very small windows. By packing buildings together, the amount of exposed surface was reduced. Pueblo structures of this type usually extend on an east-west axis, thereby reducing morning and afternoon heat impacts on the two end walls in summer and receiving a maximum amount of south sun in the winter months when its heat is welcome.

The hot-humid area, on the other hand, presented two major problems to its inhabitants: the avoidance of excessive solar radiation and the evaporation of moisture by breezes. To cope with these problems, the southern tribes built their villages to allow free air movement, and the scattered individual units were mixed into the shade of surrounding flora. The Seminoles raised large gable roofs covered with grass to insulate against the sun and throw large areas of shadow over the dwellings, which had no walls. The steep angle and extensive overhang of these roofs protected against

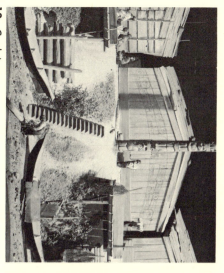

12. Cool Area.

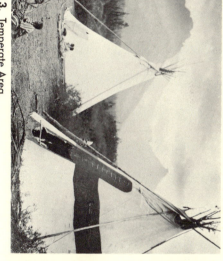

13. Temperate Area.

14. Hot-Arid area.

15. Hot-Humid area.

5

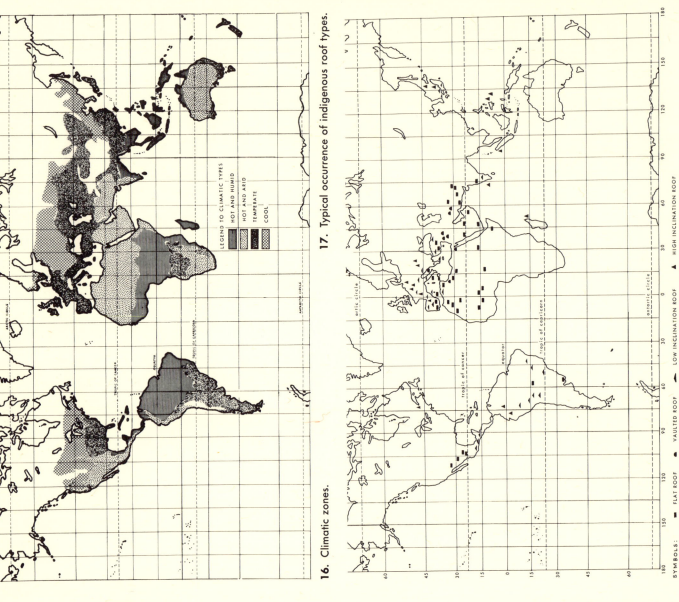

LEGEND TO CLIMATIC TYPES

▨ HOT AND HUMID
▨ HOT AND ARID
▨ TEMPERATE
▨ COOL

16. Climatic zones.

17. Typical occurrence of indigenous roof types.

SYMBOLS:  ■ FLAT ROOF  ◀ VAULTED ROOF  ▲ HIGH INCLINATION ROOF  ◀ LOW INCLINATION ROOF

rainfall, and the floors were elevated to keep them dry and to allow air circulation underneath.

As may be seen from these basic building forms used by the North American Indians in various regions, these people possessed a remarkable ability to adapt their dwellings to their particular environmental difficulties. An awareness of climate was integrated with innate craftsmanship to solve problems of comfort and protection. The results were building expressions of true regional character.

## SIMILARITIES AROUND THE WORLD

Although a global evaluation is beyond the scope of this book, the zones of climate can be traced around the earth. There are many systems for classifying them, but W. Köppen's is generally accepted. Using the relation of climate to vegetation as a criterion, he determined five basic climate zones: tropical-rainy, dry, warm-temperate, cool-snow-forest, and polar.[11] Some authors, such as Trewartha, offered modifications of these divisions based on the isotherms of the coldest months.[12] Since the detailed classifications are not directly applicable to housing, a simplified map based on Köppen's system is presented here.

For the architect's use "homoclimate," or human need, is the determining factor. That a thermostable condition has for centuries been the main goal of builders is corroborated by Jean Dollfus' sampling of characteristic dwellings around the world. He finds that building styles are defined less by national frontiers than by climate zones. Allowing for some variation in local taste and tradition, the general forms of native habitation are born of the environment.

In his first category, the great equatorial forest and tropical savannahs (Africa, Monsoon Asia, Australia, Polynesia, Amazon), he emphasizes that the roof is more essential than the

6

walls, which can be omitted altogether. Throughout this zone we find "timber skeletons, wood construction, branches, woven sticks, lath, thatch, and verdure."[13]

In cold northern forest and mountain regions, from the northwestern U.S. through Scandinavia and to the Himalayas, Dollfus groups houses of heavy timber with beam construction: These have low-pitched shingle or wooden roofs that allow dry snow to act as insulation.

In an intermediate zone, the walls consist of adobe construction covered with a thatched roof (West Africa, Andes), and here, too, are areas where nomads live in tents of felt or skins. Near to these is a great band of habitations (Mauretania, Gobi, Mexico) where the walls have a more important protecting role than the roof—in the arid zone of steppes and deserts. Here "the walls are built of stone, dried or baked clays supporting a flat roof of earth."

Between the bands of extreme climates, Dollfus divides the northern temperate zone on a line 45° N in Europe and 30° N in America. South of this, the walls constitute the principle element of the house and are built of bricks or stone and covered with slightly sloping roofs of semi-cylindrical tile (Mediterranean, Latin American, and Chinese regions). North of the line are some stone walls and a large amount of timber construction with the panels filled with mud, bricks or rough stone, or even paper. These house types have tall roofs, with an angle of 45° or more, covered with thatch or shingles.

Another significant factor that Dollfus notes: "The proportion of solid surfaces to openings in the exterior façades depends as much on popular psychology as on the climate and the materials used. In the zones of extreme temperature, for inverse reasons to safeguard against the sun or the cold, the walls are pierced only in a small proportion of their surface. And in general, rural interiors are much more stingy of air and light than those of the towns. . . . In northwest Europe the shade of urban streets sets the demand for more illumination, and it is in those gabled houses that windows attain their greatest development."[14]

It is evident that the roof is a determining element in the general form and appearance of regional house types. There is a marked correlation between zones of the climate map and the locales in which roof types commonly occur. Flat roofs appear in the hot zones, vaulted roofs are found in dry areas, and inclined roofs are found in the temperate climates with consistently dry summers. House types with higher roofs are used in the wet-temperate and cooler territories.

In the special case of the dome and vaulted roofs, the rounded form has been attributed to ancient philosophical motives.[15] It has also been suggested that it was easy to mold primitive domes with a branching tree as scaffold, or that the form is convenient where large timbers are scarce. But both domes and vaults are most popular in hot-arid regions with clear skies, where the low humidity leads to intense radiation exchange and creates extreme temperature variations between night and day. This has an underlying logic, probably discovered through centuries of experience: the envelope of a hemispherical vault is roughly three times the surface of its base, so the radiation of high sun positions is diluted on a rounded surface. This results in lower surface temperatures, which are further reduced by wind cooling. The rounded form is also suited to release the nocturnal outgoing radiation and facilitate nightly cooling. This is especially true in masonry construction, where the heavy building material, through its time lag in conducting heat, secures balanced daily thermal conditions.

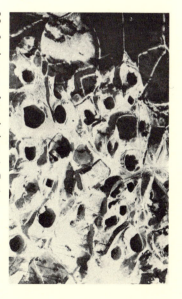

18. Settlement of troglodytes in Tunis.

19. Subterranean settlement in China.

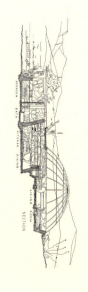

20-21. Soleri's house in Arizona.

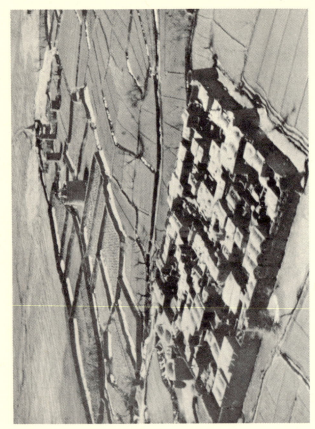

22. Village in Hot-Arid zone.

The importance of capacity insulation in extreme examples, which command a certain respect for their ingenuity, shows how concepts emerged under excessive stresses of similar nature. The habitats far away from each other, but the common denominator is low humidity with intense sun and heat, and they led to an obvious and rational solution in the cave principle. The Tunisian troglodytes of Matmata have their subterranean chambers located around open central wells, which appear on the surface in a complex organic community pattern. The more geometric-minded Chinese of Honan cut their dwellings 30 to 45 feet into the loess and reached them through hook-shaped stairs. Those solutions, however extreme, have their logical reasons. A mass of earth below the surface retains temperatures close to the yearly average, rendering relative warmth in winter and coolness in summer. This principle has its respectable followers today who advocate the Lithosphere house types. A contemporary version of earth-cooled temperature moderation shows how time-proved principles can be integrated and adapted in the light of contemporary knowledge to similar hot-arid regions.

From examples we find a remarkable correspondence between special architectural features and certain climatic zones. It is more than coincidence that groups of different continents, creeds, and cultures appear to have come independently to similar solutions in their struggle with similar environments, and to have established basic regional characteristics.

## COMMUNITY LAYOUTS AND CLIMATE

The three community units pictured give a first impression that they are as strikingly dissimilar as they are distant from each other, not only in space and time, but in level of living. A long, close contact with nature evolved solutions such as those of the Iranian village in the Oasis of Veramin, where the village huddles together to leave the least surface to the scorching heat. The geometric minimum of the individual units is echoed in the total layout, bringing an appealing unity, and the closeness yields protection through mass. The thick walls tame and delay the thermal variations. The courtyards are shaded, providing cooling wells and establishing "introvert" dwelling units looking inward from the hostile environment. This distinct order took form through the urgency of biological necessity.

In the tropical Sudan lies a Bari village which displays an entirely different character. In the near-equatorial sky the sun remains high overhead, the temperature varies little, and the hazy firmament is moisture-laden. Both radiation and rain come from above. Therefore the roof is the main element; this is emphasized by the umbrella-like cover thatched in rings. The walls lose their usual role, and the boundary of the house is loosely defined by the shade-giving roof. The winds are welcome, and buildings, like people, are lightly clad. Space can flow easily, and this fluid accessibility accounts for the pavilion-like arrangements in a spontaneous organic freedom.

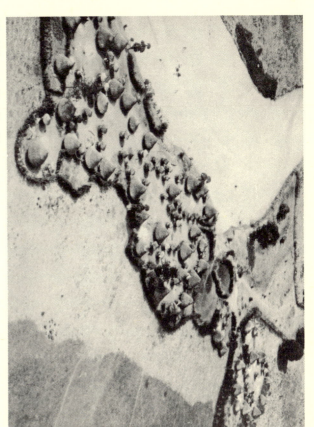

**23.** Village in Hot-Humid zone.

**24.** Housing in Temperate area.

The community of Zurich lies in the cool-temperate climate of Switzerland. Here the natural setting, however friendly, has variations that call for a carefully balanced building to act as a sun trap in the winter and a shaded shelter in the hot days, to fulfill a dual role as a summer jacket and a warm overcoat. In this climate range evolved the housing types of western civilization, with their large windows and extroverted easy communication with the natural surroundings.

Despite the diversity of these contrasting community layouts, they have something in common: all of them have marked regional characteristics, strong statements that are clear answers to their respective climatic demands.

## REGIONAL CHARACTER

The spread of populations and modern communications have accelerated the age-old interchange of ideas and technological effects. We must realize, however, that the wide dissemination of Western forms should proceed with caution. These forms evolved from the challenge of cool climates, and can pose grave problems when adopted as undigested and inappropriate symbols of cultural progress. Valuable insights into the use of native materials and genuinely original building elements may be lost with the discarding of inherited traditions. Of course these must be carefully sifted from the beliefs and customs of the region. Built-in superstitions exist, for example, in Malaya, where a trench before a house means bad luck; a room can not have views on opposite sides, which would be highly

desirable for cross-ventilation; and an entrance cannot be oriented so that a visitor's shadow would fall across the threshold. In other areas the few windows have to be closed at night against evil spirits.

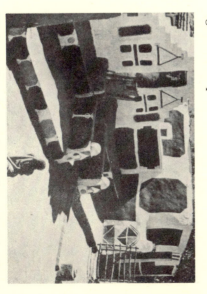

**25.** Expression of strength and sincere beauty of an African village.

9

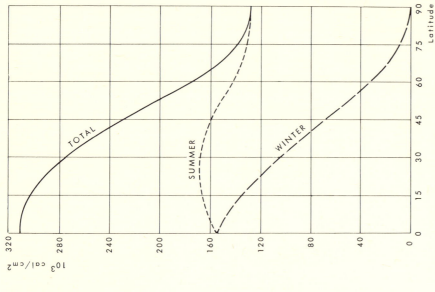

**27.** Radiation received at the ground in absence of the atmosphere at various latitudes.

cannot be found through a sentimental or imitative approach by incorporating either old emblems or the newest local fashions which disappear as fast as they appear. But if you take . . . the basic difference imposed on architectural design by the climatic conditions . . . diversity of expression can result . . . if the architect will use the utterly contrasting indoor-outdoor relations . . . as focus for design conception."[16]

## TO FIND A METHOD

The desirable procedure would be to work with, not against, the forces of nature and to make use of their potentialities to create better living conditions. The structure which in a given environmental setting reduces undesirable stresses, and at the same time utilizes all natural resources favorable to human comfort, may be called "climate balanced." Perfect balance can scarcely be achieved except under exceptional environmental circumstances. But it is possible to achieve a house of great comfort at lowered cost through reduction of mechanical conditioning. We will do well to study the broad climate layout, then apply the findings, through a specific region, to a specific structure. And one must be ever alert to regional variations.

A systematic approach to climate-balanced conditions poses an intricate problem since the procedure itself exists between the borderlines of several fields of knowledge. One can readily identify two of these fields: climatology and architecture, which contain the beginning and end of the problem. By combining these two fields, considerations for building design can be deduced. As Neutra writes:[17] "For the planning of the future, other arts and sciences, and more than one or two will be needed . . . the task of constructing many things that make up a human environment . . . cannot be

**26.** Elegance in regional expression at the Hot-Humid island climates.

On the other hand, it might be well to appraise our own practices in the light of global reevaluation. In the United States, despite the great variety of climatic conditions, building design often reflects a heedless uniformity. Housing types and building elements and designs are too often used in diverse environments with little or no relevance to their effect on human comfort, or even to the performance of materials. Undoubtedly they do not reflect the regional character, but are transplanted by a migrant population. Many causes of this wasteful uniformity can be cited, but perhaps the most decisive impact came from the technological advances in house heating and house cooling.

Walter Gropius, considering regional expression, writes " . . . true regional character

accomplished well without the use of current and available scientific knowledge. . . . Systematic biological investigation, when carefully correlated with organized policies of design, will rebound to the benefit of a broader human consumership."

A universally applicable method for architectural climate control must be based on broader foundations than have been used heretofore, and they must be accompanied by more careful analysis of a specific area. To adopt such a process one must seek out the intermediate steps.

The process of building a climate-balanced house can be divided into four steps, of which the last is architectural expression. Architectural expression must be preceded by study of the variables in climate, biology, and technology.

The first step toward environmental adjustment is a survey of climatic elements at a given location. However, each element has a different impact and presents a different problem. Since man is the fundamental measure in architecture and the shelter is designed to fulfill his biological needs, the second step is to evaluate each climate impact in physiological terms. As a third step the technological solu-

tions must be applied to each climate-comfort problem. At the final stage these solutions should be combined, according to their importance, in architectural unity. The sequence for this interplay of variables is Climate → Biology → Technology → Architecture, and in general this book will follow that sequence.

In particular, the steps of the method comprise:

1. CLIMATE DATA of a specific region should be analyzed with the yearly characteristics of their constituent elements, such as temperature, relative humidity, radiation, and wind effects. The data, if necessary, should

be adapted to the living level. And the modified effects of the microclimatic conditions should be considered.

2. BIOLOGICAL EVALUATION should be based on human sensations. Plotting the climate data on the bioclimatic chart at regular intervals will show a "diagnosis" of the region with the relative importance of the various climatic elements. The result of the above process can be tabulated on a yearly timetable, from which measures needed to restore comfort conditions can be obtained for any date.

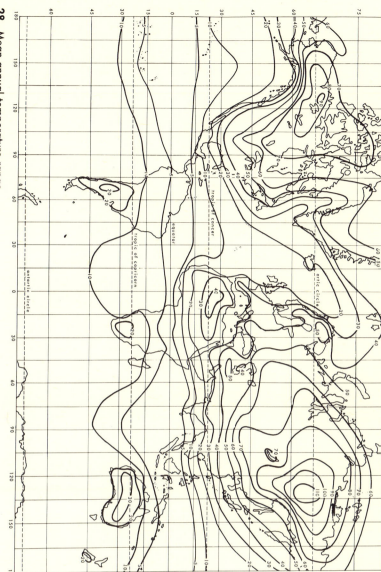

28. Mean annual temperature range.

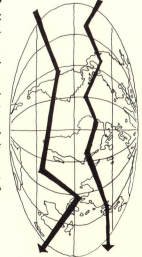

29. Horizontal correlation of climate influences.

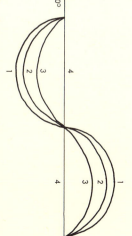

30. Flattening the temperature curve from environmental conditions (1) by microclimatology (2) and climate balance of the structure (3) to mechanical heating or cooling (4).

11

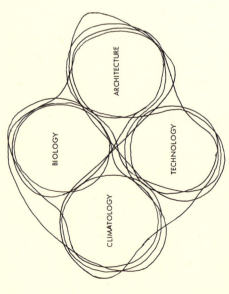

**1 CLIMATE DATA:**  **2 EVALUATION:**

CLIMATOLOGIST — COMMUNAL SERVICE

**A** REGIONAL CLIMATE DATA:
TEMPERATURE
RELATIVE HUMIDITY
WINDS

**B** CLIMATE ON LIVING LEVEL:
TEMPERATURE
RELATIVE HUMIDITY
WINDS: MODIFIED

**C** MICROCLIMATE
TEMPERATURE
RELATIVE HUMIDITY } MODIFIED
WINDS

**A** PLOTTING DATA ON THE BIOCLIMATIC CHART

**B** YEARLY NEEDS FOR: SHADE, RADIATION, REL. HUM., WINDS

**C** RELATIVE IMPORTANCE OF THE VARIOUS ELEMENTS:
COMFORT %
RADIATION, ETC. %
WINDS %

SHOWN IN VARIOUS REGIONS:

| COLD, TEMPERATE, HOT-ARID, HOT-HUMID ZONE | DIFFERENT CHARACTERISTICS, |
|---|---|

**32. Method of climate interpretation in housing.**

**31. Interlocking fields of climate balance.**

3. TECHNOLOGICAL SOLUTIONS may be sought, after the requirements are stated, to intercept the adverse and utilize the advantageous impacts at the right time and in adequate amount. This necessary function of a balanced shelter should be analyzed by *calculative methods:*

A. In *site selection* most of the factors are variable. In general, sites which show better characteristics in the winter-summer relationship are more livable.

B. In *orientation* the sun's heat is decisive both positively (in cold periods) and negatively (in hot periods). A balance can be found between the "underheated period," when we seek radiation, and the "overheated period," when we want to avoid it.

C. *Shading calculations* are based on the maxim that throughout the year in underheated times the sun should strike the building, and in overheated times the structure should be in shade. A chart of the sun's path, plus geometric and radiation calculations, can describe the effectiveness of shading devices.

D. *Housing forms* and building shapes should conform to favorable or adverse impacts of the thermal environment; accordingly certain shapes are preferable to others in given surroundings.

E. *Air movements* can be divided into the categories of winds and breezes, according to their desirability. Winds occurring at underheated periods should be intercepted, cooling breezes should be utilized in overheated periods. Indoor air movement should satisfy bioclimatic needs. Calculations based on rate of air-flow through a building in combination with inside flow patterns may be used to determine the location, arrangement, and sizes of openings.

F. *Indoor temperature balance* can be achieved to a certain degree with careful use of materials. Both time-lag and insulation characteristics of materials can be utilized for improved indoor conditions. Heliothermic planning, based on heat-flow studies, gives quantitative measures for the relative importance of the building elements. The criteria for balance are: minimum heat-flow out of building in wintertime, minimum heat-gain in the structure during the over-heated period.

4. ARCHITECTURAL APPLICATION of the findings of the first three steps must be developed and balanced according to the importance

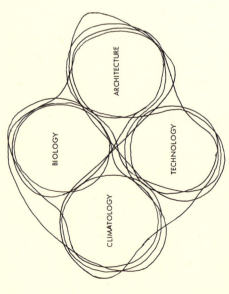

12

of the different elements. Climate balance begins at the site, and should be taken into consideration at the housing layouts, with similar careful consideration given to the individual dwelling units.

## SUMMARY

The contents of this book follow, in general, the four steps outlined. If the reader is first acquainted with the bioclimatic requirements of Chapter 2, he may the more easily follow the climatic evaluations in Chapter 3, and better understand the selective handling of climatological factors described in Chapter 4. From there on the text does not follow each climatic constituent separately; rather, with the architectural result in mind, it emphasizes architectural elements and principles. No rigid recommendations are made, since there are many ways in architecture to approach the goal of human comfort. However, to emphasize the environmental factors which motivate regional variation, comparisons are developed in most of these chapters in four diverse geographic locations, representative of the major United States climate zones. This leads to the detailed consideration of the problems of orientation, shading, form of buildings, air movement, and heliothermic planning in Chapters 6 through 10.

At this point, the investigations could close. However, architects tend to be visually inclined and do not readily imagine life in the form of cumbersome graphs. They prefer to look at assembled conclusions, so Chapter 12 summarizes the effects of climate on buildings in the four main regions, with examples illustrating possible applications.

The adaptation of building to environment has been a continuous problem throughout the centuries. Vitruvius' recognition of its importance is echoed by Le Corbusier: "The symphony of climate . . . has not been understood. . . . The sun differs along the curvature of the meridian, its intensity varies on the crust of the earth according to its incidence. . . . In this play many conditions are created which await adequate solutions. It is at this point that an authentic regionalism has its rightful place."18

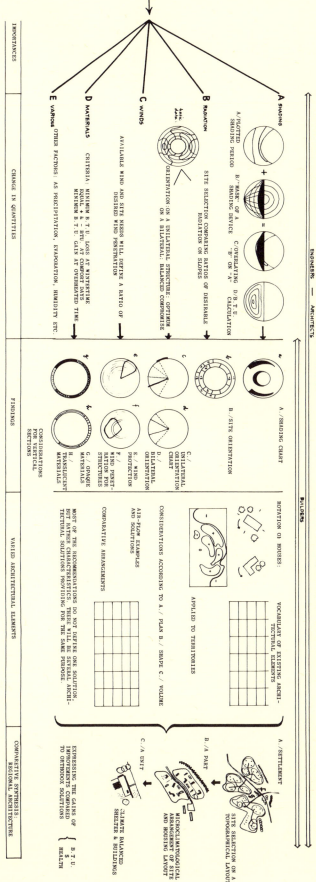

# II. THE BIOCLIMATIC APPROACH

## THE EFFECTS OF CLIMATE ON MAN

MAN's energy and health depend in large measure on the direct effects of his environment. It is a common experience to find that on some days the atmospheric conditions stimulate and invigorate our activities, while at other times they depress the physical and mental effort. It is also well known that in certain climatic areas, where excessive heat or cold prevails, energy is diminished by the biological strain of adaptation to the extreme conditions.

The measurement of climatic effects has been investigated in many ways, here two methods of evaluation may be mentioned. One method describes the negative effects of climate on man, expressed as stress, pain, disease, and death. The second defines the conditions in which man's productivity, health, and mental and physical energy are at their highest efficiency. Both approaches may be combined, to show coinciding and complementary relationships, in defining desirable or disagreeable atmospheric and thermal conditions.

The effect of climate on health has been studied on a seasonal basis by Ellsworth Huntington, who noted health and energy variables in the temperate area of the northeastern United States.[1] In the graph the two upper curves show production efficiencies in factories in Connecticut (A) and in Pittsburgh (B). Both are low in winter and rise steadily toward summer. When the summers were especially warm there was a decline in productivity, when they were cool there was no drop in productivity. In the fall, mostly in October and November, human energy seemed to reach its peak. The lower curves indicate health conditions during the same years in Connecticut (C) and Pennsylvania (D), shown as the curve of the death rate, inverted for easier comparison with the work curves. Death lags behind the incidence of illness, so that a slight delay can be read in the shift of the curves. Otherwise the fluctuations of the four curves disclose a remarkable relationship.

Huntington's studies show that the periods of highest and lowest energy occur at different times in different climatic zones.[2] At higher latitudes the most desirable period is from July to September, with winter as the unfavorable season. In temperate regions spring and fall are periods of good health, while summer and winter are relatively poor. In the low latitudes of the United States there are but two climatic periods: a short favorable winter, and a six-month decline in the rate of work and health during the summer.

Huntington points out that in Europe similar conditions prevail. In central France and in southern Germany the seasonal variations in health and strength are very like those in Boston and Detroit. In Scotland, Scandinavia, and Finland almost invariably the summer is the best health season, winter is the worst. Conversely in Italy, Spain, and Greece the harmful effect of winter decreases and that of summer increases until finally, on the south shore of the Mediterranean, winter is the best time of the year.

These observations suggest that man's physical strength and mental activity are at their best within a given range of climatic conditions, and that outside this range efficiency lessens, while stresses and the possibility of disease increase.

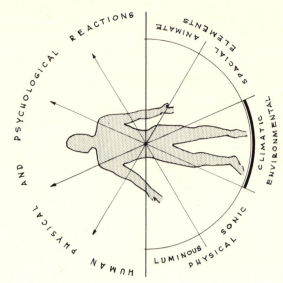

**34.** Man as the central measure in architecture.

## SHELTER AND ENVIRONMENT

The physical environment consists of many elements in a complex relationship. One can try to describe the environmental constituents as: light, sound, climate, space, and animate.[3] They all act directly upon the human body, which can either absorb them or try to counteract their effects. Physical and psychological reactions result from this struggle for biological equilibrium. Man strives for the point at which minimum expenditure of energy is

**33.** Seasonal variations in health and efficiency.

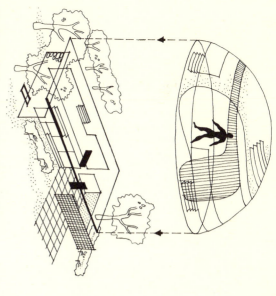

35. Theoretical approach to balanced shelter.

needed to adjust himself to his environment. Conditions under which he succeeds in doing so can be defined as the "comfort zone," wherein most of his energy is freed for productivity.

The shelter is the main instrument for fulfilling the requirements of comfort. It modifies the natural environment to approach optimum conditions of livability. It should filter, absorb, or repel environmental elements according to their beneficial or adverse contributions to man's comfort. Ideally, the satisfaction of all physiological needs would constitute the criterion of an environmentally balanced shelter. Here, however, only one element will be analyzed—the feeling of thermal balance. Without it, any definition of comfort is impossible.

The major elements of climatic environment which affect human comfort can be categorized as: air temperature, radiation, air movement, and humidity. (There are others too, such as chemical differences, physical impuri-

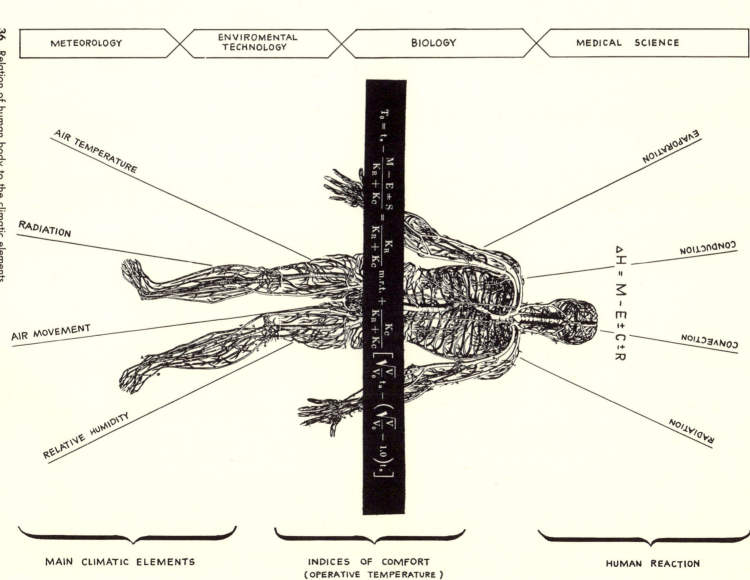

36. Relation of human body to the climatic elements.

METEOROLOGY ENVIRONMENTAL TECHNOLOGY BIOLOGY MEDICAL SCIENCE

AIR TEMPERATURE

RADIATION

AIR MOVEMENT

RELATIVE HUMIDITY

$$T_o = t_a - \frac{M - E \pm S}{K_R + K_C} = \frac{K_R}{K_R + K_C} \, m.r.t. + \frac{K_C}{K_R + K_C} \left[ \sqrt{\frac{V}{V_o}} \, t_a - \left( \sqrt{\frac{V}{V_o}} - 1.0 \right) t_s \right]$$

$$\Delta H = M - E \pm C \pm R$$

EVAPORATION

CONDUCTION

CONVECTION

RADIATION

MAIN CLIMATIC ELEMENTS

INDICES OF COMFORT (OPERATIVE TEMPERATURE)

HUMAN REACTION

15

ties, electric content in the air, and the like, not considered in this study.) They act on man in a complex relationship, which can be expressed in a calorimetric scale called the Operative Temperature ($T_o$) developed by Winslow, Herrington, and Gagge. Their equations combine air temperature, radiation, and air movements with metabolism to explain how the human body receives certain climatic elements, and how it maintains thermal stability.[4]

Means by which the body exchanges heat with its surroundings can be classified into four main processes: radiation, conduction, convection, and evaporation. It is estimated that radiation accounts for about $\frac{2}{5}$ of the heat loss of the body, convection for $\frac{2}{5}$, and evaporation for $\frac{1}{5}$; however, these proportions change with variations in the thermal conditions. Winslow and Herrington, and Bedford,[5] have discussed the body's response to thermal stresses in detail. D. H. K. Lee[6] summarized the factors involved in the heat balance of the body in the following way (see also Appendix A-1):

GAINS

1. Heat produced by:
   a) Basal processes
   b) Activity
   c) Digestive, etc. processes
   d) Muscle tensing and shivering in response to cold
2. Absorption of radiant energy:
   a) From sun directly or reflected
   b) From glowing radiators
   c) From non-glowing hot objects
3. Heat conduction toward the body:
   a) From air above skin temperature
   b) By contact with hotter objects
4. Condensation of atmospheric moisture (occasional)

LOSSES

5. Outward radiation:
   a) To "sky"
   b) To colder surroundings
6. Heat conduction away from the body:
   a) To air below skin temperature (hastened by air movement-convection)
   b) By contact with colder objects
7. Evaporation:
   a) From respiratory tract
   b) From skin

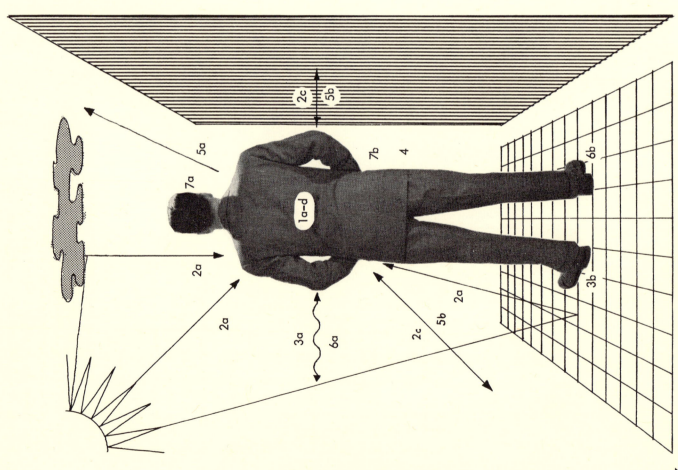

16  37. Heat exchange between man and surroundings.

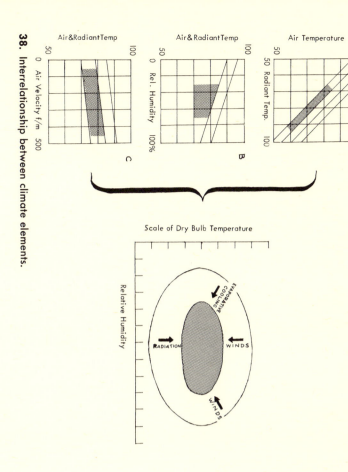

The actual relative magnitude of body heat production and heat interchange with the environment may vary within wide limits. The vital processes of the body are accompanied by considerable energy exchange. This energy is derived from the oxidation of foodstuffs and is utilized with a gross efficiency of the order of 20%, the remaining 80% of the energy is expended as heat. Even when the body is completely at rest and in warm surroundings its heat production does not fall below a certain minimum level—the basal metabolism—usually taken as about 290 Btu/hr for an average person. This figure rises to 400 Btu/hr for sedentary activities, to 760 walking 2 mph, to 1,400 walking 4 mph, and to 3,000–4,800 at maximum exertion.

The architect's problem is to produce an en-

**38. Interrelationship between climate elements.**

vironment which will not place undue stress upon the body's heat-compensation mechanism. The approach should be rephrased in terms of comfort; the presentation should be in graphic form; and, to be easily applicable, the data should derive from the empirical findings available to the practicing architect.

## THE COMFORT ZONE

Some writers consider sunstroke or heatstroke as the upper temperature limit for man's existence, with the freezing point as the lower limit.[7] The ideal air temperature may be assumed to be midway between these extremes. Experiments on animals in a variable-temperature tunnel at the John B. Pierce Founda-

tion showed that animals prefer to stay at 70° F, about midway between the points calling for maximum expenditure of energy in adjustment to the environment.[8] Therefore, some writers believe that the human being, with a body temperature averaging 98.6° F, seeking a comfortable temperature condition, picks by intuition an area where the temperature is about halfway between what he can tolerate in cold without being grossly uncomfortable, and the point which would require real effort on the part of his circulatory and sweat secretion system in order to permit him to adapt to heat.

The British Department of Scientific and Industrial Research, headed by Drs. H. M. Vernon and T. Bedford, arrived at certain conclusions in their investigations and experiments to define comfort conditions. Vernon states that the ideal temperature with slight air movement (50 fpm or less) is 66.1° F in summer, and 62.1° F in winter. Bedford gives the ideal indoor air temperature as 64.7° F in winter, and defines a comfort zone which ranges from 55.8° to 73.7° F.[9] A German suggested standard is 69.5° F with 50% relative humidity.[10] S. F. Markham proposes a range of temperature from 60° to 76° F as constituting an ideal zone, with relative humidities at noon varying from 40 to 70%.[11] C. E. P. Brooks shows that the British comfort zone lies between 58° to 70° F; the comfort zone in the United States lies between 69° and 80° F; and in the tropics it is between 74° and 85° F; with relative humidity between 30 and 70%.[12]

The Australian Commonwealth Experimental Building Station conducted physiological experiments which suggest that, in given climatic conditions, the dry-bulb temperature would provide a satisfactory index for the sensation of warmth up to the beginning of general perspiration.[13]

17

the nature of activity being carried on. Further, it depends on sex, as women in general prefer an effective temperature for comfort 1 degree higher than men. Age plays a role also in the thermal requirements as persons over 40 years of age generally prefer 1 degree ET higher than men and women below this age. Acclimatization according to geographical locations shifts the comfort zone warmer climatic conditions elevating the thermal requirements.

The comfort zone does not have real boundaries; as, diverging from the center of the comfort zone, the thermal neutrality subtly turns to a slight degree of stresses, and from this to situations of discomfort. Therefore any definite comfort perimeter outline must be based on arbitrary assumptions. In case of mechanical conditioning the desired situation should aim toward the middle of the thermal neutrality. In cases where the ambient conditions of the building strive to be balanced by natural means, evidently no such strict conditions can be required. Here the criterion was adopted that conditions wherein the average person will not experience the feeling of discomfort can constitute the perimeter of the comfort zone.

The values of effective temperature used in the chart were adjusted to the mean skin temperature index. The desirable comfort zone indicated lies between 30 and 65% relative humidity. For practical purposes the summer zone was enlarged to include those lower and higher humidity regions where no thermal stresses occur—not, however, recommended for prolonged periods. The winter comfort zone is charted somewhat lower. The use of the chart is directly applicable only to inhabitants of the temperate zone of the United States, wearing customary indoor clothing, engaged in sedentary or light muscular work, at elevations not in excess of 1,000 feet above sea

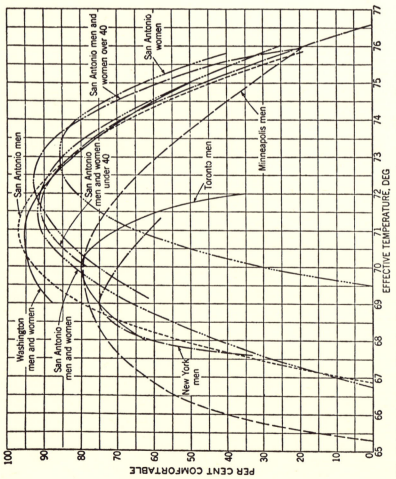

**39.** Relation between Effective Temperature and percentage observations indicating comfort.

American scientists have tried to establish a physiological measurement, combining the effects of temperature, humidity, and air movement, called the effective temperature scale (ET).[14] They place the comfort zone between 30 and 70% relative humidity. According to Houghton and Yaglou, optimum ET lies at 66°, with a range of 63–71° for both men and women (winter nonbasal, at rest, normally clothed). Yaglou and Drinker found a 71° optimum, with a range of 66–75° for men (summer nonbasal, at rest, normally clothed). Laboratory and field workers have found that the ET index overestimates the influence of humidity on sensations of warmth and com-

fort at ordinary temperatures, and underestimates this influence at very high temperatures.[15] Yaglou later offered a method for improving the ET index on a basis of mean skin temperature.[16]

The sources mentioned above were used as a basis for the outline of the "comfort zone." However, it should be mentioned that considering the range of observations and opinions there is no precise criterion by which comfort can be evaluated. Maybe it can be defined negatively as the situation where no feeling of discomfort occurs. Such a zone, which is very similar to the zone of thermal neutrality, differs with individuals, types of clothing, and level. To apply the chart to climatic regions other than approximately 40° latitude, the lower perimeter of the summer comfort line should be elevated about ¾° F for every 5° latitude change toward the lower latitudes. The upper perimeter may be raised proportionately, but not above 85° F.

Outside the comfort zone the indications of the different sensations on the chart are in agreement with C. E. P. Brooks' observations.[17] The limit to moderate work at high temperatures is indicated with a curve on the chart, which was based on D. Brunt's description.[18] This curve follows approximately the 85° ET curve. The "Difficult Environment" (93°–96° ET) and the "Impossible Environment" (95°–97° ET) curves are based on results of studies made at Pittsburgh (ASHVE-USBM) and Fort Knox (AMRL).[19]

The scale for measuring the thermal effect of clothing on the human body is based on the unit of one $Clo$.[20] $Clo$ is an arbitrary unit of clothing insulation. It is assumed to be the insulation of men's ordinary indoor clothing, capable of maintaining comfort in still air of 70°, with relative humidities less than 50%, and without much physical activity. The warmest practical clothing made has an insulation value of about 4.5 $Clo$.

## RELATION OF CLIMATIC ELEMENTS TO COMFORT

AIR MOVEMENT affects body cooling. It does not decrease the temperature but causes a cooling sensation due to heat loss by convection and due to increased evaporation from the body. As velocity of air movement increases, the upper comfort limit is raised. However, this rise slows as higher temperatures are reached.

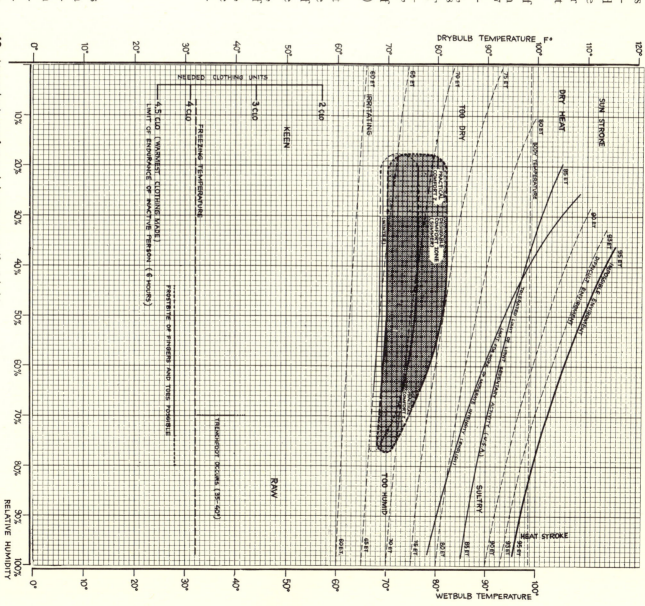

40. Atmospheric comfort and danger zones (for inhabitants of moderate climate zones).

The figure shows wind velocities theoretically needed to restore comfort when temperatures and relative humidities are outside the comfort zone. The desirable range of wind velocities is, of course, limited by the effect on the human being.[22]

| VELOCITY | PROBABLE IMPACT |
|---|---|
| Up to 50 fpm | Unnoticed |
| 50 to 100 | Pleasant |
| 100 to 200 | Generally pleasant but causing a constant awareness of air movement. |
| 200 to 300 | From slightly drafty to annoyingly drafty |
| Above 300 | Requires corrective measures if work and health are to be kept in high efficiency. |

VAPOR PRESSURE is exerted by a variable quantity of water vapor contained in atmospheric air. People usually notice a "close" or depressed feeling if vapor pressure surpasses the 15 mm mercury mark. Dr. Paul Siple states that over 15 mm vapor pressure, each additional millimeter of pressure can be counteracted with one mph (88 fpm) wind effect.[23] The John B. Pierce Foundation at Yale University has worked out more detailed calculations on this effect, but accepts the above approximation as adequate in practice. The figure shows the range from 15 to 23 mm vapor pressure counteracted with wind velocities from still air (20–30 fpm) up to 700 fpm.

EVAPORATION decreases dry-bulb temperature. The curves shown in the figure are calibrated in 5 gr moisture/lb air intervals. The temperature decrease caused by evapora-

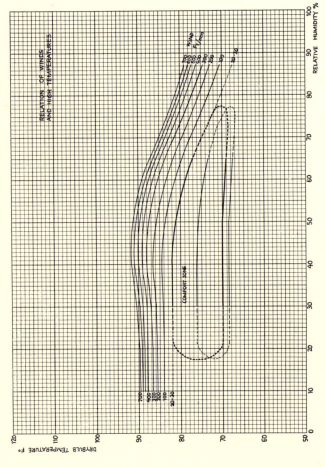

41. Relation of winds and high temperatures.

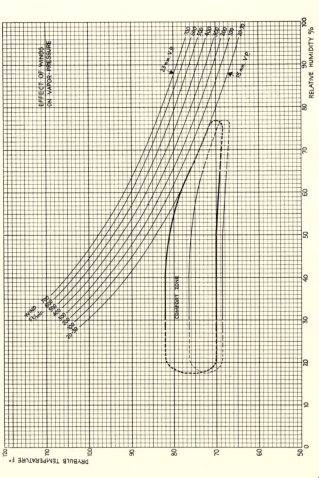

42. Effect of air movement on vapor pressure.

tion of added moisture will restore comfort temperatures to the outer limit of the comfort zone. Calculations were based on the assumption that the latent heat is supplied entirely by the air. The Carrier Psychometric Chart was used (barometric pressure 29.92 inches mercury; vapor pressures are those of water) to determine the amount of grains of moisture per pound of dry air in obtaining lower temperatures.[24]

Evaporative cooling can be achieved by mechanical means, and also, to a certain degree, through the use of trees, vegetation, pools, or fountains. It is of importance in dry and hot climate zones, where wind effect is of little help in lowering high temperatures.

RADIATION EFFECT of inside surfaces can be used to some extent to balance higher or lower air temperatures. This means that we can be comfortable at low temperatures if the heat loss of the body can be counteracted with the sun's radiation. At lower temperatures (under 70° F) a drop of 1° F in air temperature can be counteracted by elevating the mean radiant temperature by 0.8° F.[25] However, this possibility of counteraction has its limitations. In practice we shall not find more than 4° or 5° F difference between air and wall temperatures.

Radiation curves shown in the figure and expressed in Btu, refer to outdoor conditions only. Calculations indicate that 50 Btu of sun radiation can counteract a 3.85° F drop in dry-bulb temperature. (See Appendix A-2.)

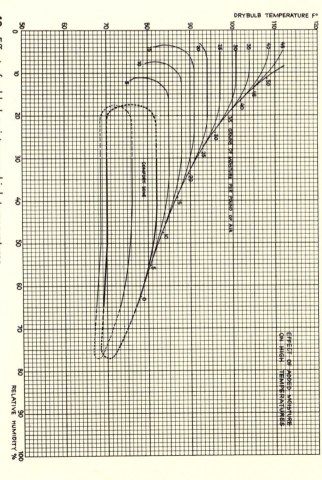

43. Effect of added moisture on high temperatures.

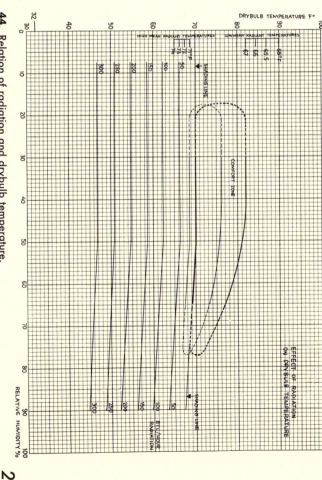

44. Relation of radiation and drybulb temperature.

27

## THE BIOCLIMATIC CHART

The effects of the climatic elements can now be assembled from these separate studies into a single chart. This chart shows the comfort zone in the center. The climatic elements around it are shown by means of curves which indicate the nature of corrective measures necessary to restore the feeling of comfort at any point outside the comfort zone. The chart is applicable to inhabitants of the moderate climate zones in the United States, at elevations not in excess of 1,000 feet above sea level, with customary indoor clothing, doing sedentary or light work.

A simplified version of the bioclimatic chart shows the relationships of the various climatic elements to each other. Climatic needs for conditions outside the comfort zone are shown in simple diagrammatic form.

The bioclimatic chart was built up with dry-bulb temperature as ordinate and relative humidity as abscissa. In the middle, we can see the summer comfort zone divided into the desirable and practicable ranges. The winter comfort zone lies a little lower. Any climatic condition determined by its dry-bulb temperature and relative humidity can be plotted on the chart. If the plotted point falls into the comfort zone, we feel comfortable in shade. If the point falls outside the comfort zone, corrective measures are needed.

If the point is higher than the upper perimeter of the comfort zone, winds are needed. How wind effects can restore the feeling of comfort and offset high temperatures is charted with the nearly parallel lines following the upper limit of the comfort zone perimeter. The numbers indicate the needed wind velocities in feet per minute value (fpm).

If the temperature is high and the relative humidity is low, we feel too dry and hot, and

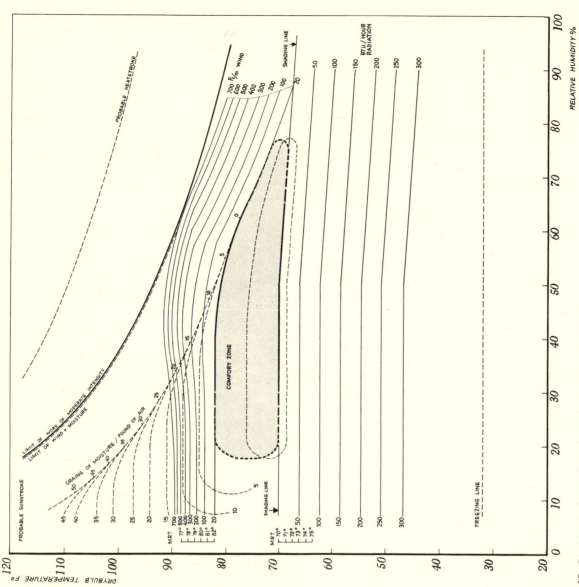

**45.** Bioclimatic Chart, for U.S. moderate zone inhabitants.

winds are of little help here. Evaporative cooling is the tool with which to fight high temperatures. The dotted lines indicate grains of moisture per pound of air needed to reduce

temperatures to the level at the upper comfort perimeter.

At the lower perimeter of the comfort zone is the line above which shading is needed.

Conversely, radiation is necessary below the line to counteract lower dry-bulb temperatures. The amount of Btu needed by "solar" action to restore the sensation of comfort is tabulated for outdoor conditions only.

At the left are charted the mean radiant temperature values (mrt) necessary to restore the feeling of comfort by either radiant heating or cooling (control of surface temperatures of the surroundings).

## USE OF THE BIOCLIMATIC CHART

No corrective measures are necessary for any point of known dry-bulb temperature and relative humidity which falls within the boundaries of the comfort zone. For any point falling outside this zone, corrective measures needed to restore the feeling of comfort can to taken directly from the chart.

For example, at dry-bulb temperature, 75° F; relative humidity, 50%, *Need* is: none, the point is already in the comfort zone.

At dry-bulb temperature, 75° F; relative humidity, 70%, *Need*: 280 fpm wind to counteract vapor pressure.

At dry-bulb temperature, 50° F; relative humidity, 56%, *Need*: 260 Btu/hr sun radiation.

At dry-bulb temperature, 87° F; relative humidity, 30%, *Need*: counteraction by either of two means: (1) 300 fpm wind; or (2) evaporative cooling by adding 8 gr moisture/lb of air.

At dry-bulb temperature, 95° F; relative humidity, 20%, *Need*: cannot be achieved with winds alone. Even 700 fpm wind would still have to be supplemented by 9 gr moisture/lb of air. However, evaporative cooling could bring down the temperature to the level of comfort by adding 22 gr moisture/lb of air. Bioclimatic evaluation is the starting point for any architectural design aiming at environ-

mental climate balance. Prevailing climatic conditions can easily be plotted on the chart, and will show the architect what corrective measures are needed to restore comfort conditions. A good many of these measures may be achieved by natural means, that is, by adapting architectural design to utilize the climatic elements. Other problems, which fall outside

the natural possibilities, will have to be remedied by mechanical means, such as air conditioning. It is the task of the architect to make utmost use of the natural means available in order to produce a more healthful and livable house, and to achieve a saving in cost by keeping to a minimum the use of mechanical aids for climate control.

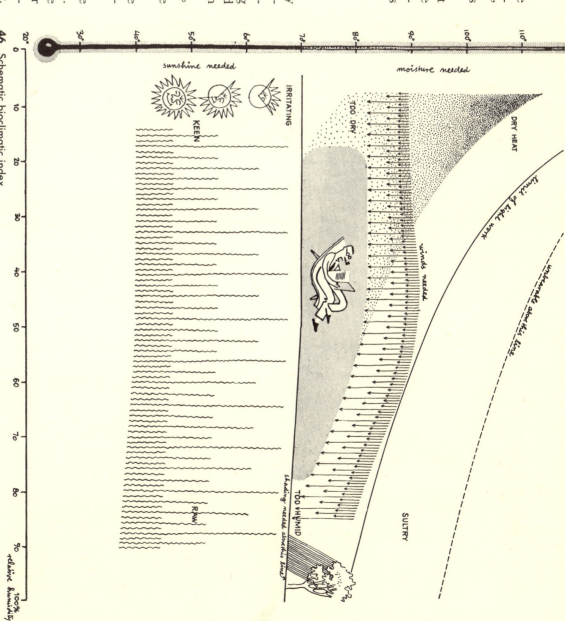

46. Schematic bioclimatic index.

# III. REGIONAL EVALUATION

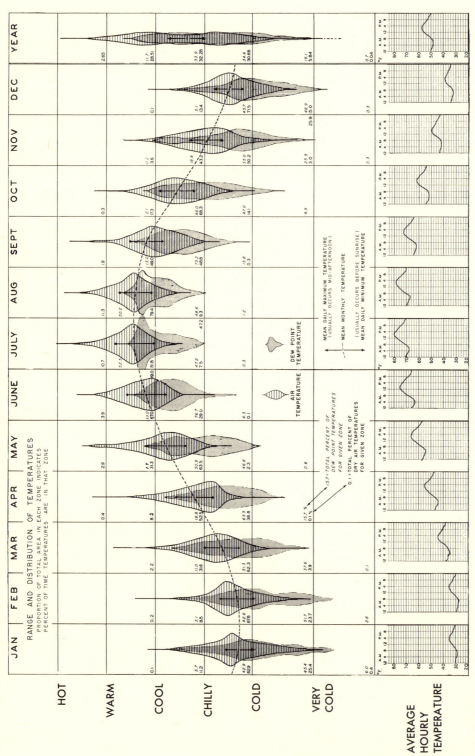

**47-48.** Regional climate analyses for metropolitan New York–New Jersey area.

## CLIMATIC EVALUATION BY REGION

THE Bioclimatic Chart maps the problems and describes the counter measures for human comfort in varying climatic conditions. To apply this, to evaluate the climatic situation of a given locale, a detailed analysis covering the complete yearly cycle is necessary. Local weather data supplied by meteorological stations may give the architect information that will enable him to construct his own evaluation. In addition, excellent regional analyses focusing on the importance of climatology in residential design have been published in connection with the *House Beautiful* climate-control project.[1] Detailed technical information, developed by Dr. Paul Siple in connection with this project has been issued by the American Institute of Architects since 1949.[2]

In the form of graphs and detailed design information, the AIA regional climate analyses contain:

A. *Thermal analysis.* In leaf-shaped graphs the range and distribution of temperatures are indicated; overlapping this the dewpoint temperatures are shown. The diurnal cycle of the average hourly temperatures and the degree days are tabulated.

# SOLAR ANALYSIS

HOURS OF SUNSHINE — AVERAGE TOTAL HOURS SUNNY OR OBSCURED — CHECK SOLAR HEAT AND SHADE REQUIREMENTS

D — AVERAGE HOURS — POSSIBLE HOURS

CLEAR DAYS — AVERAGE SUNNY DAYS AND POSSIBLE EXTREMES — CHECK POTENTIAL DAYS OF SOLAR HEAT OR SHADE REQUIREMENTS

E — SHADE REQUIREMENTS

CLOUDY DAYS — AVERAGE VERY CLOUDY DAYS AND EXTREMES — CHECK MAXIMUM WINDOW REQUIREMENTS

F

# WIND ANALYSIS

WIND DIRECTION AND VELOCITY — AVERAGE BY HOURS — CHECK IMPORTANT LOCAL MICRO-WIND VARIATIONS — CHECK SUMMER VENTILATION — WINTER FUEL AND INSULATION

J

NOTE — WIND ARROWS ON THESE GRAPHS POINT TO THE DIRECTION FROM WHICH THE WIND BLOWS THUS ↖ INDICATES WIND FROM NW

# HUMIDITY ANALYSIS

RELATIVE HUMIDITY — AVERAGE HOURLY PERCENT — CHECK ALL POORLY VENTILATED COOLER AREAS FOR CONDENSATION-CORROSION MOLD — DETERIORATION AND DISCOLORATION

S

# PRECIPITATION ANALYSIS

AMOUNT OF PRECIPITATION — AVERAGE MONTHLY TOTALS IN INCHES AND POSSIBLE EXTREMES RELATED TO MOISTURE EFFECTIVENESS — D=DRY — H=HUMID—W=WET — CHECK DRAINAGE AND IRRIGATION REQUIREMENTS

M

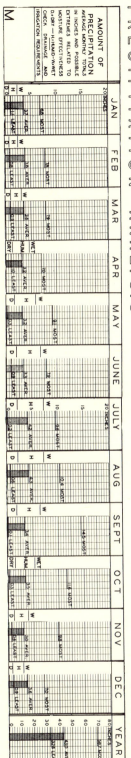
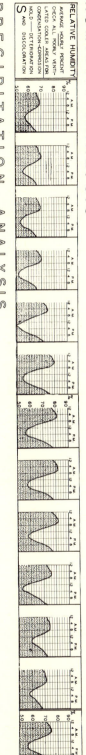

B. *Solar analysis.* The hours of sunshine broken up quantitatively for clear and cloudy days, the average amount of solar heat striking a horizontal surface, and the direction of the sun according to altitude and azimuth are charted.

C. *Wind analysis.* Wind directions and velocities, storm patterns, and gale days are tabulated.

D. *Precipitation analysis.* The amount of precipitation and snowfall, and the maximum rate of rainfall are charted. Rainy days, snow-cover days, days with heavy fogs and thunderstorms are evaluated at their average distribution.

E. *Humidity analysis.* Average hourly percentage of relative humidity occurrence and average and extremes in vapor pressure are tabulated.

The figures show an AIA Regional Climate Analysis for the metropolitan New York and New Jersey area. The charts are reproduced

25

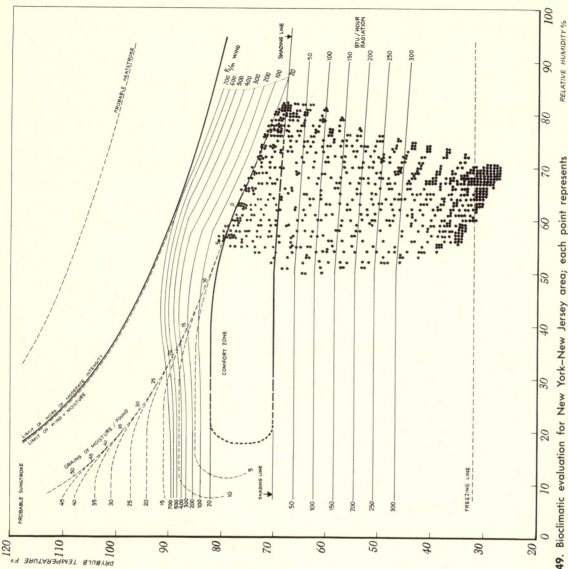

**49.** Bioclimatic evaluation for New York–New Jersey area; each point represents hourly data over ten-day periods throughout the year.

here in an abbreviated form, containing only the main climatic data pertinent to evaluations and calculations which are discussed later. (In this publication, if not otherwise indicated, the AIA charts were used as the source of climatic information.)

Since the AIA data cover general climatic conditions—or macroclimate—of a region, any specific application should be modified to some extent by the surroundings of the building in question—the microclimate. This includes the topography, exposure, obstructions, existing natural cover, and the like, of a given site. Also, since Weather Bureau observations are made at rooftop level the data should be adapted to "living level," about 6 feet above ground.[3] The meteorological data for temperature and relative humidity can be used with adequate accuracy, but the given wind velocities should be reduced considerably (see Chapter IV).

## BIOCLIMATIC NEEDS BY REGION

The regional evaluation of a climatic situation must be applied to the bioclimatic chart. Plotting of combined temperature and relative humidity data on the chart at regular intervals will show the general characteristics of a region. This can be done with data for average maximum or minimum conditions, according to the purpose. The figure shows an average yearly evaluation of the conditions for the New York–New Jersey area. Here each point represents hourly data at ten-day intervals throughout the year. From the number of points falling into different sensation categories, the importance of the various climatic elements—showing need for shading, radiation, wind, and so on—can be estimated. And from this the bioclimatic analysis can be translated to a yearly chart.

One can say in general terms that there are four major climate zones within the United States. Here are four regions selected to represent the types of cool, temperate, hot-arid, and hot-humid climates: Minneapolis, Minnesota; the metropolitan area of New York and New Jersey; Phoenix, Arizona; and Miami, Florida. Throughout the book the problems are analyzed from these key points. Although somewhat arbitrary, this choice of climate

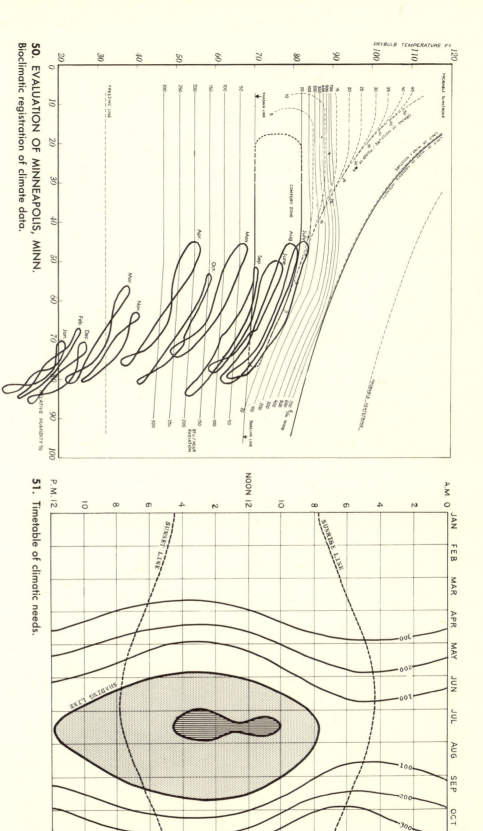

**50. EVALUATION OF MINNEAPOLIS, MINN.**
Bioclimatic registration of climate data.

**51.** Timetable of climatic needs.

samples offers the possibility of comparing diverse environments and their effects on architectural principles and building elements.

On these regional charts, the climate situation of a typical average day of each month is plotted on the bioclimatic chart. The 24-hour data of the mid-month show as closed curves. These curves are selected intervals of a continuous spiral which would move upward until July and then descend till January. It was found that such a selection is adequate for interpretation and gives a clear review of the climatic situation throughout the year.

When the bioclimatic analysis is transferred to a yearly chart, the needs are transferred into a timetable, where the varying climatic elements of any day in the year can be read vertically. With such "diagnosis of the region," the relative importance of the various needs—such as radiation (indicated in full lines up to 300 Btu/hr intensities), shading (dotted area, overheated period), or wind effects (lined indication), and so on—can be evaluated.

*Minneapolis, Minn.* Note the high slope of the daily temperature curves which indicate the variation between day and night, and the low yearly temperature distribution. Accordingly, the evaluation chart calls for radiation during most of the year (even in the early summer hours). In more than half of the underheated period, heat needs cannot be satisfied by direct natural means. During daytime hours (7 a.m.–7 p.m.) the average yearly requirements would be: 76% sun heat, 24% shade, 76% wind protection, 4% cooling breezes; 15% of the time is in shade comfort.

27

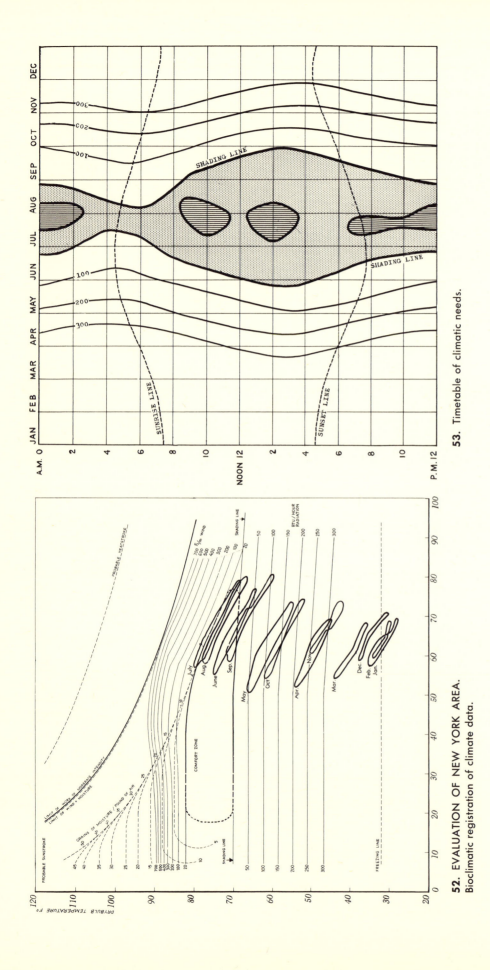

**53.** Timetable of climatic needs.

**52.** EVALUATION OF NEW YORK AREA.
Bioclimatic registration of climate data.

*New York–New Jersey area.* Both the temperature and relative humidity distribution has smaller range in winter than in the overheated summer period. The general location is at the humid side. The evaluation chart indicates a large shading period where wind effects are needed to counteract both high temperatures and vapor pressure. During the daytime hours the average yearly needs are: 72% sun heat, 28% shade, 72% wind protection, 7% breeze period; 21% of the time is in shade comfort.

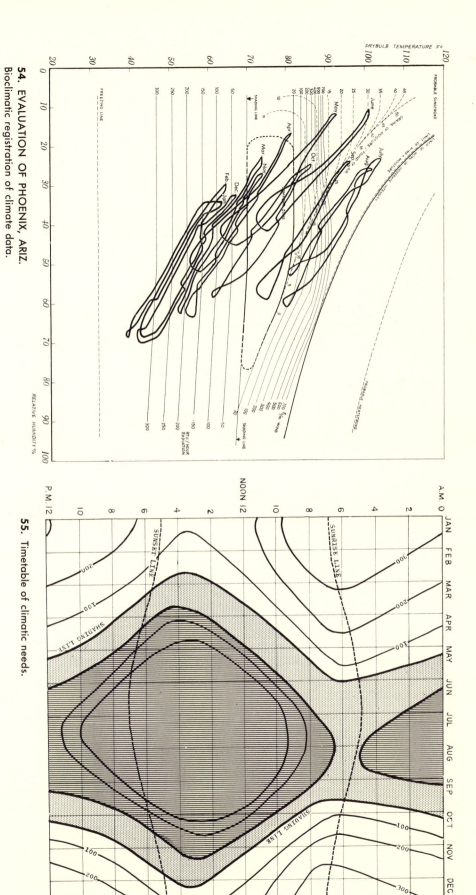

**54.** EVALUATION OF PHOENIX, ARIZ.
Bioclimatic registration of climate data.

**55.** Timetable of climatic needs.

*Phoenix, Arizona.* The diurnal temperature curves have a marked high slope indicating a large daily range of heat. The general location is at the low humidity side. Since the yearly temperature distribution lies in a relatively short range, and the winter daily maximums and summer minimums approach the comfort zone, it is highly desirable to maintain those conditions. But the evaluation chart indicates abrupt changes; there are days (such as the 1st of May) when the temperature soars from underheated levels up to such extremes

that even high air movements cannot restore comfort. Note that within the wind area (vertical-lined section) full lines indicate periods where over 300 fpm air velocities would be needed. Since too high velocities would be annoying, other remedies should be applied, such as evaporative cooling aided by the heat lag of materials. During daytime hours the average yearly needs are: 37% sun heat, 63% shade, 37% wind protection, 19% breeze period, 28% other additional cooling methods; 16% of the time is in shade comfort.

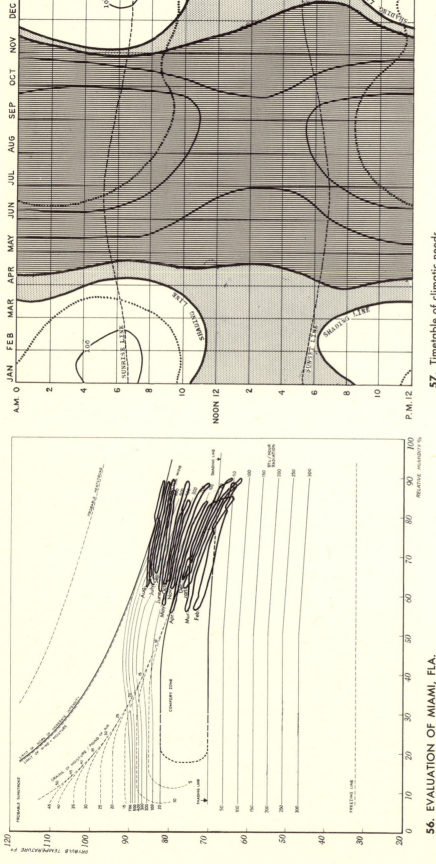

**57.** Timetable of climatic needs.

**56. EVALUATION OF MIAMI, FLA.**
Bioclimatic registration of climate data.

*Miami, Florida.* Here the daily temperature curves indicate a definite horizontal tendency. In the coldest months the daily range does not exceed 15° F and during the most overheated period decreases to a 5° variation. The yearly temperature distribution is compressed into a very close range and remains fairly constant on the side of extreme humidity. Climatic problems are practically negligible during the underheated period, as the temperature remains at overheated levels most of the year. Wind effects play an important part as relief from both high temperature and humidity; and even when temperatures would be in the comfort range, vapor pressure requires air movements. The evaluation chart indicates that throughout the year shading is required, even on the coolest day, for at least six hours. Within the wind area indication the full lines represent the 300 and 700 fpm theoretical wind velocity requirements. The dotted line refers to air movements needed to counteract vapor pressure independently of the temperature situations. During daytime hours the average yearly needs are: 12% sun heat, 88% shade, 62% breeze period (without the vapor pressure needs); 26% of the time is in shade comfort.

These regional analyses indicate the differences of these various climatic environments. The bioclimatic evaluations give a general picture of the relationship of comfort conditions and the weather situation, with detailed information on the importance of the climatic elements in their particular settings. The yearly evaluation charts indicate which element, at what time, and with what intensity each is needed to restore a feeling of comfort.

It should be mentioned that the evaluation charts convey more information than the main climatic elements. During the underheated period all possible techniques should be called into play to enhance heat preservation, or to offset radiation and heat loss. Similarly at overheated times, which call for shade protection, channels of inward radiation should be curtailed, outgoing-radiation possibilities improved, and peak heat loads moderated by emissive means.

A trained eye by merely looking at the charts may detect and "diagnose" the architectural requirements of a region. Radiation needs give an index for orientation and the size and arrangement of solar openings. The area of the overheated period designates the extent of need for shading devices. The slant of the borders of the overheated period is typical of the time-lag requirement for a structure. And the over-all level of the needs is an indication of insulation requirements.

The charts were evaluated for average climate conditions. Such criteria seem to be a valid approach for structures where the aim is to maintain a balance under usual circumstances. However, in cases where design conditions should be taken into consideration (as, for example, when calculating air movements to determine the needed sizes of openings), the charting of near maximum temperatures will give the suitable answer.

When the climatic elements and bioclimatic needs of a given site are thoroughly comprehended, it is possible to estimate the balance of natural forces that can be attained in a building. The desirable elements—sun radiation for cold periods, shade for hot times, ventilation for humid times—can be considered in relation to specific needs.

The ideal structure in the ideal location might be able to keep physical sensations wholly within the comfort range. However, in most cases the natural stresses are too large for that; the compensating forces may be blocked by the interaction of the building components, be limited by practical considerations, or be simply unavailable when needed. Only after the natural forces have been utilized, however, should the mechanical conditioning be called upon. Though partial results must be amplified by mechanical means, a structure which maintains conditions near physiological comfort requirements can be called climate-balanced.

The second part of this book (Chapters 5–11) will deal with climatic interpretation relative to architectural principles, building elements, and total structures. Before we come to this, however, the calculation methods for dealing with climatic elements should be discussed.

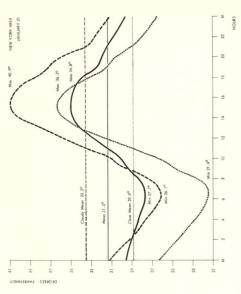

**58.** Typical winter curves; comparison between cloudy, mean, and clear day diurnal temperatures.

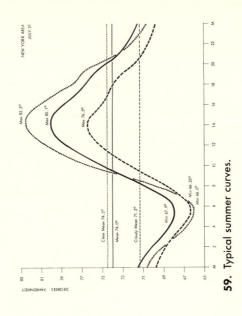

**59.** Typical summer curves.

| Altitude | 100 | 500 | 1500 | 4000 metres |
|---|---|---|---|---|
| Radiation | 0.8 | 1.2 | 1.4 | 1.6 cal/cm²/min |

The heat exchange in summer conditions, according to R. Geiger, are illustrated.[2] The relative amount of transferred heat approximately corresponds to the width of the arrows.

# IV. CLIMATIC ELEMENTS

## FACTORS IN WEATHER

WEATHER is an ensemble of all meteorological variables. At any given moment the elements appear in combination, and it is difficult to determine their relative importance in the thermal interplay. The architectural solutions to individual climatic problems should of course be similarly blended in a climate-balanced structure. To achieve this, a method for calculating the importance and relationships of climatic elements should be established and adapted to the needs of building practice.

Since the general approach of this book is based on human comfort sensations, the elements which strongly affect comfort—temperature, radiation, and wind effects—are discussed here. The effects of moisture such as rain, snow, frost, fog, and vapor pressure are treated only in the chapters on appropriate countermeasures.

Daily and yearly variations of atmospheric temperature are dominated by incoming solar energy. Hence both air temperature and radiation have to be considered for design purposes. The generally accepted design dates (February 1 and August 1) do not correspond to the solar solstice dates (December 21 and June 21). Therefore, January 21 and July 21 were accepted as design dates to correlate both conditions.

*Air Temperature.* The variation of the diurnal temperature depends on the state of the sky. On clear days a large amount of incoming radiation and a free path for outgoing radiation produce a wide daily temperature range, on overcast days the variation is less. On a seasonal basis the same holds true: clear days in summer are warmer because more solar energy is received; but a clear day in winter is usually cooler than a cloudy one, because in the longer period of nocturnal outgoing radiation heat escapes more easily through clear atmosphere. Shown in the figure are winter and summer diurnal curves for clear and cloudy days, based on data from a twenty-year average for the New York area. As the extremes of radiation gain and loss are included, the average clear-sky conditions of winter and summer are a reliable basis for average day temperature-design estimates.

The available local meteorological data on air temperatures can be used accurately enough for architectural design purposes. The differential between observation height and living level is small enough to be disregarded.

*Radiation Effects.* The solar constant is the amount of the sun's energy that falls in a unit time on a unit area 93,000,000 miles from the sun and perpendicular to its rays. The mean value is 1.94 cal/cm²/min, which is generally accepted as equivalent to 420 Btu/ft²/hr. The actual surface at ground level receives considerably less solar energy, because of a series of losses which occur when the radiation passes through the earth's atmosphere. Part of the incoming solar radiation is reflected by the surface of clouds, and part is absorbed by atmospheric ingredients. A certain amount is scattered by molecules in the atmosphere, but some of this is regained as diffuse radiation. Part of the radiation received at ground level is reflected by the earth's surface, but most of the energy is absorbed; it changes to heat and raises the temperature of the air, the ground, and surrounding objects. The intensity of the radiation received on the earth's surface increases with the height above sea level, because less is lost to the atmosphere. Observations on a clear winter day give the following values:[1]

# RADIANT HEAT TRANSFER

It is customary to divide radiant heat transfer affecting buildings into five main channels. In order of importance they are:

1. direct short-wave radiation from the sun;
2. diffuse short-wave radiation from the sky vault;
3. short-wave radiation reflected from the surrounding terrain;
4. long-wave radiation from the heated ground and nearby objects;
5. outgoing long-wave radiation exchange from building to sky.

The effect of mean radiant temperatures which affect closed spaces is discussed on page 39.

*Radiation reflected from surrounding terrain (3).* Roughly twice as much solar energy falls on a horizontal surface during overheated times as on a vertical surface; so that surrounding horizontal surfaces reflect a good amount of heat onto buildings. This heat flux can constitute a considerable load; the amount depends on the exposure and reflectivity of the immediate terrain. The table indicates the reflectivity percentages of various surfaces.[3]

PERCENTAGE OF INCIDENT SOLAR RADIATION, DIFFUSELY REFLECTED

| NATURE OF SURFACE | ESTIMATE % REFLECTED |
|---|---|
| Bare ground, dry | 10–25 |
| Bare ground, wet | 8–9 |
| Sand, dry | 18–30 |
| Sand, wet | 9–18 |
| Mold, black, dry | 14 |
| Mold, black, wet | 8 |
| Rock | 12–15 |
| Dry grass | 32 |
| Green fields | 3–15 |
| Green leaves | 25–32 |
| Dark forest | 5 |
| Desert | 24–28 |
| Salt flats | 42 |
| Brick, depending on color | 23–48 |
| Asphalt | 15 |
| City area | 10 |

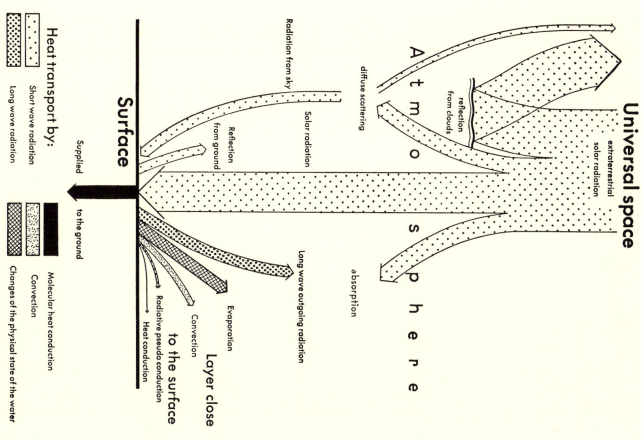

**Universal space**

Atmosphere

extraterrestrial solar radiation

reflection from clouds

diffuse scattering

Solar radiation

Radiation from sky

Reflection from ground

absorption

Long wave outgoing radiation

Evaporation

Convection

Convection

Radiative pseudo conduction

Heat conduction

Molecular heat conduction

**Surface**

Supplied

to the ground

Layer close to the surface

**Heat transport by:**

| | | |
|---|---|---|
| Short wave radiation | Molecular heat conduction |
| Long wave radiation | Convection |
| | Changes of the physical state of the water |

**60.** Heat exchange at noon for summer day. (The width of arrows corresponds to the transferred heat amounts.)

| Angle above horizon (°) | 9 p.m. | 10 p.m. | 11 p.m. | 12 p.m. | 1 a.m. | 2 a.m. | 3 a.m. | 4 a.m. | 5 a.m. | 6 a.m. |
|---|---|---|---|---|---|---|---|---|---|---|
| 0 | 88 | 85 | 82 | 82 | 82 | 79 | 78 | 78 | 76 | 79 |
| 10 | 84 | 82 | 80 | 80 | 78 | 77 | 74 | 74 | 73 | 76 |
| 20 | 82 | 79 | 76 | 76 | 76 | 73 | 72 | 70 | 71 | 72 |
| 30 | 78 | 75 | 72 | 72 | 72 | 70 | 69 | 67 | 66 | 68 |
| 40 | 75 | 71 | 70 | 72 | 68 | 65 | 63 | 63 | 63 | 65 |
| 50 | 73 | 69 | 64 | 67 | 66 | 63 | 63 | 60 | 61 | 63 |
| 60 | 72 | 68 | 64 | 65 | 64 | 62 | 61 | 59 | 57 | 60 |
| 70 | 70 | 66 | 64 | 65 | 63 | 61 | 60 | 59 | 56 | 58 |
| 80 | 67 | 64 | 63 | 64 | 61 | 61 | 59 | 57 | 55 | 57 |
| 90 | 64 | 64 | 63 | 64 | 61 | 61 | 57 | 57 | 55 | 57 |
| Air temp..... | 91 | 86 | 82 | 84 | 82 | 81 | 79 | 79 | 76 | 79 |

Vapor pressure 15 mm. Hg. Dust storm at 6 p.m. left some fine dust in the air, but night was clear.

**63.** "Sky" temperatures (°F) measured at night in summer near Yuma, Arizona.

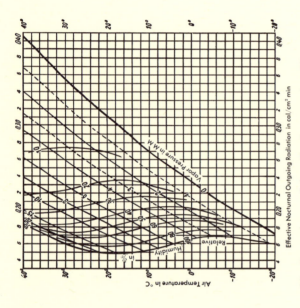

**61.** Dependence of the effective outgoing (R) on temperature (t) and water vapor content (p, in mm, f in %).

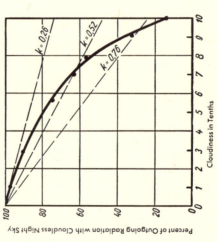

**62.** Dependence of the effective radiation on cloudiness (theory and observation).

To reduce the impact of reflected radiation, it is desirable to surround a house with surfaces of low reflectivity. The architectural layout for such arrangements can be calculated by inverting the computation method for overhangs, since the angle of the reflected rays, however diffuse, will still correspond roughly to the angle of solar incidence.

*Long-wave radiation from heated ground.* The ground and objects near a building, that are heated by the sun's rays, may rise to substantial temperatures. Observations in arid regions have found surface temperatures varying from 113° F (with air temperature at 98° F) to 144° F (with air at 116° F) on clear summer days, the ground surface temperatures as high as 160° F have been reported.[4] Building sides exposed to such conditions gain appreciable heat.

It is difficult to measure this indirect impact, since it depends not only on the materials of the building, but also on the radiation interchange which varies with the varying temperature differences between. However, indirect impact may be estimated by sampling surface temperatures and compensating for the exchange (see Chapter XI).

*Outgoing long-wave radiation.* The terrestrial heat balance implies that the yearly average of the total outgoing radiation from the earth and atmosphere is in equilibrium with the total incoming solar radiation. The outgoing radiation, however, is not uniformly intense; it varies with the seasons, and toward the poles it decreases about 10 to 20%.[5] The values for general use have been calculated by R. Geiger.[6] He indicates that the effective outgoing radiation is roughly in inverse proportion to the relative humidity—assuming a cloudless sky. With overcast conditions, radiation returned from the clouds to earth increases, and outgoing radiation decreases. F. Lauscher calculated the relationship of radiation to cloudiness; his figures also reveal a rapid decrease in outgoing radiation at heavier cloud covers.[7] Outgoing radiation is strongest toward the zenith and practically ceases toward the horizon. Data collected by observers of the U.S. Quartermaster Corps corroborate this effect.[8]

Outgoing radiation can constitute an important channel for heat disposal in housing, especially in hot-arid regions. This possibility is not adequately recognized nor significantly utilized in building practice. A practical calculation of outgoing radiation for architectural use could be developed similar to the solar calculator. However at present a lack of coordinated data hinders such development.

*Direct and diffuse solar radiation.* Solar radiation is one of the most important natural contributors to heat gain in dwellings. Therefore a quick and precise means of calculating the intensity of this radiation is of primary interest to architects.

The radiation passing through the atmosphere is "scattered"—because of suspended dust and air molecules and because part is reflected diffusely from the clouds back into space. Before it reaches the ground, solar radiation is reduced in intensity by impurities in the air and partly absorbed by some atmospheric constituents, especially carbon dioxide, water vapor and, at upper levels, ozone. The transmitted energy will thus vary according to the distance the sun's beams must travel through the atmosphere. At noon when the sun is most vertical and the distance shortest, the amount of energy received will be greatest. In early morning or late evening, when the distance is greater, less energy will be received. These situations are shown schematically. The intensities of the sun's direct energy as received at normal incidence are indicated with respect to solar altitudes. These values are representative of a clear summer day at sea-level according to Moon's proposed standard.[9] (See Appendix A-3.)

*Choosing clear sky conditions for design purposes.*
During cloudy days the ratio of diffuse to direct radiation may be 1.00 (100 per cent), while during clear days it may be only 0.15. However, the over-all heat received on a cloudy day (diffuse radiation, primarily) is much less than the over-all radiation (direct plus diffuse) on a clear day. Observations for New York in winter indicate that a vertical wall facing south receives 75% of the total solar heat during clear days, whereas on cloudy days it receives only 7%, and on partly cloudy days 18%. A somewhat similar situation is noted on clear summer days, where the average value of the ratio of diffuse to total radiation on a south-facing surface is equal to 0.26 (26% diffuse radiation).[10]

This shows that the largest portion of total radiation arrives during times when the ratio of diffuse to direct radiation is smallest, that is, during clear days. Since the architect's interest tends primarily toward design conditions, "clear sky" conditions were calculated and applied in all the discussed problems.

In addition to clear-sky values, a knowledge of average radiation is required in problems of solar openings, solar collectors, and specialized heat flow calculations. Since such information is not directly obtainable from Weather Bureau data, an empirical relationship between a parameter which is measured at Weather Bureau stations and average radiation on various surfaces is necessary. It has been found that the monthly percentage of the clear, partly cloudy, and cloudy days may be used as such a parameter.[11]

*Methods of determining insolation effects.* In order to compute radiant impacts one needs first to know the energy received at normal incidence in relation to the solar altitude. Secondly, one needs to know the incident angle to the specific surface in question, in order to reduce the energy to its cosine function.

For engineering use there exist tabulated data (such as published in the American Society of Heating and Air Conditioning Guide[12] which give values for both direct and diffuse radiation effects. Such tabulations, however convenient for practical use, can be applied directly only to the given orientations, times, and latitudes.

For architects' use the determination of the angles at which sunlight will fall on buildings at different locales, seasons, and times, model measurements are often advantageous. The usefulness of models lies in the directness with which shading or insolation effects can be observed visually. There are two general categories of such instruments; the sun-machine and the sun-dial types.

The principle of the sun-machine instruments is based on an adjustable light source (simulating the sun) to reproduce the actual insolation conditions in any given situation. Many different type of instruments have been developed for this purpose, such as the British

Building Station's "Heliodon,"[13] Professor G. M. Beal's power driven lamp device, Dr. L. W. Neubauer's "Solaranger,"[14] the Commonwealth Experimental Building Station's "Solarscope,"[15] Libbey-Owens-Ford Glass Company's "Solarscope,"[16] Cornell College of Architecture's "Solatron," John Hopkins University's "Heliodon,"[17] and others.

All these sun-machines, regardless of how ingeniously or precisely constructed, suffer from a disadvantage: the divergence of the rays of the lamp makes the measurements somewhat distorted, especially with larger (such as layouts for city planning) models.

The sun-dial types work on the characteristics of the shadow patterns. As shadows move exactly opposite the sun, a sun-dial at any given time can determine the position of the sun in reverse by its shadow. In the vast field of sun-dials, the "Shadowgrams" and "Cotangent Diagrams" are noteworthy where Kuttner,[18] Grobler,[19] and Beckett[20] have developed useable systems for architectural use. By elevating the sides of the beforementioned horizontal dial types Gunnar Pleijel constructed his practical "Little Sundial."[21] The "Shade Dial" developed by Aladar Olgyay[22] is applicable to any given latitude.

*Sun path diagrams.* There are several different systems of projecting the imaginary sky-vault with the sun paths on a plane. Some of them project it on the surface of a cylinder, others on planes parallel with the horizon. In principle there could be as many systems as map projections. However here, further investigations are based only on the so-called "sun-path diagrams," because they have more advantageous characteristics than other systems.

The diagrams of the "sun path" system show the sky-vault projected on a plane parallel to the horizon plane. On the resulting diagram the horizon line appears as a circle, and the sun-path as various curves depending on the method of projection and the proper latitude.

Recent methods of projection are the Orthographic, the Stereographic, and the Equidistant. In the equidistant projection method the altitude angles appear on the diagram equally spaced. This characteristic assures equal readability for high or low angles, and makes plotting easy. A small circle facing the observation point will be flattened out into an ellipse-like figure when it is near the edge, one diameter remaining always the same, the other increasing until it is $\pi/2$ times as great.

Irving F. Hand[23] described this method, and the Libbey-Owens-Ford Glass Company produced excellent diagrams of this projection, called the "Sun Angle Calculator."[24] The availability and wide use of this calculator in the United States is such that the diagrams in this book are constructed in the equidistant projection.

Shown are sun-path diagrams of the "Sun Angle Calculator" for 52° and 24° N. Latitudes. The curved lines indicated by days and months of the year represent the sun-paths on the dates shown. Lines "radiating" from the North Pole indicate the hours. Between the hour lines are lighter lines indicating twenty-minute intervals. With a cursor which pivots about the center point of the diagram the altitude of the sun can be read in any position.

The sun's position with reference to the horizon is usually expressed by altitude and azimuth. Altitude is the angular distance above the horizon. It has a maximum value of 90° at the zenith, which is the point overhead.

*Computation of solar energy with a radiation calculator.* The calculation of radiation through the use of tabulated data is laborious and time-consuming. Therefore, some graphic

systems have advantages over the statistical approach. Here a method is shown, developed by the author, which, for any orientation, the direct, diffuse, and total radiation effects on opaque or through glass surfaces can be determined with one reading.

The Radiation Calculator charts are based on the assumption that the magnitude of direct and diffuse radiation is a function of the solar altitude and the angle of incidence of the sun. On a sphere, equal altitude variations to a central point would show parallel circles; the variation of equal incidence angles would appear in form of concentric cones. Therefore, it is evident that for any given altitude and incidence situation, two points will correspond symmetrically to a vertical plane normal to the wall surface. Hence, all possible radiation effects can be charted in relation to a given surface on a spherical projection.

The Calculator diagrams are projected horizontally in the equidistant method. The charted energy values are representative for a clear day with unobstructed sky conditions. The direct radiation data corresponds to the Moon's standard,[25] the diffuse values to ASHVE recommendations.[26]

Since in architectural problems the irradiation of vertical and horizontal surfaces are of primary interest, the charts were developed for these exposures; however, the method can be adapted to any oblique plane, and to other conditions, such as semi-cloudy or cloudy atmospheres. The Calculator diagrams can be used for any latitude (for general practical purposes), and for all orientations. Since the total radiation falling on a surface can be read directly for any hour of the year, the flexibility and rapidity of the Radiation Calculator has its obvious advantages for use in architectural tasks.

The amounts of direct radiation falling on a

64.

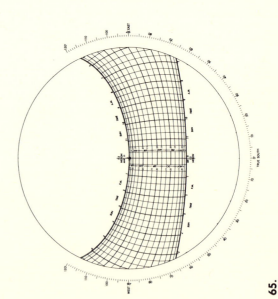

65.

SOLAR ENERGY CALCULATOR FOR OPAQUE SURFACES

SOLAR ENERGY CALCULATOR TRANSMITTED THROUGH GLASS SURFACES

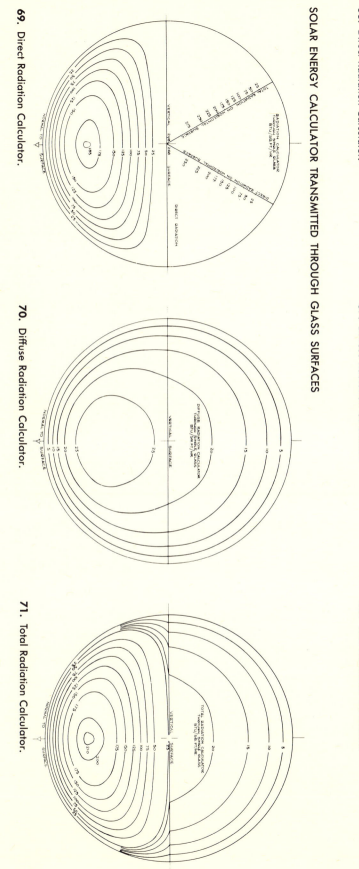

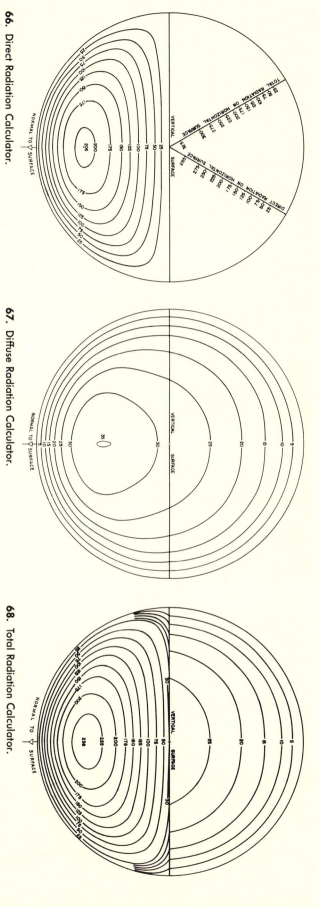

66. Direct Radiation Calculator.

67. Diffuse Radiation Calculator.

68. Total Radiation Calculator.

69. Direct Radiation Calculator.

70. Diffuse Radiation Calculator.

71. Total Radiation Calculator.

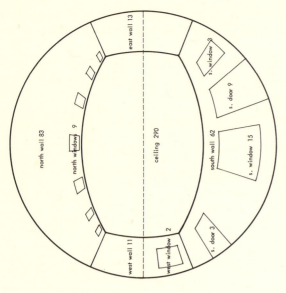

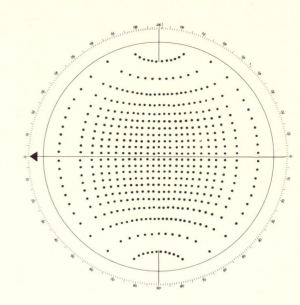

**74.** Hemispherical projection of a room.

**75.** Hemispherical radiation nomogram divided into 500 equal units.

vertical plane are shown at the lower half-circle; on the opposite side the measures indicate the sun's energies on a horizontal surface. The equi-intensity radiation lines are indicated at 25 Btu/hour/sq ft intervals. The diffuse energies are charted on a vertical surface at 5 Btu/hour/sq ft intervals. Note that the vertical surface receives sky radiation even when the sun's angle of incidence exceeds 90°. Total radiation amounts received by a vertical surface are shown, with tabulations for the added energy amounts of both the direct and diffuse radiation. The calculator diagrams show transmitted energies through single glass surfaces of direct, diffuse, and total radiation. Here for transmittance of the glass at normal incidence for direct radiation 0.91 was taken; for diffuse radiation a general transmittance of 0.82 was used.

For practical application the intensity diagrams are charted on transparent overlays. These may be superimposed on a sun-path diagram to read directly the amount of energy being received.

Two examples show the application of the Radiation Calculator. The first diagram illustrates the Calculator position set for 40° N latitude to read total radiation effects on a vertical surface facing south-east direction. The second example illustrates the calculator set to read the total radiation falling on a horizontal surface 9:20 A.M. at June 21.

*Mean radiant temperature.* Discounting solar radiation and evaporation effects, heat sensation in a closed space depends not only on ambient air temperatures but also on heat impacts radiating from the surrounding surfaces. The total effect of such radiation is expressed as the mean-radiant-temperature impact (MRT). This heat flux will be positive when the surrounding surfaces are warmer than the body surface temperature; and it will

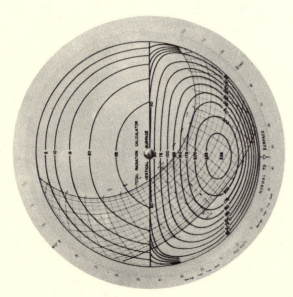

**72.** Calculation of radiation effects on a vertical surface.

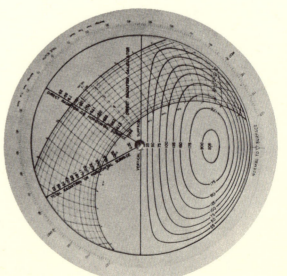

**73.** Calculation of radiation effects on a horizontal surface.

be negative (heat loss from the body) if the mean radiant temperature is lower than the average surface body temperature. Mean radiant temperature and ambient air temperature are dependent on each other, but they are not usually equal. The sensible heat relationship of temperature and radiation has been explored by several researchers, who generally concur that 1.25° F increase in room temperature will compensate for 1° F decrease in MRT.[27]

In a room composed of interior and exterior walls and windows, surface temperatures may vary considerably from point to point. Accordingly the resulting mean radiant temperatures and the sensation of heat will vary with positions within the room. Since the mathematical calculations determining this effect are quite lengthy, a graphic method is developed here as an approach to the problem.

For any given observation point, radiation effects are proportionate to their distance from the radiating panel. By projecting the surrounding radiative objects on a theoretical sphere in which the center is the observation point, the relative magnitude of the surface impacts can be plotted. For this purpose the equidistant projection method proved practical as did a surface protractor (see Chapter VII) for plotting. The size of the projected surfaces can be calculated with the hemispherical surface nomogram. Here the hemisphere was divided into 500 equal squares. The points shown on the nomogram designate the centers of these squares. By superimposing a projected surface over the nomogram and counting the encompassed points within, the relative magnitude of its radiation impact is found. An example is given of an applied calculation, where the numbers on the projected areas refer to fractions of the 1,000 total spherical units.

Thus the calculation of sensible heat effect to a location point will be:

$$T_s = T_a \text{ (ambient air temperature)} \pm MRT$$

temp. difference per 1.272 (or 1.25).

_Wind._ For wind calculations several factors have to be considered. First is the decrease in measured wind speeds at levels close to the ground, second is the modification of the operative wind pattern by local topography and the immediate surroundings, third is the comfort evaluation—the desired breezes versus the unwanted winds.

The wind effects of the free atmosphere are modified and slowed down at low levels, and at ground surface the air is almost at rest. Geiger has worked out an equation to express the variation of wind velocities with height.[28] However, the U.S. Quartermaster Corps method has been applied here.[29] This develops a smooth diurnal curve, giving reduction factors which can be safely applied to all days in the year.

For example, the New York–New Jersey wind evaluation is illustrated. The meteorological data were gathered at 47 feet; the velocities can be reduced to the 6-foot "living level." The necessary curves for the reduction process, the average velocities and wind directions at the measured height, and the effect of the reduced wind velocities at 6 feet, are shown on the next two pages.

The effects of wind on housing have to be considered both on the outside (because of convection transfer and infiltration) and within the dwelling itself. For comfort balance, air movements have to be evaluated as both positive and negative. They should be blocked as much as possible from penetrating structures during underheated periods, but they should be admitted and utilized at overheated times. If the overheated diagram is superimposed on

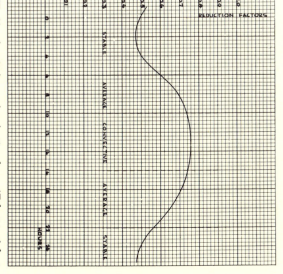

77. Hourly wind speed reduction from 47 feet to 6 feet height.

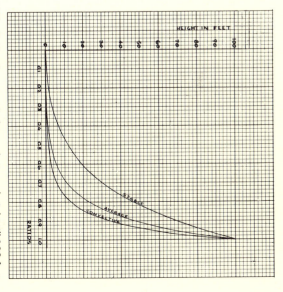

76. Ratio of mean wind speed at any height fill 100 feet under average, stable, and convective conditions.

78. Average wind velocity and direction at about 50 feet height, in New York–New Jersey area.

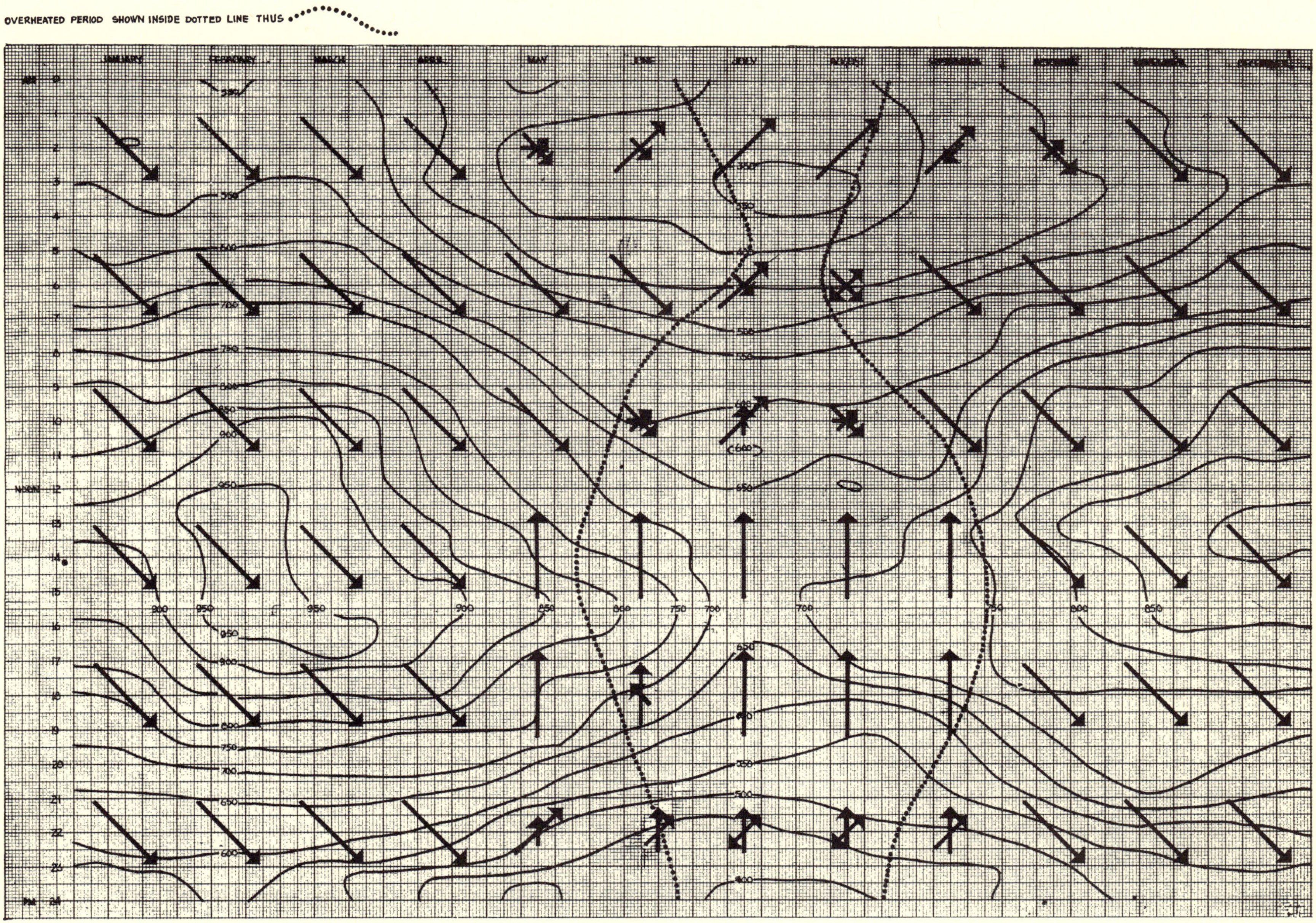

79. Average wind velocity and direction at 6 feet height, in New York–New Jersey area.

the wind chart, desirable breezes can be distinguished from unwanted winds, and their directions and velocities easily summarized. Depending on their characteristic duration and velocity, they can also be expressed as orientation vectors.

The charted wind data are evaluated under average conditions. However, the need for cooling and relief from vapor pressure in periods of high absolute humidity should be considered in planning design conditions. To set a maximum it is customary to use outdoor temperature data, from a period of years, which were equalled or exceeded not more than 5% of the time in the summer months.[30] Such maximum conditions would constitute the criteria for sizes of openings to counteract undesirable climate situations.

Maximum-velocity air flows, however, would be too high for comfort, so a limit should be set, of 300 fpm in daytime and 200 fpm at night, for air movements inside a structure. If this does not balance the heat or vapor pressure conditions, mechanical conditioning should be called into play.

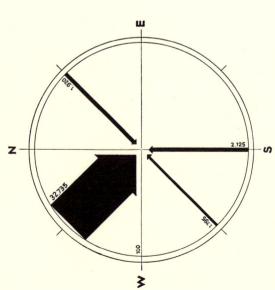

80. Wind analyses for New York–New Jersey area. Winds occurring during the underheated period.

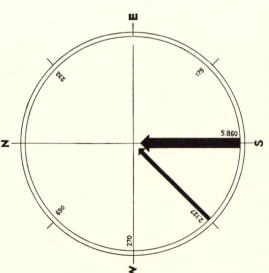

81. Breezes prevailing during the overheated period. The numbers represent the total amount of 4 hourly data x the ft min air movement velocity throughout the year at average conditions.

PART  2 INTERPRETATION IN ARCHITECTURAL PRINCIPLES

# V. SITE SELECTION

## MICROCLIMATIC EFFECTS

WE ARE inclined to think of climate as a certain condition uniformly distributed over a large area. This impression is partly because weather data are collected at points where "undisturbed conditions" prevail, and partly because large-scale maps depict equal mean temperatures in a few smooth lines. However, at ground level multifold minute climates exist side by side, varying sharply with the elevation of a few feet and within a distance of a mile. Nature demonstrates this in late winter with melting snow-cover patterns, and in early spring when north sides of hills may be frozen and brown while southerly slopes turn green with awakening vegetation. Plants are sensitive indicators of favorable circumstances. This effect is well known to farmers, who prefer southern slopes for growing grapes or cultivating orchards. The difference between the kind of plants which would grow on either side of a hill, if nature were allowed to select, would be as great as the difference between locales a hundred miles north and south of one another.[1] Further, every elevation difference, character of land cover, every water surface, induces variations in a local climate.

These effects within the large scale "macroclimate" form a small-scale pattern of "microclimates." Deviations in climate play an important part in architectural land utilization. First, in site selection, favorable locations should be considered. Second, a less favorable site may be improved by windbreaks and surrounding surfaces that induce an advantageous reaction to temperature and radiation impacts.

Extensive studies on microclimatology were done by Geiger,[2] and by Landsberg.[3] These provide detailed information on the subject. The purpose of this chapter is to discuss some of the most important climate effects on sites from the point of view of the architect.

## EFFECT OF TOPOGRAPHY

Temperature in the atmosphere decreases with altitude. The temperature drop in the mountains can be approximated as 1° F for each 330-foot rise in summer, and for each 400-foot rise in winter. This effect is important in tropical lands where temperatures become more favorable at higher altitudes. The location of the capitals of some Latin American republics reflect this. Mexico City lies over 7,000 feet above sea level, and the new capital for Brazil is being built at an elevation of 3,500 feet.

As mountains affect the macroclimate, small differences in terrain can create remarkably large modifications in the microclimate. Cool air is heavier than warm, and at night the outgoing radiation causes a cold-air layer to form near the ground surface. The cold air behaves somewhat like water, flowing toward the lowest points. This "flood of cold air" causes "cold islands," or "cold air puddles." Accordingly, elevations that impede the flow of air affect the distribution of the nocturnal temperatures by dam action; and concave terrain formations become cold-air lakes at night. The same phenomenon is enlarged when a large volume of cold air flow is involved, as in valleys. Geiger describes and illustrates that with a diagrammatic cross section.[4] The plateau, valley walls, and bottom surface cool off at night. Air flow occurs toward the valley floor.

On the valley slopes a series of smaller circulations mix with the neighboring warm air, causing intermediate temperature conditions. Accordingly, the temperatures at the plateau

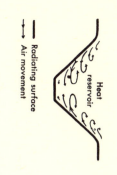

82-83. Cold air pool.

Radiating surface
Air movement
Heat reservoir
Cold lake

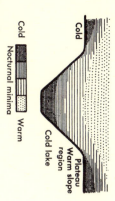

Cold
Nocturnal minima
Warm

84. Warm slope zone.

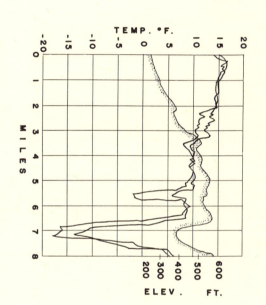

85. Effect of land formation on temperature distribution.

will be cold, at the valley floor very cold, but the higher sides of the slopes will remain warm. This area, often indicated by vegetation, is referred to as the warm slope (thermal belt). In the temperate zone the thermal belt is most advantageous for placing a dwelling. However, if this location is exposed to crest winds that may offset higher temperatures, a more desirable place would be approximately halfway up the slope.

A characteristic example of the effect of land formation on temperatures was recorded by Middleton and Millar in Toronto, Canada.[5] They measured the temperatures along a profile at right angles to the Lake Ontario shore on a clear winter night. Near the lake the highest temperatures were recorded, gradually decreasing with the distance from it. The graph indicates the temperature differences between valley bottoms and their crests. Only seven miles from the lake a temperature drop of 34° F was recorded. Such differences cannot be neglected in the choice of a building site.

RADIATION EFFECTS. The quantity of solar radiation also has a dominant effect on climate. The ancient Greeks associated insolation exposure with climate so much that the latter word derives from the verb "to slope." A hillside receives radiation impact depending on the inclination and direction of the slope. This radiation varies, of course, depending on the season and the degree of cloudiness.

Because of its importance the quantity of radiation impact on various slopes will be treated here in detail. The tabulated data was developed for the specific conditions of the New York–New Jersey region. In the calculations a method was adapted where weighted percentage-correction factors were used according to the Blue Hills Observatory data for both cloud-free and for average conditions (typical for the month).[6] The following assumptions are implicit in these radiation calculations: there is no asymmetry in the curve of daily intensity of solar radiation; differences in radiation intensity resulting from the slightly elliptical orbit of the earth may be disregarded; the regions to which these calculations apply are near sea level.

Tables A-F contain the results of the calculations for clear-sky diffuse radiation; clear-sky direct radiation; clear-sky total radiation for design purposes, and average direct radiation; average total radiation for heat-gain data under average conditions. The summations show daily radiation amounts received on a surface of one square foot. The values are given for the 21st of each month for eight orientations. For site selection purposes only the small-slope inclinations are of importance. However, for the sake of completeness, data from the horizontal to the vertical, in eight angles of inclination are recorded.

## TABLE A.—Direct Radiation for Clear Skies

40° N. Lat.  Radiation: Direct Clear  
(New York-New Jersey area)  
Total daily B. t. u./sq. ft.

**0° Inclination**

| Month | S. | SE./SW. | E./W. | NE./NW. | N. |
|---|---|---|---|---|---|
| Dec. 21 | 532 | 532 | 532 | 532 | 532 |
| Jan. 21 or Nov. 21 | 588 | 588 | 588 | 588 | 588 |
| Feb. 21 or Oct. 21 | 953 | 953 | 953 | 953 | 953 |
| Mar. 21 or Sept. 21 | 1392 | 1392 | 1392 | 1392 | 1392 |
| Apr. 21 or Aug. 21 | 1889 | 1889 | 1889 | 1889 | 1889 |
| May 21 or July 21 | 2185 | 2185 | 2185 | 2185 | 2185 |
| June 21 | 2300 | 2300 | 2300 | 2300 | 2300 |

**10° Inclination**

| Month | S. | SE./SW. | E./W. | NE./NW. | N. |
|---|---|---|---|---|---|
| Dec. 21 | 741 | 686 | 525 | 385 | 309 |
| Jan. 21 or Nov. 21 | 800 | 737 | 574 | 451 | 363 |
| Feb. 21 or Oct. 21 | 1177 | 1106 | 942 | 781 | 704 |
| Mar. 21 or Sept. 21 | 1573 | 1535 | 1382 | 1235 | 1173 |
| Apr. 21 or Aug. 21 | 1999 | 1920 | 1870 | 1777 | 1719 |
| May 21 or July 21 | 2153 | 2220 | 2165 | 2128 | 2096 |
| June 21 | 2298 | 2306 | 2279 | 2262 | 2238 |

**20° Inclination**

| Month | S. | SE./SW. | E./W. | NE./NW. | N. |
|---|---|---|---|---|---|
| Dec. 21 | 931 | 760 | 519 | 241 | 96 |
| Jan. 21 or Nov. 21 | 981 | 863 | 561 | 299 | 142 |
| Feb. 21 or Oct. 21 | 1352 | 1232 | 900 | 616 | 457 |
| Mar. 21 or Sept. 21 | 1708 | 1607 | 1340 | 1044 | 899 |
| Apr. 21 or Aug. 21 | 2054 | 1992 | 1806 | 1612 | 1502 |
| May 21 or July 21 | 2181 | 2180 | 2083 | 1984 | 1938 |
| June 21 | 2241 | 2249 | 2188 | 2062 | 2107 |

**30° Inclination**

| Month | S. | SE./SW. | E./W. | NE./NW. | N. |
|---|---|---|---|---|---|
| Dec. 21 | 1065 | 910 | 490 | 99 | — |
| Jan. 21 or Nov. 21 | 1127 | 960 | 561 | 192 | — |
| Feb. 21 or Oct. 21 | 1494 | 1313 | 887 | 450 | 194 |
| Mar. 21 or Sept. 21 | 1779 | 1650 | 1278 | 844 | 633 |
| Apr. 21 or Aug. 21 | 2028 | 1979 | 1723 | 1383 | 1232 |
| May 21 or July 21 | 2091 | 2095 | 1985 | 1787 | 1714 |
| June 21 | 2100 | 2118 | 2079 | 1949 | 1889 |

**45° Inclination**

| Month | S. | SE./SW. | E./W. | NE./NW. | N. |
|---|---|---|---|---|---|
| Dec. 21 | 1258 | 1003 | 486 | 39 | — |
| Jan. 21 or Nov. 21 | 1299 | 1053 | 531 | 131 | — |
| Feb. 21 or Oct. 21 | 1525 | 1351 | 835 | 328 | — |
| Mar. 21 or Sept. 21 | 1794 | 1617 | 1177 | 628 | 191 |
| Apr. 21 or Aug. 21 | 1991 | 1846 | 1560 | 1063 | 813 |
| May 21 or July 21 | 1818 | 1860 | 1753 | 1343 | 1334 |
| June 21 | 1808 | 1884 | 1841 | 1592 | 1544 |

**60° Inclination**

| Month | S. | SE./SW. | E./W. | NE./NW. | N. |
|---|---|---|---|---|---|
| Dec. 21 | 1344 | 1019 | 401 | 26 | — |
| Jan. 21 or Nov. 21 | 1368 | 1080 | 440 | 52 | — |
| Feb. 21 or Oct. 21 | 1602 | 1333 | 700 | 205 | — |
| Mar. 21 or Sept. 21 | 1706 | 1519 | 1036 | 477 | 3 |
| Apr. 21 or Aug. 21 | 1647 | 1631 | 1346 | 794 | 272 |
| May 21 or July 21 | 1457 | 1585 | 1515 | 1092 | 842 |
| June 21 | 1407 | 1579 | 1590 | 1223 | 1013 |

**75° Inclination**

| Month | S. | SE./SW. | E./W. | NE./NW. | N. |
|---|---|---|---|---|---|
| Dec. 21 | 1334 | 997 | 309 | 13 | — |
| Jan. 21 or Nov. 21 | 1344 | 1037 | 361 | 39 | — |
| Feb. 21 or Oct. 21 | 1497 | 1207 | 628 | 130 | — |
| Mar. 21 or Sept. 21 | 1469 | 1296 | 935 | 325 | — |
| Apr. 21 or Aug. 21 | 1272 | 1322 | 1109 | 591 | 87 |
| May 21 or July 21 | 985 | 1218 | 1250 | 841 | 298 |
| June 21 | 905 | 1182 | 1281 | 905 | 485 |

**90° Inclination**

| Month | S. | SE./SW. | E./W. | NE./NW. | N. |
|---|---|---|---|---|---|
| Dec. 21 | 1250 | 917 | 235 | 10 | — |
| Jan. 21 or Nov. 21 | 1235 | 911 | 235 | 24 | — |
| Feb. 21 or Oct. 21 | 1314 | 1013 | 459 | 95 | — |
| Mar. 21 or Sept. 21 | 1138 | 1067 | 788 | 227 | — |
| Apr. 21 or Aug. 21 | 830 | 994 | 872 | 407 | 41 |
| May 21 or July 21 | 469 | 844 | 998 | 588 | 161 |
| June 21 | 407 | 807 | 978 | 673 | 237 |

---

## TABLE B.—Diffuse Radiation for Clear Skies

40° N. Lat.  Radiation: Diffuse clear  
(New York-New Jersey area)  
Total daily B. t. u./sq. ft.

**0° Inclination**

| Month | S. | SE./SW. | E./W. | NE./NW. | N. |
|---|---|---|---|---|---|
| Dec. 21 | 143 | 143 | 143 | 143 | 143 |
| Jan. 21 or Nov. 21 | 159 | 159 | 159 | 159 | 159 |
| Feb. 21 or Oct. 21 | 216 | 216 | 216 | 216 | 216 |
| Mar. 21 or Sept. 21 | 291 | 291 | 291 | 291 | 291 |
| Apr. 21 or Aug. 21 | 375 | 375 | 375 | 375 | 375 |
| May 21 or July 21 | 427 | 427 | 427 | 427 | 427 |
| June 21 | 451 | 451 | 451 | 451 | 451 |

**10° Inclination**

| Month | S. | SE./SW. | E./W. | NE./NW. | N. |
|---|---|---|---|---|---|
| Dec. 21 | 156 | 148 | 141 | 135 | 136 |
| Jan. 21 or Nov. 21 | 172 | 170 | 161 | 156 | 153 |
| Feb. 21 or Oct. 21 | 233 | 229 | 221 | 209 | 204 |
| Mar. 21 or Sept. 21 | 309 | 303 | 288 | 278 | 273 |
| Apr. 21 or Aug. 21 | 381 | 378 | 373 | 365 | 350 |
| May 21 or July 21 | 453 | 435 | 427 | 416 | 402 |
| June 21 | 457 | 458 | 453 | 448 | 423 |

**20° Inclination**

| Month | S. | SE./SW. | E./W. | NE./NW. | N. |
|---|---|---|---|---|---|
| Dec. 21 | 170 | 158 | 118 | 130 | 128 |
| Jan. 21 or Nov. 21 | 185 | 178 | 136 | 150 | 144 |
| Feb. 21 or Oct. 21 | 247 | 244 | 202 | 199 | 193 |
| Mar. 21 or Sept. 21 | 320 | 314 | 271 | 268 | 257 |
| Apr. 21 or Aug. 21 | 401 | 394 | 357 | 342 | 338 |
| May 21 or July 21 | 441 | 440 | 412 | 407 | 398 |
| June 21 | 457 | 457 | 427 | 424 | 423 |

**30° Inclination**

| Month | S. | SE./SW. | E./W. | NE./NW. | N. |
|---|---|---|---|---|---|
| Dec. 21 | 183 | 166 | 118 | 128 | 122 |
| Jan. 21 or Nov. 21 | 198 | 188 | 139 | 143 | 137 |
| Feb. 21 or Oct. 21 | 264 | 252 | 200 | 193 | 185 |
| Mar. 21 or Sept. 21 | 329 | 320 | 273 | 254 | 241 |
| Apr. 21 or Aug. 21 | 402 | 395 | 350 | 340 | 319 |
| May 21 or July 21 | 428 | 437 | 405 | 395 | 376 |
| June 21 | 441 | 449 | 423 | 415 | 402 |

**45° Inclination**

| Month | S. | SE./SW. | E./W. | NE./NW. | N. |
|---|---|---|---|---|---|
| Dec. 21 | 203 | 180 | 118 | 122 | 116 |
| Jan. 21 or Nov. 21 | 210 | 199 | 138 | 137 | 135 |
| Feb. 21 or Oct. 21 | 272 | 261 | 200 | 184 | 179 |
| Mar. 21 or Sept. 21 | 333 | 319 | 268 | 245 | 229 |
| Apr. 21 or Aug. 21 | 391 | 388 | 344 | 316 | 294 |
| May 21 or July 21 | 405 | 413 | 391 | 370 | 349 |
| June 21 | 407 | 419 | 406 | 379 | 371 |

**60° Inclination**

| Month | S. | SE./SW. | E./W. | NE./NW. | N. |
|---|---|---|---|---|---|
| Dec. 21 | 222 | 182 | 140 | 119 | 113 |
| Jan. 21 or Nov. 21 | 218 | 206 | 160 | 132 | 128 |
| Feb. 21 or Oct. 21 | 275 | 265 | 200 | 174 | 172 |
| Mar. 21 or Sept. 21 | 320 | 315 | 281 | 233 | 219 |
| Apr. 21 or Aug. 21 | 354 | 363 | 347 | 297 | 274 |
| May 21 or July 21 | 370 | 380 | 388 | 353 | 322 |
| June 21 | 374 | 389 | 403 | 369 | 341 |

**75° Inclination**

| Month | S. | SE./SW. | E./W. | NE./NW. | N. |
|---|---|---|---|---|---|
| Dec. 21 | 214 | 179 | 133 | 116 | 107 |
| Jan. 21 or Nov. 21 | 214 | 203 | 154 | 129 | 124 |
| Feb. 21 or Oct. 21 | 263 | 252 | 187 | 170 | 161 |
| Mar. 21 or Sept. 21 | 296 | 301 | 248 | 220 | 204 |
| Apr. 21 or Aug. 21 | 324 | 335 | 327 | 282 | 258 |
| May 21 or July 21 | 329 | 353 | 362 | 327 | 297 |
| June 21 | 337 | 357 | 372 | 344 | 313 |

**90° Inclination**

| Month | S. | SE./SW. | E./W. | NE./NW. | N. |
|---|---|---|---|---|---|
| Dec. 21 | 199 | 173 | 133 | 112 | 105 |
| Jan. 21 or Nov. 21 | 205 | 190 | 151 | 125 | 122 |
| Feb. 21 or Oct. 21 | 242 | 236 | 201 | 165 | 158 |
| Mar. 21 or Sept. 21 | 272 | 288 | 248 | 213 | 204 |
| Apr. 21 or Aug. 21 | 296 | 309 | 302 | 296 | 252 |
| May 21 or July 21 | 308 | 323 | 332 | 315 | 289 |
| June 21 | 314 | 325 | 344 | 325 | 307 |

---

## TABLE C.—Total Radiation for Clear Skies

40° N. Lat.  Radiation: Total clear  
(New York-New Jersey area)  
Total daily B. t. u./sq. ft.

**0° Inclination**

| Month | S. | SE./SW. | E./W. | NE./NW. | N. |
|---|---|---|---|---|---|
| Dec. 21 | 675 | 675 | 675 | 675 | 675 |
| Jan. 21 or Nov. 21 | 747 | 747 | 747 | 747 | 747 |
| Feb. 21 or Oct. 21 | 1169 | 1169 | 1169 | 1169 | 1169 |
| Mar. 21 or Sept. 21 | 1683 | 1683 | 1683 | 1683 | 1683 |
| Apr. 21 or Aug. 21 | 2264 | 2264 | 2264 | 2264 | 2264 |
| May 21 or July 21 | 2612 | 2612 | 2612 | 2612 | 2612 |
| June 21 | 2751 | 2751 | 2751 | 2751 | 2751 |

**10° Inclination**

| Month | S. | SE./SW. | E./W. | NE./NW. | N. |
|---|---|---|---|---|---|
| Dec. 21 | 897 | 834 | 666 | 520 | 445 |
| Jan. 21 or Nov. 21 | 972 | 907 | 735 | 607 | 516 |
| Feb. 21 or Oct. 21 | 1410 | 1335 | 1163 | 990 | 908 |
| Mar. 21 or Sept. 21 | 1882 | 1838 | 1670 | 1513 | 1446 |
| Apr. 21 or Aug. 21 | 2380 | 2298 | 2243 | 2142 | 2069 |
| May 21 or July 21 | 2606 | 2655 | 2592 | 2544 | 2498 |
| June 21 | 2725 | 2764 | 2732 | 2710 | 2661 |

**20° Inclination**

| Month | S. | SE./SW. | E./W. | NE./NW. | N. |
|---|---|---|---|---|---|
| Dec. 21 | 1101 | 918 | 637 | 371 | 224 |
| Jan. 21 or Nov. 21 | 1166 | 1041 | 710 | 449 | 286 |
| Feb. 21 or Oct. 21 | 1599 | 1476 | 1102 | 815 | 650 |
| Mar. 21 or Sept. 21 | 2028 | 1921 | 1611 | 1312 | 1156 |
| Apr. 21 or Aug. 21 | 2455 | 2386 | 2163 | 1964 | 1840 |
| May 21 or July 21 | 2622 | 2620 | 2495 | 2391 | 2336 |
| June 21 | 2698 | 2706 | 2615 | 2563 | 2530 |

**30° Inclination**

| Month | S. | SE./SW. | E./W. | NE./NW. | N. |
|---|---|---|---|---|---|
| Dec. 21 | 1208 | 1076 | 608 | 227 | 122 |
| Jan. 21 or Nov. 21 | 1325 | 1148 | 700 | 335 | 137 |
| Feb. 21 or Oct. 21 | 1758 | 1565 | 1087 | 643 | 379 |
| Mar. 21 or Sept. 21 | 2108 | 1970 | 1551 | 1098 | 874 |
| Apr. 21 or Aug. 21 | 2430 | 2374 | 2073 | 1723 | 1551 |
| May 21 or July 21 | 2519 | 2532 | 2390 | 2183 | 2090 |
| June 21 | 2541 | 2567 | 2502 | 2364 | 2291 |

**45° Inclination**

| Month | S. | SE./SW. | E./W. | NE./NW. | N. |
|---|---|---|---|---|---|
| Dec. 21 | 1461 | 1183 | 604 | 161 | 116 |
| Jan. 21 or Nov. 21 | 1509 | 1252 | 669 | 268 | 135 |
| Feb. 21 or Oct. 21 | 1797 | 1612 | 1035 | 512 | 179 |
| Mar. 21 or Sept. 21 | 2127 | 1936 | 1445 | 873 | 420 |
| Apr. 21 or Aug. 21 | 2382 | 2234 | 1904 | 1379 | 1107 |
| May 21 or July 21 | 2223 | 2277 | 2144 | 1713 | 1683 |
| June 21 | 2215 | 2303 | 2247 | 1971 | 1915 |

**60° Inclination**

| Month | S. | SE./SW. | E./W. | NE./NW. | N. |
|---|---|---|---|---|---|
| Dec. 21 | 1566 | 1201 | 541 | 145 | 113 |
| Jan. 21 or Nov. 21 | 1586 | 1286 | 600 | 184 | 128 |
| Feb. 21 or Oct. 21 | 1877 | 1598 | 900 | 379 | 172 |
| Mar. 21 or Sept. 21 | 2026 | 1834 | 1317 | 710 | 222 |
| Apr. 21 or Aug. 21 | 2001 | 1994 | 1693 | 1091 | 546 |
| May 21 or July 21 | 1827 | 1965 | 1903 | 1445 | 1164 |
| June 21 | 1781 | 1968 | 1993 | 1592 | 1354 |

**75° Inclination**

| Month | S. | SE./SW. | E./W. | NE./NW. | N. |
|---|---|---|---|---|---|
| Dec. 21 | 1548 | 1176 | 445 | 129 | 107 |
| Jan. 21 or Nov. 21 | 1558 | 1240 | 515 | 149 | 124 |
| Feb. 21 or Oct. 21 | 1760 | 1459 | 815 | 300 | 161 |
| Mar. 21 or Sept. 21 | 1765 | 1597 | 1203 | 545 | 204 |
| Apr. 21 or Aug. 21 | 1596 | 1657 | 1436 | 873 | 345 |
| May 21 or July 21 | 1314 | 1571 | 1612 | 1168 | 595 |
| June 21 | 1242 | 1539 | 1653 | 1249 | 798 |

**90° Inclination**

| Month | S. | SE./SW. | E./W. | NE./NW. | N. |
|---|---|---|---|---|---|
| Dec. 21 | 1449 | 1090 | 368 | 122 | 105 |
| Jan. 21 or Nov. 21 | 1440 | 1101 | 386 | 149 | 122 |
| Feb. 21 or Oct. 21 | 1556 | 1249 | 660 | 260 | 158 |
| Mar. 21 or Sept. 21 | 1410 | 1355 | 1036 | 440 | 204 |
| Apr. 21 or Aug. 21 | 1126 | 1303 | 1174 | 673 | 293 |
| May 21 or July 21 | 777 | 1167 | 1330 | 903 | 450 |
| June 21 | 721 | 1132 | 1322 | 998 | 544 |

Table D.—*Direct Radiation for Average Conditions*

40° N. Lat. Radiation: Direct average
(New York-New Jersey area)
Total daily B. t. u./sq. ft.

| Month | S. | SE. SW. | E. W. | NE. NW. | N. |
|---|---|---|---|---|---|
| **0° Inclination** | | | | | |
| Dec. 21 | 261 | 261 | 261 | 261 | 261 |
| Jan. 21 or Nov. 21 | 288- 312 | 288- 312 | 288- 312 | 288- 312 | 288- 312 |
| Feb. 21 or Oct. 21 | 505- 562 | 505- 562 | 505- 562 | 505- 562 | 505- 562 |
| Mar. 21 or Sept. 21 | 682- 835 | 682- 835 | 682- 835 | 682- 835 | 682- 835 |
| Apr. 21 or Aug. 21 | 963-1039 | 963-1039 | 963-1039 | 963-1039 | 963-1039 |
| May 21 or July 21 | 1180-1202 | 1180-1202 | 1180-1202 | 1180-1202 | 1180-1202 |
| June 21 | 1219 | 1219 | 1219 | 1219 | 1219 |
| **10° Inclination** | | | | | |
| Dec. 21 | 363 | 336 | 257 | 189 | 151 |
| Jan. 21 or Nov. 21 | 392- 424 | 361- 391 | 281- 304 | 220- 239 | 178- 192 |
| Feb. 21 or Oct. 21 | 624- 694 | 586- 633 | 499- 556 | 414- 461 | 373- 415 |
| Mar. 21 or Sept. 21 | 771- 944 | 752- 921 | 677- 829 | 605- 741 | 575- 704 |
| Apr. 21 or Aug. 21 | 1019-1099 | 980-1055 | 954-1029 | 906- 977 | 877- 945 |
| May 21 or July 21 | 1163-1184 | 1199-1221 | 1169-1191 | 1149-1170 | 1132-1153 |
| June 21 | 1200 | 1222 | 1208 | 1199 | 1186 |
| **20° Inclination** | | | | | |
| Dec. 21 | 456 | 372 | 254 | 118 | 47 |
| Jan. 21 or Nov. 21 | 481- 520 | 423- 457 | 281- 304 | 147- 158 | 70- 75 |
| Feb. 21 or Oct. 21 | 717- 798 | 653- 727 | 477- 531 | 326- 363 | 242- 270 |
| Mar. 21 or Sept. 21 | 837-1025 | 787- 964 | 657- 804 | 512- 626 | 441- 539 |
| Apr. 21 or Aug. 21 | 1048-1130 | 1016-1096 | 921- 993 | 822- 887 | 766- 826 |
| May 21 or July 21 | 1178-1200 | 1177-1199 | 1125-1146 | 1071-1091 | 1047-1066 |
| June 21 | 1188 | 1192 | 1160 | 1134 | 1117 |
| **30° Inclination** | | | | | |
| Dec. 21 | 532 | 446 | 240 | 49 | ------- |
| Jan. 21 or Nov. 21 | 552- 597 | 470- 509 | 275- 297 | 94- 102 | ------- |
| Feb. 21 or Oct. 21 | 792- 881 | 696- 775 | 470- 523 | 239- 266 | 103- 114 |
| Mar. 21 or Sept. 21 | 872-1067 | 809- 990 | 626- 767 | 414- 506 | 310- 380 |
| Apr. 21 or Aug. 21 | 1034-1115 | 1009-1088 | 879- 948 | 705- 761 | 628- 678 |
| May 21 or July 21 | 1129-1150 | 1131-1152 | 1072-1092 | 965- 983 | 926- 943 |
| June 21 | 1113 | 1123 | 1102 | 1033 | 1001 |
| **45° Inclination** | | | | | |
| Dec. 21 | 616 | 491 | 238 | 19 | ------- |
| Jan. 21 or Nov. 21 | 637- 688 | 516- 558 | 260- 281 | 64- 69 | ------- |
| Feb. 21 or Oct. 21 | 807- 898 | 716- 797 | 443- 493 | 174- 194 | ------- |
| Mar. 21 or Sept. 21 | 879-1076 | 792- 970 | 577- 706 | 308- 377 | 94- 115 |
| Apr. 21 or Aug. 21 | 1015-1095 | 941-1015 | 796- 858 | 542- 585 | 415- 447 |
| May 21 or July 21 | 982-1000 | 1007-1025 | 947- 964 | 725- 739 | 720- 734 |
| June 21 | 958 | 999 | 976 | 844 | 818 |
| **60° Inclination** | | | | | |
| Dec. 21 | 659 | 499 | 196 | 13 | ------- |
| Jan. 21 or Nov. 21 | 670- 725 | 529- 572 | 216- 233 | 25- 28 | ------- |
| Feb. 21 or Oct. 21 | 849- 945 | 706- 786 | 371- 412 | 109- 121 | ------- |
| Mar. 21 or Sept. 21 | 836-1024 | 744- 911 | 508- 622 | 234- 286 | 1- 1 |
| Apr. 21 or Aug. 21 | 840- 906 | 832- 897 | 686- 740 | 405- 437 | 139- 150 |
| May 21 or July 21 | 787- 801 | 856- 872 | 818- 833 | 589- 601 | 455- 463 |
| June 21 | 746 | 837 | 843 | 648 | 537 |
| **75° Inclination** | | | | | |
| Dec. 21 | 654 | 489 | 151 | 6 | ------- |
| Jan. 21 or Nov. 21 | 659- 712 | 508- 550 | 176- 190 | 19- 21 | ------- |
| Feb. 21 or Oct. 21 | 793- 883 | 640- 712 | 308- 377 | 69- 77 | ------- |
| Mar. 21 or Sept. 21 | 720- 881 | 635- 778 | 458- 561 | 159- 195 | ------- |
| Apr. 21 or Aug. 21 | 649- 700 | 674- 727 | 566- 610 | 301- 325 | 44- 48 |
| May 21 or July 21 | 532- 542 | 658- 670 | 675- 688 | 454- 463 | 161- 164 |
| June 21 | 480 | 626 | 679 | 480 | 257 |
| **90° Inclination** | | | | | |
| Dec. 21 | 613 | 449 | 115 | 5 | ------- |
| Jan. 21 or Nov. 21 | 605- 655 | 446- 483 | 115- 125 | 12- 13 | ------- |
| Feb. 21 or Oct. 21 | 696- 775 | 537- 598 | 243- 271 | 50- 56 | ------- |
| Mar. 21 or Sept. 21 | 558- 683 | 523- 640 | 386- 473 | 111- 136 | ------- |
| Apr. 21 or Aug. 21 | 423- 457 | 507- 547 | 445- 480 | 208- 224 | 21- 23 |
| May 21 or July 21 | 253- 258 | 456- 464 | 539- 549 | 318- 323 | 87- 86 |
| June 21 | 216 | 428 | 518 | 357 | 129 |

Table E.—*Diffuse Radiation for Average Conditions*

40° N. Lat. Radiation: Diffuse average
(New York-New Jersey area)
Total daily B. t. u./sq. ft.

| Month | S. | SE. SW. | E. W. | NE. NW. | N. |
|---|---|---|---|---|---|
| **0° Inclination** | | | | | |
| Dec. 21 | 202 | 202 | 202 | 202 | 202 |
| Jan. 21 or Nov. 21 | 224 | 224 | 224 | 224 | 224 |
| Feb. 21 or Oct. 21 | 304 | 304 | 304 | 304 | 304 |
| Mar. 21 or Sept. 21 | 423 | 423 | 423 | 423 | 423 |
| Apr. 21 or Aug. 21 | 583 | 583 | 583 | 583 | 583 |
| May 21 or July 21 | 671 | 671 | 671 | 671 | 671 |
| June 21 | 701 | 701 | 701 | 701 | 701 |
| **10° Inclination** | | | | | |
| Dec. 21 | 220 | 209 | 198 | 188 | 191 |
| Jan. 21 or Nov. 21 | 242 | 239 | 226 | 218 | 216 |
| Feb. 21 or Oct. 21 | 328 | 322 | 311 | 293 | 287 |
| Mar. 21 or Sept. 21 | 465 | 448 | 425 | 403 | 390 |
| Apr. 21 or Aug. 21 | 599 | 590 | 582 | 567 | 541 |
| May 21 or July 21 | 685 | 685 | 673 | 656 | 628 |
| June 21 | 712 | 715 | 708 | 700 | 656 |
| **20° Inclination** | | | | | |
| Dec. 21 | 239 | 223 | 165 | 173 | 169 |
| Jan. 21 or Nov. 21 | 260 | 251 | 190 | 205 | 190 |
| Feb. 21 or Oct. 21 | 362 | 348 | 282 | 272 | 254 |
| Mar. 21 or Sept. 21 | 481 | 466 | 416 | 378 | 362 |
| Apr. 21 or Aug. 21 | 632 | 616 | 558 | 522 | 515 |
| May 21 or July 21 | 693 | 689 | 650 | 634 | 616 |
| June 21 | 710 | 710 | 670 | 656 | 656 |
| **30° Inclination** | | | | | |
| Dec. 21 | 258 | 233 | 165 | 171 | 161 |
| Jan. 21 or Nov. 21 | 279 | 265 | 191 | 191 | 178 |
| Feb. 21 or Oct. 21 | 385 | 363 | 280 | 264 | 244 |
| Mar. 21 or Sept. 21 | 499 | 481 | 411 | 348 | 323 |
| Apr. 21 or Aug. 21 | 634 | 621 | 542 | 507 | 466 |
| May 21 or July 21 | 671 | 683 | 636 | 603 | 584 |
| June 21 | 693 | 695 | 660 | 634 | 618 |
| **45° Inclination** | | | | | |
| Dec. 21 | 298 | 253 | 165 | 160 | 153 |
| Jan. 21 or Nov. 21 | 310 | 285 | 188 | 178 | 178 |
| Feb. 21 or Oct. 21 | 398 | 386 | 274 | 245 | 236 |
| Mar. 21 or Sept. 21 | 507 | 488 | 391 | 334 | 303 |
| Apr. 21 or Aug. 21 | 607 | 601 | 527 | 452 | 414 |
| May 21 or July 21 | 631 | 640 | 605 | 555 | 508 |
| June 21 | 628 | 637 | 625 | 570 | 552 |
| **60° Inclination** | | | | | |
| Dec. 21 | 326 | 264 | 190 | 148 | 140 |
| Jan. 21 or Nov. 21 | 320 | 299 | 217 | 170 | 169 |
| Feb. 21 or Oct. 21 | 402 | 391 | 272 | 227 | 224 |
| Mar. 21 or Sept. 21 | 481 | 473 | 397 | 305 | 281 |
| Apr. 21 or Aug. 21 | 554 | 556 | 501 | 402 | 365 |
| May 21 or July 21 | 564 | 576 | 582 | 504 | 453 |
| June 21 | 562 | 585 | 607 | 529 | 480 |
| **75° Inclination** | | | | | |
| Dec. 21 | 314 | 259 | 184 | 143 | 127 |
| Jan. 21 or Nov. 21 | 316 | 295 | 206 | 158 | 146 |
| Feb. 21 or Oct. 21 | 384 | 364 | 252 | 212 | 194 |
| Mar. 21 or Sept. 21 | 444 | 438 | 371 | 280 | 258 |
| Apr. 21 or Aug. 21 | 484 | 502 | 456 | 367 | 328 |
| May 21 or July 21 | 480 | 517 | 512 | 442 | 395 |
| June 21 | 486 | 514 | 523 | 476 | 421 |
| **90° Inclination** | | | | | |
| Dec. 21 | 291 | 245 | 177 | 135 | 118 |
| Jan. 21 or Nov. 21 | 289 | 276 | 201 | 150 | 136 |
| Feb. 21 or Oct. 21 | 341 | 336 | 268 | 196 | 190 |
| Mar. 21 or Sept. 21 | 383 | 377 | 328 | 260 | 249 |
| Apr. 21 or Aug. 21 | 424 | 436 | 404 | 338 | 308 |
| May 21 or July 21 | 421 | 445 | 445 | 407 | 373 |
| June 21 | 430 | 444 | 462 | 420 | 395 |

Table F.—*Total Radiation for Average Conditions*

40° N. Lat. Radiation: Total average
(New York–New Jersey area)
Total daily B. t. u./sq. ft.

| Month | S. | SE. SW. | E. W. | NE. NW. | N. |
|---|---|---|---|---|---|
| **0° Inclination** | | | | | |
| Dec. 21 | 463 | 463 | 463 | 463 | 463 |
| Jan. 21 or Nov. 21 | 512- 536 | 512- 536 | 512- 536 | 512- 536 | 512- 536 |
| Feb. 21 or Oct. 21 | 809- 866 | 809- 866 | 809- 866 | 809- 866 | 809- 866 |
| Mar. 21 or Sept. 21 | 1105-1258 | 1105-1258 | 1105-1258 | 1105-1258 | 1105-1258 |
| Apr. 21 or Aug. 21 | 1546-1622 | 1546-1622 | 1546-1622 | 1546-1622 | 1546-1622 |
| May 21 or July 21 | 1851-1873 | 1851-1873 | 1851-1873 | 1851-1873 | 1851-1873 |
| June 21 | 1920 | 1920 | 1920 | 1920 | 1920 |
| **10° Inclination** | | | | | |
| Dec. 21 | 583 | 572 | 455 | 377 | 342 |
| Jan. 21 or Nov. 21 | 634- 666 | 600- 630 | 507- 530 | 438- 457 | 394- 408 |
| Feb. 21 or Oct. 21 | 952-1022 | 908- 975 | 810- 867 | 707- 754 | 660- 702 |
| Mar. 21 or Sept. 21 | 1236-1409 | 1200-1369 | 1102-1254 | 1008-1144 | 965-1094 |
| Apr. 21 or Aug. 21 | 1618-1698 | 1570-1645 | 1536-1611 | 1473-1544 | 1418-1486 |
| May 21 or July 21 | 1848-1869 | 1884-1906 | 1842-1864 | 1805-1826 | 1760-1781 |
| June 21 | 1912 | 1937 | 1916 | 1899 | 1842 |
| **20° Inclination** | | | | | |
| Dec. 21 | 695 | 595 | 419 | 291 | 216 |
| Jan. 21 or Nov. 21 | 741- 780 | 674- 708 | 471- 494 | 352- 363 | 260- 265 |
| Feb. 21 or Oct. 21 | 1079-1160 | 1001-1075 | 759- 813 | 598- 635 | 496- 524 |
| Mar. 21 or Sept. 21 | 1318-1506 | 1253-1430 | 1073-1220 | 890-1004 | 803- 901 |
| Apr. 21 or Aug. 21 | 1680-1762 | 1632-1712 | 1479-1551 | 1344-1409 | 1281-1341 |
| May 21 or July 21 | 1871-1893 | 1866-1888 | 1775-1796 | 1705-1725 | 1663-1682 |
| June 21 | 1898 | 1902 | 1830 | 1790 | 1773 |
| **30° Inclination** | | | | | |
| Dec. 21 | 790 | 679 | 405 | 220 | 161 |
| Jan. 21 or Nov. 21 | 831- 876 | 735- 774 | 466- 488 | 285- 193 | 178 |
| Feb. 21 or Oct. 21 | 1177-1266 | 1059-1138 | 750- 803 | 503- 530 | 347- 358 |
| Mar. 21 or Sept. 21 | 1371-1566 | 1290-1471 | 1037-1178 | 762- 854 | 633- 703 |
| Apr. 21 or Aug. 21 | 1668-1749 | 1630-1709 | 1421-1490 | 1212-1268 | 1094-1144 |
| May 21 or July 21 | 1800-1821 | 1814-1835 | 1708-1728 | 1568-1586 | 1510-1527 |
| June 21 | 1806 | 1818 | 1762 | 1667 | 1619 |
| **45° Inclination** | | | | | |
| Dec. 21 | 914 | 744 | 403 | 179 | 153 |
| Jan. 21 or Nov. 21 | 947- 998 | 801- 843 | 448- 469 | 242- 247 | 178 |
| Feb. 21 or Oct. 21 | 1205-1296 | 1102-1183 | 717- 767 | 419- 439 | 236 |
| Mar. 21 or Sept. 21 | 1386-1583 | 1280-1458 | 968-1097 | 642- 711 | 397- 418 |
| Apr. 21 or Aug. 21 | 1622-1702 | 1545-1616 | 1323-1385 | 994- 103 | 7829- 861 |
| May 21 or July 21 | 1613-1631 | 1647-1665 | 1552-1569 | 1280-1294 | 1228-1242 |
| June 21 | 1586 | 1636 | 1601 | 1414 | 1370 |
| **60° Inclination** | | | | | |
| Dec. 21 | 985 | 763 | 386 | 161 | 140 |
| Jan. 21 or Nov. 21 | 990-1045 | 828- 871 | 433- 450 | 195- 198 | 169 |
| Feb. 21 or Oct. 21 | 1251-1347 | 1097 1177 | 643- 684 | 336- 348 | 224 |
| Mar. 21 or Sept. 21 | 1317-1505 | 1217-1384 | 905-1019 | 539- 591 | 282-282 |
| Apr. 21 or Aug. 21 | 1394-1460 | 1388-1453 | 1187-1241 | 807- 839 | 504-515 |
| May 21 or July 21 | 1351-1365 | 1432-1448 | 1400-1415 | 1093-1105 | 908-916 |
| June 21 | 1308 | 1422 | 1450 | 1177 | 1017 |
| **75° Inclination** | | | | | |
| Dec. 21 | 968 | 748 | 335 | 149 | 127 |
| Jan. 21 or Nov. 21 | 975-1028 | 803- 845 | 382-396 | 177-179 | 146 |
| Feb. 21 or Oct. 21 | 1177-1267 | 1004-1076 | 560-629 | 281-289 | 194 |
| Mar. 21 or Sept. 21 | 1164-1325 | 1073-1216 | 829-932 | 439-475 | 258 |
| Apr. 21 or Aug. 21 | 1133-1184 | 1176-1229 | 1022-1066 | 668-692 | 372-376 |
| May 21 or July 21 | 1012-1022 | 1175-1187 | 1187-1200 | 896-905 | 556-559 |
| June 21 | 966 | 1140 | 1202 | 956 | 678 |
| **90° Inclination** | | | | | |
| Dec. 21 | 904 | 694 | 292 | 140 | 118 |
| Jan. 21 or Nov. 21 | 894- 944 | 722- 759 | 316-326 | 162-163 | 136 |
| Feb. 21 or Oct. 21 | 1037-1116 | 873- 934 | 511-539 | 246-252 | 190 |
| Mar. 21 or Sept. 21 | 941-1066 | 900-1017 | 714-801 | 371-396 | 249 |
| Apr. 21 or Aug. 21 | 847- 881 | 943- 983 | 849-884 | 546-562 | 329-331 |
| May 21 or July 21 | 674- 679 | 901- 909 | 984-994 | 725-730 | 460-462 |
| June 21 | 646 | 872 | 980 | 777 | 521 |

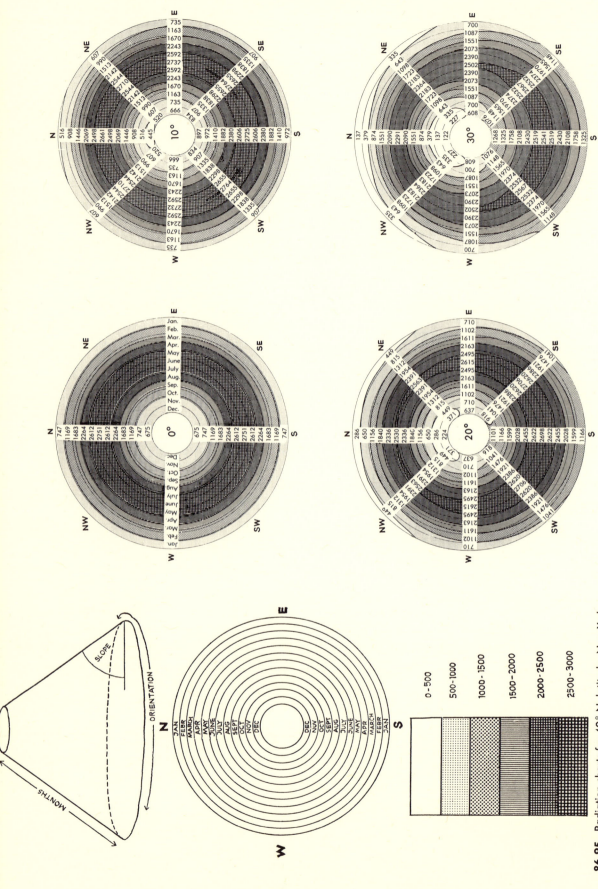

**86-95.** Radiation charts for 40° N. latitude, New York–New Jersey area.

When daily "clear sky" radiation values for the New York–New Jersey area are transposed on to a graph, the charts are designed as a truncated cone to show the relationship of time element to orientation. Different quantities of radiation are charted on the horizontal projection of the cone. The divisions of radiation intensities (by Btu/ft²/day) are indicated with different patterns. The charts indicate radiation effects on all orientations in eight inclinations from horizontal (0° slope) to vertical (90° slope).

Average radiation conditions are important in evaluating sites. In selecting advantageous locations, one should seek inclined surfaces which receive larger amounts of radiation during underheated periods, and less at overheated times, than a horizontal site. To ap-

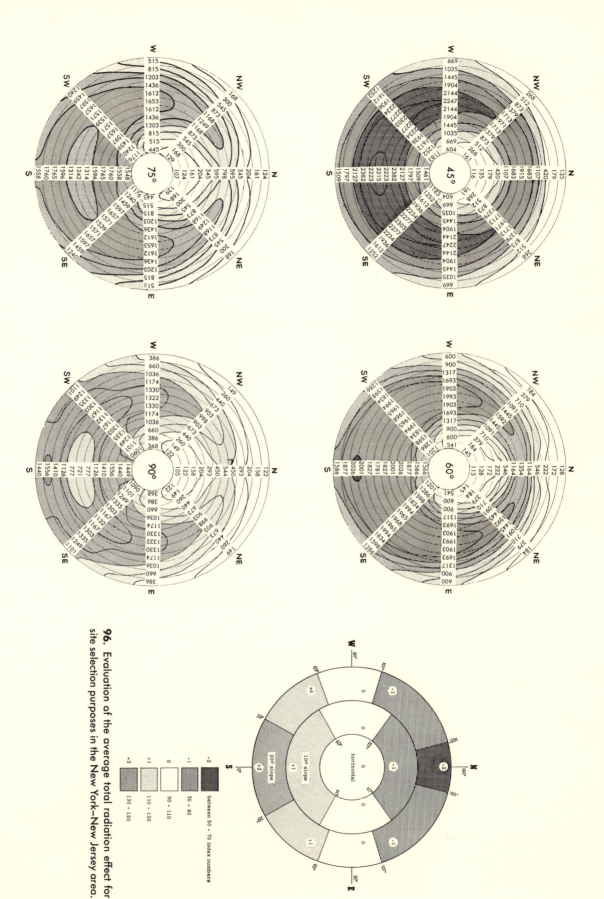

proximate those conditions in the following calculations the three coldest months (Dec. 7 to Mar. 7) and the three hottest months (June 7 to Sept. 7) of the year were taken as a yardstick. In the evaluations, slopes steeper than 20° were not investigated since generally they are considered unsuitable for ordinary building purposes. The results of the investigation are summarized, where for 10° and 20° slopes toward all orientations the radiation impacts are grouped into five arbitrary categories. These categories can also be expressed as radiation time factors, since the same radiation intensities received on southern slopes will be received on level sites a few weeks later. In other words, a sloped site which receives 20% more winter radiation than a level site, will be two weeks ahead in the arrival of spring.

96. Evaluation of the average total radiation effect for site selection purposes in the New York–New Jersey area.

49

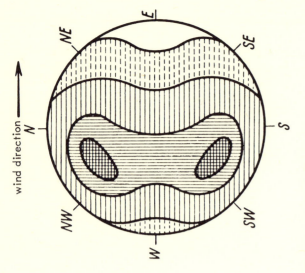

wind direction →

N NE E SE S SW W NW

**97.** Wind pattern around a hill.

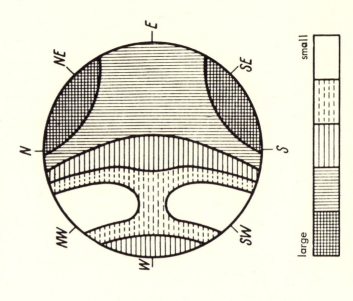

N NE E SE S SW W NW

**98.** Effect of wind speed on a hill.

large [ ] small

**99.** Precipitation distribution on a hill.

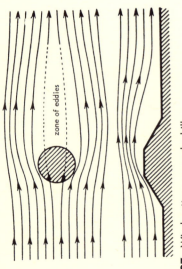

zone of eddies

**97.** Wind pattern around a hill.

Likewise, a sloped site receiving 40% more winter radiation will be 3½ weeks ahead. It is therefore assumed that as far as radiation is concerned, slopes with index numbers from 110 to 130 are 2 weeks closer, and slopes with index numbers from 130 to 150 are 3½ weeks closer, to spring, than are horizontal sites. Sites with index numbers smaller than 100 will have a later spring.

It should be noted here that since only radiation was taken into account, the graphs are symmetrical. However, bearing in mind the fact that mornings are cooler and afternoons warmer, preference in the choice of two territories with the same index number should be given the one toward the east rather than the west.

A hill has modification effects on both wind and precipitation distribution. Observation and measurements on these were done by Geiger.[7] A wind flow is diverted by a hill in both its horizontal and vertical stream patterns, causing higher speeds near the hilltop on the windward side and less turbulent wind conditions on the lee slope. The resultant wind distribution on a hill creates high velocity areas

below and at the sides on the crest; the lowest speeds are near the bottom of the hill in the wind "shadow."

Precipitation on the windward side is carried over a hill by the wind which strikes the slope, and falls on the lee side, where irregular weak air movements prevail. However, high mountains cause exactly reversed precipitation distributions. When air is forced to ascend on the windward side, this produces adiabatic processes of condensation and precipitation. This pattern of rainfall shapes the climatic character of the California coast. The water-laden Pacific Ocean winds bring about 20 inches of rainfall to the seaside valley. The rising air on the slope of the Sierras causes a deposit of more than 50 inches. The descending air at the eastern slope, compressed and warmed by the drop, sucks up moisture instead of releasing it. Thus the arid character of the Nevada side, where Reno receives only 6 inches of rain yearly. A similar effect prevails on the Riviera, where the protecting Alps shut out the cold north winds; and the descending air, heated by compression, provides mild winters.

## NATURAL AND BUILT-UP SURROUNDINGS

Water, having a higher specific heat than land, is normally warmer in winter and cooler in summer, and usually cooler during the day and warmer at night, than the terrain. Accordingly, the proximity of bodies of water moderates extreme temperature variations, and in winter raises the minimums, in summer lowers the heat peaks. In the Great Lakes region this effect raises the average January temperatures about 5° F, the absolute minimum temperatures about 10° F, and the annual minima about 15° F. Average July temperature is decreased about 3° F, and the annual absolute maximum is depressed about 5° F.[8] In the diurnal temperature variations, when the land is warmer than the water, low cool air moves over the land to replace the updraft. During the day, such offshore breeze may have a cooling effect of 10°. At night the direction is reversed. The effects depend on the size of the water body, and are more effective along the lee side.

The natural cover of the terrain tends to moderate extreme temperatures and stabilize conditions through the reflective qualities of various surfaces (discussed in the previous chapter). Plant and grassy covers reduce temperatures by absorption of insolation, and cool by evaporation. This reduction can amount to 1,500 Btu/sq ft/season.[9] It is generally found that temperatures over grass surfaces on sunny summer days are about 10° to 14° cooler than those of exposed soil. Other verdure may further reduce high temperatures; temperature under a tree at midday was observed to be 5° lower than in the unshaded environment.[10]

Conversely, cities and man-made surfaces tend to elevate temperatures, as the materials used are usually of absorptive character. Landsberg refers to observations, where asphalt surfaces reached 124° F in 98° air temperatures. He also measured the temperature distribution on a bright summer day in Washington, D.C., which varied 8° F within horizontal distances of a few miles. At night the differences in temperature were even larger; some suburban territories had temperatures 11° F lower than those downtown.[11] A schematic drawing illustrates the effect of "city climate." Note how closely the temperature lines follow built-up areas.

If one considers that a 9° difference in average temperature occurs in the United States roughly over a 9° latitude distance change, the importance of carefully selected sites becomes evident. Therefore, zoning should be differentiated according to the desirability in living conditions, based on microclimatic survey. Sites can be further improved by layout, windbreaks, and shade-tree arrangements. These aspects will be discussed in more detail in Chapters VII and IX.

## CRITERIA FOR SITE SELECTION

In various environments, according to the specific bioclimatic needs of a region, different topographic exposures will be desirable for habitation, and other human activities.

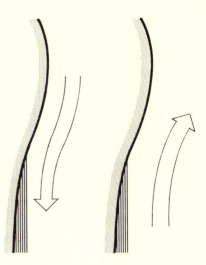

100. Air movements near a waterbody.

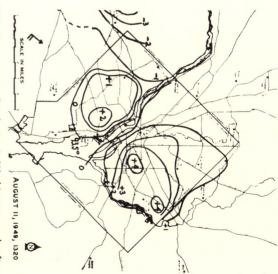

101. Temperature distribution in Washington, early afternoon in summer.

AUGUST 11, 1949, 1320

SCALE IN MILES

of lower portions of a slope. The upper topographical locations of a "warm slope" become advantageous provided there is adequate windbreak sheltering. Breeze utilization in warm periods grows in importance. This need not conflict with winter wind protection, as prevailing seasonal wind directions often do not coincide. In the temperate zone the varying needs of sun-heat gain and shade protection should be carefully considered.

In the hot-arid zone desirability of heat loss overrules the demands of the cool periods. Lower hillside locations, benefiting from cool air flow, are preferable if arrangements are made to avoid the flow during underheated times by "dam" action. A "courtyard" type of solution coincides with the need of capturing the air of the immediate surroundings that is cooled by the outgoing night radiation. Wind effects have relatively small importance. The large daily temperature range makes easterly exposures desirable for daily heat balance. In a large portion of the year afternoon shade is required; accordingly sites with ESE exposure are preferred in the hot-arid zone.

In hot-humid areas air movement constitutes the main comfort-restoring element. Sites offset from the prevailing wind direction, but exposed to high air-stream areas near the crest of a hill, or high elevations on the windward side near a ridge, are preferable. East and west sides of a hill receive more radiation than other orientations where the sun rays come in a more oblique angle. Therefore southern and northern slope directions are more desirable. However, wind-flow effects will remain the dominating consideration, as shading might be provided by other means.

The foregoing considerations of regional site selections are projected on schematic hill formations.

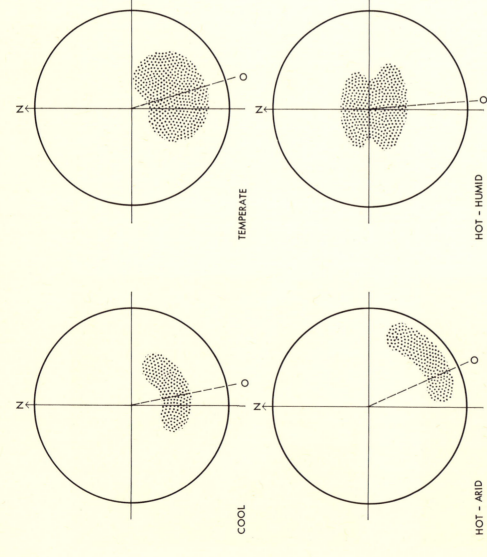

TEMPERATE

HOT - HUMID

COOL

HOT - ARID

**102. Desirable site locations in various zones.**

In the cool zone, where heat conservation is the main objective, protected sites are preferable. The lower part of the "thermal belt," on slopes placed in "wind shadow" areas but well exposed to winter insolation, offers advantageous positions. Orientation somewhat east of south secures balanced heat distribution. Accordingly, sites about halfway up a slope located in a SSE direction would offer the best

location for desirable cool-zone habitation. In the temperate zone, location requirements are not so strict as in the cold zone; however, they are broader in scope, inasmuch as needs for both over- and underheated periods must be correlated. Desirable site exposure tends to move farther east of south, as does the orientation index. The cool-air-flow effect is less important, allowing the utilization

52

# VI. SOL-AIR ORIENTATION

## BOUND TO THE SUN

EARLY man was bound to the sun's cycle and the rise of the beneficent sun was honored ritually in many groups by facing important buildings towards its dawning rays. The sun's movements were studied in Egypt, and temples and tombs in many periods found to be accurately aligned either with the cardinal directions, or their subdivisions.

Later, however, man no longer reacted to the sun mainly as a symbol; his interest had turned to its therapeutic and psychological effects. In his treatise "On Architecture" Vitruvius recognizes salubrious placement as the principle factor in a city and offers several instructions for such placement. Among such precepts is his statement that towns "if they looked toward the Midi or the Occident would not be salubrious because, during the summer, the meridional section of the sky grows warm at sunrise, and burning in the middle of the day; on the same account, those which look towards the Occident grow warm in the middle of the day and burning in the evening. Also, bodies deteriorate in such places because of this alternating heat and cold." He was rightly concerned with both the quality and the regularity of sunshine. The planner's view of orientation came nearer to the biological definition: "a change of position exhibited by certain protoplasmic bodies within the cell in relation to external influences, as light, heat...."

The total problem of orientation for buildings is composed of many factors: local topography, the requirements of privacy, the pleasures of a view, reduction of noise, and the climatic factors of wind and solar radiation.

(Wind directions and their effect on orientation are discussed in Chapter IX.) A large part of the architect's task is to position a building so as to take best advantage of the sun's value for thermal effect, hygiene, and psychological benefits.

Just as the seasons are strongly differentiated by the inclination of the earth's axis toward the sun, the orientation of a building is affected by the quantities of solar radiation falling on different sides at different times. In winter at 40° latitude a southern exposure receives nearly three times as much total sun energy as the east or west sides; while in summer the radiation falling on south plus north sides is only half of that absorbed by the east plus west elevations. At lower latitudes these ratios are even more pronounced, and can easily mean the difference between comfort and distress.

No doubt early mankind noted the adaptations of certain plant life to thermal stresses. Many plants besides the common sunflowers and marigolds are phototropic; the leaves of Convolvulus sepium may turn as much as 270° to follow the sun. Conversely, a form of wild lettuce called the "Compass Plant" (Latuca scariola) orients its leaves parallel to the sun's rays, to reduce the impact of radiation. A strong reflecting surface on another axis, however, can force the plant away from its consistent North-South orientation.[2]

Shown, in plan, is the sequence of blooming of a 15-year-old pine tree standing in the open.[3] The definite predominance of early buds toward South-Southwest defines the "heat-axis," the joint influence of sunshine, and high afternoon temperature.

Clues such as these, plus long experience and practical knowledge, must have guided

103.  Solar orientation in plant life.

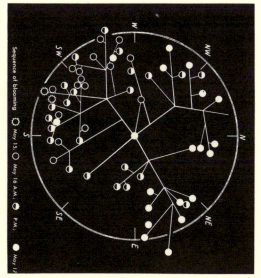

104.  Sequence of blooming of a free-standing pine tree.

the builders of Pueblo Indian towns such as Acoma, which is oriented slightly east of south, with long streets of massed dwelling units running east-west. In these row houses the radiation-vulnerable east and west sides are practically eliminated by being joined together, and leave only the north and south elevations to receive solar impacts.

The Egyptians and Classical builders were, of course, keenly conscious of solar orientation, probably as much for reasons of health as of their sun-dominated religions. The Cardo, or axis, of the standard Roman camp, consistently ranged not more than 30° from the meridian.[4]

**105. Acoma.**

N

## RECENT THEORIES

With the development of techniques for measuring radiation and the accumulation of factual data, the approach to orientation was made on a calculative basis. These measurements became the foundation for a number of solar-orientation theories.

Augustin Rey, J. Pidoux and C. Bardet[5] devised a "heliothermic" value as a basis for their theory of orientation. This value consists of the product of the duration of the insolation and the median temperature predominating during that time. Using this product they calculated yearly heat intensities at various orientations, and from these calculations arrived at a heliothermic axis which is 19° east of north.

Making calculations on sun intensities, Felix Marboutin[6] arrived at the following conclusions:

1. For best living conditions (warmth in winter, coolness in summer) principal façades of buildings should face south;
2. façades facing southeast and southwest offer the advantage of regularity of insolation, but they are colder in winter and warmer in summer than façades facing south;
3. east and west exposures are warmer in summer and colder in winter than are south, southeast, and southwest exposures.

Gaston Bardet[7] devised an orientation chart based on Marboutin's theory. Bardet finds south to be the preferred orientation, allowing variations up to 30° to the southeast and southwest.

A chart published by Jean Lebreton[8] defines orientations from south to 25° east of south as preferred, with orientations up to southeast classified as good conditions, and south to southwest classified as tolerable conditions.

Gaetano Vinaccia[9] searched for a position that would give equal radiation conditions to all four sides of a rectangular block of dwellings. He found an "equisolar axis," 32° from the east towards NE-SW and oriented his dwelling block with the two long sides parallel to that axis.

Ludwig Hilberseimer[10] concludes that east and west orientations are the least advantageous, that southeast and southwest are reasonably satisfactory and that south is the most advantageous. When southeast and southwest orientations are combined in a single dwelling unit, however, they are to be preferred to a due south orientation.

According to Henry Wright[11] a building should face 25° west of south to have the best orientation in the New York area. However, he used exaggerated values in his radiation calculations which make them unreliable.

A number of recent theories relating to "solar" houses have preferred true south orientation. This undoubtedly does yield the greatest amount of radiation at the winter solstice and the least amount of insolation at the summer solstice, but these theories do not consider daily temperature variations which make solar heat more necessary in the early morning and sometimes undesirable in the late afternoon. Theories urging maximum sunshine in every room do not apply to regions and seasons which are already overheated.

## SOL-AIR APPROACH

The "Sol-Air" approach to orientation recognizes that air temperature and solar radiation act together to produce one sensation of heat in the human body. Thus, to utilize the sun's rays fully, their thermal impacts must be considered in conjunction with heat convection, and the total effect measured by its ability to maintain temperature levels near the "comfort zone."

The importance of the sun's heat will, then, vary according to regions and seasons. Under cold conditions its additional radiation will be

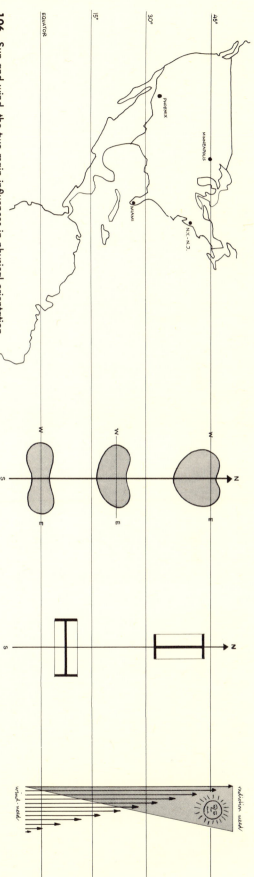

welcome and a building should be positioned to receive as much radiation as possible, while under conditions of excessive heat, the orientation of the same building should decrease undesirable solar impacts. By means of the bioclimatic chart these two conditions can be defined as the underheated and overheated periods of the year. An optimum orientation for a given site would give maximum radiation in the underheated period while simultaneously reducing insolation to a minimum in the overheated period.

The variation in orientation produced by regional requirements is diagrammatically presented in the accompanying illustration. In northern latitudes, the air is generally cool and there is a great need for the sun's heat. Consequently, buildings should be oriented so as to receive the maximum amount of radiation throughout the year. However, the same building in the south, where the air is heavy with heat, should turn its axis to avoid the sun's unwanted radiation and pick up cooling breezes instead.

The effects of solar radiation upon various

orientations are illustrated here by rotating a vertical surface around the compass at 30° intervals and calculating the resultant thermal impacts. The charts on the following page give these results for 40° N latitude, which were based on data from the New York–New Jersey area. Each of the charts shows:

1. Average direct radiation received in the underheated period ($R_u$) and the overheated period ($R_o$) of one year in thousand Btu.

2. Daily total clear-sky radiation in a year in Btu/ft² for the three coldest months (Dec. 7 to March 7) and the three warmest months (June 7 to Sept. 7). $R_o$ and $R_u$ indicate total amounts of radiation, but the curves show the distribution of Btu in time.

3. Typical hourly sol-air index, consisting of the temperature curve on March 21, plus the impact of radiation. This was calculated using the sol-air method, with an absorptivity derived from the bioclimatic chart. It shows the distribution of radiation in relation to the daily temperature curve. If radiation is received in the forenoon (as in the case of orientations toward the east) the curve shows a

rather even distribution of heat. If radiation is received in the afternoon (as in the case of orientations toward the west) the temperature peak and the radiation peak are added together. This results in a heavy heat impact in

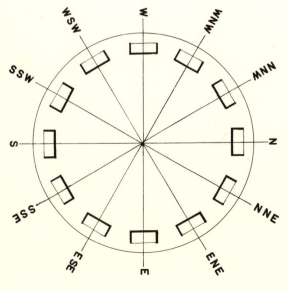

**107.** Explanatory orientation diagram used in the evaluations.

55

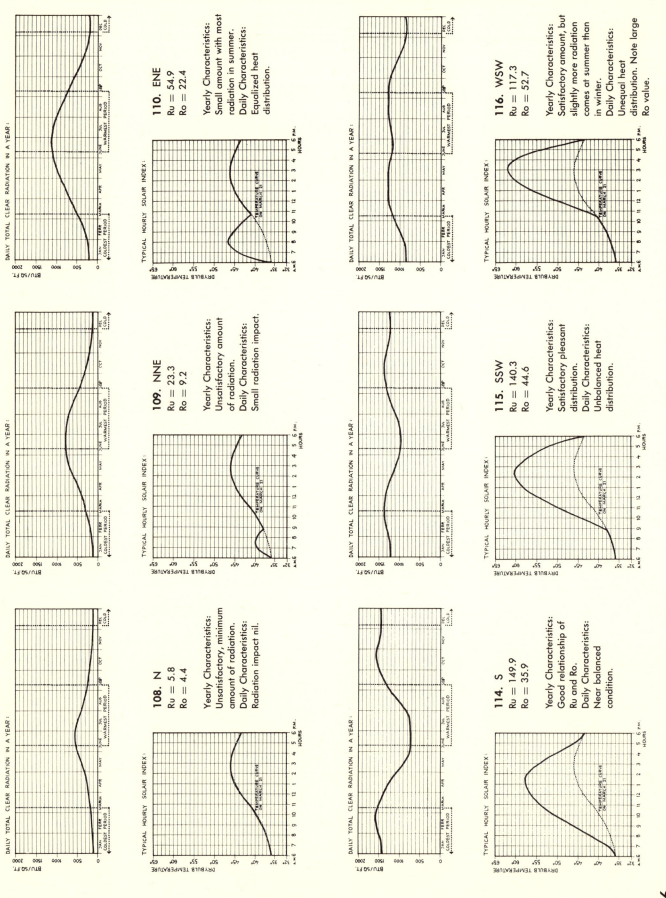

DAILY TOTAL CLEAR RADIATION IN A YEAR :

BTU/SQ. FT.

**110. ENE**
Ru = 54.9
Ro = 22.4

Yearly Characteristics:
Small amount with most radiation in summer.
Daily Characteristics:
Equalized heat distribution.

TYPICAL HOURLY SOLAIR INDEX :

DRYBULB TEMPERATURE

TEMPERATURE CURVE ON MARCH 21

HOURS

**116. WSW**
Ru = 117.3
Ro = 52.7

Yearly Characteristics:
Satisfactory amount, but slightly more radiation comes at summer than in winter.
Daily Characteristics:
Unequal heat distribution. Note large Ro value.

**109. NNE**
Ru = 23.3
Ro = 9.2

Yearly Characteristics:
Unsatisfactory amount of radiation.
Daily Characteristics:
Small radiation impact.

**115. SSW**
Ru = 140.3
Ro = 44.6

Yearly Characteristics:
Satisfactory pleasant distribution.
Daily Characteristics:
Unbalanced heat distribution.

**108. N**
Ru = 5.8
Ro = 4.4

Yearly Characteristics:
Unsatisfactory, minimum amount of radiation.
Daily Characteristics:
Radiation impact nil.

**114. S**
Ru = 149.9
Ro = 35.9

Yearly Characteristics:
Good relationship of Ru and Ro.
Daily Characteristics:
Near balanced condition.

DRYBULB TEMPERATURE

BTU/SQ.FT.

TYPICAL HOURLY SOLAIR INDEX:

DAILY TOTAL CLEAR RADIATION IN A YEAR:

TEMPERATURE CURVE ON MARCH 21

HOURS

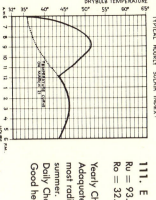
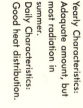
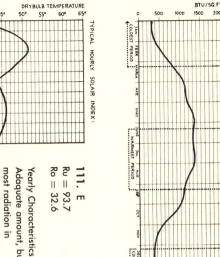
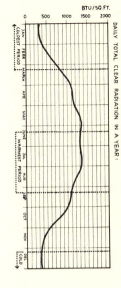
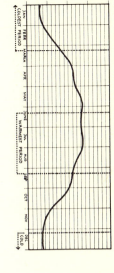

**111. E**
Ru = 93.7
Ro = 32.6

Yearly Characteristics:
Adequate amount, but most radiation in summer.
Daily Characteristics:
Good heat distribution.

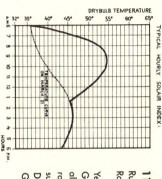

**112. ESE**
Ru = 132.4
Ro = 37.6

Yearly Characteristics:
Good distribution, although little more radiation come at summer than in winter.
Daily Characteristics:
Good heat distribution.

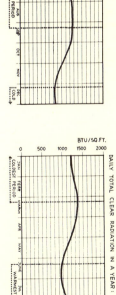

**113. SSE**
Ru = 150.8
Ro = 34.1

Yearly Characteristics:
Good distribution. Ru and Ro relationship very satisfactory.
Daily Characteristics:
Good balanced condition.

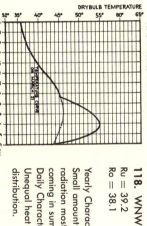

**117. W**
Ru = 74.4
Ro = 57.9

Yearly Characteristics:
Adequate amount, but most radiation comes in summer.
Daily Characteristics:
Badly unequal heat distribution. Note large Ro.

**118. WNW**
Ru = 39.2
Ro = 38.1

Yearly Characteristics:
Small amount of radiation most of it coming in summer.
Daily Characteristics:
Unequal heat distribution.

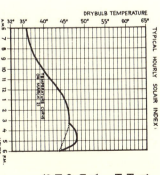
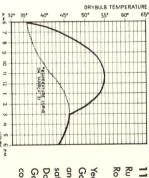
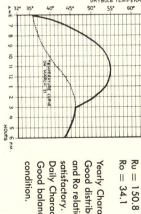
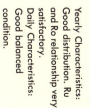

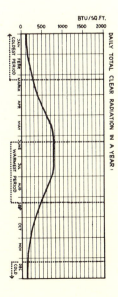

**119. NNW**
Ru = 18.7
Ro = 13.8

Yearly Characteristics:
Unsatisfactory amount of radiation.
Daily Characteristics:
Small radiation impact.

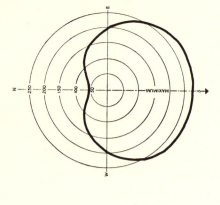

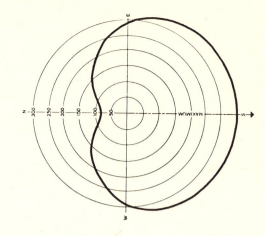

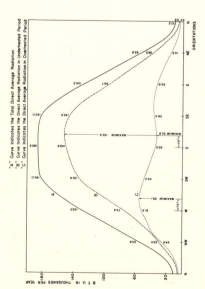

120. Yearly radiation received on vertical surfaces at different orientations in New York–New Jersey area.

the afternoon compared with the low temperatures in the forenoon.

These detailed radiation impacts can be plotted on a single chart. The one given here shows the total yearly direct average radiation impacts in the New York area (curve A) received on a vertical surface at all different orientations. This is the sum of the radiation received during the underheated period (curve B) and the radiation received during the overheated period (curve C). The optimum orientation is found where radiation is at maximum during the underheated period, and minimized during the overheated period.

## REGIONAL ADAPTATION

The orientation evaluation for the New York–New Jersey area, using total (direct and diffuse) radiation data, is shown on axial charts. The first circle gives the total yearly radiation with its maximum intensity pointing to the south. The second circle gives the amount of insolation received during the underheated period, where the maximum radiation intensity shifts from the south by 17½° toward east. The third circle gives the amount of radiation received during the overheated period, where the maximum occurs 17½° south of west. This leads to the conclusion that the optimum orientation will be at 17½° east of south for this region. "Good" and "satisfactory" orientations (fifth circle) were also derived from the radiation values occurring during the overheated (O) and underheated (U) periods (fourth circle).

The second example illustrates the orientation evaluation for Phoenix, Arizona. Here the total amount of radiation is larger, not only because of the difference in latitude, but also because of the larger proportion of clear weather. The New York–New Jersey area receives 60% of the possible yearly sunshine, while Phoenix receives 84%. In the warmer climate of Phoenix the underheated period is much shorter, the overheated period longer; the radiation circles show the difference. It can be seen that the desirable direction in the underheated period lies 32° east of south; and the undesirable radiation maximum in the overheated period is 22° south of west. Because the avoidable heat maximum in the overheated period and the desirable radiation axis in the underheated period do not fall perpendicular to one another, an adjustment is necessary. The adjustment weighing heat and cold stresses and durations was made here with a $1\frac{1}{3}-\frac{1}{3}$ ratio in favor of the overheated period, resulting in an "optimum" orientation for Phoenix of 25° east of south.

Evaluation of orientation on a yearly basis, depends on the surface which receives relatively the most radiation impact during the underheated season ($R_u$) and the least in overheated ($R_o$) times.

58

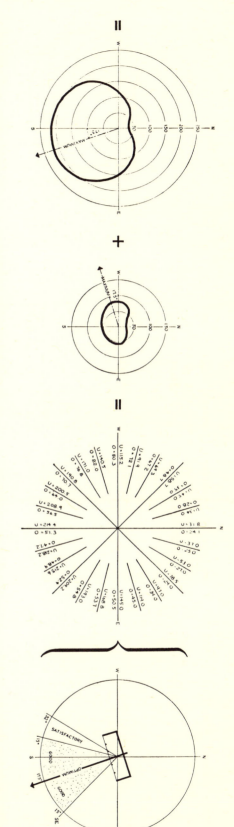

2. But in the cold months maximum radiant gain is from the east of south. (Total solar radiation in underheated period—average radiation received on vertical surface toward all orientations, underheated period.)

3. And in the hot months when you do not want sun heat the biggest sun gain is far to the west of south. (Total solar radiation in overheated period—average radiation received on a vertical surface toward all orientations, underheated period.)

4. This is the compass evaluation for total radiation during both overheated and underheated periods. (U denotes underheated; O denotes overheated).

5. The evaluation in this case is easy, since the worst summer condition and the best winter condition are at right angles to each other, an ideal situation.

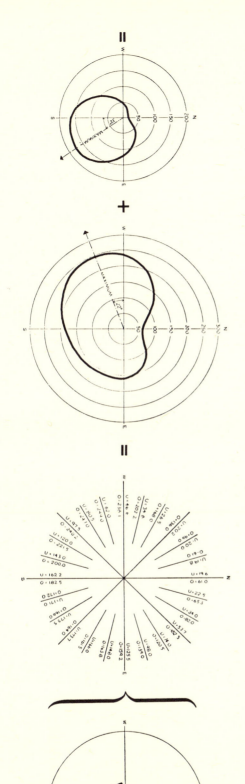

2. Insolation, underheated period.

3. Insolation, overheated period.

4. Total insolation in underheated and overheated periods.

5. The compromise places the optimum sol-air orientation 25° east of south.

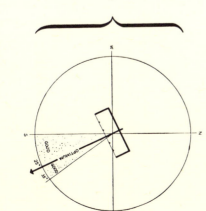

The second problem with regard to orientation is the daily heat balance. Ideally, we would have temperatures in the comfort zone and constant throughout the day. The orientation which most nearly produces these requirements is closest to balanced conditions.

The daily sol-air effect, the combination of temperature and radiation, is illustrated for the New York area in four seasons at different orientations. In each case the base line (curve A) represents the daily dry bulb air temperature variations and the superimposed conditions. In each case the daily dry bulb air temperature variations and the superimposed sun heat. Curve B shows the sol-air effect for an orientation 17½° east of south, curve C shows the same for an orientation due south, and curve D illustrates an orientation 25° west of south.

The curve which is most symmetrical about the noon axis denotes the most equal heat distribution throughout the day. Seasonally, the curve which embraces the largest amount of heat during cold periods, and is lower, or drops when the air becomes overheated is more advantageous.

Notice that curve B (east of south) distributes the heat most equally in all seasons; in summer (July 21) when the whole day is overheated only curve B drops, while the other orientations still gain radiation. When the solar wall is oriented toward the southeast it is most valuable, because radiation comes in the forenoon when the air is colder. In curve B the temperature peaks are symmetrical to the radiation peaks, tempering the extremes, so this position can be called a balanced orientation. Charts drawn for southeasterly orientations in other climatic regions register similarly balanced daily situations.

## REGIONAL APPLICATION

The method of sol-air orientation is applied to four typical climate zones in the United States, showing the total amount of radiation

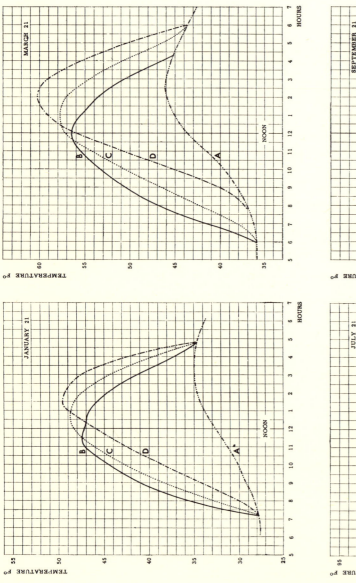

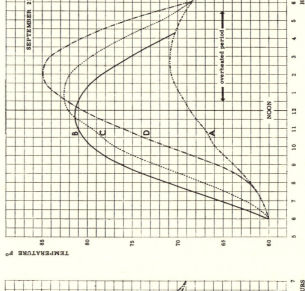

**123.** Heat effect for four typical days of the year. "A" indicates the daily drybulb temperature change. "B" curve indicates the solair impact on a vertical surface oriented 17½° East of South. "C" curve indicates the solair impact on a vertical surface oriented 25° West of South. "D" curve indicates the solair impact on a South-facing surface.

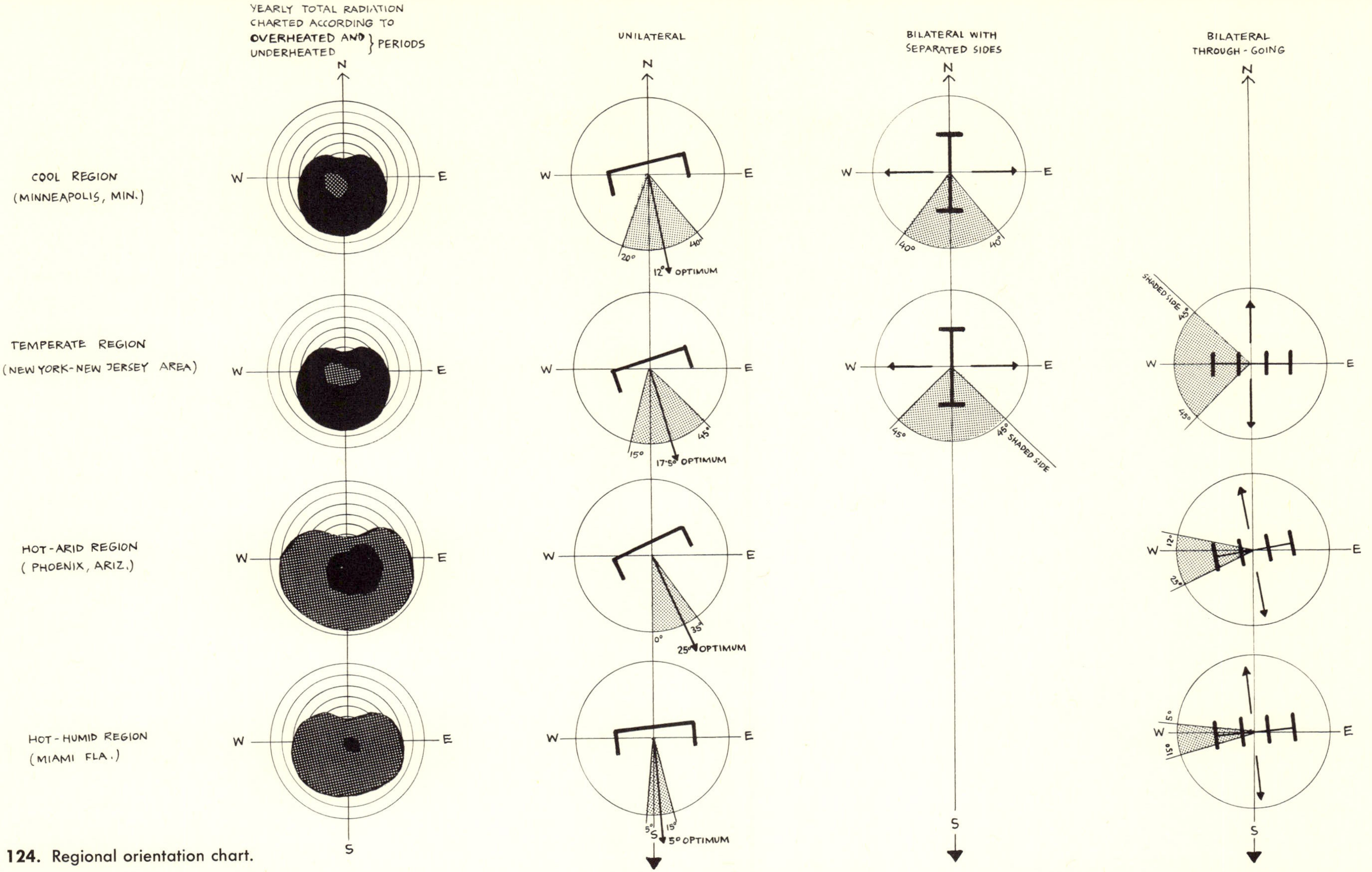

**124. Regional orientation chart.**

COOL REGION (MINNEAPOLIS, MINN.)

TEMPERATE REGION (NEW YORK-NEW JERSEY AREA)

HOT-ARID REGION (PHOENIX, ARIZ.)

HOT-HUMID REGION (MIAMI FLA.)

YEARLY TOTAL RADIATION CHARTED ACCORDING TO OVERHEATED AND UNDERHEATED PERIODS

UNILATERAL

BILATERAL WITH SEPARATED SIDES

BILATERAL THROUGH-GOING

received in the overheated and underheated periods of a year in the lefthand column. In the cool and temperate regions the maximum vectors are at right angles to each other, making evaluation easy. In the hot-arid regions compromise is necessary. The hot-humid zone requires orientation perpendicular to the axis of the overheated period. These optimum orientation positions are shown in the second column.

In many cases the living areas of a building must face orientations other than the optimum zone. This occurs if a building is not a "unilateral" type, but has living areas facing in different directions. The most common type is the "bilateral," where the living areas face in opposite directions. These can be "back-to-back," or the "through" type in which the two sides belong to the same apartment.

In the third column the bilateral types in the cool and temperate zones have a large range of positioning. As the axis turns toward the west, the heat distribution on the sides will be equalized, but the west side will receive less sunlight. At most easterly axis positions, however, the west side should be protected from summer radiation. The back-to-back building type is unsuitable for more southerly latitudes and should be replaced by the "through" type of bilateral buildings.

61

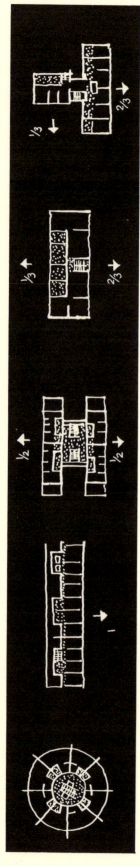

no orientation    unilateral    bilateral    weighted    multilateral

**125.** Building shapes with directional orientations.

Naturally, many other building shapes exist, some of which are illustrated. Here the important side is not readily apparent, and each wall must be assigned a proportionate importance. Once the proportion has been set up, the optimum orientation can be evaluated by drawing a parallelogram of the forces. The result will be an adjusted exposure for the important sides. From this it can be seen that two buildings with the same shape but differently arranged living areas and glass surfaces will require different orientations to take the best advantage of the sun's impacts.

For the floor plan itself many recommendations exist for room exposures. As an illustration, a table is shown, composed by Jeffrey E. Aronin,[12] suggesting sun orientations for various rooms in residential buildings above the 35° latitude.

Most importantly, to secure desired conditions in living areas, the times during which they are used (such as in dayrooms or bedrooms) or their specific hourly occupancy (such as in schools, summer houses, or office buildings) should be considered in the evaluation of orientation.

One other factor should be mentioned in connection with orientation; namely, the germicidal action of radiation. For this reason some building codes require that all living areas should receive at least two hours of insolation in 250 days of the year. The American Public Health Association Committee on the Hygiene of Housing recommends that orientation and spacing of buildings meet the following performance standard: "At the winter solstice, at least one-half of the habitable rooms of a dwelling should have a penetration of direct sunlight of one-half hour's duration during the noon hours when the sun is at its maximum intensity."[13] This standard, although commendable, does not define any orientation, being dependent on the plan and spacing of the buildings. It can be used, however, as a control measure in specific cases.

Finally, the treatment of the exposed surfaces is important also. If an elevation is properly protected, or equipped with shading devices (such as trees, balconies, etc.) radiation in the overheated period ($R_o$) will count less than in the underheated period ($R_u$). If the elevations have large exposed glass surfaces, $R_o$ will be a more decisive factor than $R_u$. The relationship between the $R_o$ and $R_u$ values, therefore, depends also on the treatment of the elevations.

In architectural practice, thoughtful adaptation will be necessary to find the most advantageous orientation conditions for each individual design.

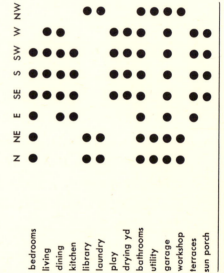

| | N | NE | E | SE | S | SW | W | NW |
|---|---|---|---|---|---|---|---|---|
| bedrooms | ● | ● | ● | ● | | | | |
| living | | | | ● | ● | ● | ● | ● |
| dining | | ● | ● | ● | | | | |
| kitchen | | ● | ● | ● | | | | |
| library | | | | ● | ● | ● | | |
| laundry | | ● | ● | | | | | |
| play | | ● | ● | ● | ● | | | |
| drying yd | | | ● | ● | ● | ● | | |
| bathrooms | | ● | ● | ● | | | | |
| utility | ● | ● | | | | | ● | ● |
| garage | ● | ● | | | | | ● | ● |
| workshop | ● | ● | | | | | ● | ● |
| terraces | | | | ● | ● | ● | ● | |
| sun porch | | | ● | ● | ● | ● | | |

**126.** Suggested sun orientation for rooms.

# VII. SOLAR CONTROL

## THE STRUCTURE

THE age-old problems of controlling the reception of solar radiation in buildings have been sharply enlarged by the modern developments in architectural planning and construction. Traditional massive bearing-walls, which combined the function of support with protection from light and heat, have been supplanted by clear structural members devoted to load-bearing (the skeleton) and covered with curtain-walls (the skin) made of many materials.

The skin of a building performs the role of a filter between indoor and outdoor conditions, to control the intake of air, heat, cold, light, sounds, and odors. It is generally agreed that air, temperature, wind, and sound are best controlled within the wall itself, while light is easier to control inside the building shell, and heat radiation is most efficiently halted before it reaches the building envelope proper.

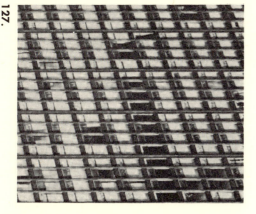

127.

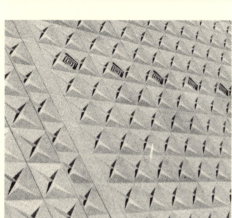

128.

129.

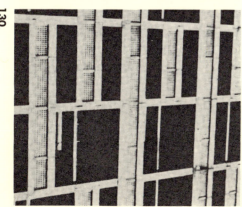

The materials of a building skin play a decisive part in the utilization and control of solar rays. Some examples are compared here for their relative performance as radiation filters.

The first example is a full glass window-wall. With its straight approach, appealing as it is, the wall has to absorb all the penalties of the environmental variations, since the bare glass pane offers very little (around 12%) protection from radiation.

A diametrically opposite example, is the fully opaque curtain wall. In some cases this envelops a building totally, leaving the entirely independent interior free for man-made conditioning. No doubt this solution has its rightful place in specific and peculiar situations, but a fully engineered atmosphere divorced from nature leaves known psychological deficiencies and most probably has still undiscovered drawbacks.

The use of heat-intercepting glass permits the use of large window-walls with less heat penetration than allowed by ordinary glass. A relatively light-colored heat-absorbing glass intercepts over 40% of the radiant energy. This is a considerable aid in summer cooling, but unfortunately it also represents a loss of useful heat in winter.

The last example illustrates a radiation-control solution with shading devices. The method is fundamentally sound. Interception of the energy happens at the right place—before it attacks the building. In this way the obstructed heat is reflected and can dissipate into the outside air. Shading devices give by far the most efficient performance, since by shaping them according to the changing seasonal sun-path, both summer shading and winter heat gain can be achieved.

Location, latitude, and orientation all contribute to the formulation of an effective device. In addition, the sun-breaker can express a strong spatial character, add new elements to the architectural vocabulary, and phrase a truly regional consciousness.

130.

137.

139.

138.

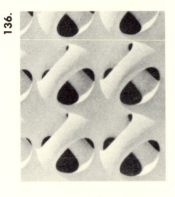

136.

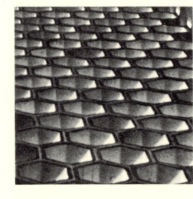

135.

133.

132.

131.

134.

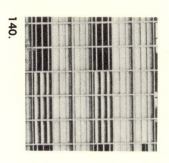

142.

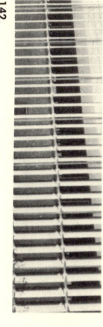

140.

143.

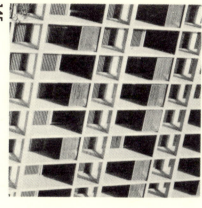

145.

141.

144.

146.

The materials which provide a screen between man and the natural environment offer rich possibilities for visual expression. Many materials only elaborate the surface, others invite a play of light and shadow or add to the spatial composition, while some constitute their own architectural entities. To their plastic appearance they add visual ties of rhythm, light, color, and texture.

The elements shown are independent of direct scale, leaving only the geometrical relationships to be their masters. As compositions, the screens offer large variations. This diversity is not incidental. Their character is representative of positive functions, as the dominant patterns are basically designs of their specific uses.

Some patterns let the air movement through (Fig. 131), and provide shade with more (Fig. 132) or less (Fig. 133) privacy. Some use the wind to cool the wall and defend it by half shade (Fig. 134). Patterns might be geometrical (Fig. 135) or use the fluid play of the *claire-obscure* of the light (Figs. 136-137). This can be horizontal (Fig. 138) by ingenious utilization of spatial constructions. The shading elements of elevations in combination with deep balconies (Fig. 139) provides rich texture. Horizontal devices can be closed in character (Fig. 140), but nearly similar shading effect can be reached with butterfly-light balconies (Fig. 141). Some orientations call for vertical shading members with movable (Fig. 142) or with fixed fins (Fig. 143) which dominate the appearance of the elevation. In certain locations the eggcrate sun-breaker provides the needed coolness by screening before the glass (Fig. 144), or by creating with twofold depth (Figs. 145, 146) the elevation itself.

The motifs vary, but are subordinate to the sun, whose strength and angles, according to orientation and location, prescribe the regional patterns.

65

## TRANSMISSION OF RADIATION AND HEAT

To contrast a solid wall with a glass window as a radiation transmitter seems a rather one-sided competition, since one is opaque and the other transparent to the rays. It is more realistic to compare their roles as heat barriers with their full thermal performance. Periodic heat-flow calculations were used for this purpose to integrate convection, conduction, and radiation effects.

For this comparison in Miami, Florida, an average clear summer day (July 21) was chosen. Both surfaces have a west exposure. The first graph shows the heat transmission of a wall consisting of a lightly painted insulated wood frame construction. The other graph shows the heat transmission of a single glass pane. The daily total heat transmission of the wall (solid line) amounts to 40 Btu/ft², and to 27 Btu/ft² in shade (dotted line). The daily total transmission of the glass pane is 1,227 Btu/ft² in sun, 346 Btu when shaded. In this case the glass is more than 30 times as vulnerable to sunlit conditions as the opaque wall. But by shading the glass, this heat impact can be reduced to one-third. Of course, these vulnerability ratios differ according to latitude, orientation, time of the year and other conditions.

The direct radiation transmitted varies markedly with the angle of incidence, remaining fairly steady until about 50° but dropping sharply after 60°. Here are the data for a single glass (with 0.90 transmittance at normal incidence) and a double glass ($T_n = 0.81$) window:[1]

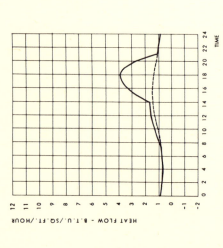

**147.** Heattransmission of a wooden wall.

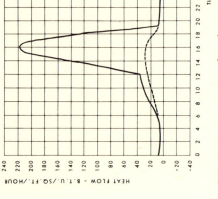

**148.** Heattransmission of a glass pane.

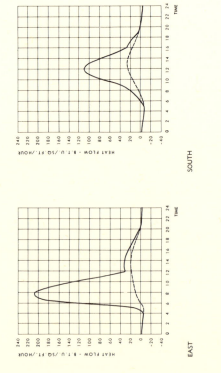

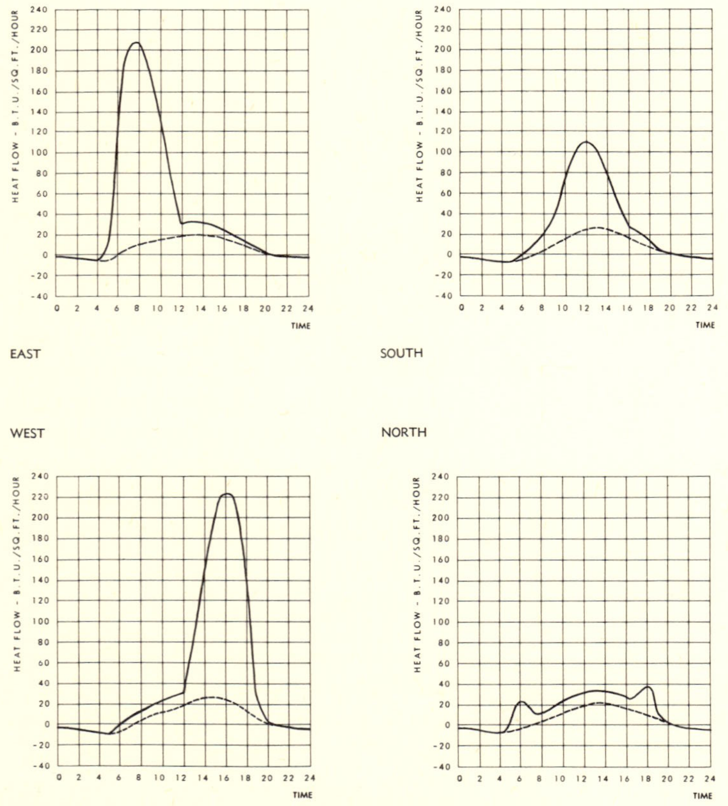

EAST

SOUTH

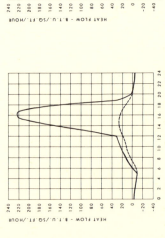

WEST

NORTH

**149.** Heattransmission for differently exposed glass surfaces.

| Angle of Incidence | Single-Glazed Window | Double-Glazed Window |
|---|---|---|
| 0° | 0.90 | 0.81 |
| 20° | 0.90 | 0.81 |
| 40° | 0.89 | 0.80 |
| 50° | 0.87 | 0.77 |
| 60° | 0.82 | 0.71 |
| 70° | 0.77 | 0.59 |
| 80° | 0.44 | 0.29 |
| 90° | 0.00 | 0.00 |

The transmittance of diffuse radiation is independent of the sun's position (for the above single glass 0.82, for double window 0.72).

As a summation of the heat-transmission problem, charts are shown illustrating the flow effect of four differently oriented glass surfaces, during an average clear summer day (July 21) in the New York area. The daily total Btu flowing through a square foot of single glass surface is as follows:

| | Sunlit | Shaded |
|---|---|---|
| East | 1,097 | 134 |
| South | 601 | 138 |
| West | 1,097 | 134 |
| North | 305 | 123 |

The totals show large variations according to orientations with especially important differences to the east and west. On the average, shading devices in this area reduce the sun loads to one-fifth, resulting in appreciable economies.

## METHODS OF SHADE PROTECTION FOR GLASS SURFACES

The aim of this chapter is to evaluate solar protection methods for external shading devices and to describe the method of their calculation. However, to place such devices and their effectiveness in a proper perspective a survey is shown here as to the effectiveness of other possible shading applications. *

* This section was developed for the Educational Facilities Laboratories of the Ford Foundation and released by permission.

To compare the effective solar protection of the different methods the Shading Coefficient was used as a measure. The Shading Coefficient is the ratio of the total solar heat gain from the transmitted, absorbed, and reradiated energy by the shade and glass combination compared to the total solar heat gain due to transmission, absorption, and reradiation by a single unshaded common window glass.

To evaluate the Shading Coefficient the transmitted radiation percentage of the shade-glass combination was related to a value 1.00 as a basic index for an unshaded regular double-strength (DS) window glass.

As the sun's position in the sky and therefore in relation to the surface changes constantly; the proportion of direct to diffuse incident solar energy varies according to orientation and time of day, as does the solar heat transmission of the shading materials. However, for the use of the evaluation comparison these variations may be neglected.[2]

As the many different types of shading methods that exist had to be correlated into a single index, some adaptations, such as the following, were employed:

At the flat surface shading materials (i.e. tinted glass, sheeted and coated glass surfaces, etc.), the customary normal incident angle was taken for transmission value. Such evaluation takes those materials somewhat in disadvantage in the categorization. The designations of "light" and "dark" refer to materials with at least 50% and 20% light transmission, respectively.

The values for blinds are based upon their effect at several orientations, where it was assumed that the slats are adjusted to prevent the direct sun rays.[3]

The values of shading screens were calculated for all orientations, and the average performance taken.

The curtain data is from fenestration fabrics of 6 and 8 oz/sq yd weight.[4]

At the values of trees it was assumed that they were positioned strategically so that direct sun does not strike the window.[5]

The values for the fixed shading devices are the average daily transmission performance of a well-designed efficiency to the orientations mentioned.

Because of the number of variables involved in the calculations, the coefficients must be considered as approximate values, and application should be used with proper interpretation.

## CONCLUSIONS ON SHADING EFFECTIVENESS

The sun protection effect for glass surfaces depends on several factors: the reflectivity of solar radiation of the applied material and its color coating (A), the location of the shade protection which influences the reradiation and convection heat impacts (B), and the specific arrangement of the applied shading method (C). Because of the interplay of the above factors, it is difficult to separate the influences; however, generalized conclusions about their effect can be drawn.

A. Influence of color, and material.

It is well known that light colors reflect sun impact and dark colors absorb it. The judgment of the eye gives an approximate measure of the relation of color to the absorbtion value. Data on some typical surface materials are shown in a more detailed list in Chapter X. on the subject):

67

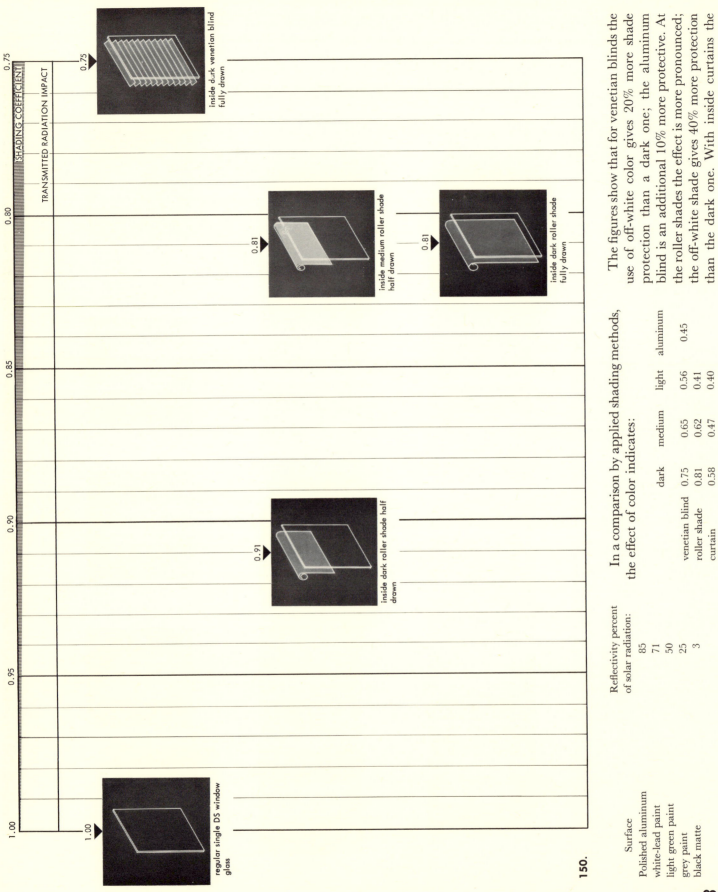

SHADING COEFFICIENT

TRANSMITTED RADIATION IMPACT

1.00  0.95  0.90  0.85  0.80  0.75

regular single DS window glass — 1.00

inside dark roller shade half drawn — 0.91

inside medium roller shade half drawn — 0.81

inside dark roller shade fully drawn — 0.81

inside dark venetian blind fully drawn — 0.75

150.

The figures show that for venetian blinds the use of off-white color gives 20% more shade protection than a dark one; the aluminum blind is an additional 10% more protective. At the roller shades the effect is more pronounced; the off-white shade gives 40% more protection than the dark one. With inside curtains the

| Surface | Reflectivity percent of solar radiation: |
|---|---|
| Polished aluminum | 85 |
| white-lead paint | 71 |
| light green paint | 50 |
| grey paint | 25 |
| black matte | 3 |

In a comparison by applied shading methods, the effect of color indicates:

| | dark | medium | light | aluminum |
|---|---|---|---|---|
| venetian blind | 0.75 | 0.65 | 0.56 | 0.45 |
| roller shade | 0.81 | 0.62 | 0.41 | |
| curtain | 0.58 | 0.47 | 0.40 | |

151.

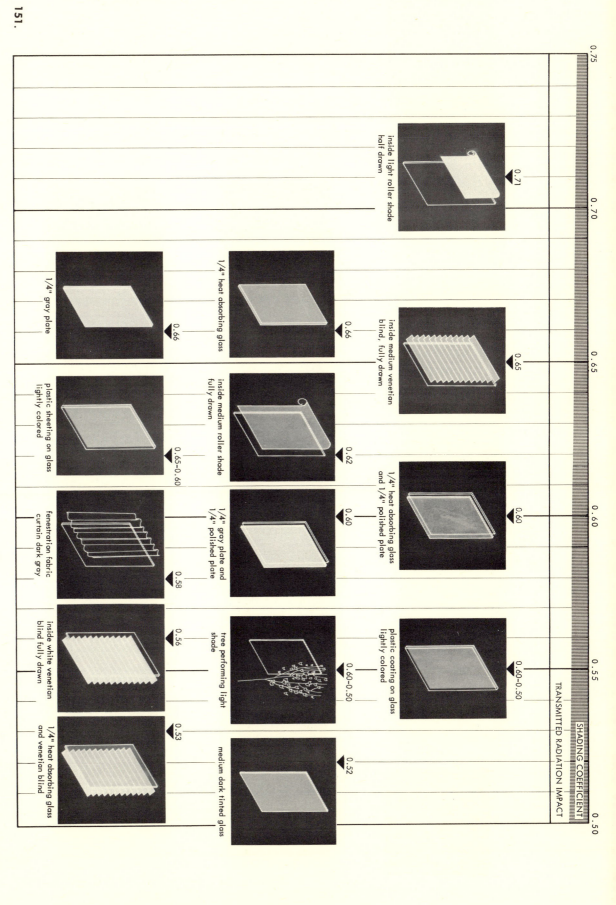

difference is not so wide; the light one is 18% more effective than the dark one.

B. Location of shade protection.

Inside shading protecting devices can only intercept the solar energy which just passed through the glass surface and can eliminate only that portion of the radiant energy which can be reflected through the glass again. Some of the energy striking an interior device is absorbed, convected, and reradiated into the room.

If the interception occurs in or at the surface of the glass, part of the energy will be reflected back at the entry layer, part of it transmitted, and a part absorbed. The absorbed portion will be convected and reradiated both to the outside and into the interior of the room.

The exterior protecting devices dispose the convected and reradiated portion of the energy to the outdoor air.

From the above it is evident that the shade

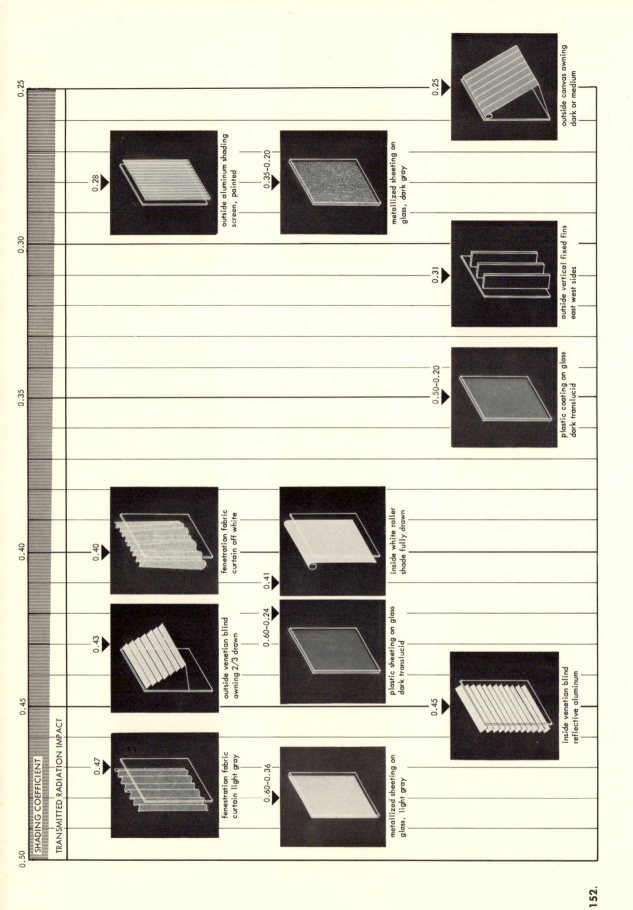

**SHADING COEFFICIENT**

**TRANSMITTED RADIATION IMPACT**

0.50  0.45  0.40  0.35  0.30  0.25

0.47 — fenestration fabric curtain light gray
0.43 — outside venetian blind awning 2/3 drawn
0.40 — fenestration fabric curtain off white
0.28 — outside aluminum shading screen, painted

0.60–0.36 — metallized sheeting on glass, light gray
0.60–0.24 — plastic sheeting on glass dark translucid
0.41 — inside white roller shade fully drawn
0.35–0.20 — metallized sheeting on glass, dark gray

0.45 — inside venetian blind reflective aluminum
0.50–0.20 — plastic coating on glass dark translucid
0.31 — outside vertical fixed fins east west sides
0.25 — outside canvas awning dark or medium

152.

70

protection is dependent on its location, and its effectiveness increases accordingly as it is positioned after, on, or before the glass surface in that order.

For example:

|  | metal venetian blind | canvas shade |
|---|---|---|
| Shade installed inside the glass | 0.45 | 0.62 |
| Shade installed outside the glass | 0.15 | 0.25 |

As an overall value one could conclude that the effectiveness increases 35% by using outside shade protection instead of an inside one.

C. Effectiveness of various shading methods.

The different methods of shade protection can only become categorized under certain assumptions, such as to take certain values (as medium color or 50% light transmissions) as a measure. With such restrictions the order of effectiveness is as follows at the right.

The charts above indicate the various shade protection devices in order of their Shading Coefficients.

venetian blind — coating on glass surface
roller shade — trees
tinted glass — outside awning
insulating curtain — outside fixed shading device
outside shade screen — outside moveable shading device
outside metal blind

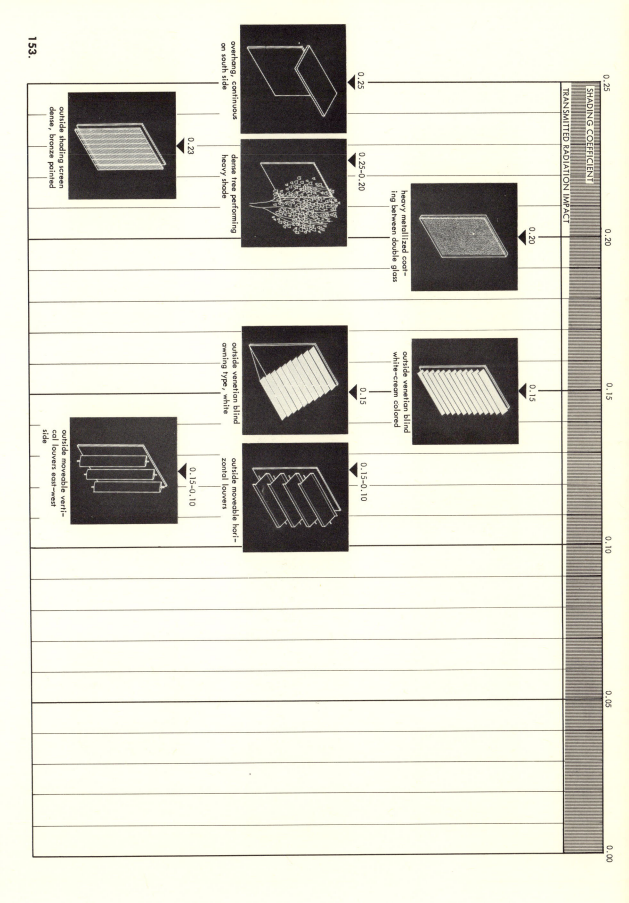

SHADING COEFFICIENT
TRANSMITTED RADIATION IMPACT

0.25    0.20    0.15    0.10    0.05    0.00

overhang, continuous on south side — 0.25
dense tree performing heavy shade — 0.25–0.20
heavy metallized coating between double glass — 0.20
outside shading screen dense, bronze painted — 0.23
outside venetian blind white-cream colored — 0.15
outside venetian blind awning type, white — 0.15
outside moveable horizontal louvers — 0.15–0.10
outside moveable vertical louvers east-west side — 0.15–0.10

Thus a design criterion can be established: One ton of refrigeration equals 12,000 Btu/hr. This equals a heat load that may fall on 100 square feet of easterly or westerly oriented walls. If this heat load is intercepted, one ton of air-conditioning capacity can be saved, for each 100 square feet of wall.

In the New York area a single glass surface on July 21 on a clear day will transmit direct sun radiation into the building, in Btu/ft²/hr:

|  | ORIENTATION | | |
|---|---|---|---|
|  | East | South | West |
| 5 a.m. | 23 | ... | ... |
| 6 a.m. | 126 | ... | ... |
| 7 a.m. | 177 | ... | ... |
| 8 a.m. | 185 | 2 | ... |
| 9 a.m. | 160 | 19 | ... |
| 10 a.m. | 108 | 45 | ... |
| 11 a.m. | 43 | 58 | ... |
| 12 Noon | ... | 72 | ... |
| 1 p.m. | ... | 58 | 43 |
| 2 p.m. | ... | 44 | 108 |
| 3 p.m. | ... | 19 | 160 |
| 4 p.m. | ... | 2 | 185 |
| 5 p.m. | ... | ... | 177 |
| 6 p.m. | ... | ... | 126 |
| 7 p.m. | ... | ... | 23 |

## ECONOMY OF SHADING DEVICES

The importance of sun control can be shown by comparing the amounts of heat entering a building through its various components. Curves can be made of the diurnal variation of heat-flow through unit areas of differently oriented building elements. Total heat can be calculated by summing up the products of the unit transmissions and the areas involved. The total heat flow through the components of a standard house of conventional wood-frame construction, on an average summer day in July in the New York–New Jersey area are shown.

The relative importance of the components with respect to undesirable heat gains is apparent. The windows account for the greatest amounts of heat entering the building and therefore shading them offers the greatest protection. Second in importance is the roof, and the infiltration and the window conduction follow. Wall materials and opaque vertical enclosures play a relatively small part unless they are not properly insulated. It is well known that only a synthesized integration of all components will result in a "climate-balanced" shelter; nevertheless, this emphasizes the importance of sun control.

This importance, naturally, will change relative to the size and type of the building, and therefore a separate analysis must be made for each problem. To take another approach, compare the cost of air-conditioning of an unshaded building to that of a shaded one, and add to the latter the cost of the shading device. This comparison will show the economic balance of the device.

For design purposes this process can be reversed. Knowing the sun's heat entering through a unit surface, and the cost of the air-conditioning necessary to counterbalance this amount, one can determine the cost of a device which will break even economically.

The cost of air-conditioning can be estimated as:

A. Installation cost, where one Btu of air-conditioning varies between $.05 and $.07. (Prices quoted in these pages are as of 1957.)

B. Operating cost, which runs around 5% of the installation cost per year.

From the instantaneous heat-gain there is still the question of transforming this value to cooling load. It has been realized that, due to storage effect and lag, not all of the peak heat gain to a structure would appear as an instantaneous and simultaneous peak cooling-load. Some experts take the average of the three maximum hours of heat gain as peak cooling-load; some take 70% of the peak heat gain.

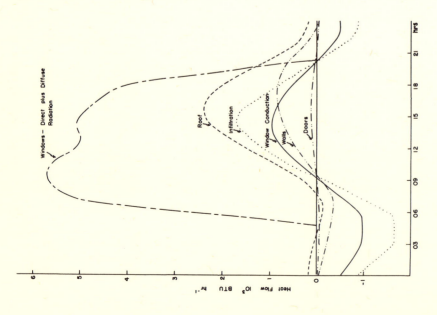

**154.** The figure shows the result of an analysis of the heat flow through the various components of a typical single story residence structure.[51] A conventional low cost house was selected as an example. The importance of the winter heating period in the climate of the New York–New Jersey area, where the house was assumed to be located, limited the selection of the wall and roofing materials to those with a low heat-conductivity. Consequently, the building consists of frame construction with wood siding on insulating board sheathing with 2 inches of mineral wool insulation and a ⅜ inch gypsum board inner surface. The roof consists of asphalt shingles (absorptivity to Solar radiation = 0.7) on solid wood sheathing. The ceiling of gypsum board is backed by 3 inches of batt-type insulation. The windows are of ordinary (type B) glass with a transmittance for solar radiation of 0.77 at normal incidence, set practically flush with the exterior wall. Half-drawn, dark-colored pull shades are assumed to be behind the windows. The total effective areas of this house are: walls 866, roof 768, windows 139, doors 38 square feet.

Following these methods, and taking their mean values, the peak cooling load produced by direct sun radiation has been determined for the New York area:

| | East | South | West |
|---|---|---|---|
| Saveable cooling load in Btu's/sq ft | 157 | 57 | 157 |

The above figures do not include diffuse radiation, which also will be partially cut out by the shading device.

Calculating the installation cost, and adding to it two years of operating cost, the savings in air-conditioning costs produced by a shading device can be estimated:

| | East | South | West |
|---|---|---|---|
| Possible savings per square foot of window area. | $8.60–$10.40 | $3.00–$3.80 | $8.60–$10.40 |

Thus a design criterion can be established: a properly designed shading device will break even economically, if it costs as much as the above figures. It it costs less, it will save money. In practice the cost of shading devices is usually less than the figures quoted.

Shown here in schematic diagrams are various standard types of shading. The first, A, is a curtain wall unit without any projection, for comparison purposes only, while B to F show different types of devices. The cost of a curtain wall "A" differs according to the type; if it is a closed wall or if it has openable windows. The cost of a fixed type varies between $3.50 and $4.50 per square foot, while the same with openable ventilating units vary from $4.50 to $7.00 per square foot. The additional cost of a horizontal solid shading device, B.1, is about $2.20 to $2.60 per square foot of window surface, while a louvered type, B.2, is between $3.60 and $4.60. The cost of vertical fixed device, C, is between $4.40 and $6.00, and a movable device, D, is between $8.00 and $10.00 per square foot of window surface.

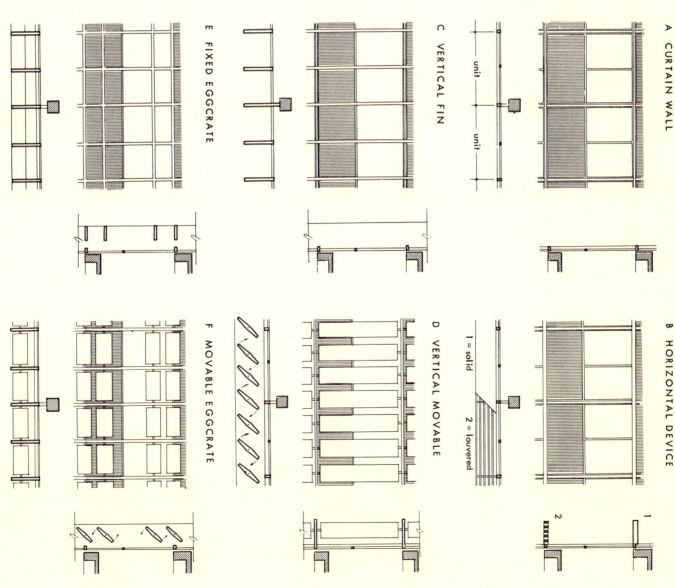

A CURTAIN WALL

B HORIZONTAL DEVICE

C VERTICAL FIN

D VERTICAL MOVABLE

1 = solid

2 = louvered

E FIXED EGGCRATE

F MOVABLE EGGCRATE

155. Standard types of shading devices.

73

Eggcrate types cost between $6.40 and $8.50 if they are fixed as E, and if movable as F their cost varies between $8.00 and $10.50 per square foot of window surface.

The horizontal shading device protects southern orientations efficiently, while the other types work well toward east and west, where the more expensive movable types might be utilized.

It is evident that shading devices might not only pay their way, but save in cost, but only with proper design, the importance of which cannot be over-emphasized. Varied orientations have different heat impacts, and the counterbalance of the heat impacts will affect either the cost of the mechanical cooling or that of the shading device.

Careful architectural planning, while considering cost of mechanical cooling and shading devices, will include:

1. The arrangement of the whole building layout, determining the orientation of the elevations.
2. The size and distribution of the openings, which determine the heat transmission of the elevations.
3. The proper design of the shading devices, which will result in economy only if they work efficiently.

A few practical aspects should be added to the considerations above. Exterior devices may conduct heat into a structure on windless, hot days, especially if they are made of dull-finished materials. Conversely on windy, cold days they may carry heat away from the walls as a cooling radiator. This can be avoided, if the devices are insulated from the building. The simplest solution to this is to connect the device to the building only at necessary points, leaving an open airspace in between. This open slot also serves as an escape hatch for banked-up warm air.

A further consideration is the snow and ice problem. In higher latitudes and on elevations facing streets or public areas this may create a hazard. Projecting the lowest horizontal overhang furthest out from the façade can solve this problem. The problem of maintenance is always present, with or without shading devices; its solution, like the others, would seem to lie in the thoughtfulness of the architectural design.

## SHADING EFFECTS OF TREES AND VEGETATION

The old custom of surrounding homes with embracing trees has deeper roots than a desire for the enjoyment of nature's esthetic variety. Besides satisfying the instinctive need for protection, trees also contribute much to the immediate physical environment. They reduce air-borne sounds with great efficiency, if densely planted. The viscous surface of leaves catches dust and filters the air. Vegetation can also secure visual privacy and reduce annoying glare effects.

But an especially beneficial effect of trees is their thermal performance. In winter evergreen windbreaks can reduce the heat loss from buildings and discourage drifting snow. In summer the surface of grass and leaves absorb radiation, and their evaporation processes can cool air temperatures. Above all, they provide generous shade at the right seasons. This trait makes deciduous trees especially valuable when placed close to buildings, since one aim of solar control is not to interfere with the winter sunshine. Vines also constitute

another of nature's automatic heat-control devices, cooling by evaporation and providing shade. This combination makes them valuable for sunny walls in hot weather.

Both vines and trees should be selected for their appearance as well as shading performance. (Of course climatic and soil conditions of a given site should be checked.) The type of tree to be used in a given location is very important. One must keep in mind two things: the shape and character of the tree itself both in winter and summer, and the shape of its shadow for a natural shading device.

It is desirable to transplant shade trees in as large a size as practicable. Certainly, for a tree to give results in a comparatively few years it should be fifteen to twenty feet high when planted. It does not, however, take some trees as long to mature to their full usefulness as is often assumed; generally when a fast-growing five-year tree is planted in a new location, it takes only five more years to grow to 80% of its full shading effect.

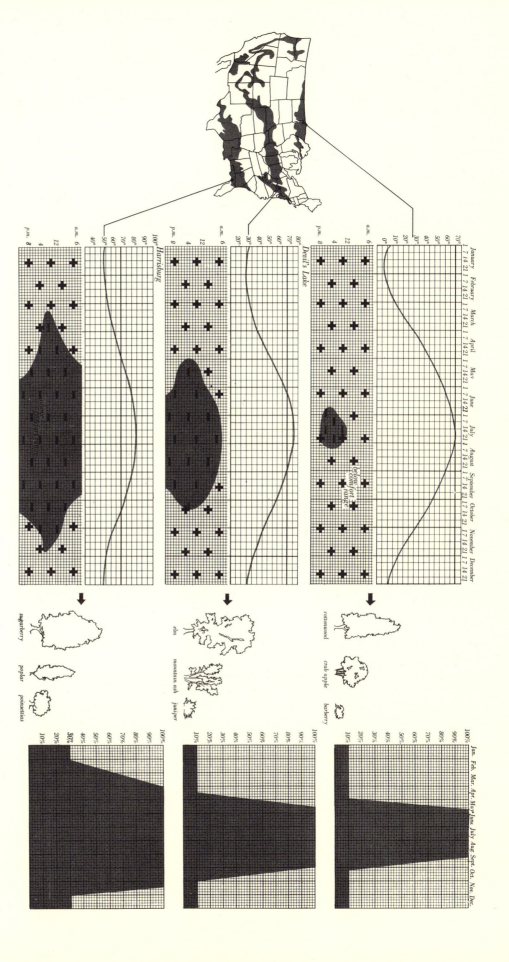

**156.** Yearly temperature variations in three locations in the United States with shading periods of native trees.

In the figures above the yearly temperature variations are charted for three locations in the United States: Devils Lake, N.D.; Harrisburg, Pa.; and Pensacola, Fla. Charted under the yearly temperature curve for each of these cities is a record of the 24 hours of the average day for each month. On this, the overheated period, when shade is needed, is outlined in darker

tone. On the right-hand side trees and shrubs that are native to the given locations are indicated. On the far right the shading period of the trees is shown on a chart where the vertical scale indicates the percentage of shade which occurs in months designated on the horizontal scale.

It seems evident from this chart that, al-

though in each case the leaves arrive on the branches of the trees somewhat early for shading, the time of the full bloom period and of the shading needs in the given areas correspond very closely. They cooperate elastically with human needs even in their yearly variations. In cold spring the leaves arrive later, in warm summer last longer—within a variation of six weeks.

75

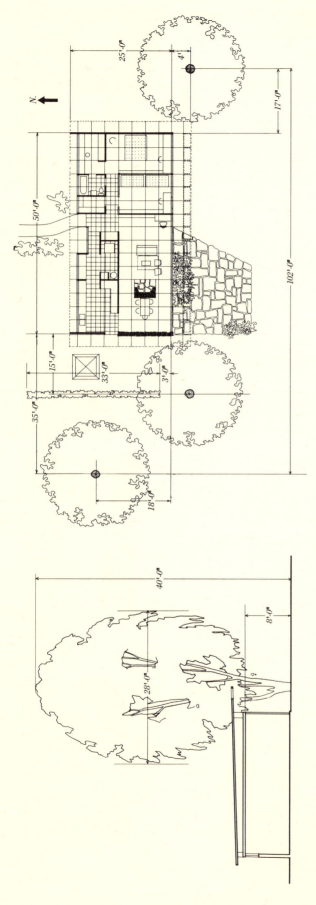

**157-158.** Section and plan of a house showing the location of vegetation and overhang measurement.

Among deciduous shade trees, the maple and ash produce more or less circular shadow effects during the summer, with an ascending branch pattern in winter. The linden is spherical, but is dense and twiggy without its leaves. The honey locust and tulip tree have oblong shapes. The white oak is horizontally oblong, with an open-branched structure in winter. The lombardy poplar is columnar in appearance, the American elm vase shaped.

Among the small flowering trees one can find a great variety of forms, such as the upright-growing crabapple, the dogwood with its horizontal branches, the vase-shaped honeysuckle, the rounded spirea, the columnar enkianthus, or the broad-spreading dwarf Japanese quince. Each of these shapes has a definite im-

plication in its shading effect. The exact location of trees and vegetation can be determined with their shading masks through the use of a protractor. The projected mask of the trees should cover the outlined overheated period.

To achieve efficient shading, trees have to be placed strategically. As the sun passes in the morning and late afternoon at a low altitude, trees give their best performance on the east-south-east and on west-south-west sides. Low sun-rays cast long shadows, which can be utilized effectively on the sides otherwise difficult to protect from the sun's heat. At midday the sun's path is high and the rays can be intercepted easily with an overhang; at this time of day the trees on the south side perform poorly, casting their shadows near themselves.

The section and plan of a house with planting shows an arrangement for temperate climates. Here the early morning sun may relieve the coolness of daybreak. After 8 A.M., the east side gets protection from the single tree at the southeast corner. At noon an overhang shields the building. In the early afternoon the tree on the southwest corner protects the west side. For complete shade coverage there is another tree to the west. This is placed at a greater distance from the house, as the setting sun lengthens the shadows. The west hedge is intended to catch the last low-angle evening rays. The photographs of a model on the opposite page show how these trees will cast their shadows during the consecutive hours of a summer day from dawn to dusk.

159. Summer shading from dawn to dusk.

77

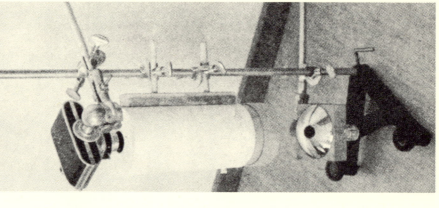

161. The "Horizontograph."

162. The "Globoscope."

## OBSTRUCTION OF SURROUNDINGS

In the foregoing the path of the sun has been discussed as an uninterrupted movement on the sky-vault, starting and ending on the horizon line. In reality it is seldom seen in this way, except in extreme cases, as from a ship at sea. Generally, there will be interfering objects, which will obstruct parts of the total view of the sky-vault from a given point of observation. These obstructions might be unchangeable objects, such as mountains or structures already built around a site. But they might be changeable, and even designable, as shading devices on a façade seen from the window.

The photographs show a well known and often seen place, Rockefeller Plaza in New York, from a seldom used observation point. It was photographed from the middle of the skating rink, once in daytime and once at night, using a Robin Hill camera with an equidistant lens system. The horizon line appears as a circle on the outside edge of the picture and the sky-vault is obscured by the outlines of the surrounding buildings. It is quite evident that the sun will shine on the point from which the photograph was taken only when it is not obstructed by buildings or other objects. These photographs are, then, shading masks, which may be used to calculate the amount of sun that will fall on the point of observation.

Other methods for determining the obstruction pattern,[6] or shading mask, are based on the principle that a vaulted mirror surface will reflect the sky-vault and may be observed by eye or photographed. Then these observations or pictures can be overlaid or transferred to sun-path diagrams.[7]

160. Rockefeller Plaza in daytime and at night.

**163.** Minneapolis, Minnesota, 44° N. latitude.

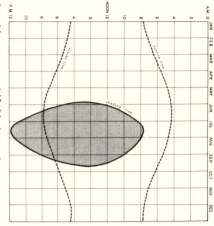

**164.** New York-New Jersey area, 40° N. latitude.

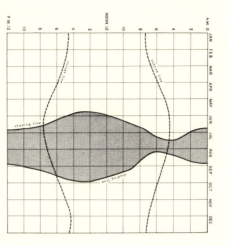

**165.** Phoenix, Arizona, 32° N. latitude.

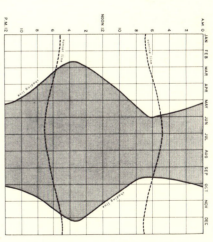

**166.** Miami, Florida, 24° N. latitude.

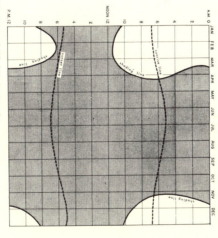

## SUMMARY OF METHOD

In order to use shading masks for design purposes, it is necessary first to define the times—hours and seasons—and then to define the direction—orientation and altitude—where shading is needed.

STEP 1, to Define the Times When Shading is Needed: Data should be collected for the daily temperature changes throughout a year at the place in question. Average daily temperatures should be used with hourly or two-hourly data for each month of the year. The

temperatures which fall over the bottom line of the comfort zone (70° in the temperate zone, and rising as the latitude decreases) will define the overheated period. This can be tabulated on a chart where the hourly and monthly divisions serve as ordinates.

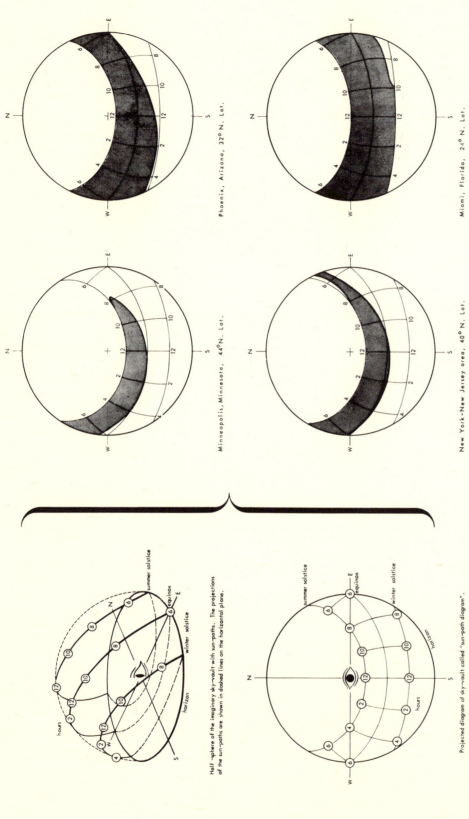

Phoenix, Arizona, 32° N. Lat.

Miami, Florida, 24° N. Lat.

Minneapolis, Minnesota, 44° N. Lat.

New York–New Jersey area, 40° N. Lat.

Half-sphere of the imaginary sky-vault with sun-paths. The projections of the sun-paths are shown in dashed lines on the horizontal plane.

Projected diagram of sky-vault called "sun-path diagram".

**167.** Sun-path and projection. Overheated periods transferred to sun-path diagrams.

STEP 2, to Determine the Position of the Sun When Shading is Needed: On a sun path diagram the curved lines represent the movements of the sun for the dates shown. Lines "radiating" from the North Pole indicate the hours; the lighter lines show 20-minute intervals. The sun's position is usually expressed by altitude, or angular distance above the horizon, and az-imuth, or angular distance measured along the horizon in a clockwise direction. When the overheated period is transferred to this chart, the resulting sun-path diagram will not only show the position of the sun, but will indicate whether shading is desirable at a given time.

By the nature of the diagram, each line represents two dates when the sun has the same path during a year. The plotted over-heated period will have areas (indicated in dark tone) to show when shading is needed on both of these dates, and other areas (in light tone) to show when shading is needed on only one of them, which is usually the autumn date. This diagram provides the basis for the evaluation of shading devices.

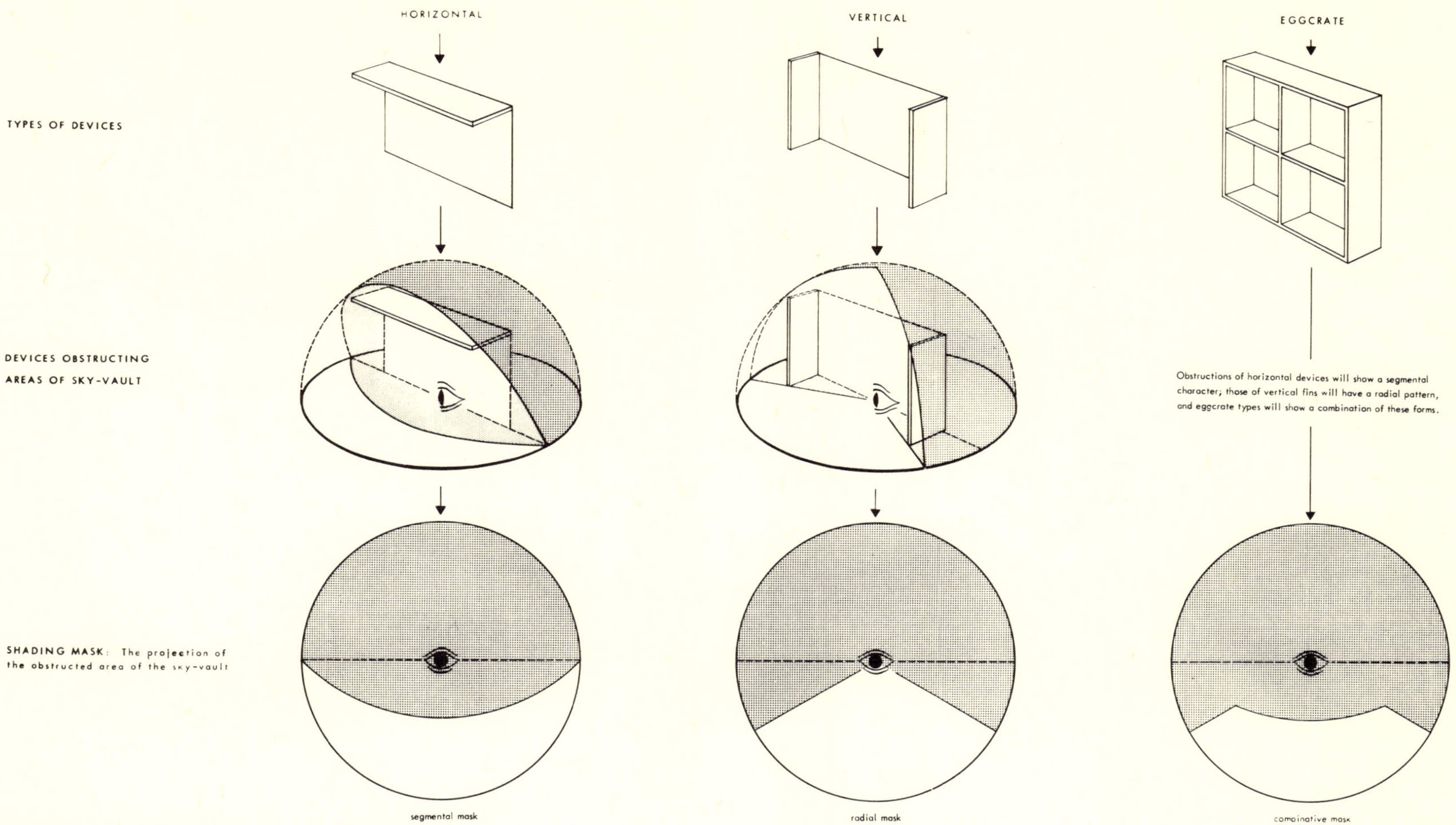

HORIZONTAL

VERTICAL

EGGCRATE

segmental mask

radial mask

combinative mask

Obstructions of horizontal devices will show a segmental character; those of vertical fins will have a radial pattern, and eggcrate types will show a combination of these forms.

**168.** Basic types of shading devices and their projections.

STEP 3, to Determine the Type and Position of a Shading Device for the Overheated Period: Masks can be drawn for any shading device; even for very complex ones, by geometrical methods. A protractor serves to plot the projection of a device onto the sky-vault much as the shading mask of the surroundings are charted.

Since the masks are a conventionalized geometric description, they are independent of latitude, orientation and time. Once plotted for a specific device, the shading mask can be used in any situation. Shading devices can be tabulated according to their masks in three main categories.

*Horizontal overhangs:* their typical mask characteristics are segmental areas.

*Vertical louvers:* their typical shading masks are bounded by radial lines.

*Eggcrate types:* basically combinations of horizontal and vertical devices; their mask characteristics are, accordingly, a combination of these.

The characteristics of a shading mask are independent of the scale of the device; the ratio of the depth of the device to the proper dimension of the wall surface is the determining factor. This is expressed by the angle, which shows this ratio in a plane normal to the wall. The shading effect, and therefore the mask, depends on this angle. A very small-scaled device, like the "cool-shade" or an outside venetian blind, will have the same shading mask as a balconied apartment house if their angles are the same.

STEP 4, to Evaluate the Shading Device: Two masks can be shown: one for 100% shading, in which case the total wall surface is in shade, and one for 50% shading, when only the half of the surface is in shade. The mask of a shading device with its 100% and 50% diagrams superimposed on the sun-path diagram and the plotted overheated period will show the times when the sun will be intercepted by this device. As a rule of thumb, it can be said that if the 50% border of the shading mask covers the overheated periods shown on the sun-path diagram, the shading device will work

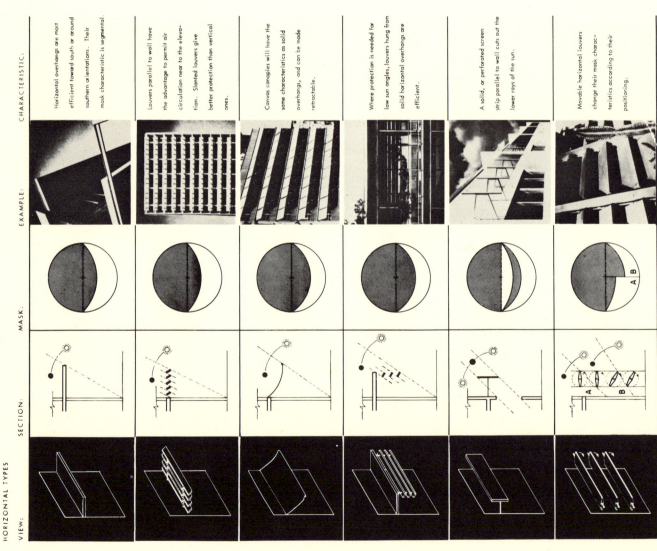

HORIZONTAL TYPES

VIEW:　　SECTION:　　MASK:　　EXAMPLE:　　CHARACTERISTIC:

Horizontal overhangs are most efficient toward south, or around southern orientations. Their mask characteristic is segmental.

Louvers parallel to wall have the advantage to permit air circulation near to the elevation. Slanted louvers give better protection than vertical ones.

Canvas canopies will have the same characteristics as solid overhangs, and can be made retractable.

Where protection is needed for low sun angles, louvers hung from solid horizontal overhangs are efficient.

A solid, or perforated screen strip parallel to wall cuts out the lower rays of the sun.

Movable horizontal louvers change their mask characteristics according to their positioning.

169.  Examples of various types of shading devices.

82

well. For detailed evaluation, of course, radiation calculations will be needed.

The process of evaluation can be reversed for design purposes. With the use of a sun-path diagram with the overheated period plotted on it, a proper overlapping mask can be determined and an appropriate shading device for the situation developed. Since various devices have the same mask, and therefore the same shading characteristics, there will be many technically correct solutions for each situation. To choose between them is the designer's task; here the domain of creative design begins.

VERTICAL TYPES

VIEW:　　PLAN AND SECTION:　　MASK:　　EXAMPLE:　　CHARACTERISTIC:

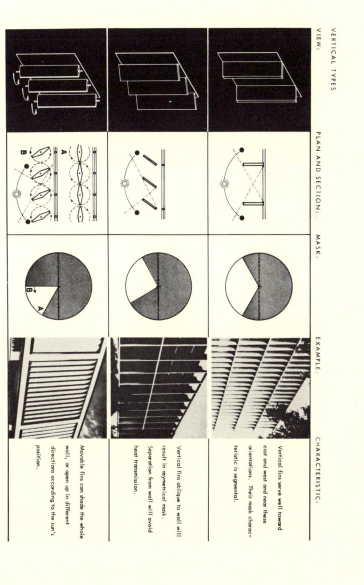

Vertical fins serve well toward east and west and near these orientations. Their mask characteristic is segmental.

Vertical fins oblique to wall will result in asymetrical mask. Separation from wall will avoid heat transmission.

Movable fins can shade the whole wall, or open up in different directions according to the sun's position.

EGGCRATE TYPES

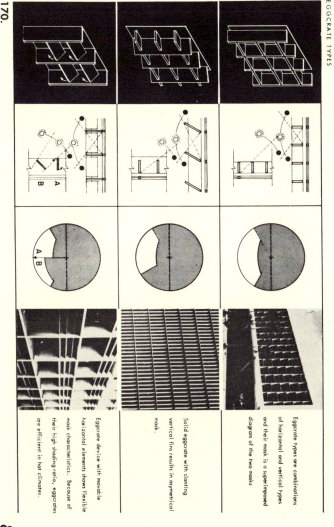

Eggcrate types are combinations of horizontal and vertical types and their mask is a superimposed diagram of the two masks.

Solid eggcrate with slanting vertical fins results in asymetrical mask.

Eggcrate device with movable horizontal elements shows flexible mask characteristics. Because of their high shading ratio, eggcrates are efficient in hot climates.

# VIII. ENVIRONMENT AND BUILDING FORMS

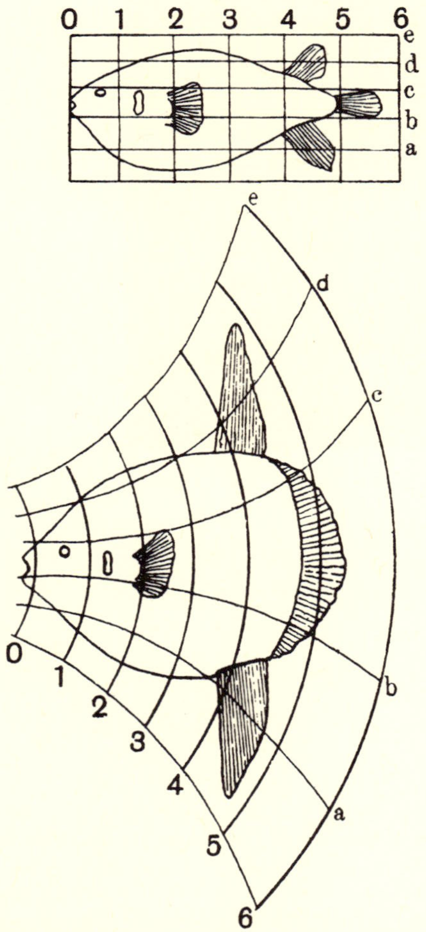

## MORPHOLOGY IN NATURE

IT IS a recognized fact that the forces of nature have a direct effect on the formation of objects.

In natural history the rule is universal that only species are fit to survive which are in harmony with their environment, balanced with their tissue materials, and adapted to all internal and external forces to which they are exposed.

The living organisms occupy a field of force which is never simple and which indeed is of immense complexity. As sometimes in physics, the knowledge of form leads to the interpretation of forces that molded it, at other times the knowledge of the forces at work guides a better insight into the form itself. Therefore, the conception of form is ultimately the understanding of the forces that gave rise to it, as a representation of a form is a diagram of forces in equilibrium.

In organic life the forces, therefore the adaptation to them, are under a dynamically continuous change. "Ignorato motu, ignoratur Natura," wrote Oliver Lodge. This constant change constitutes the base of the theory of transformation, that is, when the same "genus" under different circumstances deforms in proportion, differs in relative magnitude, or in "excess and defect."

In the diagram a Diodon, or porcupine-fish is shown. Deforming its vertical coordinates into a system of concentric circles, and the horizontal coordinates into approximate hyperbolas, the new network shows a representation of the closely allied but very different looking sunfish, Orthagoriscus Mola, shaped by the influence of his chosen habitat.

Turning from the complexity of the zoological world, plant life shows a closer relationship to the specific thermal environmental problem. The plant morphology in various climates seems to bear an analogy to the formation of buildings, as a few of the shaping forces (such as temperature range) are somewhat similar to human environmental needs.

The illustrative examples of cross sections of leaves (shown at the opposite page with typical sections, however not necessarily drawn from the same plants as shown above) can draw attention to interesting synonymity. According to either favorable or adverse environment, plants open or close their surfaces. The plants of cool and hot-arid regions show similarities with their massive sections; i.e., large content with relatively small surface. This is their defense response against the excessive cold or torrid heat. Conversely, the plants of more temperate zones are free to communicate with their seasonal environments, and the growth of hot-humid vegetation is liberal in size and shape.

In the approach to regional building characteristics described further, the two main thermal factors—the combined effect of air temperature and radiation—lead the investigations. Since not the particular local conditions but rather the general regional character was aimed for, the effect of air movement in the convection calculations was held as a constant and directionless value. The results point towards shapes under which specific conditions stand up better, hence are preferable in their thermal environments.

**171.** Diodon. Orthagoriscus. Transformation in biology through environmental impacts.

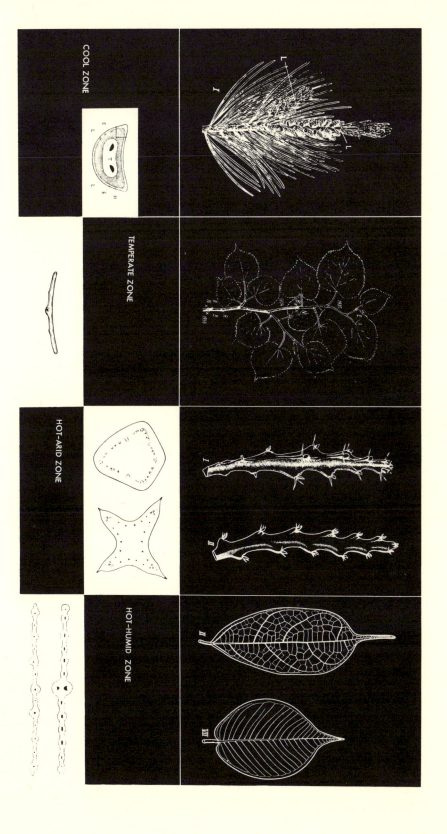

COOL ZONE

TEMPERATE ZONE

HOT-ARID ZONE

HOT-HUMID ZONE

These calculations are based on quantity, and the evaluation is expressed in this manner. However, it is felt that the significance of the observations lies in the inherent tendency of the shaping itself, in the peculiarity of desired densities, in forms related to types of habitats, and in the qualities which as a consequence shall influence and may govern the basic architectural compositions in the various climatic zones.

FORMATION OF LEAVES IN DIFFERENT ENVIRONMENTS. Leaf cross sections show environmental effect in plant morphology.

In the Cool Zone, Pine needles are slightly flattened cylinders of such construction that they may withstand cold, drought, winds, and other unfavorable conditions. Forms are compact.

In the Temperate Zone the upper side of the leaf is transparent and the greater part of the light enters through its surface. Friendly seasonal environment encourages the leaf to open to considerable size.

In the Hot-arid Zone the environment puts serious strains on the plants to which they are not very well suited. They adapt themselves by reduction of the leaf surfaces (actually they are green stems) and the branches, and show an exaggerated development of masses of thinwalled cells. Forms are massive for protection.

In the Hot-humid zone conditions are favorable for plant life in wet, warm, hothouse climate. Under protective shade quite liberal shapes develop. There is freedom in growth. Leaf surfaces expand roughly two and a half times as large as those in temperate climate.

## IMPACT OF EXTERNAL THERMAL FORCES ON BUILDINGS

To investigate the effects of climate on buildings, similar factors that influence the forms of plants can be considered in the human environment.

Let us return to the four locations chosen as typical of the main U.S. climate zones, which were evaluated in Chapter III. These areas represent cool, temperate, hot-arid, and hot-humid environments. In Table VIII-1 the coldest (January 21) and the warmest (July 21) days were chosen in each region as indexes for winter and summer conditions. The radiation effect on the various sides of a building can be expressed in Btu/ft²/day as follows (see also Appendix A-4):

TABLE VIII-1

| | | Btu/ft²/day | |
|---|---|---|---|
| | | Winter | Summer |
| Minneapolis | E | 416 | 1314 |
| | S | 1374 | 979 |
| | W | 416 | 1314 |
| | N | 83 | 432 |
| | Roof | 654 | 2536 |
| New York | E | 517 | 1277 |
| | S | 1489 | 839 |
| | W | 517 | 1277 |
| | N | 119 | 430 |
| | Roof | 787 | 2619 |
| Phoenix | E | 620 | 1207 |
| | S | 1606 | 563 |
| | W | 620 | 1207 |
| | N | 140 | 452 |
| | Roof | 954 | 2596 |
| Miami | E | 734 | 1193 |
| | S | 1620 | 344 |
| | W | 734 | 1193 |
| | N | 152 | 616 |
| | Roof | 1414 | 2568 |

It appears that, in the upper latitudes, the south side of a building receives nearly twice as much radiation in the winter as in the

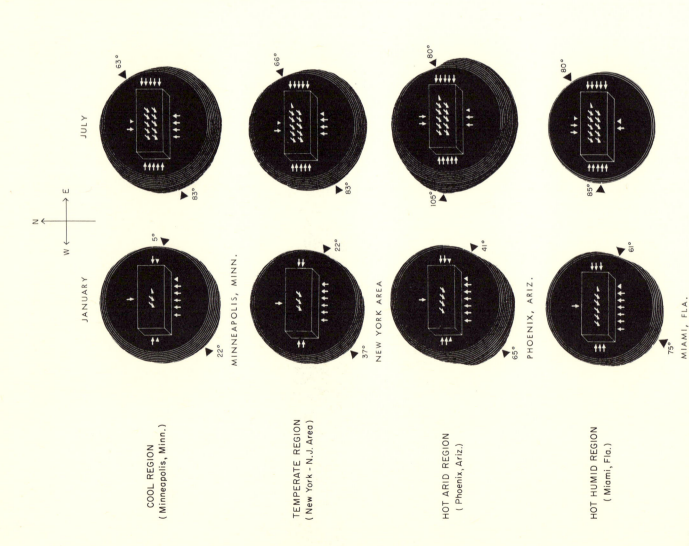

JANUARY    JULY

N
W ← → E

COOL REGION
( Minneapolis, Minn. )
MINNEAPOLIS, MINN.

TEMPERATE REGION
( New York - N.J. Area )
NEW YORK AREA

HOT ARID REGION
( Phoenix, Ariz.)
PHOENIX, ARIZ.

HOT HUMID REGION
( Miami, Fla. )
MIAMI, FLA.

173. Impact of external thermal forces on buildings.

86

summer. The effect is even more pronounced at the lower latitudes, where the ratio is about one to four. Also, in the upper latitudes, the east and west sides receive about 2½ times more radiation in summer than in winter. This ratio is not as large in the lower latitudes; but it is noteworthy that in summer there these sides receive two to three times as much radiation as the south elevation. On the west side high temperature impacts are augmented by the afternoon radiation effects. In all latitudes the north side receives only a small amount of radiation, and this comes mainly in the summer. But in low latitudes the north side receives in summer nearly twice the impact of the south side. The amount of radiation received on a horizontal roof surface in summertime exceeds all other sides. The roof heat-impact demands special attention, as its area is roughly equal to all the wall surfaces of the house added together.

The table shows that the various sides of a house receive markedly different thermal impacts. The changes in value, above the seasonal rise common to all sides, define the radiation according to orientation.

The relative importance of the regional thermal stresses must be clarified to show the part they play in shaping a structure. General low temperature tends to press buildings into a compact form, and heavy radiation impacts tend to elongate the shapes, mostly in the east-west direction.

## CRITERION OF OPTIMUM SHAPE

It can be taken as a rule that the optimum shape is that which loses the minimum amount of outgoing Btu in winter, and accepts the least amount of incoming Btu in summer. It is widely believed that a square building has the best characteristics of preserving the heat in winter and remaining cool in summer. This convection is based on the fact that a square building combines the largest practical volume with the smallest outside surface. The principle may be valid for older types of buildings where, because of relatively small window openings, the radiation effect is negligible. With the large contemporary openings, this concept becomes a fallacy.

The thermal impacts on the interior of the building should be computed on a quantitative basis. The combined effect of the temperature and radiation can be expressed with the sol-air temperature on the outside surface of the building. The effect of this on the interior surface can be calculated by the heatflow method.

In case of glass surfaces the solar-heat-gain method was used with the following equation:

$$c = I_D(T_D \times \alpha_D) + I_d(T_d \times \alpha_d) + U(t_o - t_i)$$

Where the symbols in the equations designate:

U = overall coefficient of heat transfer Btu/ft²/hr

t_o = outdoor air temperature

t_i = indoor air temperature

$t_m$ = 24-hr cyclic average sol-air temperature

$t_e^*$ = sol-air temperature earlier to time lag

$\lambda$ = amplitude decrement factor

$\alpha$ = absorptivity of weather side of wall. Subscripts D and d refer to direct and diffuse incident solar radiation

I = incident solar radiation, Btu/ft²/hr. Subscripts D and d refer to direct and diffuse incident solar radiation

T = transmittance coefficient of solar radiation. Subscripts D and d refer to direct and diffuse.

*Application.* To investigate the shaping effect of the thermal environment a house type was chosen and placed hypothetically in the four regional climates that have been analyzed. The selected house consists of usual insulated frame construction ($U = 0.13$), with 40% glass (single pane) on the south side, and with 20% glass surfaces on all other sides. Although all the conclusions apply directly to this specific type of house, other types will behave more or less similarly. Very well insulated houses, or buildings with shading devices on the south side will show even more strongly the deformation effects described. Conversely, buildings with relatively small window openings, or in full shade, will show less need for elongation.

As a reference for comparison, a 1000 square foot house with equal sides was computed first. Only the heat impacts through the four sides were calculated, as the impact through a horizontal roof remains constant regardless of the form. The hour-by-hour calculated heat flows were added to make a total daily (24-hour) summation. The square house showed

Let us call the interior heat effects "c," and the sides of the house "x" and "y."

Then the area of a given plan is: A = xy

if we search for the form which gives the best performance, this can be expressed as: $x\Sigma c_1 + y\Sigma c_2 =$ minimum

where $c_1$ and $c_2$ are the thermal forces of the opposite sides. Putting this in form of the Langrangean multiplier:

$$\Sigma c_1 - \lambda y = 0 \qquad then \quad \Sigma c_1 = \lambda y$$
$$\Sigma c_2 - \lambda x = 0 \qquad\qquad \Sigma c_2 = \lambda x$$

the optimum form can be expressed as:

$$\frac{\Sigma c_1}{\Sigma c_2} = \frac{y}{x}$$

When an inverse relationship exists between the thermal impacts and the sizes of the sides of the structure, the optimum form represents the thermal forces in equilibrium.

*Method of Calculation.* The interior heat effects (c) are here calculated with periodic heat-flow method using the following equation in case of opaque materials:[2]

$$c = U(t_m - t_i) - \lambda U(t_e^* - t_m)$$

the following incoming and outgoing heat amounts at the different locations:

| | Total Btu impact/day | |
|---|---|---|
| | Winter | Summer |
| Minneapolis | −352.400 | 196.600 |
| New York | −194.300 | 190.300 |
| Phoenix | 42.500 | 338.500 |
| Miami | 171.800 | 231.000 |

Those results of the house with the square plan now can be compared with houses of the same construction, characteristics, and same square-foot area, but with different forms: some elongated in an east-west, some in a north-south direction. In the tabulations the left-hand column refers to the east-west versus north-south relationship of the sides of the building.

MINNEAPOLIS

| | Total Btu impact/day | |
|---|---|---|
| Ratio | Winter | Summer |
| 5:1 | −491.300 | 295.500 |
| 4:1 | −455.600 | 272.500 |
| 3:1 | −418.000 | 247.400 |
| 2:1 | −380.200 | 220.800 |
| 1.5:1 | −363.600 | 207.700 |
| 1:1 | −352.400 | 196.600 |
| 1:1.5 | −355.500 | 193.300 |
| 1:2 | −366.800 | 196.600 |
| 1:3 | −395.200 | 206.400 |
| 1:4 | −425.500 | 220.600 |
| 1:5 | −455.400 | 235.000 |

NEW YORK

| | Total Btu impact/day | |
|---|---|---|
| Ratio | Winter | Summer |
| 5:1 | −300.900 | 296.300 |
| 4:1 | −275.300 | 272.000 |
| 3:1 | −247.900 | 245.600 |
| 2:1 | −221.100 | 217.300 |
| 1.5:1 | −207.000 | 203.400 |
| 1:1 | −194.300 | 190.300 |
| 1:1.5 | −189.000 | 184.700 |
| 1:2 | −190.700 | 185.500 |
| 1:3 | −199.600 | 193.300 |
| 1:4 | −211.000 | 203.600 |
| 1:5 | −222.900 | 214.500 |

*Minneapolis:* Winter optimum is received with a form 1:1.1, summer optimum 1:1.4. As the stresses in wintertime are about twice as large as in summer, and the duration of the overheated period is only 20% of the year, the winter index was adopted. The elasticity of the shape is 1:1.3.

*New York:* Winter optimum is 1:1.56, in summer 1:1.63. Adopted index 1:1.6. Elasticity 1:2.4.

*Phoenix:* Summer optimum is 1:1.26. In the wintertime, because of the large solar effect, there is no specific limit but a large southern side is desirable. As the summer stresses are nearly eight times as large as the winter ones; the optimum shape shall be accordingly 1:1.3, elasticity 1:1.6.

*Miami:* Summer optimum is 1:1.7, in winter 1:2.69. Here again the winter shape is quite liberal, but of less importance because of the very short underheated period. Adopted optimum is 1:1.7, elasticity 1:3.

From the above the following observations can be drawn:

1. The square house is not the optimum form in any location.

2. All shapes elongated on the north-south axis work both in winter and summer with less efficiency than the square one.

3. The optimum lies in every case in a form elongated somewhere along the east-west direction.

PHOENIX

| | Total Btu impact/day | |
|---|---|---|
| Ratio | Winter | Summer |
| 5:1 | −15.400 | 489.600 |
| 4:1 | −7.600 | 452.400 |
| 3:1 | 2.600 | 413.100 |
| 2:1 | 16.700 | 372.200 |
| 1.5:1 | 26.800 | 353.100 |
| 1:1 | 42.500 | 338.100 |
| 1:1.5 | 59.900 | 337.200 |
| 1:2 | 73.300 | 344.800 |
| 1:3 | 95.700 | 367.900 |
| 1:4 | 113.900 | 394.000 |
| 1:5 | 129.800 | 419.700 |

MIAMI

| | Total Btu impact/day | |
|---|---|---|
| Ratio | Winter | Summer |
| 5:1 | 160.100 | 364.400 |
| 4:1 | 155.800 | 334.200 |
| 3:1 | 152.900 | 301.100 |
| 2:1 | 154.100 | 265.900 |
| 1.5:1 | 158.900 | 248.200 |
| 1:1 | 171.800 | 231.000 |
| 1:1.5 | 191.300 | 223.200 |
| 1:2 | 209.500 | 223.400 |
| 1:3 | 243.400 | 231.500 |
| 1:4 | 273.800 | 243.400 |
| 1:5 | 301.300 | 256.000 |

## CONCLUSIONS FOR "BASIC FORMS" OF HOUSES

To define the most desirable form of a house in the given environment the criterion of "optimum shape" was applied. However, to leave a certain latitude wherein the proportions of a plan can be considered as generally good, the criterion of "elasticity" was adapted. The upper limit of variation from the optimum was arbitrarily defined here as the elongated shape that is subjected to the same heat impacts as a square form.

These criteria applied to the given locales result in the following conclusions:

A graphical presentation of the calculations is shown. On the graph at the left the heat amounts received by different building shapes are charted. The numerical values of the heat amount received by the square house both in winter and summer were considered as starting reference points, and therefore located on the zero line. The heat amounts received by other forms (see top) are charted from this line rela-

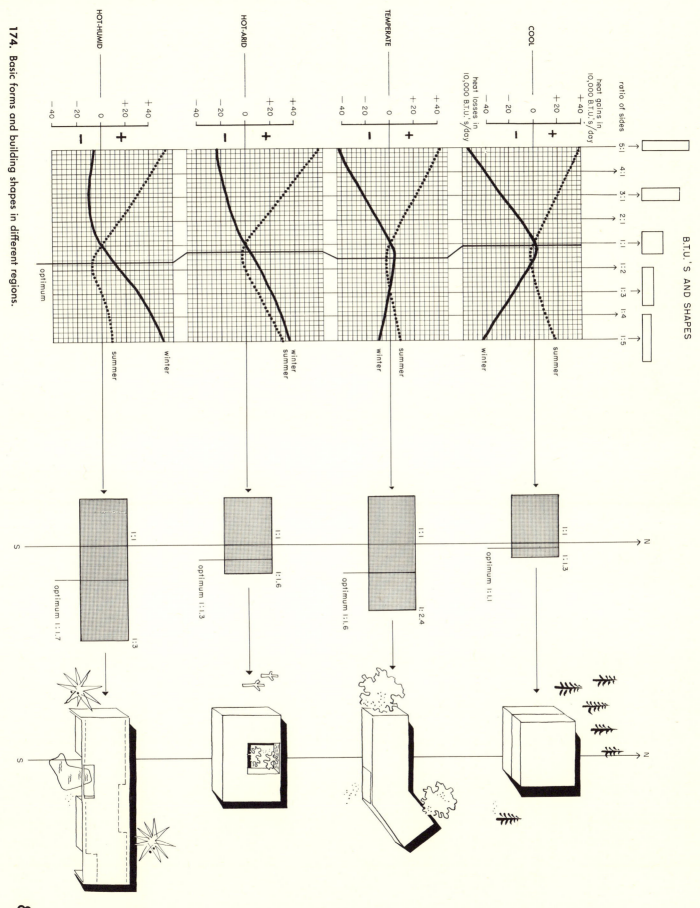

**174.** Basic forms and building shapes in different regions.

tive to it. The middle column illustrates the optimum and elasticity basic forms compared to the square area. At the right are architectural interpretations of the basic forms.

*Regional Effects on House Shapes.* The optimum shape was defined above as the one which has the minimum heat gain in summer and the minimum heat loss in winter. Hence it is obvious that the form of houses should vary with the region, and that the effects of thermal forces may be expressed in architectural terms, within the "limit of elasticity."

In the *cool zone* the low winter temperature overrules the sun's effort to elongate the structure in the east-west direction, and presses it into a nearly square shape. In large houses the cubical form can be enchanced by a two-story structure.

In the *temperate region*, where the temperature range permits more flexible plans to materialize, an elongated form is desirable. The thermal stresses, even on wings extending in a north-south direction, impose less penalty than in the other zones. Therefore this region can afford cross-shaped or freeform buildings; however, an east-west elongation is definitely desirable.

In the *hot-arid region* under winter conditions the house could have an elongated form, but it is returned to a squarish shape by strong summer stresses. However, by cutting out part of the cube and filling the hole with shade (walls, trees, trellis) and with cooled air (evaporative cooling, lawn, trees, pool, fountain effect) the environment is changed for the better (microclimate). Around such a "gardenette" the plan can be free (the ancient peristilium or the old patio type). Accordingly, the basic plan changes here to an inward-looking scheme.

In the southern *hot-humid region* the sun attacks the east and west ends of a house and

forces it into a slender elongated structure. The temperatures are not excessive, and such a shape can be used beneficially for wind effects (counteraction of vapor-pressure). Free plans can also be evolved here, as long as the house is under protective shade.

The same form enlarged four times, however, will scale down its surface ratio to 1:4, and the environmental impacts in proportion. Floating icebergs survive for a considerable time in water over the melting point, since their mass is immensely large relative to their exposed surface.

It is evident that the volume effect can be utilized architecturally for the alleviation of over-all thermal pressures. Some calculations show that, while in houses more than 90% of the cooling load is due to weather factors, in large buildings the same effects amount to less than 60%.[3] In such cases the form and orientation is of secondary importance.

The over-all Btu impact (calculated on a theoretical unit) in Minnesota in the winter (−1704 Btu) is nearly two times greater than in the summer (886). In the New York area the winter impact (−1008) is larger than that of the summer. Conversely in Phoenix the summer stress is the determining factor (1590), as it is in Miami (1092), where the winter impact is relatively negligible.

The range of stresses in Minnesota and Phoenix is about 1½ times as great as in Miami or New York. Therefore, to build up volume effect by masses is of eminent importance in both cold and hot-arid areas where the adverse impacts are excessive.

From past experience in the cold climates, this seems obvious, but it might be less so in the hot-arid regions. To illustrate indigenous solutions in such climates, two native examples show composite-dwelling structures, which under milder impacts would certainly be

separated into single units. Although they are in quite different geographical locations, the same excessive impacts of hot-arid environment urged them to congregate and pile together in collective mass protection. In the milder zones of temperate and hot-humid regions, the need for volume effect has less importance.

It should be added that rearrangement of the form of a given volume will not reduce the total thermal stresses *per se* by more than 10%.

## REGIONAL EFFECTS ON LARGE BUILDING SHAPES

Where spatial freedom exists, a desired form can be developed for its own sake in the case of dwellings. But in larger buildings, other factors play a more important part in forming the structure, such as the logic of circulation, the over-all need for space, and economy of organization. The building as an envelope of specific group action expresses those internal forces, leaving less consideration to the shaping tendencies of external climatic elements. However, some general principles can be stated for large buildings.

In the *cool zone* closed compact forms are preferable, such as "point-houses" of squarish character, or bilateral ("back-to-back") building plans on the north-south axis, because of their relatively dense cubature. Elongated unilateral ("through") buildings are not advantageous. The environmental pressure favors higher buildings in this region.

In the *temperate zone* there is the least stress from any specific direction. The smallest penalty is received from this climate, allowing considerable freedom in form; however, shapes on the east-west axis are preferable.

**175.** Volume effect:

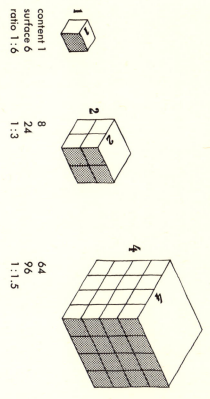

| | | | |
|---|---|---|---|
| content | 1 | 8 | 64 |
| surface | 6 | 24 | 96 |
| ratio | 1:6 | 1:3 | 1:1.5 |

In the *hot-arid zone* massive shapes are advantageous. Cubical forms, or those slightly elongated toward the east-west axis are most adaptable. High buildings are preferable.

In the *hot-humid zone* buildings freely elongated in the east-west direction are advantageous. Buildings located on the north-south axis receive greater penalty than they would in other climatic zones.

## MORPHOLOGY OF TOWN STRUCTURES

The "tissue-pattern" of town layouts is an interwoven synthesis of many factors. Its organism reflects political and social tendencies as much as materialistic and technical requirements. From all those shaping factors which are merged together into a composite picture, sometimes it seems difficult to analyze the climatic environment as a separate element.

However, in a town layout the same tendencies and characteristics can be found which were influential in determining single building units. As it is influenced by the same forces, its texture not only is built up as a conglomeration of different shapes, but also reflects mass-building tendencies on a larger scale. The density of a city layout will vary according to friendly or adverse climatic conditions.

In a *cool environment* the layout tries to provide shelter against the winds. Large building units are closely grouped, but spaced to utilize beneficial sun-heat effects. The houses tend to join in order to have less surface exposed to heat loss. The town structure is an *insolated dense* layout.

In the temperate zone plans are open, nature and the houses merge. The town structure utilizes the possibilities of a *free* arrangement.

In the hot-arid zone the walls of the houses and the gardens provide shade to the living areas and to the street, like a horizontal eggcrate device for shading. Unit dwellings are arranged around closed courtyards like cooling wells, and are grouped together to achieve defense in volume. Here the town layout reacts against the heat with *shaded dense* structure.

In *hot-humid areas* the buildings are freely elongated, and this freedom is accentuated in the layouts. The houses are separated to utilize the air movements; shade trees become

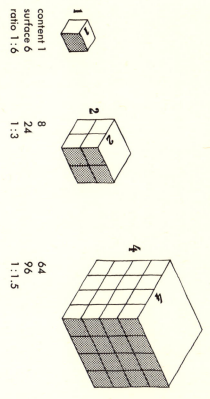

**176.** Arab village, Metameur, Tunis.

**177.** Indian Pueblo, Taos, New Mexico. Native adaptation of volume utilization.

**91**

important elements. The character of the town fabric becomes *scattered* and loose.

Human habitation has an integrated correlation with its environment. In its final appearance it seems simple, although it is composite in itself, coordinating countless subordinate actions. The same fundamental laws dominate its characteristics as govern the adaptations of even the small-scale organisms, such as wood structures or cell molecules.

No matter how we approach the question—through mathematics, physiological considerations, or via the accumulated experiences of tradition—the answer will be the same: where the natural setting is friendly the shapes communicate with the environment and try to merge with it; under adverse influences the form closes its sensitive surfaces and tries to maintain the equilibrium of its own internal life.

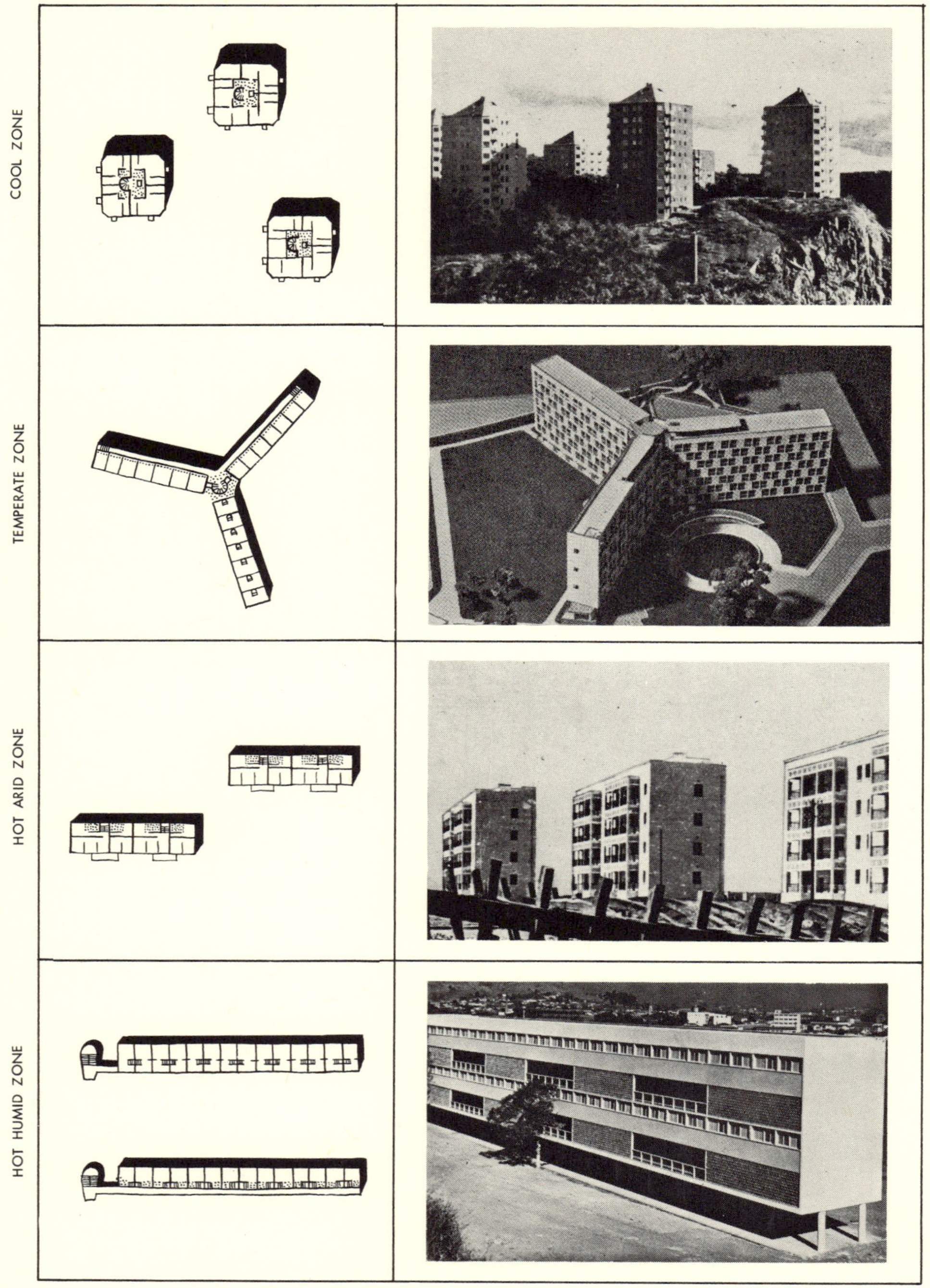

178.
Backstrom & Reinius, Stockholm.

Skinner, Baily & Lubetkin, Finsbury

Zehrfuss, Turus

Reidy, Pedregulho

BUILDINGS IN DIFFERENT CLIMATE REGIONS

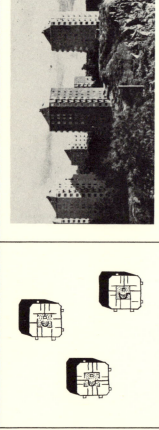

COOL ZONE

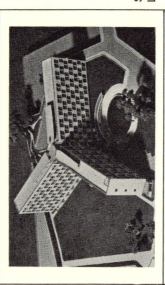

TEMPERATE ZONE

HOT ARID ZONE

HOT HUMID ZONE

92

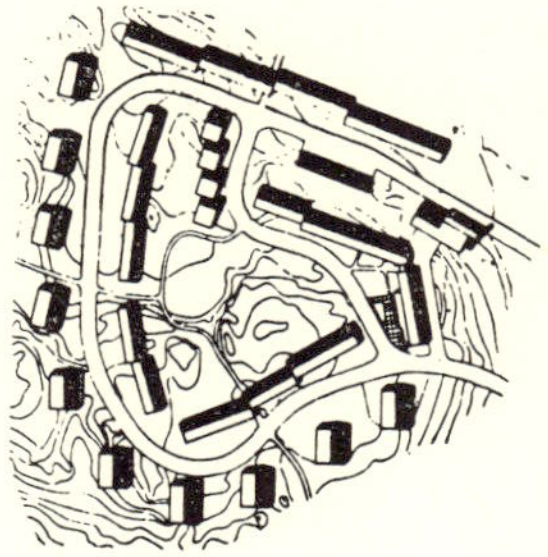

COOL ZONE

Hockaraegen, Stockholm

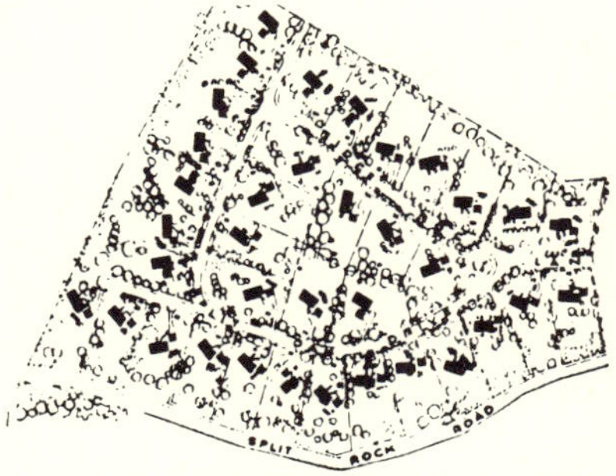

TEMPERATE ZONE

Furno & Harrison, East Norwich, L.I., N.Y.

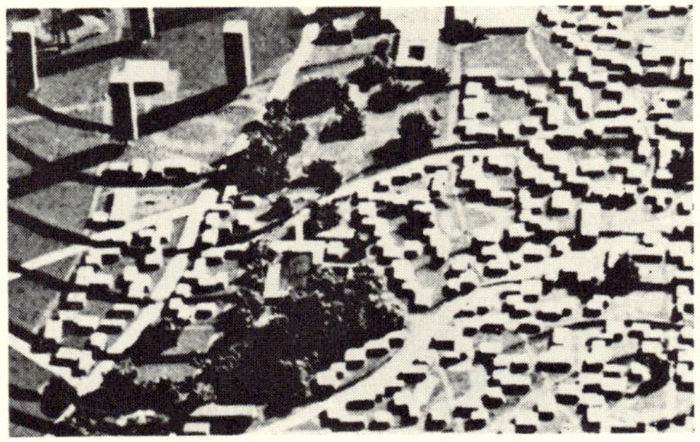

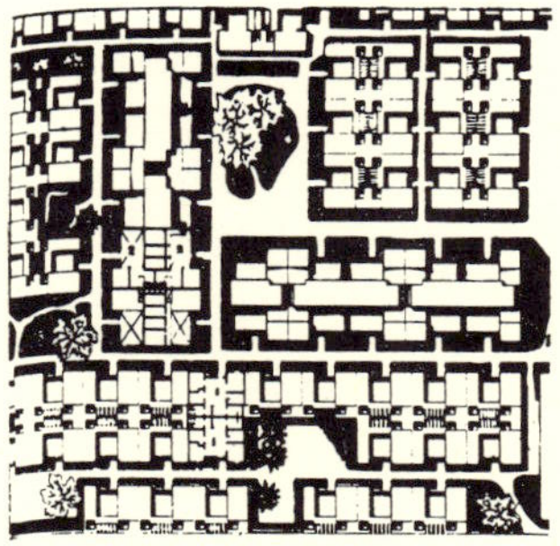

HOT-ARID ZONE

Wiener & Sert, Chimbote, Peru

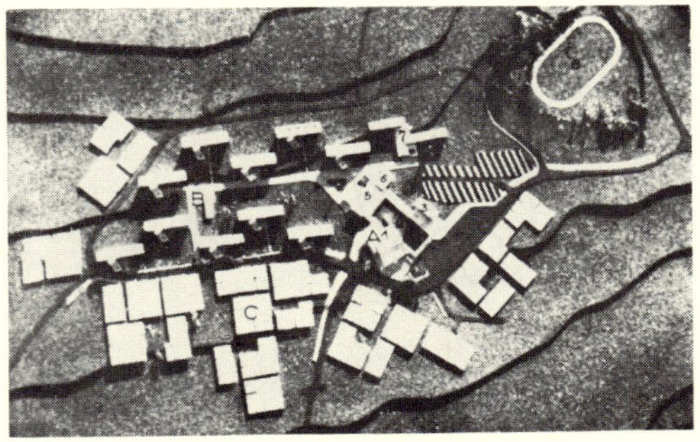

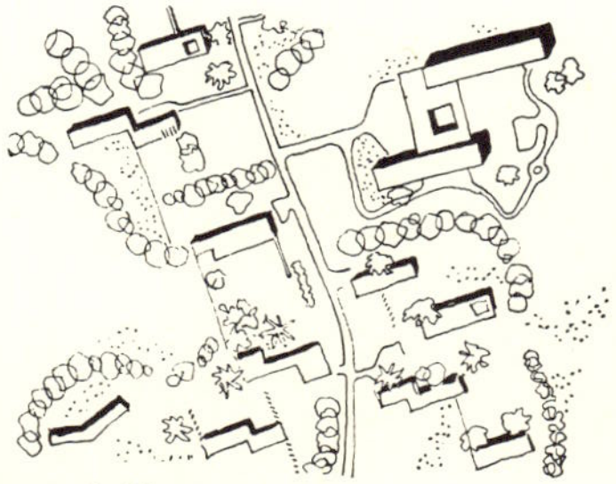

HOT-HUMID ZONE

Olgyay & Olgyay

**179.**
Gegenbach, Kolsdal, Norway

Stevenage City Plan, England

Tasteman, Morocco

Rudolph, Revere House, Fla.

# IX. WIND EFFECTS AND AIR FLOW PATTERNS

## WIND AND ARCHITECTURE

THE unequal distribution of the sun's heat on the earth's surface produces variations in density in the atmospheric mass. The rising air of the equatorial zone descends around the 30° latitudes, to be pushed toward the south and the north where it later meets the cold polar flow. This flow system, set in motion by the earth's rotation, is complicated by the earth's inclination, resulting in seasonal variations. The unequal distribution of continents and oceans also causes distortions in the series of atmospheric pressure belts. And geographical characteristics lend local peculiarities to the prevailing winds.

Builders of the past have used protective measures against the troublesome effects of wind, and arrangements took advantage of its benefits. In windswept places the least exposure is the general rule, and sheltered locations are sought. Huddling for protection is the motivation for the closeness of the towns in the Swiss Alps. The weather sides are often specially protected, such as the shingled "tavaillons" in the Jura Mountains. In hot-climate zones ventilation has particular importance as a remedy against high temperatures and humidities. Town layouts on the African shore of the Mediterranean show street arrangements which bring the coolness of the sea breezes into the heart of the city.[1] Persian houses orient large openings, the "iwanes," in the direction of beneficial air movements.[2] In Spain and India the use of light latticework lets the slightest breeze bring

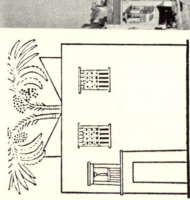

180, 181, 182. Capturing the breezes in the hot areas, in North Africa, in Egypt, in Pakistan.

refreshment into the structure, and performs much the same function as the porches of the West. The close-packed Egyptian houses use roof ventilators, the "Mulguf," to catch air currents. Ventilation towers in Charga give the Persian town an architectural accent, while in the valley of the Indus the town of Hyderabad is strangely silhouetted with air-shafts and wind scoops standing erect on the roofs.

## WIND ANALYSIS

Desirable air movements should be utilized for cooling in hot periods, and as a relief from vapor pressure during times of high absolute humidity. Conversely, air movements should be blocked and avoided during the cold season. The yardstick for evaluating wind movements is provided by a bioclimatic analysis for the region (Chapter III), which divides the year into overheated and underheated periods and defines the comfort needs.

Before investigating possible arrangements that will give wind protection or will utilize air movements beneficially, it is necessary to consider the orientation of the building.

## LOCAL FACTORS IN WIND ORIENTATION

Adaptation for wind orientation is not of great importance in low buildings; where the use of windbreaks, the arrangement of openings in the high and low-pressure areas, and

These examples refer to predominantly cool or hot conditions. However, in most climatic zones varying periods prevail, and accordingly a careful wind analysis is required.

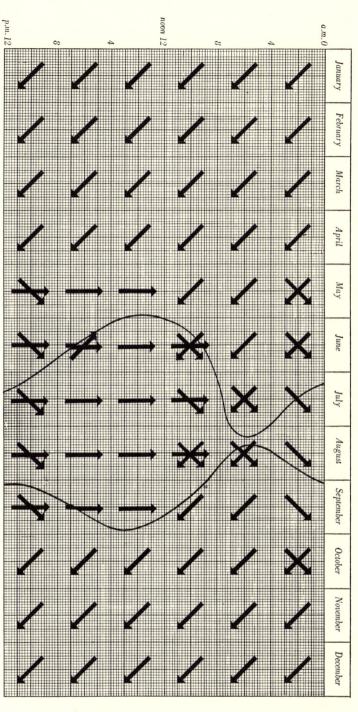

a.m. 0
4
8
noon 12
4
8
p.m. 12

| January | February | March | April | May | June | July | August | September | October | November | December |
|---|---|---|---|---|---|---|---|---|---|---|---|

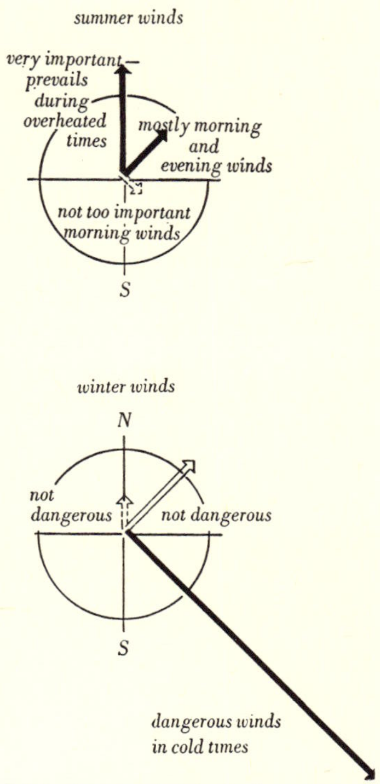

184. Summarized wind vectors.

very important prevails during overheated times

mostly morning and evening winds

not too important morning winds

summer winds

S

winter winds

S

N

dangerous winds in cold times

not dangerous

not dangerous

the directional effect of the window inlets can help to ameliorate the airflow situation. However, for non-airconditioned high buildings, such as apartment houses, office buildings, or hospitals—where surrounding terrain has little effect on the upper stories—careful considera- tion has to be given to wind orientation. In order to evaluate the specific effects of wind on human comfort conditions, both the annual and monthly variations of prevalence, velocity, and the temperature of the winds must be analyzed by direction.

Such a precise study of the climatic condi- tions was evolved by the Department of City Planning, Baltimore, Md., where solar orienta-

tion was modified by the application of the local specific wind factors. The method devel- oped in that study by I. S. Wiener is described here in abbreviated form.[3] For the evaluation three types of wind data are necessary:

1. Prevalence of winds in terms of percentage of time,
2. Velocity in mph,
3. General characteristics, such as cool and hot breezes.

A breakdown of wind characteristics by monthly prevalence and velocity for each of the eight main directions is plotted. Average monthly prevalence and velocities by time and

direction are charted in separate graphs. This permits an easy interpretation of the relative importance of winds by direction, and correla- tions between prevalence and velocity. In the evaluations desirable breezes were categorized as air movements occurring when air tempera- tures were above 75° F. The overheated period in this case was taken to prevail from the end of May to the middle of September. Con- versely, air movements were rated as undesira- ble during the cold and transitional periods from the beginning of November to the be- ginning of March.

The method of modifying solar orienta- tions consists of three

by the resultant wind factors consists of three

95

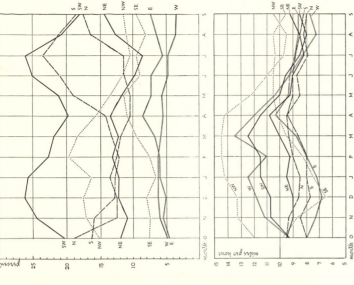

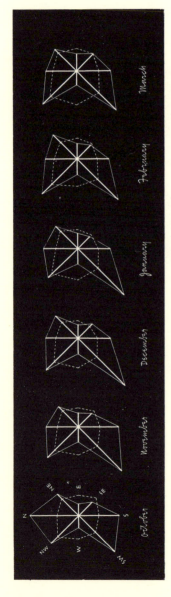

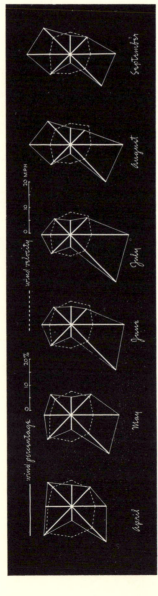

**185.** Surface winds: frequency of directions and average velocity.

**186.** Average monthly percentage of wind by time and direction.

**187.** Average monthly velocity by direction.

phases: (A) Derivation of scoring effect for wind factors; (B) Scoring for solar orientation; (C) Concluding the orientation resulting from combined sun and wind scoring.

STEP A: Averages of prevalence (P) and velocity (V) are computed on the averages of the peak winter and summer months. Scoring is based on the assumption that all winds in winter are undesirable, consequently have minus value; those in summer are desirable with plus value. The resultant wind score (W$_s$) consists of the modification of the wind volume (PV) according to the thermal property of the wind. The variable thermal coefficients (C$_{Th}$) of the wind are categorized as:

| Thermal characteristics in winter | medium | cool | cold |
|---|---|---|---|
| Thermal coefficient (C$_{Th_1}$) | 1.00 | 1.25 | 1.50 |

| Thermal characteristics in summer | medium | warm | hot |
|---|---|---|---|
| Thermal coefficient (C$_{Th_2}$) | 1.00 | 1.25 | 1.50 |

Winter (W$_{s1}$) and summer (W$_{s2}$) scores are computed separately by direction, and are subsequently added to get the net yearly (W$_{st}$) score by direction:

$$W_{st} = W_{s1} + W_{s2}$$

which equation can be written in full detail as:

$$W_{st} = -(P_1 V_1 C_{Th_1}) + \left(V_2 - \frac{V_2 C_v}{P_2}\right) \left[\frac{P_2 V_2}{P_2 \left(V_2 - \frac{V_2 C_v}{P_2}\right)}\right] \div C_{Th_2}$$

where
P$_1$ = average winter prevalence
P$_2$ = average summer prevalence
V$_1$ = average winter velocity
V$_2$ = average summer velocity
C$_{Th_1}$ = thermal winter coefficient
C$_{Th_2}$ = thermal summer coefficient
C$_v$ = variable velocity coefficient

The absolute wind scores thus obtained are expressed in percentages.

STEP B: Scoring for solar orientation by direction. The desirability of solar orientation may be determined by directions in terms of highest and lowest desirability (+100 and −100 respectively) according to the char-

acteristics for the given climatic zone. For Baltimore the solar orientation scoring (S$_s$) by direction was taken as follows:

| Direction | N | NE | E | SE | S | SW | W | NW |
|---|---|---|---|---|---|---|---|---|
| Summer score (S$_s$) | −100 | 0 | +50 | +100 | +100 | +50 | 0 | −50 |

STEP C: The combined sun and wind orientation scoring. In order to determine the final orientation scoring, the relative importance of sun factors and wind factors for orientation has to be evaluated. In this particular case the relative sun-score value was considered twice the value of the wind score. (The sun factor in orientation will gain in relative importance in the northern regions and lose its importance—provided there is adequate shading—in the tropical zone.)

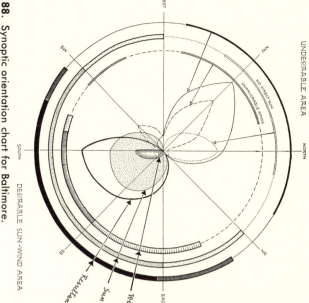

**188.** Synoptic orientation chart for Baltimore.

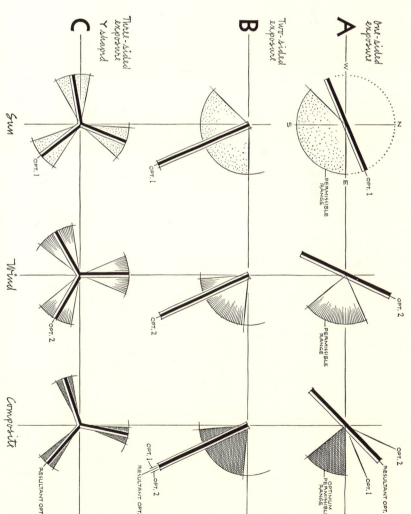

**189.** Application of method for three different building types at Baltimore.

The absolute resultant orientation score ($R_{sa}$) will be:

$$R_{sa} = W_{st}C_w \div S_s$$

where:

$W_{st}$ = resultant wind score
$S_s$ = sun score
$C_w$ = wind importance coefficient (here taken as 0.5)

The resultant scores are then expressed in percentages.

For application purposes a synoptic chart was plotted showing the sectors of relative desirability and undesirability in terms of wind, sun, and overall resultant scores. The general principle governing the application of the synoptic chart to specific cases involves the superimposition of the optimum and permissible ranges of orientation for solar and wind factors respectively, as scaled off from the chart. The overlapping ranges will determine the resultant range of orientation.

The application of the method for Baltimore is shown for three different types of buildings:

A. With desired exposure on one side of a building.

B. With desired exposure on two sides of a building.

C. With desired exposure on three sides of a Y-shaped building.

The described method can be applied to other localities, modified according to their specific climatic conditions.

## WINDBREAKS

Large air masses cannot be altered in their motion which is dictated by differences of air pressure. However, velocities near the living, or ground, level can be controlled to a certain extent. The frictional drag of vegetation and the resistance and obstruction created by trees can cause diversions in the air flow which may be utilized beneficially. Besides their aesthetic and shade-giving properties, the value of tree windbreaks lies in their ability to reduce wind velocities. This mechanical effect brings perceptible changes both in the temperature and

97

| Object | Distance at 0.1 H to— | | |
|---|---|---|---|
| | 75% reduction | 50% reduction | 25% reduction |
| Vertical plate | 13.0 H | 15.5 H | 21.5 H |
| Triangular shape | 10.5 H | 15.0 H | 20.5 H |
| Cylindrical shape | 7.0 H | 9.0 H | 14.0 H |
| Model trees | — | 13.5 H | 27.0 H |

humidity of the air, in evaporative effects and in the formation of snowdrifts, thus significantly affecting the growth of plants. For this reason most data and observations on shelterbelts originate from agricultural studies and experiments.

A windbreak, according to C. G. Bates' description,[4] diverts the air currents upward, and while they soon turn back and again sweep the ground, an area of relative calm is created near the ground. The most protected part of this area is fairly close to the windbreak on the leeward side; it becomes more exposed as the distance from the windbreak increases until a point is reached where the air currents have again reached full velocity. There is a smaller calm area on the windward side, especially if the windbreak is quite dense. If it is open, so that the wind can sweep under the trees, the windward side has little protection. On the leeward side such openness will result

in a smaller protected area located farther from the windbreak.

The type of windbreak used has a definite effect on the resultant airflow pattern and on the area of protection. Solid wind barriers, or walls, cause eddies over the top which reduce their effectiveness. In general, three belts with greater density and thickness will produce a larger effect in wind protection.

Wind tunnel experiments on the effect of barrier shape on flow patterns for solids and trees were studied in models at the Kansas Agricultural Experiment Station.[5] The tests were conducted at 25 mph constant velocities. The velocity-profile maps drawn from the experiments are shown. The indicated velocities $U_p/U_c$ are dimensionless ratios, where $U_p$ is the velocity in the tunnel with a barrier, and $U_c$ the velocity at a corresponding point in a clear tunnel. The table summarizes the more important results indicated in the figure:

On the basis of these findings N. P. Woodruff points out that although there is no 75% reduction for trees, because of the jet-movement of air through them, they cause a more extended area of protection than any of the other shapes. This is marked by the 27 H distance to a 25% reduction and the relatively great distance between a 25% and a 50% reduction in velocity. The vertical plate secures the second best protection, reducing the velocities approximately 44% more than the cylinder when near the object and 25% at positions farther from it. The plate also reduces the velocity approximately 10% more than does the triangular shape at both the near and far distances. The findings show that the windward reduction in velocity is relatively insignificant for all the barriers.

Architectural interest in wind protection lies not only in outdoor comfort conditions, but also in its effects on house heating. The general functional relationship for the heating load, the wind velocity, the temperature difference for the house, and the location of the shelter-belt can be expressed in a three-variable equation[6]

$$\frac{Q}{T_\triangle} = 1.3 \ (10^{0.018L0.07u})$$

where

$Q$ = heating load in Btu per hour
$T_\triangle$ = difference between inside and outside temperature in °F
$L$ = distance from belt to house in barrier heights H
$u$ = wind velocity in mph.

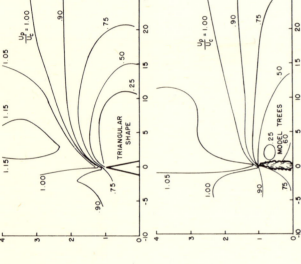

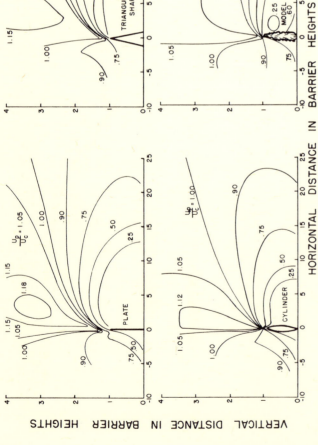

VERTICAL DISTANCE IN BARRIER HEIGHTS

HORIZONTAL DISTANCE IN BARRIER HEIGHTS

190. Air flow around four barriers of varying shape.

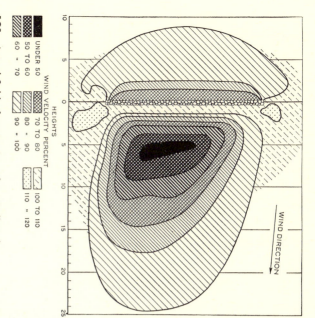

**191. Actual field of protection of a windbreak.**

WIND VELOCITY PERCENT

UNDER 50
50 TO 60
60 " 70
70 " 80
80 " 90
90 " 100
100 TO 110
110 " 120

HEIGHTS

WIND DIRECTION

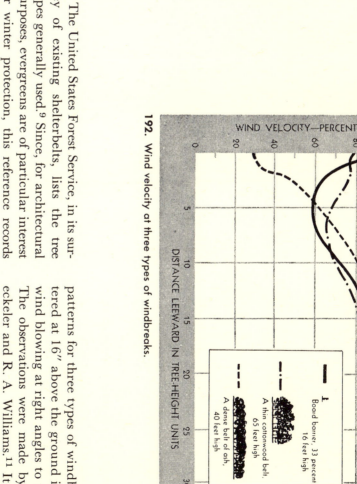

**192. Wind velocity at three types of windbreaks.**

WIND VELOCITY—PERCENT

DISTANCE LEEWARD IN TREE-HEIGHT UNITS

Board barrier, 33 percent solid, 16 feet high

A thin cottonwood belt, 65 feet high

A dense belt of ash, 40 feet high

Calculations indicate[7] that the heating load of an unprotected house with a 20 mph wind is approximately 2.4 times as great as that for a 5 mph wind under the same temperature conditions. The heating load for a protected house at 20 mph wind velocities, was approximately twice as great as for a similar house exposed to 5 mph wind effects. This indicates that a shelter-belt's effectiveness increases at higher wind velocities.

The Lake States Forest Experimental Station conducted experiments in Nebraska with two identical test houses.[8] One was exposed to the winds; the other protected from it. As the exact fuel requirements were recorded, it was possible to calculate the savings. Under 70° F constant house temperature the amount of fuel saved by the protected house was 22.9%, and occurred at five heights from the barrier. With greater density near the barrier. With good protection on three sides of the house it was estimated that the fuel saving might have run as high as 30%.

The United States Forest Service, in its survey of existing shelterbelts, lists the tree types generally used.[9] Since, for architectural purposes, evergreens are of particular interest for winter protection, this reference records only the conifer trees.

The wind-shadow effect of windbreaks is illustrated here in two drawings. The horizontal velocity distribution pattern was charted by the Lake States Forest Experimental Station.[10] The slat windbreak was constructed of 6" boards with 12" spaces in the lower half, but only 3" spaces in the upper half, to give a resistance similar to old trees with very few limbs near the ground. The wind was measured 16" above ground, with 13 mph open wind velocities. The lowest velocity was 47% and occurred at five heights from the barrier. With greater density near the barrier the low point moves closer.

The second chart shows the zone-of-influence

patterns for three types of windbreaks registered at 16" above the ground in a 15 mph wind blowing at right angles to the barriers. The observations were made by J. H. Stoeckeler and R. A. Williams.[11] It can be seen that the wind velocity near a dense belt of green ash may be reduced to as low as 30% of the original velocities; for a thin, rather open cottonwood belt, it is about 66% of that in the open; for a board barrier the maximum velocity reduction is about 58%. All three windbreaks show the same effect out to about 30 times their height; however, the effect beyond 20 H is minor.

*Windbreaks for Multiple-Housing Layouts.* The first consideration in the placement of the windbreaks is with reference to the object or area of protection. The principles are applied here to a neighborhood unit in the New York–New Jersey area. The housing layout is com-

**99**

*Wind Direction and Housing Layouts.* Buildings positioned perpendicular to the wind direction receive on their exposed side the full sweep of the velocities. Positioned at 45° the wind velocity is reduced to 50%; some calculations use 66% as the correction factor. Building rows spaced at a distance equal to seven times their respective heights secure satisfactory ventilation effect for each unit. The wind has a tendency, however, to leap-frog long parallel unit arrangements. Buildings planned in row arrangements cause a wind shadow over the subsequent units, which is reinforced by the tendency of the wind to channel through free spaces and pass by the later units. An arrangement of staggered units takes advantage of the bouncing pattern of the wind since the houses direct the flow to subsequent structures. Note that the direction of flow is perpendicular to the third row of houses. The first type of layout is desirable for avoiding winter wind effects; the second pattern secures equal summer breeze distribution. As winter winds and summer breezes more often than not come from different directions, both conditions may be satisfied.

*Effect of Landscaping on Areas Adjacent to Structures.* The immediate surroundings near low structures have definite effects both on airflow patterns and on wind velocities. This frees the building to a certain extent from rigid orientation requirements. The landscape design elements, including plant materials, trees and shrubs, walls and fences, can create high and low pressure areas around a house with reference to its apertures. Care should be taken that arrangements do not eliminate the desirable cooling breezes during overheated periods, and planting should be designed to direct and accelerate beneficial air movements into the building.

Field tests and model experiments on the

**194.** Winter sheltering effect.

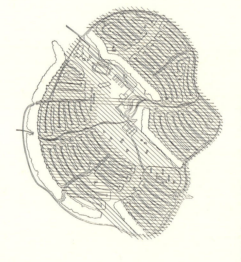

**195.** Summer breeze penetration.

**193.** Community layout in New York–New Jersey area.

posed of four residential colonies of about 1200 people each, grouped around a central area which contains commercial, administrative, cultural, sports, and recreational facilities. The winter winds which come from the northwest are blocked by dense evergreen belts planted to the northwest of the residential areas. Wind shadow is indicated with different values corresponding to percentage of protection. Northwest streets are offset, or sheltered to keep them from becoming wind channels. In summer winds are welcome. The streets are slanted to the south and southwest (the directions of the prevailing summer breezes), and are led through the settlement, as much as other planning and traffic problems allow. Since winter protection and summer ventilation of the individual houses near the periphery is considered of primary importance, the central section of the layout is left open for the communal area.

100

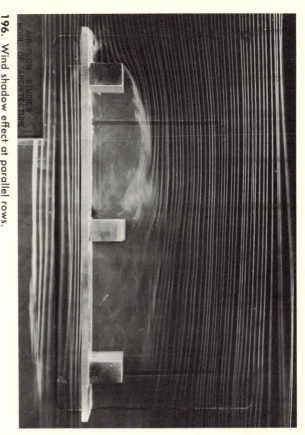

**196.** Wind shadow effect at parallel rows.

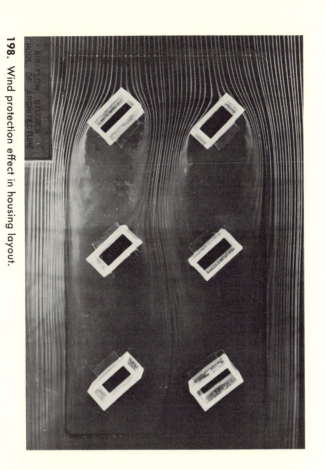

**198.** Wind protection effect in housing layout.

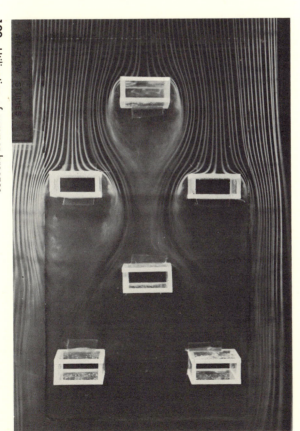

**197.** Wind protection with linear housing arrangement.

**199.** Utilization of summer breezes.

# FLOW PATTERNS INSIDE BUILDINGS

The forces producing natural ventilation in buildings can be categorized as: 1, air movements produced by pressure differences; 2, air change caused by difference in temperature. Either force may act alone, in conjunction with, or in opposition to, the other, depending upon atmospheric conditions and building design.

*Ventilation by Wind Forces.* A house placed in the air stream slows down and piles up the moving air at its windward side, causing an area of relatively high pressure. The flow enveloping the building creates low-pressure areas on the sides adjacent to the windward face. At the leeward side a wind shadow with relatively low pressure is produced. This wind shadow gradually will be filled with the surrounding air, so that at a distance of about twice the height of the building the air is at rest. Flowing from there both in reverse toward the building and away from it, the wind resumes its original velocity at a distance about seven times the height of the building. The air-flow patterns created around the house are determined by the geometry of the building, and are independent of air speeds. A vertical section of the wind pattern is similar to that enveloping the plan shown here, where the positive and negative signs indicate the high and low pressure areas.

The pressure differences on windward and leeward sides can contribute to air flow inside the building. Placement of openings is most effective when the inlet faces a high, the outlet a low-pressure area. The rate of air change is governed by pressure differences and by the effectiveness of the exposed openings. The approximate rate of air change, when the direction of wind is normal to the building side and the areas of inlets and outlets are equal, can be expressed as:[13]

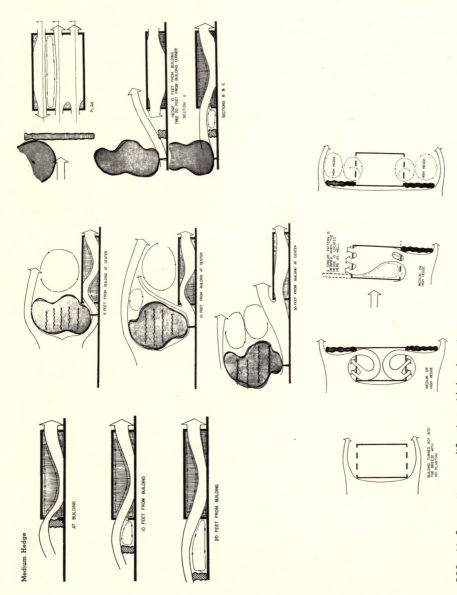

Medium Hedge

AT BUILDING

10 FEET FROM BUILDING

20 FEET FROM BUILDING

5 FEET FROM BUILDING AT CENTER

10 FEET FROM BUILDING AT CENTER

30 FEET FROM BUILDING AT CENTER

PLAN

HEDGE 10 FEET FROM BUILDING
TREE 20 FEET FROM BUILDING CORNER
SECTION A

SECTIONS B & C

HIGH HEDGE

MEDIUM OR HIGH HEDGE

MEDIUM OR HIGH HEDGE

BUILDING TURNED 90° INTO THE BREEZE WITH NO PLANTING

SIMILAR PATTERN WHEN THE HEDGE IS LOCATED HERE AS WELL.

**200.** Air flow pattern modification with landscaping.

modified air-flow patterns produced by various planting combinations were studied at the Texas Engineering Experiment Station. The figures represent some of the findings of Robert F. White.[12] The effect on the inside air pattern of a medium hedge both near and far from the building is illustrated. The foliage mass of the trees serves as a block to the passage of air, consequently the speed of air movement directly underneath the tree is increased. Shown are the effect of a 30′ high tree, with a spread 25′ wide and 5′ above

ground, on the flow pattern, and the effect of tree and hedge combinations. If the hedge is placed near the building, the inside flow of the structure can be modified markedly. At sections B and C the somewhat elevated pattern flows conventionally, while at section A the air stream diverted upward by the tree causes reversed flow in the building. The directional effect of hedges on flow pattern is illustrated in two examples. When placing wind barriers on one or on both leeward sides of a building the wind pressures cause flow within the structure.

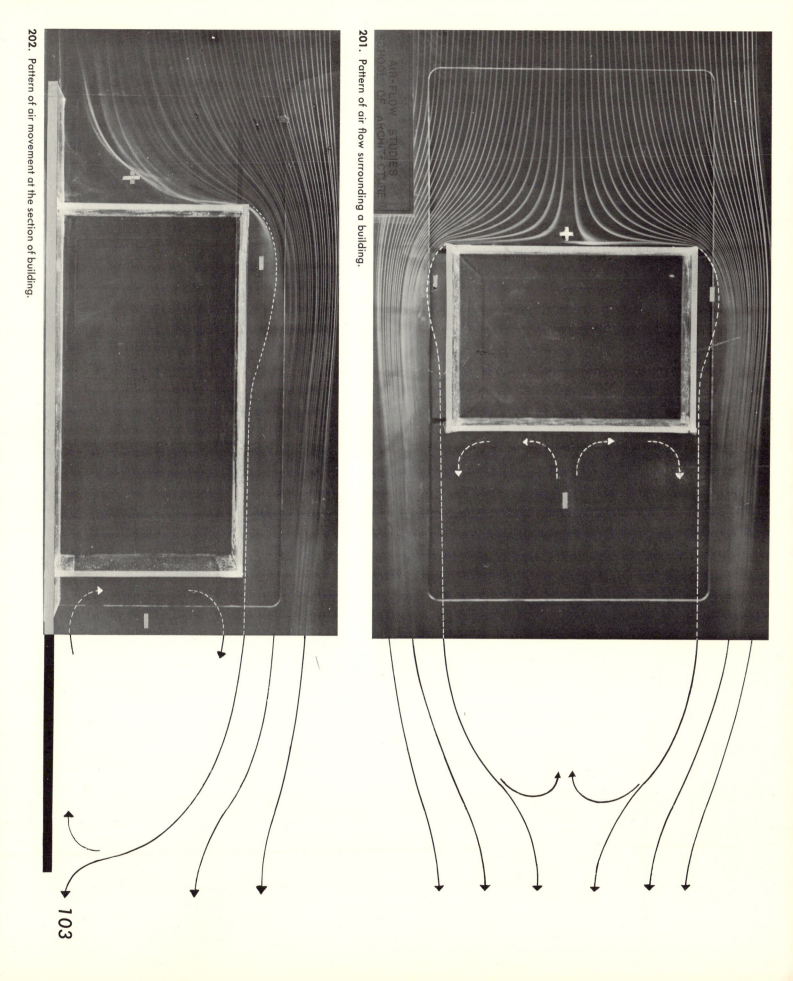

**201.** Pattern of air flow surrounding a building.

**202.** Pattern of air movement at the section of building.

103

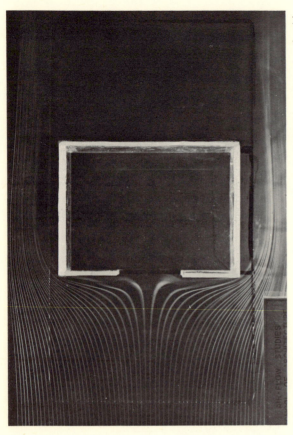

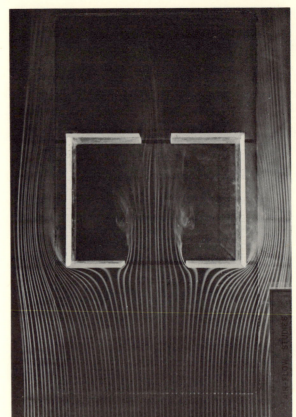

**203.** To receive air movements a house must have both inlet openings (preferably where the ram pressure is positive) and outlet openings (on negative, or suction areas). Here, as outlet is missing, no airflow occurs in the building.

**206.** Large inlet with small outlet combination makes high velocities occur beyond the building; therefore its cooling effect is lost.

$$Q = 3150 \, AV$$

where

Q = rate of air flow, cu ft/hr
A = area of inlets, sq ft
V = wind velocity, mph.

This expression requires adjustment in cases where the area of outlets are appreciably different from the area of inlets as:

| Area of outlets / Area of inlets | Value to be substituted for 3150 in above expression |
|---|---|
| 1:1 | 3150 |
| 2:1 | 4000 |
| 3:1 | 4250 |
| 4:1 | 4350 |
| 5:1 | 4400 |
| 3:4 | 2700 |
| 1:2 | 2000 |
| 1:4 | 1100 |

*Characteristics of Air Flow.* It is obvious that in structures where outlet is not provided no airflow will occur inside the building. Similarly, it is evident that large openings placed opposite each other, and positioned at the high and low pressure areas respectively, will provide the maximum air changes within the structure. However, for summer cooling comfort sufficient speed is of more importance than the amount of air change. By using a smaller sized inlet opening, "Venturi effect" occurs, securing maximum air speeds within the structure. Note the increased velocity lines inside the building as compared to the outside wind speeds. The reversed arrangement, with large inlet and small outlet, is inefficient because the high speed occurs behind and outside the building.

*Inertia Effect.* An inlet and outlet placed symmetrically will result in a straight inside-flow pattern since the external pressures are equal. With asymmetrically arranged open-

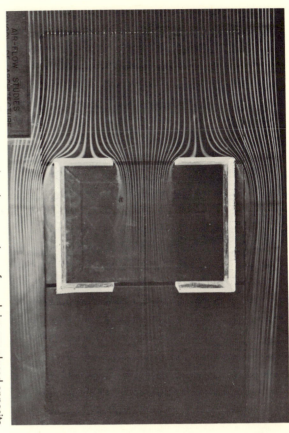

**204.** Maximum air flow occurs where large openings of equal size are placed opposite of each other. Note the considerable amount of flow with slightly higher speeds than that of the outside.

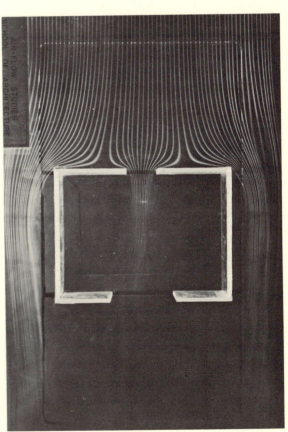

**205.** Highest speeds occur in the building when a small inlet is combined with a large outlet. Note high velocities after the inlet.

**207.** In case of an offset, asymmetrical indoor flow occurs. The side pressure outside the inlet directs flow at an angle.

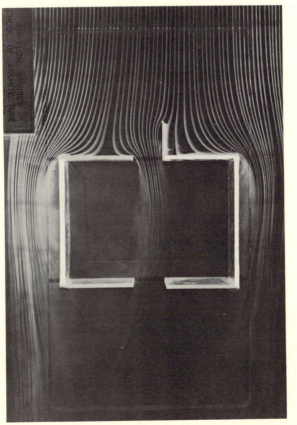

**208.** Asymmetrical flow occurs when the outside force vectors result in side pressure to initial flow. Here the effect of a casement window is shown.

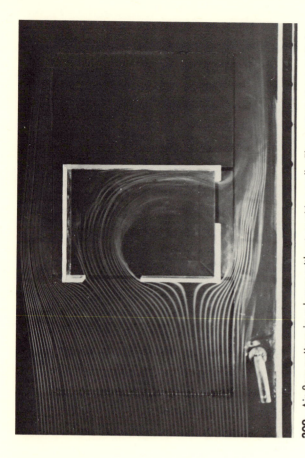

**209.** Air flow pattern in a house without partition walls. Flow enters at an angle because of external side pressure. Inertia carries it in the same direction until it finds the outlet in a smooth curve.

**212.** Flow is intercepted by partitions; blocking slows flow effect to considerable extent. Cooling effect becomes meager.

ings, in accordance with the difference in component pressure forces, the air will enter the building at an oblique angle. The inside flow will tend to follow its original direction by inertia until, overcome by differences in pressure, it will turn toward the outlet. Similar asymmetrical flow patterns occur when one of the outside pressures is intercepted (as by a casement window).

*Divisions Inside the House.* The inside flow pattern is the function of the apertures, and is largely independent of other geometric characteristics of a room. Straight flow secures the speediest air movement, and any change in direction slows the effect. Any abrupt course change caused by furniture, equipment, or partitions will cut air speeds markedly. Therefore, the placing of internal divisions should be arranged in consideration with the flow pattern.

The laminar flow stream is bordered by turbulent eddies which cause a slow cartwheel motion in the relatively stagnant air mass surrounding the flow. If a partition is placed outside the stream, the rate and pattern of the flow will remain unchanged. If the same partition is placed in the stream pattern, the flow will be interrupted and slowed down, causing a meager supply of ventilation in both rooms. Similar conditions can be observed in experiments where a structure is divided into three spaces. Divisions which conform to the pattern of flow secure adequate ventilation, those which interrupt it perform poorly.

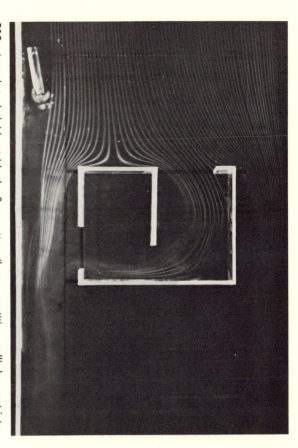

**210.** Any obstacle laid outside the flow pattern (here a partition wall) does not interfere with the flow direction, as the main air stream is about eight times as powerful as the cartwheeling eddies.

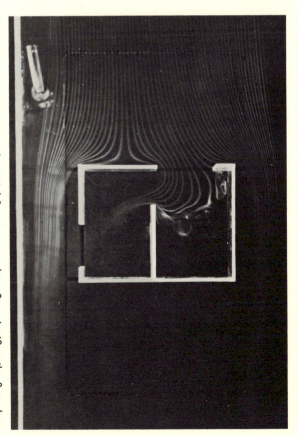

**211.** Partition intercepting the initial flow pattern alters flow significantly; flow slows down, upper room does not receive air movement, lower room receives only meager flow.

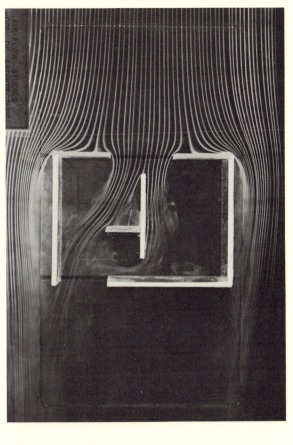

**213.** Partitions parallel to initial flow splits pattern, but result remains at adequate high speeds.

**214.** Partition perpendicular to initial flow alters pattern; back room is meagerly supplied at cooling speed.

215. Low inlet; outlet is placed near ceiling. Air flow pattern has pleasant downward direction despite high outlet.

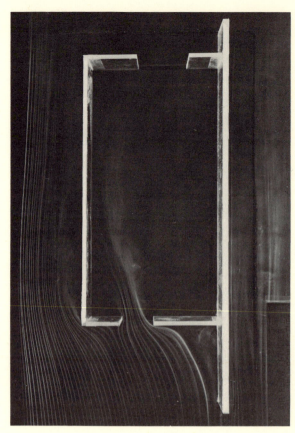

218. Arrangement with high inlet placement. Note that unequal outside wall surfaces exert upward force, resulting in loss of cooling effect of the air flow pattern.

EXPLANATORY NOTES TO THE VELOCITY TESTS

The tests were conducted in a two-dimensional wind tunnel, with models built of plexiglas. The streamlines are the paths of kerosene smoke entering the tunnel at the left hand side through a series of nozzles. Smooth and continuous lines indicate laminar flow. The distance between streamlines can be directly related to the air speeds. Where the lines are close, high speeds occur indicating low pressure areas; where the lines are far apart, the speed is low with high pressure regions.

The testing was greatly facilitated by the cooperation of David C. Hazen of the Department of Aeronautical Engineering and by the use of low wind velocity tunnel at the Forrestal Research Center of Princeton University. The approach and method of testing rely heavily on the excellent pioneer work and detailed studies developed in this field by the Texas Engineering Experiment Station,[17] where especially William W. Caudill, Bob H. Reed, and Ben H. Evans kindly provided much information and many suggestions.

*Location of Outlet and Inlet Openings.* A relatively large ratio of outlet to inlet size secures the speediest, and hence most cooling, air flow within a building. The location of the outlet is irrelevant to the pattern of the incoming flow, and speeds will be retarded only if energy is consumed by directional changes. This effect is shown in examples where the inlet position remains the same, but the outlet is placed at ceiling height, midway, or near floor level. Note that both amount and pattern of air flow remain constant.

On the other hand, where the outlet position is held constant, but the inlet is placed at high, middle, or low positions, the pattern of flow is directed upward to the ceiling, slightly downward, or toward the floor. If the air flow is to be effective and produce a cooling effect for the occupants, the stream has to be directed to the living zone. The placement of the inlet governs the flow pattern within the structure, and this can be regulated not only by the positioning but by the arrangement and type of inlet.

108

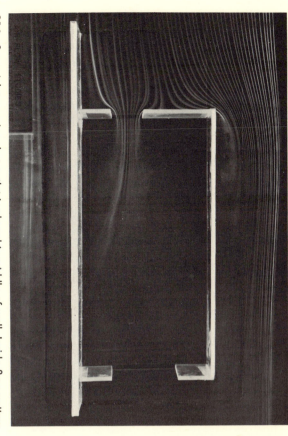

**216.** Same inlet opening, but outlet is placed in middle of wall. Inside flow pattern remains the same as before.

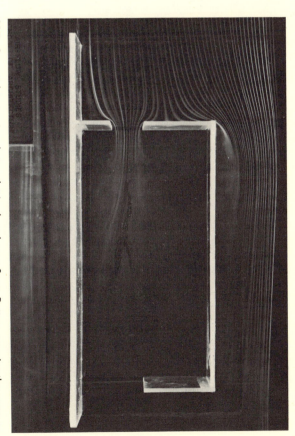

**217.** Same inlet opening, but outlet is placed near floor. Pattern remains the same as before. Conclusion: the location of the outlet has no effect on the internal air flow pattern.

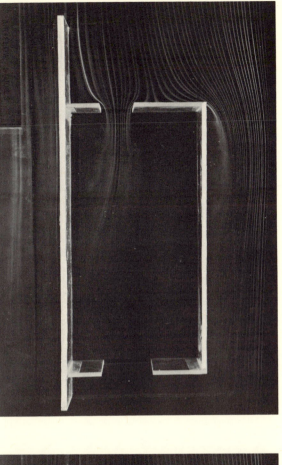

**219.** Outlet opening as before, but low placement of inlet results in a pleasant downward flow pattern.

**220.** Outlet opening as before, but inlet placed down causes flow to sweep floor surface. Conclusion: placement of inlet opening has major role on the internal air flow pattern.

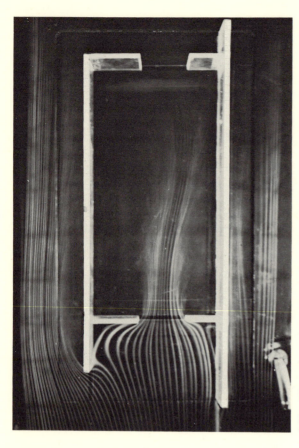

**221.** Effect of overhang on air flow. Note that overhang collects air streams which otherwise would escape; thus enhances incoming flow effect.

**224.** Pivoted window in upward position. This arrangement is unsatisfactory as air flow is directed away from living zone.

*Directional Effect of Inlet Attachments.* Features outside the building near the inlet opening can influence the flow pattern markedly. An overhang at ceiling height intercepting and diverting air masses toward the inlet improves the ventilation effect. Similar solid overhangs, when placed directly above the window opening, cause the air to flow toward the ceiling because they eliminate outside pressure effects from above. Since the air bypasses the living zone, this effect is unfavorable. The same overhang modified by a slot equalizes the pressures; thereby lowering the flow pattern to a more useful level.

The type of window opening, like a hose nozzle, deflects and modifies the incoming flow. Casement, folding, projected, and awning window types all have their specific diverting effects.[14] Here a horizontal-pivoted window effect is shown in two positions; turning downward, the flow is satisfactory. In reverse position, the flow is directed toward the ceiling. Jalousies have the same directional effect on the flow pattern.

*Ventilation by Temperature Differential.* Temperature differences existing between the air inside and that outside the building, due to the weight disparity, cause the warmer air column to rise by displacement gravitation. The higher the temperature difference, the larger the height between the inlet and outlet and the greater their size; the more vigorous will be the "stack effect." The approximate rate of such air change when the area of in-

110

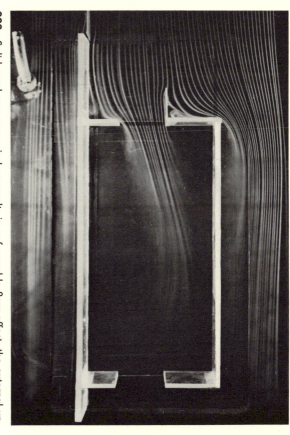

222. Solid overhang over window results in unfavorable flow effect; the external unequal ram pressure directs flow upward away from living zone.

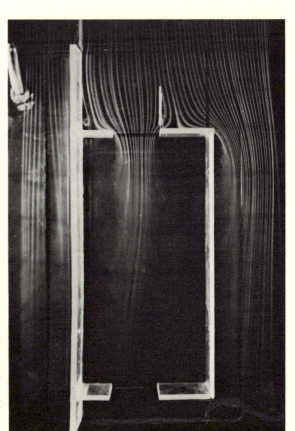

223. Overhang with slot equalizing the external pressures results in desirable air flow pattern.

225. Pivoted window in downward position. Air flow pattern is satisfactory.

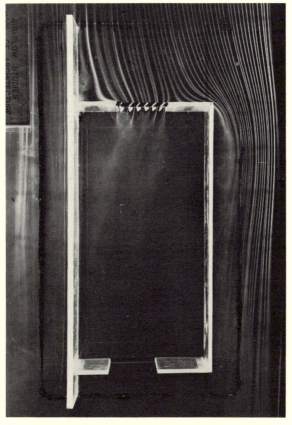

226. Effect of downward position venetian blind results in well-directed, diffused air pattern.

lets is equal to the area of outlets can be expressed as:[15]

$$Q = 540A\sqrt{H(t_i - t_o)}$$

where

Q = rate of air flow, cu ft/hr
A = area of inlets, sq ft
H = height between inlets and outlets, ft
$t_i$ = average temperature of indoor air at height H, °F
$t_o$ = temperature of outdoor air, °F

This expression requires adjustment in cases when the area of outlets is appreciably different from the area of inlets according to the following ratios:

| $\dfrac{\text{Area of outlets}}{\text{Area of inlets}}$ | Value to be substituted for 540 in above expression |
|---|---|
| 5 | 745 |
| 4 | 740 |
| 3 | 720 |
| 2 | 680 |
| 1 | 540 |
| 3/4 | 455 |
| 1/2 | 340 |
| 1/4 | 185 |

Air change by gravitation is one of the motives for the use of high ceilings in warm environments. The central hall, or staircase arrangements in multi-storied southern houses was a time-honored recognition of the stack effect. Today's recommendations emphasize the need for ventilation of lofts and attics. According to T. S. Rogers,[16] the total vent areas under gable, hip, or flat roofs (of less than 5000 sq ft) should be one sq ft for each 150 sq ft of attic area for summer comfort. In the lower latitudes the ratio should be elevated to 1:100.

However, the relatively low air speeds of normal rise are inadequate to achieve relief from high temperatures or to ameliorate the discomfort caused by vapor pressure conditions. When these occur the utilization of wind forces is needed.

# SUMMARY OF PROCEDURES IN WIND CONTROL

1. The yearly air movements can be divided into the categories of winds and breezes according to the underheated and overheated periods.
2. On the basis of duration and velocity characteristics, the air movements can be expressed as orientation vectors.
3. Wind protection can be provided by windbreaks and positioning of buildings.
4. Natural ventilation can be utilized by:
   A. orientation of building (not necessarily perpendicular to wind direction),
   B. use of surrounds to create low and high pressure zones,
   C. locating inlets in high, outlets in low, pressure areas,
   D. small inlet and large outlet sizes,
   E. inlets which direct the flow to the living zone,
   F. undisturbed inside flow, open plan.

It is desirable that inside air speed satisfy bioclimatic requirements based on design temperatures. The approximate mean inside air speed can be expressed as:

$$V_i = \frac{C}{P}m$$

where

$V_i$ = mean inside speed, ft/min
C = number of air changes, cu ft/min
P = airflow pattern, cu ft
m = mean distance between inlet and outlet, ft

As the number of air changes can be calculated from the rate of air flow (Q), this expression provides an estimation of the resultant inside air speeds and furnishes a measure for the aperture sizes needed under specific climatic conditions.

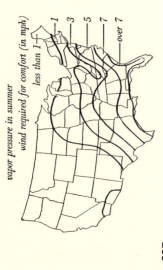

*vapor pressure in summer*
*wind required for comfort (in mph)*

less than 1
1
3
5
7
over 7

227.

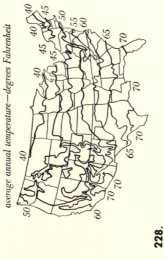

*average annual temperature—degrees Fahrenheit*

228.

# X. THERMAL EFFECTS OF MATERIALS

## OPAQUE MATERIALS AND INDOOR TEMPERATURE BALANCE

ALL external heat impacts must pass through the building shell before they affect indoor temperature conditions. As heat flows into the shell material the process is comparable to the absorption of moisture by a porous material; successive layers of the structure become "saturated" with heat until finally the effect is felt on the inside surface. The more or less sinusoidal fluctuating daily temperature loads as they percolate through the structural elements become distorted in amplitude and are delayed in time. Both these functions of the material can be utilized favorably to approach balanced conditions in the interior of a structure.

The aim of this inquiry is to define the material requirements for an opaque shell which, by damping and distribution, will balance the external thermal impacts of various regions and exposures. These qualities may be determined by investigating the processes and properties that allow for surface control, touching briefly the related problems of moisture and deterioration, and examining in detail the factors of heat transmission and time-lag characteristics.

Anyone who has entered a large stone church on a hot summer day may have experienced its comforting coolness. In such structures the large mass of the masonry materials absorbs and reflects the coolness of the previous night, resulting in a delayed temperature approximating a seasonal average. A similar effect is evident in such "crypto-climatic" examples as the pyramids, where the interior space is negligible in relation to the immense mass of heavy material. The interior tomb chamber will constantly be close to the yearly average outdoor temperature. In the subterranean homes of the Troglodytes analogous conditions prevail, since the mass of earth keeps temperatures near isotherm conditions. Historic houses sturdily built of heavy wall materials for reasons other than thermal stability, nevertheless react well from that standpoint. By comparison, the structures of today are extremely light and thin, and the question of temperature balance arises urgently.

Under many conditions light structures are quite undesirable, being at the mercy of external forces just as light boats are tossed about on a high sea.

## HEAT ENTRY ON THE SURFACE

The thermal forces acting on the outside of a structure are combinations of radiation and convective impacts. The radiation component consists of incident solar radiation and of radiant heat exchange with outdoor surroundings and with the sky. The convective heat impact is a function of exchange with the surrounding air temperature, and may be accelerated by air motion.

Under warm and sunlit conditions heat input will take place; and during cold periods, at night, or on surfaces surrounded by low-temperature objects, the heat exchange will work negatively, resulting in heat loss from the exposed surface. An equation for the rate of heat entry into the outer side of a building surface is indicated in the notes.[1]

*To Control Heat Entry.* The first line of heat control lies at the surface. Since the surface temperature of a sunlit material will be higher than that of the air, air movements over an exposed surface will reduce the external heat impact, and are particularly beneficial under hot conditions. The exchange effect can be increased by diluting the radiation over a larger area by means of curved surfaces (such as vaults and domes), or corrugated uneven surfaces (such as alternating recessed brick layers), which will also simultaneously increase the rate of convection transfer.

The selective absorptivity and emissivity characteristics of materials are another very effective defense against radiation impacts, and especially important in overheated conditions. Materials which reflect rather than absorb radiation and which more readily release the absorbed quantity as thermal radiation will cause lower temperatures within the structure.

The sun's energy, by the time it falls upon a building, has been cut down by the atmosphere and arrives through several different channels. The solar radiation consists of visible (wavelength 0.3 to 0.7 microns) and short infrared radiation (1.7 to 2.5 microns). Since this energy is concentrated near the visible part of the spectrum, the criterion of reflectivity is in regard to color values. White materials may reflect 90% or more, black materials 15% or less, of radiation received.

On the other hand, the thermal exchange with the surroundings consists of longer infrared wavelengths (over 2.5, usually from 5 to 20 microns. This range can also be classified as 9 microns). The characteristics of materials in regard to reflectivity of long-wave infrared heat depends more on the density of surface and on molecular composition than on color.

The characteristics of some typical surface materials, in regard to reflectivity and thermal emissivity of both solar and thermal radiation, are given below.

REACTION OF MATERIALS TO SOLAR AND THERMAL RADIATION

| SURFACE | PER CENT OF REFLECTIVITY | | PER CENT OF EMISSIVITY |
| --- | --- | --- | --- |
| | Solar radiation | Thermal radiation | Thermal radiation |
| Silver, polished | 93 | 98 | 2 |
| Aluminum, polished | 85 | 92 | 8 |
| Whitewash | 80 | — | — |
| Copper, polished | 75 | 85 | 15 |
| Chromium plate | 72 | 80 | 20 |
| White lead paint | 71 | 11 | 89 |
| White marble | 54 | 5 | 95 |
| Light green paint | 50 | 5 | 95 |
| Aluminum paint | 45 | 45 | 55 |
| Indiana limestone | 43 | 5 | 95 |
| Wood, pine | 40 | 5 | 95 |
| Asbestos cement, aged | | | |
| 1 year | 29 | 5 | 95 |
| Red clay brick | 23–30 | 6 | 94 |
| Gray paint | 25 | 5 | 95 |
| Galvanized iron, aged | | | |
| (oxidized) | 10 | 72 | 28 |
| Black matte | 3 | 5 | 95 |

Data taken principally from Handbook of Chemistry and Physics, Dept. Scient. & Ind. Research (England), Coblentz, Cammerer, Drysdale.

The highly selective behavior of materials under solar and thermal radiation can be utilized in relation to climatic circumstances. In zones where the underheated period is extensive, low reflectivity for solar radiation is advantageous. In areas where overheated periods alternate with cool periods, both reflectivity and absorptivity is desirable at different times. Architecturally this can be solved by taking advantage of the seasonal paths of the sun; the low winter rays can reach deepest dark-colored absorptive surfaces, and the summer rays of high elevation may be intercepted by building elements of high reflectivity. In zones where hot conditions prevail, the net effect of reflectivity combined with the emissive thermal radiation characteristic of the material has to be considered.

If surfaces exposed to the irradiation of the sun and to clear sky are whitewashed, painted white or built of light-colored materials such as marble, they will remain cooler than surfaces of polished metal such as aluminum. Despite the fact that the aluminum has a higher reflectivity to solar radiation the effect is outbalanced by the emissive capability of the white surface which loses heat by thermal radiation toward the sky. This principle accounts for the white exteriors of tropical buildings. However, if the same materials are exposed not only to the sun but to hot ground—where the white surface is not capable of losing heat by emissivity—the polished aluminum will be the cooler of the two materials. The application of both processes is utilized by airplanes, where the upper part exposed to solar radiation is painted white, while the lower portion remains metallic.

## MOISTURE EFFECTS

Materials absorb moisture according to their hygroscopic qualities. In general, organic substances have higher absorptive properties than inorganic materials. With increased moisture content, materials show higher heat transmittance because of the relatively high thermal conductivity of water. Experiments show the effect of hygroscopic moisture on the thermal conductivity of inorganic materials in relation to volume, of organic materials in direct proportion to their weight.

A moisture problem, which is unrelated to thermal performance but must be mentioned, is the set of critical conditions that can arise from condensation effects. Air with a high content of water vapor penetrates through materials or through the hollow spaces of a structure toward areas of lower vapor pressure. Usually the direction of flow is from the warm inside to the colder outside. Reverse flow exists from hot outdoor conditions toward cooler indoor spaces. Theoretically condensation should take place where the moisture-laden air comes to its dew-point temperature inside the structure. T. S. Rogers describes the methods of eliminating condensations in the structure:[3] (1) by reducing the amount of moisture content indoors, (2) by providing a "vapor barrier" or vapor-resistant surface on the warm side of the dew-point zone, (3) by venting the cold side to the outer air, (4) by using materials on the cold side that are at least five times more porous to vapor than those assembled on the warm side. In general the importance of vapor control increases toward the cold climate zones.

## DETERIORATION OF MATERIALS

Every climate zone has its specific destructive atmospheric agencies. Here only brief mention is made of the main problems which, though inconsequential to thermal behavior, are an essential part of the total picture.

The process of chemical deterioration depends mostly on the presence of water, rainfall, and high relative humidity.[4] This at freezing temperatures in cold zones causes frost effects, in hot ones coupled with high temperatures it produces dews. Temperature difference by itself primarily affects building materials physically, with dimensional movements that contribute to cracking. Important secondary effects are evoked by chemical reactions and various other phenomena that are accelerated logarithmically by an elevation of temperature.[5] Radiation causes deterioration partly by heightening temperatures on the exposed surfaces, partly by the photo-chemical action of the rays (which at lower latitudes is intensified by the slightly enhanced ultraviolet band). Biological agencies (such as algal growth, molds, fungi) require moisture for their existence; very little deterioration occurs unless the relative humidity is in excess of 70%.[6] Subterranean types of termites, in some regions "dry-wood" species, are the most destructive source of damage in cellulose products without adequate protection.

## HEAT TRANSMISSION OF MATERIALS

The most important thermal-control characteristic of materials is their transmission behavior. The daily heat-load variation causes a corresponding oscillation inside the structure, but with two differences; (1) the inside cycle will be damped, that is, the variations will be smaller (decrease in amplitude) (2) the inside cycle will lag behind the outside cycle (shift in phase).

The first effect is caused by the insulation value of the material, characterized by "U" factor (overall heat transfer coefficient expressed in Btu/hr/sq ft). The lower the U-value, the better the insulation effect. This interference with the passage of heat is commonly referred to as "resistance insulation" as it reduces the heat flow.

The second effect depends on the heat-storage value of the material, characterized by the volumetric specific heat ($\rho \times c$, density times specific heat). The larger the heat storage value, the slower the temperature change that is propagated through the material. This delay is called the "time lag" of the construction; it gives an opportunity to store peak heat loads and release them at low temperature periods. This effect simultaneously reduces the amplitude of impact and is generally called "capacity insulation."

Both characteristics are present in materials to various degrees, depending on their

thermal diffusivity. This can be defined by the following equation:

$$D = k/\rho c$$

where  D = thermal diffusivity (ft²/hr)
k = thermal conductivity (Btu/ft² hr °F)
$\rho$ = density (lb/ft³)
c = specific heat (Btu/lb °F)

As still air is one of the best insulators, materials which enclose, trap, or contain thin films of clinging air have low heat-transfer characteristics and generally are light in weight. Conversely, materials with large time lags are usually dense in quality, and hence the effect is often directly associated with their weight (see tables for comparative data).

In design the appropriate use of both insulation and time lag effects is eminently important for interior heat balance.

## RESISTANCE INSULATION OR HEAT CAPACITY EFFECTS

To evaluate the desirable thermal behavior characteristics for materials in a given climatic region, a study of the yearly temperature condition, a study of the yearly temperature conditions with their relation to comfort conditions is needed. From the yearly maximum temperature range a direct relationship can be established to the needed insulation value; and from the daily temperature range a parallel correlation with heat-capacity requirements can be confirmed. On the latter, Leroux[7] recommends that in zones where the diurnal range is 6 to 8° C (11 to 14° F) the construction should be of 300 kg of heavyweight material, such as concrete or masonry, per cubic metre of the building; for a range of 10 to 12° C (18 to 22° F) 600 to 700 kg per cubic metre; and over 20° C (over 36° F) 1200 kg or more per cubic metre. These recommendations, although correct in principle, have been criticized for application in particular.[8] We will offer below a more detailed approach to the problem.

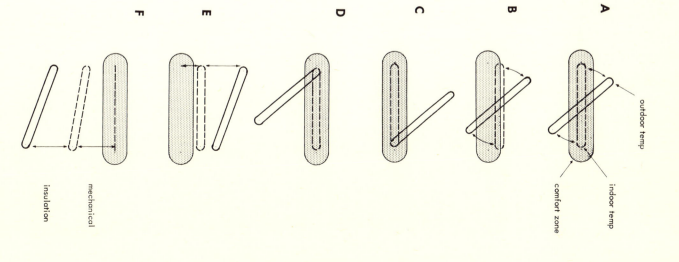

A

B

C

D

E

F

outdoor temp

indoor temp

comfort zone

insulation

mechanical

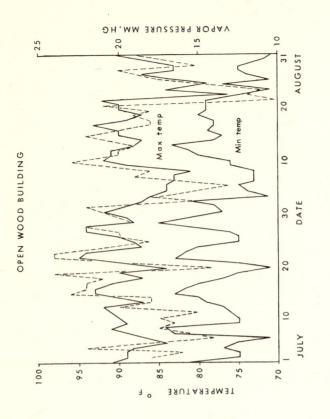

OPEN WOOD BUILDING

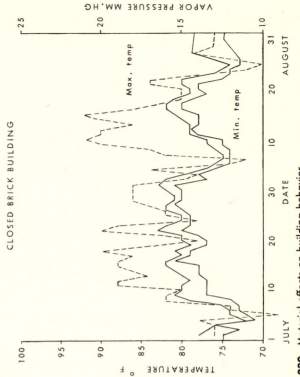

CLOSED BRICK BUILDING

**230.** Material effects on building behavior.

The relationship of comfort conditions and diurnal temperature variation can be illustrated with regard to desirable material characteristics in some typical examples. Heat capacity is essential when the slope of the daily temperature curve (which is equivalent to amplitude) is steep and the resulting flattened daily curve remains in (A), or near (B) in the comfort zone. Where the mean outdoor temperature is expected to be 85° F or higher, heavyweight construction by itself would stabilize temperatures in the discomfort range. However, with steep curves there is the possibility of using low diffusivity materials to absorb the thermal conditions near to comfort situations (C and D), and to maintain them during the extreme periods of the day (with measures such as closing openings to trap shade temperatures or heat peaks).

Both heat capacity and resistance insulation values are required in zones where seasonal and daily variations are excessive (E). Under conditions where the seasonal temperatures are extreme (F) the importance lies in the insulation value, and comfort conditions have to be maintained by mechanical means. Here the daily temperature variation is relatively negligible; however, if it is rather steep, internally placed heat capacity materials can provide a diurnal balancing effect.

Two examples illustrate the marked differences in buildings of different materials under similar conditions. Shown is a comparison between an open, light structure and a heavy, closed one, in locations where the wooden building fluctuates with the ambient outside temperature, reaching 25° daily amplitudes. The closed brick house stabilizes the indoor conditions with low mean temperatures where the maximum diurnal cycle does not exceed 9° variations.[9]

# TIME LAG AND CALCULATION METHODS

*Daily Heat Balance of Structures.* In an example a comparison is shown between the behavior of light and heavyweight structures under the same climatic circumstances. The calculations were made for a housing development in Baghdad, Iraq. The upper left graph shows the heat transmission curves for wood construction walls (U = 0.268, lag 2 hrs, color light) under sunlit conditions in midsummer (July 21). The curves on the lower left indicate heat flow behavior of 9″ native Iraq brick walls under the same conditions but with 10 hrs time-lag characteristics. Note that although the total daily heat transmission of the building components at both structures is the same (having equal insulation values), the amplitude and the period of transmission is markedly different. The total daily heat flow behavior of the structures is summarized in the upper right graph; under it the shade-temperature curve illustrates the corresponding outdoor conditions. Note that the light structure heats up during the hot daytime hours (from 7 AM till 7 PM) transmitting 450.5 Btus through the differently oriented unit surfaces, while the heavyweight structure transmits only 331.4 Btus during the same period. Here the heavyweight components are markedly advantageous in the daytime heat balance.

## CALCULATION METHOD FOR TIME LAG REQUIREMENTS

The "shift in phase" effect of capacity insulation provides the leeway to delay outside impacts from heat load periods to a cooler time phase, and to transmit the nighttime low temperatures to the daytime heat peak. Generally it can be said that in zones of high diurnal

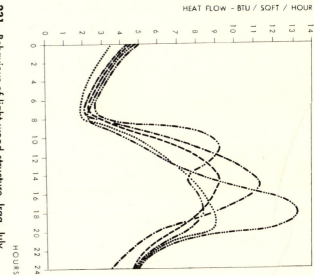

**231.** Behaviour of light wood structure, Iraq, July.

HEAT FLOW – BTU / SQFT / HOUR

TOTAL HEAT FLOW – BTU / HOUR

Light construction

heavy construction

HOURS

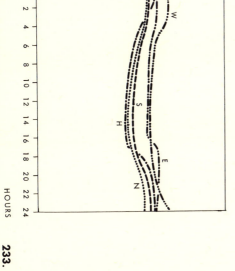

**232.** Behavior of 9″ brick structure, Iraq, July.

HEAT FLOW – BTU / SQFT / HOUR

HOURS

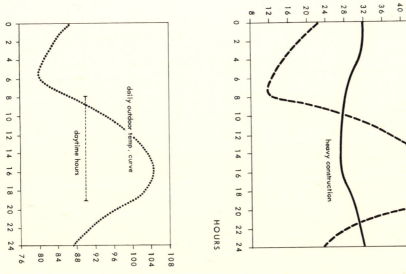

**233.** Thermal behaviour comparison of the structures, Iraq, July.

daily outdoor temp. curve

daytime hours

HOURS

The sol-air temperature impacts on the differently oriented surfaces are indicated. Here the accumulated heat load concentrating at the early afternoon hours is evident. In order to shift the impacts to cooler periods different exposures require different time lags. The heaviest load falls on the horizontal surface (roof), needing a shift of 11 to 12 hours. The load on the east exposure would need from a minimum 12 to an optimum 17 hour shift to avoid delivering its heat during peak hours, which indeed would be an extreme requirement. Therefore, the practical solution is to have no lag at all for the east, and to let the impact be felt at the inside while the daytime temperatures are still low. The south side has little importance; the desirable shift is minimum 7 hours, optimum 10 hours. The west side which receives the heaviest load among the wall surfaces should have a minimum lag of 5, an optimum shift of 10 hours. The north wall has the least importance with regard to lag characteristics, however a 5 to 10 hours' delay helps somewhat in the daily heat distribution. The sol-air effect distribution delayed by optimum time lag requirements is shown.

The consequent total heat impacts in a construction unit resulting from the use of optimum time lags are compared with an unbalanced structure. The chart, it should be remembered, is computed with sol-air values excluding the insulation effect of the materials, hence directly applicable only for lag calculations. In the graph the full line indicates the impacts conveyed by the heavy construction, the broken line that of the light structure. The relationship of the curves with the outdoor temperature is illustrated by a dotted line. Note that during all daytime hours (7 AM to 7 PM) the heavy structure will transmit lower temperatures to the interior than the light construction. In the evening, when the light structure cools off, the outdoor temperature

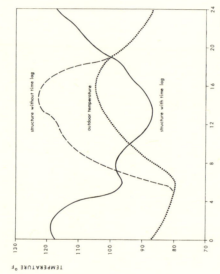

**236.** Comparison of heat impact on structures with and without use of time lag, Phoenix, July.

variation an approximate half-day time-lag shift (that is, the delay of night coolness to the day and the day warmth to the nighttime) will result in daily thermal balance. However, as the sun's impact heats the various surfaces at different hours, the problem has to be studied in detail.

Such an analysis is applied for Phoenix, Arizona summer conditions (July 21, at clear day, average temperature conditions, $\alpha = 0.7$).

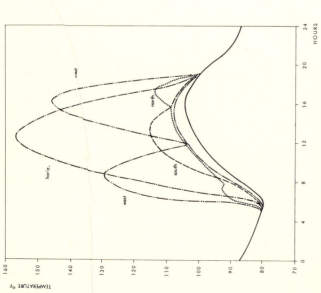

**234.** Sol-air surface temperatures, Phoenix, July.

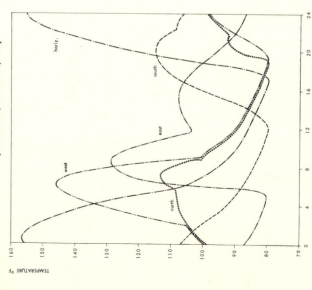

**235.** Rearranged sol-air impacts according to desirable time lags, Phoenix, July.

118

drop offers the possibility for the heavy construction to utilize ventilative cooling. The graph also indicates that under the analysed comfort conditions the most balanced indoor situation would occur in a house designed so that daytime living areas were built of heavy materials and nighttime areas of light materials.

## OVERALL HEAT TRANSMISSION COEFFICIENT (U) AND TIME LAG CHARACTERISTIC DATA FOR HOMOGENEOUS WALLS[10]

| Material | Thickness, Inches | U value, Btu/sq ft/hr | Time lag, Hours |
|---|---|---|---|
| Stone | 8 | 0.67 | 5.5 |
| | 12 | 0.55 | 8.0 |
| | 16 | 0.47 | 10.5 |
| | 24 | 0.36 | 15.5 |
| Solid Concrete | 2 | 0.98 | 1.1 |
| | 4 | 0.84 | 2.5 |
| | 6 | 0.74 | 3.8 |
| | 8 | 0.66 | 5.1 |
| | 12 | 0.54 | 7.8 |
| | 16 | 0.46 | 10.2 |
| Common Brick | 4 | 0.60 | 2.3 |
| | 8 | 0.41 | 5.5 |
| | 12 | 0.31 | 8.5 |
| | 16 | 0.25 | 12.0 |
| Face Brick | 4 | 0.77 | 2.4 |
| Wood | ½ | 0.68 | 0.17 |
| | 1 | 0.48 | 0.45 |
| | 2 | 0.30 | 1.3 |
| Insulating Board | ½ | 0.42 | 0.08 |
| | 1 | 0.26 | 0.23 |
| | 2 | 0.14 | 0.77 |
| | 4 | 0.08 | 2.7 |
| | 6 | 0.05 | 5.0 |

In the above table the U value is based upon an outdoor surface conductance of 4.0, and an indoor surface conductance of 1.65 Btu/sq ft/hr. For composite constructions to the individual sums of the time lags an additional estimated lag should be added. It is customary for two layer and light construction walls to add ½ hour more; for three or more layers, or very heavy constructions, one hour additional lag is preferred.

# BALANCED INSULATION

The reduction of heat flow is most efficiently achieved by the resistance-insulation property of the material. The desired insulation magnitude is in direct relationship to the difference between outside thermal conditions and comfort requirements. This relationship can be based conveniently on the design temperatures of the locality; and expressed as the "insulation index." However, different exposures, as a result of the sol-air action, have different temperature impacts, diminishing or adding to the thermal heat load. By using "balanced insulation" values to account for these differences, interior thermal conditions may be equalized.

The calculation method for balanced insulation effect is illustrated for four localities. In the middle of the graphs is the plan of a structure. Clockwise at each side the hours of the day are indicated. In the main directions the winter and summer sol-air temperatures are charted on unfolded elevations. The temperature curves, computed for sunny days at average conditions for light surfaces, are related to winter (70°) and summer (74°) comfort conditions. The section of the structure is shown below to indicate roof impacts.

The design condition for each season was selected according to the duration of underheated (when from 7 AM to 7 PM the temperature is mostly under 70°) and overheated days in the year. This underheated versus overheated relationship was found to be: in Minneapolis 75% to 25%, in New York 72% to 28%, in Phoenix 37% to 63%, and in Miami 12% to 88%. Accordingly, in Minneapolis and New York the cold condition (Jan. 21), and in Phoenix and Miami the hot condition (July 21), were selected as design criteria.

The daily temperature fluctuations relative to comfort conditions constitute the main

objective in regard to balancing. The average daily deviation from 70° (in winter) or 74° (in summer) gives the measure for relative insulation values in cases where the seasonal impacts impose marked stresses on specific sides, such as the horizontal surface (R = roof) in summer at higher latitudes, the evaluations were calculated on a yearly basis. This results in the following relationships at different exposures:

| | E | S | W | N | R |
|---|---|---|---|---|---|
| Minneapolis | 50† | 42† | 53† | 50† | 57* |
| New York | 35† | 27† | 38† | 35† | 40* |
| Phoenix | 32‡ | 28‡ | 28‡ | 33‡ | 45‡ |
| Miami | 18‡ | 13‡ | 14‡ | 19‡ | 30‡ |

The values marked with † were related to winter loads; those with ‡ to summer loads; values indicated with * were adapted according to the duration and impact of winter and summer loads.

## SUMMARY

*Regional Insulation Requirements.* The previous considerations can be depicted for the four localities analysed. The general magnitude of insulation values here are expressed with the "insulation index." This, as has been discussed, depends on the outdoor temperatures encountered. The generally accepted design temperatures for heating and cooling loads are those recommended by the American Society of Heating and Airconditioning Engineers.[11] These values in Minneapolis are −20° F in winter, 95° in summer; resulting in a deviation of 90° from winter comfort condition (70°), and 21° from the summer comfort (74°) requirement. In New York the same conditions are 0° and 95°, with deviations of 70° and 21° respectively. In Phoenix 25° and 105° result in deviations of 45° and 31°. In

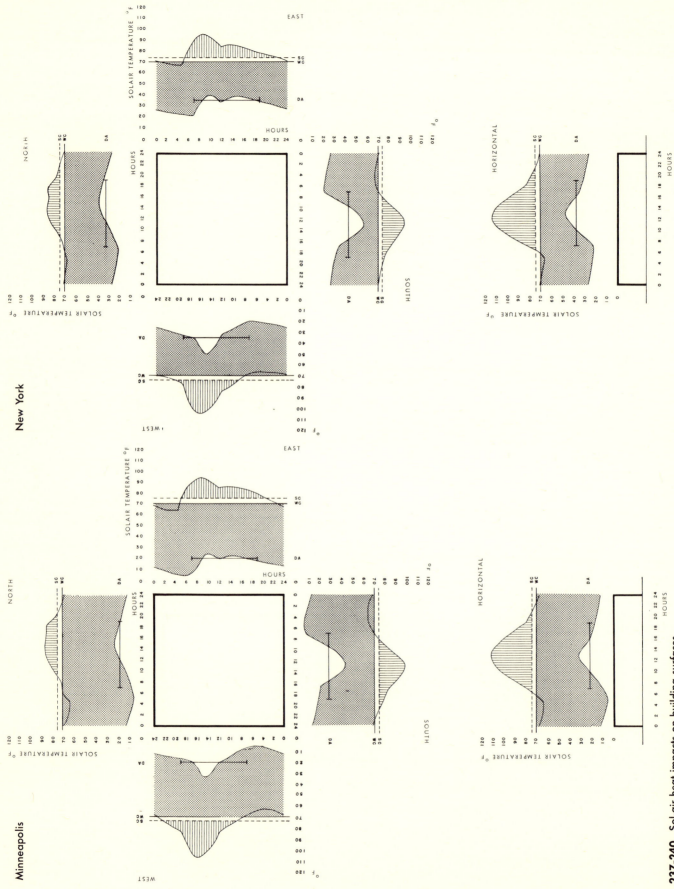

New York

Minneapolis

237-240. Sol-air heat impacts on building surfaces.

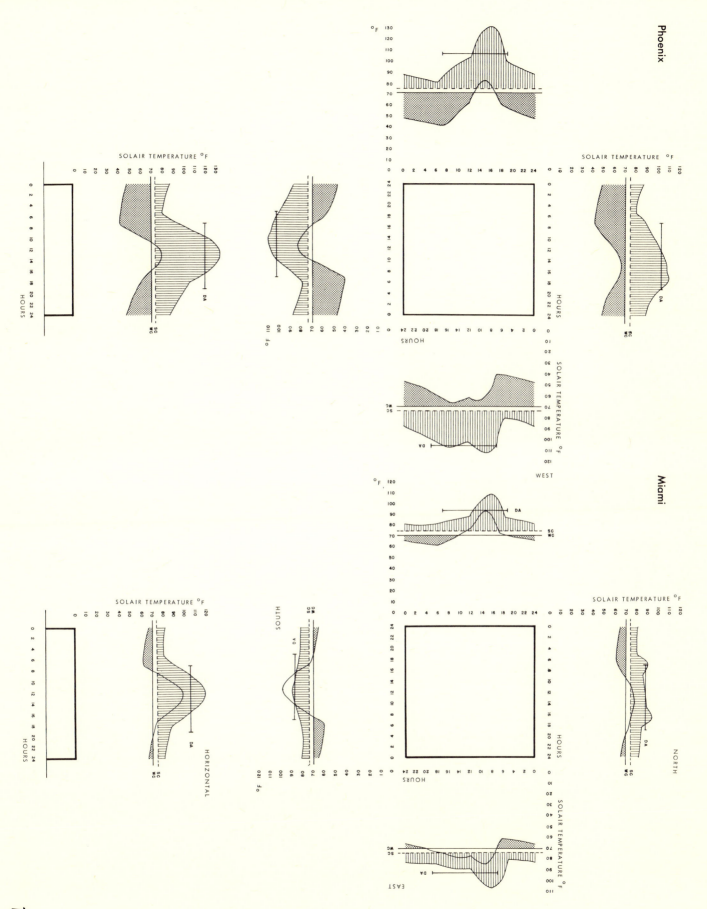

Phoenix

Miami

SOLAIR TEMPERATURE °F

SOLAIR TEMPERATURE °F

SOLAIR TEMPERATURE °F

SOLAIR TEMPERATURE °F

WEST

SOUTH

NORTH

EAST

HORIZONTAL

HOURS

HOURS

121

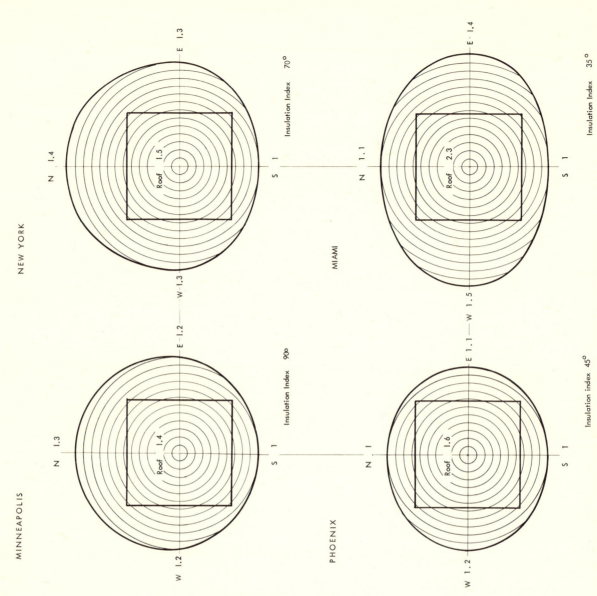

NEW YORK

Insulation Index 70°

N 1.4  Roof 1.5  E 1.3  W 1.3  S 1

MIAMI

Insulation Index 35°

N 1.1  Roof 2.3  E 1.4  W 1.5  S 1  E 1.1

MINNEAPOLIS

Insulation Index 90°

N 1.3  Roof 1.4  E 1.2  W 1.2  S 1

PHOENIX

Insulation index 45°

N 1  Roof 1.6  E 1.1  W 1.2  S 1

**241.** Insulation values according to orientation for balanced heat effect.

Miami the 35° and 91° encountered deviate 35° and 17° from comfort conditions. From the above thermal stresses the maximum deviations were adopted to indicate the desired value of the "insulation index" for each locale.

However, the general insulation index has to be interpreted according to the variety of heat load experienced by the different exposures of the structure. The recommended comparative values of insulation toward any orientation are illustrated on the charts with concentric circles. The values shown are the results of sol-air computations; therefore, in locations where exceptionally strong directional winds prevail, this should be taken into consideration by elevating the convection component accordingly. The measurements of magnitudes are indicated relative to the south side value. Only the main directions are indicated with numerical values; any other orientation can be read by the concentric circles in the polar chart.

*Desirable Time-Lag Characteristics in Regions.* The low diffusivity characteristics of materials can be used effectively to equalize and displace in time the sinusoidal daily thermal impacts. The desired magnitude of such capacity insulation may be related to the total weight of the structure with the function of the diurnal amplitude variation. However, by computing the heatflow effects element by element, the daily heat load distribution can be balanced by shifting the impacts to off-load hours.

A summary of the desirable time lag characteristics is illustrated here for four localities. In the graphs a schematic building is placed in center. The radial lines refer to the hours. The advantageous lag characteristics for the main orientations are indicated with arrows.

In Minneapolis the delay of the western impact has importance, with some interior

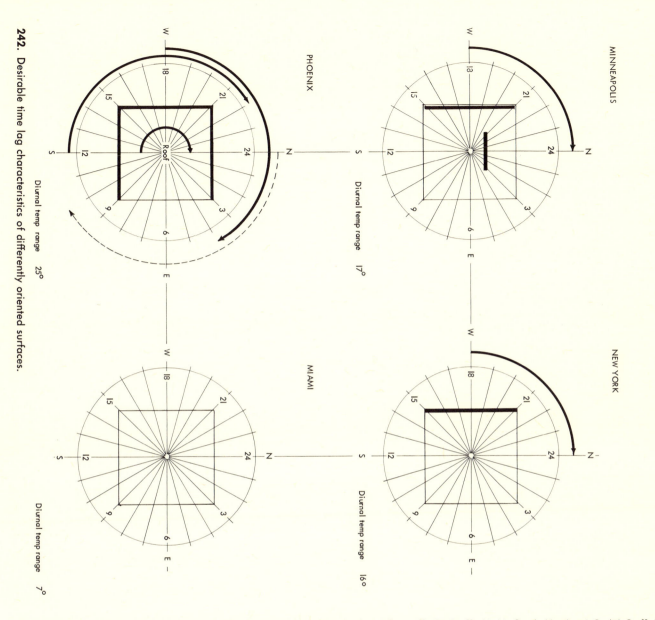

242. Desirable time lag characteristics of differently oriented surfaces.

balancing, which, toward higher latitudes, gains in usefulness. In the cool zone masses should be placed internally rather than at the exterior. In New York the most significant heat load strikes the western side, where a delay of six hours will contribute to thermal balance. In Phoenix the large diurnal variation generally calls for heavy walls, with relatively little importance on the north, and with no lag requirements on the east. The delay effect of the roof in the hot-arid region is, however, a task difficult to fulfill, although it is preeminently important. In Miami the small daily variations do not warrant delays; and heavy masses may stabilize temperatures at high vapor pressure conditions. Light constructions are therefore preferable here.

*Conclusion for Material Characteristics for Various Latitudes.* From the previous considerations a generalized synopsis can be drawn for the various climatic regions. The ordinate designates climatic zones with their approximate latitudes are illustrated. The upper abscissa is marked with temperature values which refer to the insulation needs. The deviation from comfort conditions in the various zones is marked with a curve, with the calculated values shown in full and the approximated ones in dotted lines. The lower abscissa indicates the daily diurnal temperature ranges. This relates to the curve of the time-lag index. As might be expected, the amount of insulation needed becomes greater as the climatic conditions turn cooler and design temperatures diverge from comfort requirements. The amount of weight required for desirable time-lag performance may be seen to vary with the amount of daily temperature fluctuation, with the greatest range occurring in hot and dry areas.

Methods for applying these principles are shown in the schematic house plans on the

123

right side of the graph. In tropical, humid environments, materials used should be lightweight and have low insulation values. The climate typical of tropical islands requires little insulation, but because of larger daily temperature fluctuation, mass located inside the structure will stabilize diurnal temperature conditions. In hot, humid areas where there is little daily variation, light insulation with no lag will give good performance. The requirements of a hot, dry area are much more stringent since there is a wide variation between day and night impacts. This calls for protecting the daytime living areas with heavy, heat-delaying masses and omitting capacity insulation at the sleeping areas so that they respond readily to the coolness of evening. In temperate areas the mass should be located on the west side so as to delay the heat impact of late afternoon, while resistance insulation is needed for the other sides of the structure. Cool areas require higher insulation values with a heavy western wall and with interior mass to balance daily temperature fluctuations. In cold surroundings, structures should be characterized by heavy walls to maintain temperature equilibrium, preferably with outside insulation to reduce heat-flow escape. At very high latitudes, where the daily variation becomes relatively negligible in comparison to the outside-temperature deviation from comfort, the insulation value will be the only criterion.

According to their location and orientation to thermal impacts, some areas receive "more winter" in underheated periods and "hotter summer" in overheated periods. This requires differing insulation values, while the corresponding weight of the structure is defined by the daily temperature range. These combined characteristics indicate a rational variation in the use of materials according to the requirements of each region and orientation.

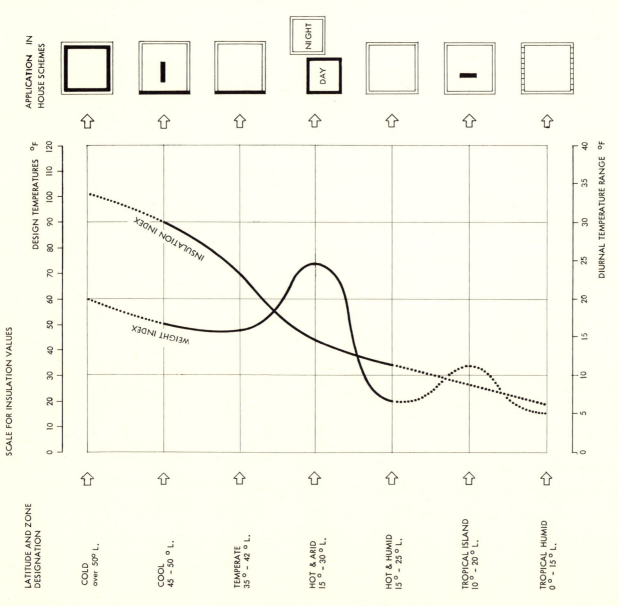

243. Regional importance of time lag and insulation values.

124

PART 3 APPLICATION

# XI. HELIOTHERMIC PLANNING

## COMFORT CRITERIA

THE aim in designing a structure thermally is to establish an indoor environment which most nearly approaches comfort conditions in a given climatic setting. In architectural terms this means that the planning and structure of a building should utilize natural possibilities to improve conditions without the aid of mechanical apparatus.

But how much benefit can be gained by application of the different principles—how much can the physical architectural features alter the actual thermal situation? It is evident that any improvement exercised by the structure itself will show up in the promotion of comfort, which is difficult to define exactly. However, a rendering of the question in more tangible terms would illuminate the problem: any heat energy captured in underheated periods will reduce heating costs; any quantity of heat kept from reaching the interior in overheated times will lessen the expenditure for cooling.

In the previous chapters various single aspects were discussed; but it remains necessary to correlate the findings. The material must be brought together by a common denominator in order to clarify the way in which these factors work together.

A breakdown of the total heat behavior into its component parts enables an analysis of a structure element by element, leading to a knowledge of the relative importance of the parts as related to the whole. It also makes it possible to evaluate situations which overlap or run against each other, indicating measures that should be taken in a specific situation.

## CALCULATING THERMAL BEHAVIOR OF STRUCTURES

The correlation of components, which affect thermal load inputs and their change during transmission through a structure until they appear as heat load outputs at the interior surface, is in itself an intricate problem. This is further complicated by the wide cyclical changes of outdoor conditions, which are usually out of phase with each other and constantly varying in magnitude, and also by the unsteady state of indoor temperature levels. Furthermore, the interior thermal exchange between objects, and the tendency for inside structural elements and contents to store and subsequently release heat, make it difficult to define the resultant thermal conditions occurring in the structure.

Many methods for calculating instantaneous heat loads on the basis of heat conduction solutions have been developed and are available. The method as presented by the American Society of Heating and Air-Conditioning Engineers[1] was adapted for the computations used in this study. For outside heat impacts on opaque surfaces the sol-air temperature formula, which combines radiation and temperature effects into a single parameter was used.[2] See Appendix A-5.

In the applied computations, one air-change per hour was used for usual constructions, and half an air-change per hour was calculated to account for the infiltration in weather-stripped buildings. Latent heat gain was not included in the computations.

On behalf of the total thermal summation

a conservative amount was added to account for the heat generated inside the house. It was presumed that from 8 AM till 4 PM one person, and at other times tree persons, would be contributing sensible body heat (195 Btu/hr per person). Lights and other electric appliances were supposed to be in use from 6 to 7 AM and from 6 to 11 PM. Cooking was presumed at 8 AM, and again from 5 to 6 PM. A small load of washing was supposed to take place in the morning hours. In the modified houses the heat loads generated by these appliances were reduced according to their possible ventilation rate.

The computations, because of limitations, imposed an imperfect account of long-wave radiation exchange, the neglect of storage effect for the complete structure, and the use of equal wind velocity coefficients for all sides in convection calculations. Nevertheless, they can be considered as an adequate measure with which to estimate the relative performances of various building arrangements.

## METHOD OF APPROACH FOR HELIOTHERMIC PLANNING

The heat-flow calculation method in engineering use is applied to already-designed structures to determine the heating or cooling loads resulting at nearly maximum thermal conditions. The architectural approach to thermal problems, however, emphasizes the creation of a structure that under general conditions avoids extreme thermal fluctuations, and thereby retains a balanced state close to comfort criteria. Accordingly, the architectural

departure from standard engineering procedure consists of:

A. Selecting dates representative of typical yearly climatic conditions. Here the average clear-sky (not design) data of January 21 and July 21 were used as illustrative days for underheated and overheated times respectively.

B. The regular method was followed for the sol-air temperature and structural heat transmission calculations. Then the method was reversed; selected from the transmission curves were those which at different orientations had desirable behavior under the given conditions (i.e., minimum heat gain in summer, low heat loss in winter). The "balanced house" schemes represent the summation of such reconstructed heat flow curves.

C. As a yardstick for improvement and an evaluation of the importance of architectural elements and principles, findings were related to an arbitrary structure called here "orthodox house." The deviation from such a norm, either positively or negatively, can represent an index for "thermal livability" and can be expressed in percentages.

The selected "orthodox house" is one of 1225/sq ft insulated wood frame construction, with approximately 20% window area distributed equally relative to the floor surface. The behavior of this house was calculated in different environments for comparison purposes.

For the "balanced house" evaluations the same net proportions in wall, floor area, and glass surfaces were still maintained. Conventional measures were still maintained, such as the application of east and west windows on squarish houses, despite their thermal disadvantages. Material characteristics were altered only in cases where the advantages were verifiable.

The comparative results express conservative data since the orthodox house is a structure which is neutral to its climatic surroundings, and not as unbalanced as a house laid out on the north-south axis would be. Furthermore, the comparisons are on a full 24-hour basis, not just on given hours or peak-temperature-load data, which would result in larger values. However, in the calculations for the balanced houses it was supposed that they would incorporate and utilize the findings described in previous chapters.

The calculation method for the New York area example is described in detail, while houses of other regions, although computed similarly, are presented in abbreviated form. As the houses of the hot-arid and hot-humid zones have special requirements, applied examples are shown in addition to the calculations.

CALCULATION OF SOL-AIR IMPACTS. The graphs illustrate sol-air temperature values at different orientations on various surfaces in the New York area both for winter (Jan. 21) and summer (July 21) under average clear-day conditions. In computing the solar heat impacts the radiation calculator data was used.

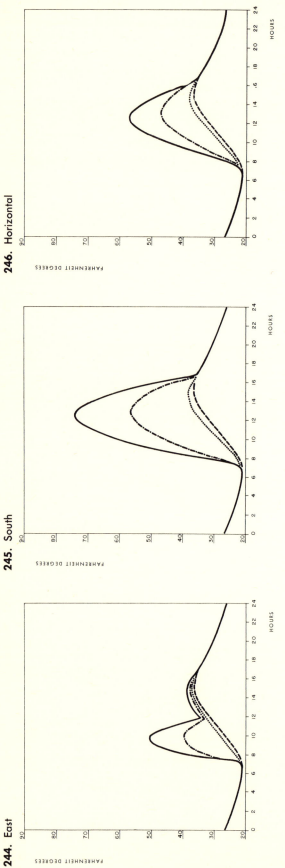

**244. East**

FAHRENHEIT DEGREES

**245. South**

FAHRENHEIT DEGREES

**246. Horizontal**

FAHRENHEIT DEGREES

HOURS

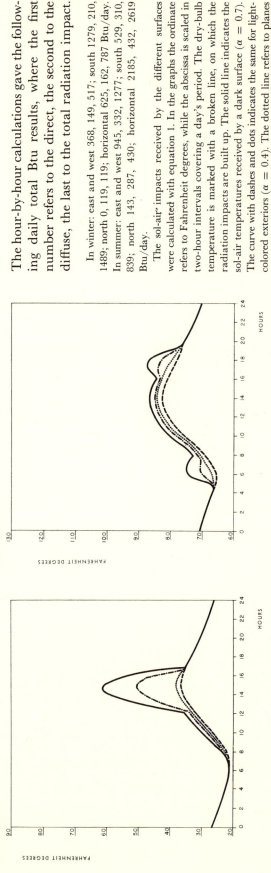

**247. West**

FAHRENHEIT DEGREES

**248. North**

FAHRENHEIT DEGREES

HOURS

The hour-by-hour calculations gave the following daily total Btu results, where the first number refers to the direct, the second to the diffuse, the last to the total radiation impact.

In winter: east and west 368, 149, 517; south 1279, 210, 1489; north 0, 119, 119; horizontal 625, 162, 787 Btu/day. In summer: east and west 945, 332, 1277; south 529, 310, 839; north 143, 287, 430; horizontal 2185, 432, 2619 Btu/day.

The sol-air impacts received by the different surfaces were calculated with equation 1. In the graphs the ordinate refers to Fahrenheit degrees, while the abscissa is scaled in two-hour intervals covering a day's period. The dry-bulb temperature is marked with a broken line, on which the radiation impacts are built up. The solid line indicates the sol-air temperatures received by a dark surface ($\alpha = 0.7$). The curve with dashes and dots indicates the same for light-colored exteriors ($\alpha = 0.4$). The dotted line refers to planes ($\alpha = 0.7$) in shade where, departing from the usual procedures, it was assumed that half of the diffuse radiation impact would reach the surface.

**128** Sol-air impacts in winter, New York area, Jan. 21.

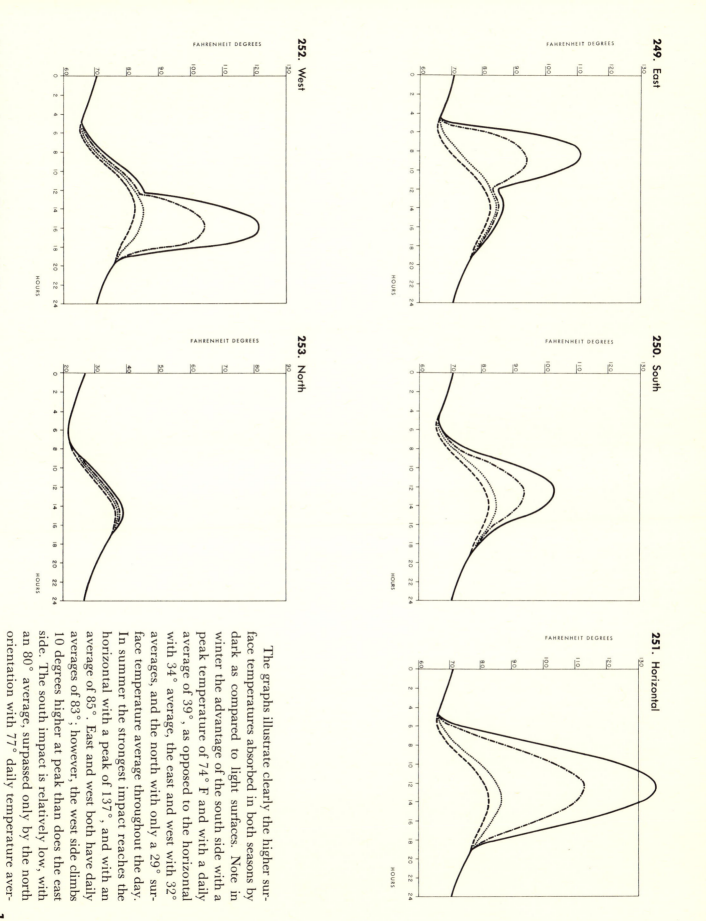

**249.** East

FAHRENHEIT DEGREES

HOURS

**250.** South

FAHRENHEIT DEGREES

HOURS

**251.** Horizontal

FAHRENHEIT DEGREES

HOURS

**252.** West

FAHRENHEIT DEGREES

HOURS

**253.** North

FAHRENHEIT DEGREES

HOURS

Sol-air impacts in summer, New York area, July 21.

The graphs illustrate clearly the higher surface temperatures absorbed in both seasons by dark as compared to light surfaces. Note in winter the advantage of the south side with a peak temperature of 74° F and with a daily average of 39°, as opposed to the horizontal with 34° average, the east and west with a daily average of 32° averages, and the north with only a 29° surface temperature average throughout the day. In summer the strongest impact reaches the horizontal with a peak of 137°, and with an average of 85°. East and west both have daily averages of 83°; however, the west side climbs 10 degrees higher at peak than does the east side. The south impact is relatively low, with an 80° average, surpassed only by the north orientation with 77° daily temperature average.

129

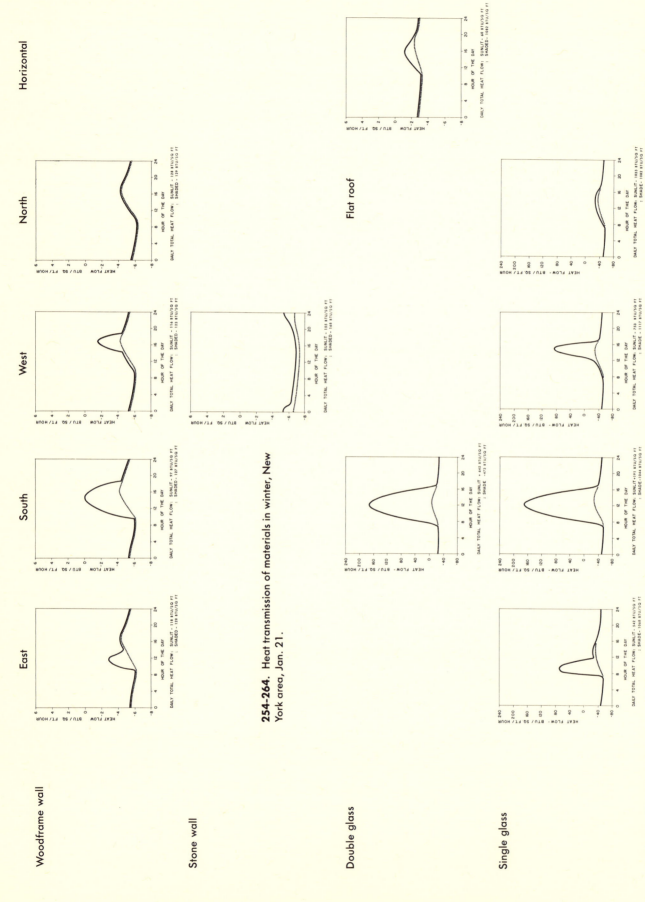

**254-264.** Heat transmission of materials in winter, New York area, Jan. 21.

HEAT TRANSMISSION OF MATERIALS. The graphs illustrate the heat transmission characteristics of various materials in the New York area during winter and summer. The resultant charts are ordered according to orientations denoted on the top. The transmission values were computed hour by hour with equations 2, 3, and 4. In the graphs the ordinate registers the magnitude of heat flow in Btu/hr/sq ft. Note that for glass surfaces, the heat flow scale is 20 times larger than that of the other materials, because of the large transmittance

Woodframe wall

Stone wall

**265-275.** Heat transmission of materials in summer, New York area, July 21.

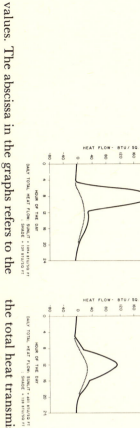

East

South

West

North

Horizontal

Double glass

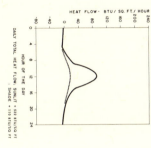

Flat roof

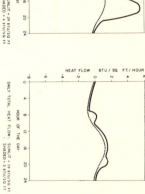

Single glass

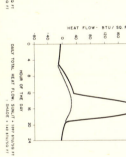
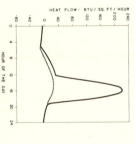

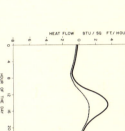
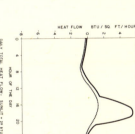
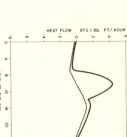

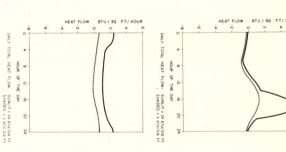

values. The abscissa in the graphs refers to the hours of the day. The solid line indicates the heat transmission under sunlit, the dotted line under shaded conditions. Under the graphs the total heat transmission values are summed up in Btu. The heat transmission curves, from which some typical examples are shown here, were used to calculate the behavior of the "orthodox" house; and a selection of curves, according to their advantageous characteristics, led to the evaluation of a "climate-balanced" structure.

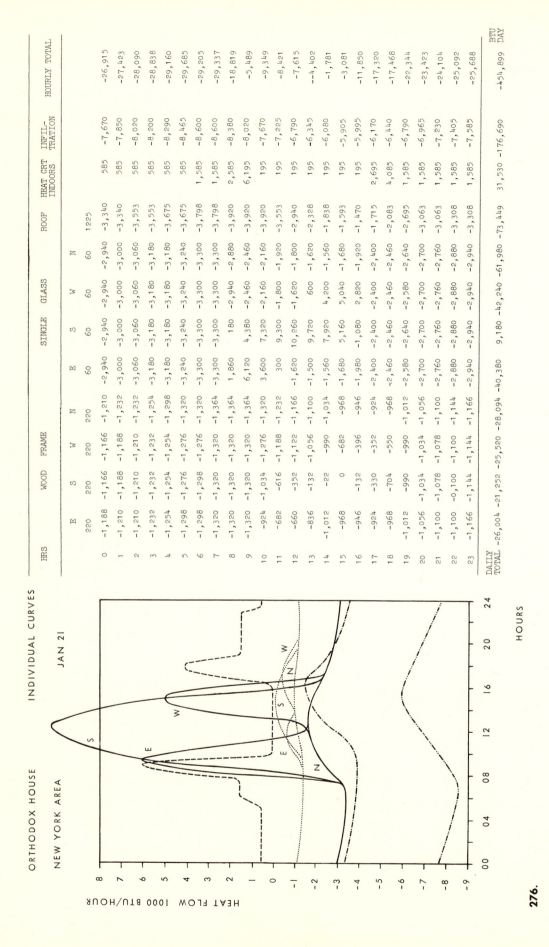

ORTHODOX HOUSE · INDIVIDUAL CURVES

NEW YORK AREA · JAN 21

HEAT FLOW 1000 BTU/HOUR — HOURS

**276.**

| HRS | WOOD FRAME | | | | SINGLE GLASS | | | | ROOF | HEAT CRT INDOORS | INFILTRATION | HOURLY TOTAL |
|---|---|---|---|---|---|---|---|---|---|---|---|---|
| | E 220 | S 220 | W 220 | N 220 | E 60 | S 60 | W 60 | N 60 | 1225 | | | |
| 0 | -1,188 | -1,166 | -1,166 | -1,210 | -2,940 | -2,940 | -2,940 | -2,940 | -3,340 | 585 | -7,670 | -26,915 |
| 1 | -1,210 | -1,188 | -1,188 | -1,232 | -3,000 | -3,000 | -3,000 | -3,000 | -3,340 | 585 | -7,850 | -27,423 |
| 2 | -1,210 | -1,210 | -1,210 | -1,232 | -3,060 | -3,060 | -3,060 | -3,060 | -3,553 | 585 | -8,020 | -28,090 |
| 3 | -1,232 | -1,232 | -1,232 | -1,254 | -3,180 | -3,180 | -3,180 | -3,180 | -3,553 | 585 | -8,200 | -28,838 |
| 4 | -1,254 | -1,254 | -1,254 | -1,298 | -3,180 | -3,180 | -3,180 | -3,180 | -3,675 | 585 | -8,290 | -29,160 |
| 5 | -1,298 | -1,276 | -1,276 | -1,320 | -3,240 | -3,240 | -3,240 | -3,240 | -3,675 | 585 | -8,465 | -29,685 |
| 6 | -1,298 | -1,298 | -1,276 | -1,320 | -3,300 | -3,300 | -3,300 | -3,300 | -3,798 | 1,585 | -8,600 | -29,205 |
| 7 | -1,320 | -1,320 | -1,320 | -1,364 | -3,300 | -3,300 | -3,300 | -3,300 | -3,798 | 1,585 | -8,600 | -29,337 |
| 8 | -1,320 | -1,320 | -1,320 | -1,364 | 1,860 | 180 | -2,940 | -2,880 | -3,920 | 2,585 | -8,380 | -18,819 |
| 9 | -1,320 | -1,320 | -1,320 | -1,364 | 6,120 | 4,380 | -2,460 | -2,460 | -3,920 | 6,195 | -8,020 | -5,489 |
| 10 | -924 | -1,034 | -1,276 | -1,320 | 3,600 | 7,320 | -2,160 | -2,160 | -3,920 | 195 | -7,670 | -9,349 |
| 11 | -682 | -616 | -1,188 | -1,232 | 300 | 9,300 | -1,800 | -1,920 | -3,553 | 195 | -7,225 | -8,421 |
| 12 | -660 | -352 | -1,122 | -1,166 | -1,620 | 10,260 | -1,620 | -1,800 | -2,940 | 195 | -6,790 | -7,615 |
| 13 | -836 | -132 | -1,056 | -1,100 | -1,500 | 9,720 | 600 | -1,620 | -2,328 | 195 | -6,345 | -4,402 |
| 14 | -1,012 | -22 | -990 | -1,034 | -1,560 | 7,920 | 4,200 | -1,560 | -1,838 | 195 | -6,080 | -1,781 |
| 15 | -968 | 0 | -682 | -968 | -1,680 | 5,160 | 5,040 | -1,680 | -1,593 | 195 | -5,905 | -3,081 |
| 16 | -946 | -132 | -396 | -946 | -1,980 | -1,080 | 2,820 | -1,920 | -1,470 | 195 | -5,995 | -11,850 |
| 17 | -924 | -330 | -352 | -924 | -2,400 | -2,400 | -2,400 | -2,400 | -1,715 | 2,695 | -6,170 | -17,320 |
| 18 | -968 | -704 | -550 | -968 | -2,460 | -2,460 | -2,460 | -2,460 | -2,083 | 4,085 | -6,440 | -17,468 |
| 19 | -1,012 | -990 | -990 | -1,012 | -2,580 | -2,640 | -2,580 | -2,640 | -2,695 | 1,585 | -6,790 | -22,344 |
| 20 | -1,056 | -1,034 | -1,034 | -1,056 | -2,700 | -2,700 | -2,700 | -2,700 | -3,063 | 1,585 | -6,965 | -23,423 |
| 21 | -1,100 | -1,078 | -1,078 | -1,100 | -2,760 | -2,760 | -2,760 | -2,760 | -3,063 | 1,585 | -7,230 | -24,104 |
| 22 | -1,100 | -0,100 | -1,100 | -1,144 | -2,880 | -2,880 | -2,880 | -2,880 | -3,308 | 1,585 | -7,405 | -25,092 |
| 23 | -1,166 | -1,144 | -1,144 | -1,166 | -2,940 | -2,940 | -2,940 | -2,940 | -3,308 | 1,585 | -7,585 | -25,688 |
| DAILY TOTAL | -26,004 | -21,252 | -25,520 | -28,094 | -40,380 | 9,180 | -42,240 | -61,980 | -73,449 | 31,530 | -176,690 | -454,899 BTU DAY |

## THERMAL BEHAVIORS

**STRUCTURES IN TEMPERATE AREAS**

"ORTHODOX HOUSE" IN TEMPERATE ZONE. The selected house norm is a structure which has neutral features in regard to the climatic environment. The square (35' × 35') house has a floor area of 1225 sq ft. Each side has a 280 sq ft surface consisting of 220 sq ft dark colored wood frame construction (α = 0.7, U = 0.13) and two 5' × 6' windows totaling 60 sq ft of glass area. A 21 sq ft door is placed on the north side. Flat roof construction (α = 0.7, U = 0.07) covers the total 1225 sq ft area.

The thermal behavior of the structure in New York in winter is illustrated, with the heatflow budget itemized at the righthand side. There the ordinate refers to the hours of the day. Horizontally the columns indicate the materials arranged according to exposures. At the far right the hourly total heat flow for the structure is shown. Under each column the

132

| HRS | WOOD FRAME E | S | W | N | SINGLE GLASS E | S | W | N | ROOF | HEAT CRT INDOORS | INFILTRATION | HOURLY TOTALS |
|---|---|---|---|---|---|---|---|---|---|---|---|---|
| | 220 | 220 | 220 | 220 | 60 | 60 | 60 | 60 | 1225 | | | |
| 0 | -2 | -31 | -11 | -42 | -240 | -240 | -240 | -240 | 585 | 585 | -617 | -833 |
| 1 | -13 | -33 | -24 | -55 | -240 | -240 | -240 | -240 | 245 | 585 | -706 | -961 |
| 2 | -37 | -68 | -48 | -81 | -360 | -360 | -360 | -360 | 245 | 585 | -882 | -1,848 |
| 3 | -51 | -79 | -64 | -95 | -420 | -360 | -420 | -420 | 123 | 585 | -1,058 | -2,319 |
| 4 | -73 | -106 | -86 | -121 | -240 | -240 | -360 | -240 | 123 | 585 | -1,235 | -2,956 |
| 5 | -97 | -130 | -110 | -145 | -480 | -480 | -480 | -480 | 0 | 585 | -1,411 | -1,368 |
| 6 | -121 | -156 | -134 | -172 | 8,040 | 0 | -60 | -60 | 0 | 585 | -1,411 | 8,771 |
| 7 | -33 | -176 | -156 | -139 | 11,760 | 480 | 300 | 840 | -120 | 1,585 | -1,147 | 13,194 |
| 8 | 510 | -150 | -114 | 33 | 12,540 | 900 | 660 | 780 | -245 | 2,585 | -794 | 16,705 |
| 9 | 829 | -33 | -61 | 26 | 11,040 | 2,400 | 960 | 1,080 | 368 | 6,195 | -265 | 22,539 |
| 10 | 926 | 53 | 9 | -9 | 8,220 | 4,560 | 1,380 | 1,380 | 1,225 | 195 | 353 | 18,292 |
| 11 | 911 | 290 | 97 | 73 | 4,380 | 5,640 | 1,620 | 1,380 | 2,082 | 195 | 794 | 17,702 |
| 12 | 779 | 517 | 174 | 174 | 1,800 | 6,720 | 1,740 | 1,620 | 3,063 | 195 | 1,147 | 18,131 |
| 13 | 563 | 658 | 264 | 244 | 1,860 | 5,880 | 1,800 | 1,860 | 3,798 | 195 | 1,411 | 21,353 |
| 14 | 317 | 763 | 317 | 295 | 1,860 | 4,620 | 1,860 | 1,860 | 4,287 | 195 | 1,499 | 25,073 |
| 15 | 348 | 746 | 660 | 332 | 1,620 | 4,980 | 8,700 | 1,740 | 4,655 | 195 | 1,411 | 26,587 |
| 16 | 352 | 680 | 957 | 341 | 1,620 | 3,000 | 13,320 | 1,560 | 4,532 | 195 | 1,235 | 26,299 |
| 17 | 330 | 528 | 1,168 | 326 | 1,440 | 1,680 | 12,600 | 1,680 | 4,287 | 195 | 1,058 | 27,132 |
| 18 | 290 | 343 | 1,208 | 286 | 780 | 840 | 8,880 | 2,280 | 3,675 | 2,695 | 706 | 23,373 |
| 19 | 249 | 249 | 1,157 | 348 | 240 | 240 | 1,680 | 660 | 2,940 | 4,085 | 529 | 9,877 |
| 20 | 183 | 152 | 814 | 341 | 120 | 240 | 120 | 120 | 2,082 | 1,585 | 265 | 5,902 |
| 21 | 119 | 101 | 227 | 145 | -60 | -60 | -60 | -60 | 1,102 | 1,585 | -88 | 2,951 |
| 22 | 84 | 59 | 75 | 48 | -120 | -120 | -120 | -120 | 613 | 1,585 | -353 | 1,631 |
| 23 | 33 | 9 | 24 | -4 | -240 | -240 | -240 | -240 | 490 | 1,585 | -441 | 736 |
| DAILY TOTAL | 6,396 | 4,186 | 6,365 | 2,149 | 65,640 | 36,120 | 65,820 | 18,300 | 39,450 | 31,530 | 0 | 275,956 BTU/DAY |

daily total is summarized. At the lefthand side a chart indicates graphically the heat flow curves resulting from these calculations.

The results indicate that different heat losses arise from the following sources: wood-frame construction, east 5%, south 4%, west 5%, north 6%; window areas, east 8%, west 8%, north 13%. Heat loss through the roof is 15%, through infiltration 36%. There is a small 2% heat gain through the south window, and the heat created indoors amounts to a 6% positive gain, as related to the total sum of losses.

The summer thermal behavior of the orthodox house was calculated similarly, and the heat-flow results are indicated. The heat budget figures denote that the heat gain results from the following sources: woodframe wall, east 2%, west 2%, north 1%; window areas, east 24%, south 13%, west 24%, north 7%. Heat gain through the roof is 14%, and the heat created indoors amounts to 11% of the total.

277.

HEAT FLOW 1000 BTU/HOUR

HOURS

| HRS | WOOD FRAME E 186 | S 213 | N 333 | STONE WALL W 186 | SINGLE GLASS E 30 | W 30 | N 30 | DOUBLE GLASS S 150 | ROOF 1225 | HEAT GRT INDOORS | INFILTRATION | HOURLY TOTAL |
|---|---|---|---|---|---|---|---|---|---|---|---|---|
| 0 | −1,004 | −1,129 | −1,832 | −1,004 | −1,470 | −1,470 | −1,470 | −3,600 | −3,430 | 585 | −3,837 | −19,661 |
| 1 | −1,023 | −1,150 | −1,865 | −1,060 | −1,500 | −1,500 | −1,500 | −3,600 | −3,430 | 585 | −3,925 | −19,968 |
| 2 | −1,023 | −1,172 | −1,865 | −1,190 | −1,530 | −1,530 | −1,530 | −3,750 | −3,553 | 585 | −4,010 | −20,568 |
| 3 | −1,042 | −1,193 | −1,898 | −1,190 | −1,590 | −1,590 | −1,590 | −3,900 | −3,553 | 585 | −4,101 | −21,062 |
| 4 | −1,060 | −1,214 | −1,965 | −1,209 | −1,590 | −1,590 | −1,590 | −3,900 | −3,675 | 585 | −4,145 | −21,353 |
| 5 | −1,097 | −1,235 | −1,998 | −1,209 | −1,620 | −1,620 | −1,620 | −3,900 | −3,675 | 585 | −4,233 | −21,622 |
| 6 | −1,097 | −1,257 | −1,998 | −1,228 | −1,650 | −1,650 | −1,620 | −4,050 | −3,798 | 1,335 | −4,300 | −21,343 |
| 7 | −1,116 | −1,278 | −2,031 | −1,228 | −1,650 | −1,650 | −1,650 | −4,050 | −3,798 | 1,335 | −4,300 | −21,416 |
| 8 | −1,135 | −1,278 | −2,065 | −1,246 | 930 | −1,470 | −1,440 | 3,600 | −3,920 | 1,585 | −4,190 | −10,629 |
| 9 | −1,135 | −1,278 | −2,065 | −1,246 | 3,060 | −1,230 | −1,230 | 13,050 | −3,920 | 795 | −4,010 | 791 |
| 10 | −781 | −1,001 | −1,998 | −1,246 | 1,800 | −1,080 | −1,080 | 19,650 | −3,920 | 195 | −3,837 | 6,702 |
| 11 | −577 | −596 | −1,865 | −1,246 | 150 | −900 | −960 | 24,300 | −3,553 | 195 | −3,616 | 11,332 |
| 12 | −558 | −341 | −1,765 | −1,264 | −810 | −810 | −900 | 25,950 | −2,940 | 195 | −3,396 | 13,361 |
| 13 | −707 | −128 | −1,665 | −1,264 | −750 | 300 | −810 | 24,750 | −2,328 | 195 | −3,175 | 14,418 |
| 14 | −856 | −21 | −1,565 | −1,264 | −780 | 2,100 | −780 | 20,400 | −1,838 | 195 | −3,043 | 12,548 |
| 15 | −818 | 0 | −1,465 | −1,283 | −840 | 2,520 | −840 | 14,100 | −1,593 | 195 | −2,955 | 7,021 |
| 16 | −800 | −128 | −1,432 | −1,283 | −990 | 1,410 | −960 | 4,650 | −1,470 | 195 | −2,999 | −3,807 |
| 17 | −781 | −320 | −1,399 | −1,265 | −1,200 | −1,200 | −1,200 | −2,850 | −1,715 | 1,445 | −3,087 | −13,572 |
| 18 | −818 | −682 | −1,465 | −1,246 | −1,230 | −1,230 | −1,230 | −3,000 | −2,083 | 2,585 | −3,219 | −13,618 |
| 19 | −856 | −959 | −1,532 | −1,228 | −1,290 | −1,290 | −1,320 | −3,150 | −2,695 | 1,335 | −3,396 | −16,381 |
| 20 | −893 | −1,001 | −1,598 | −1,190 | −1,350 | −1,350 | −1,350 | −3,300 | −3,063 | 1,335 | −3,484 | −17,244 |
| 21 | −930 | −1,044 | −1,665 | −1,172 | −1,380 | −1,380 | −1,380 | −3,450 | −3,063 | 1,335 | −3,616 | −17,745 |
| 22 | −949 | −1,065 | −1,732 | −1,097 | −1,440 | −1,440 | −1,440 | −3,450 | −3,308 | 1,335 | −3,704 | −18,290 |
| 23 | −986 | −1,108 | −1,765 | −1,023 | −1,470 | −1,470 | −1,470 | −3,600 | −3,308 | 1,335 | −3,793 | −18,658 |
| DAILY TOTAL | −22,042 | −20,578 | −42,493 | −28,881 | −20,190 | −21,120 | −30,990 | 96,900 | −73,629 | 20,630 | −88,371 | −230,764 BTU DAY |

278.

"Balanced House" in Temperate Zone. The modified structure detailed here utilizes some principles described in the foregoing chapters. In general the house is similar to the orthodox one, having the same floor area (1225 sq ft), the same total glass surface, the same heat-transmission values. Changes were made in materials at the south-facing window by double glazing (U = 0.55), and on the western side by using a stone wall. The stone, although high in transmission value (U = 0.23), has an advantageous influence on the heat-capacity balancing through time-lag. The form of the structure was changed from square to proportions 1:1.68 on the east-west axis. The openings were rearranged, concentrating larger glass areas (150 sq ft) near the south, but leaving (30 sq ft) windows on all other orientations for conservative measures despite their relatively disadvantageous heat behavior. Applied overhangs secure shade in summer, while the east and west wall surfaces are shaded mostly by trees, and thus calculated for half shade. The roof color was changed to

## INDIVIDUAL CURVES — BALANCED HOUSE — NEW YORK AREA — JULY 21

| HRS | WOOD FRAME E (186) | WOOD FRAME S (213) | WOOD FRAME N (333) | STONE WALL W (186) | SINGLE GLASS E (30) | SINGLE GLASS W (30) | SINGLE GLASS N (30) | DOUBLE GLASS S (150) | ROOF (1225) | HEAT CRT INDOORS | INFILTRATION | HOURLY TOTAL |
|---|---|---|---|---|---|---|---|---|---|---|---|---|
| 0 | -21 | -43 | -66 | 269 | -120 | -120 | -120 | -300 | 147 | 585 | -309 | -98 |
| 1 | -33 | -64 | -100 | 270 | -120 | -120 | -120 | -450 | 147 | 585 | -353 | -358 |
| 2 | -61 | -85 | -133 | 264 | -180 | -180 | -180 | -450 | 74 | 585 | -358 | -787 |
| 3 | -67 | -85 | -167 | 223 | -120 | -180 | -180 | -450 | 74 | 585 | -441 | -1196 |
| 4 | -86 | -128 | -200 | 168 | -180 | -210 | -210 | -600 | 0 | 585 | -529 | -1599 |
| 5 | -105 | -149 | -233 | 140 | -210 | -240 | -240 | -600 | 0 | 585 | -618 | -1788 |
| 6 | -125 | -170 | -266 | 122 | -240 | -240 | -240 | -600 | 0 | 585 | -706 | -152 |
| 7 | -118 | -192 | -300 | 122 | -266 | -270 | -210 | 0 | -72 | 1585 | -706 | 831 |
| 8 | 33 | -170 | -266 | 112 | -240 | -240 | -120 | 450 | -147 | 1335 | -574 | 2160 |
| 9 | 135 | -106 | -167 | 102 | -210 | -150 | 30 | 900 | 221 | 1335 | -397 | 3037 |
| 10 | 195 | -64 | -100 | 102 | 0 | 0 | 120 | 1350 | 735 | 1335 | -133 | 4600 |
| 11 | 234 | 21 | 33 | 93 | 180 | 90 | 240 | 1800 | 1249 | 195 | 177 | 6422 |
| 12 | 243 | 107 | 166 | 83 | 300 | 300 | 390 | 2100 | 1838 | 195 | 397 | 7586 |
| 13 | 230 | 170 | 233 | 83 | 570 | 570 | 480 | 2700 | 2279 | 195 | 574 | 8456 |
| 14 | 197 | 234 | 333 | 74 | 600 | 600 | 480 | 2700 | 2572 | 195 | 706 | 8405 |
| 15 | 229 | 256 | 400 | 83 | 660 | 660 | 540 | 2700 | 2793 | 195 | 750 | 8892 |
| 16 | 232 | 277 | 433 | 83 | 720 | 720 | 570 | 2700 | 2572 | 195 | 706 | 7587 |
| 17 | 215 | 256 | 400 | 112 | 720 | 720 | 510 | 2100 | 2205 | 1445 | 529 | 7869 |
| 18 | 193 | 213 | 366 | 140 | 600 | 600 | 450 | 1350 | 1764 | 2585 | 353 | 7525 |
| 19 | 161 | 192 | 300 | 158 | 480 | 480 | 330 | 900 | 1249 | 1335 | 265 | 4835 |
| 20 | 108 | 128 | 200 | 177 | 270 | 330 | 150 | 450 | 661 | 1335 | 133 | 3660 |
| 21 | 79 | 85 | 133 | 196 | 90 | 150 | 60 | 300 | 368 | 1335 | -44 | 2355 |
| 22 | 45 | 43 | 67 | 233 | -30 | 60 | -30 | 150 | 294 | 1335 | -177 | 1584 |
| 23 | 6 | 0 | 0 | 261 | -120 | -60 | -120 | -300 | — | 1335 | -221 | 1015 |
| DAILY TOTAL | 1919 | 726 | 1066 | 3670 | 4170 | 4200 | 3690 | 16500 | 23670 | 20630 | 000 | 80241 BTU/DAY |

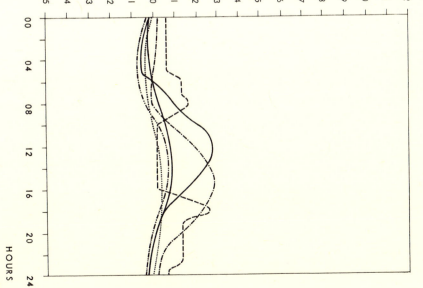

HEAT FLOW 1000 BTU/HOUR — HOURS (00, 04, 08, 12, 16, 20, 24)

The total winter heat loss escapes through the following channels: woodframe construction, east 6%, south 6%, north 12%; western stone wall 8%; single-pane window, east 6%, north 9%. Heatloss through the roof is 21%, through infiltration 26%. The double-pane south window admits a heat gain of 28%, and the heat created indoors adds a 6% gain.

In summer the heat gain results from the following sources in percentages: woodframe wall; east 2%, south 1%, north 1%; western stone wall 5%; single pane window, east 5%, west 6%, north 5%; double-pane south window admits 21%. The roof adds 29%, and heat created indoors amounts to 26% of the total.

a white surface with ventilated construction. The heat sources within the house were calculated with exhaust ventilation. It was supposed that weatherstripping would cut the infiltration to half an air-change per hour.

The heatflow tabulations and transmission graphs for winter and summer conditions are constructed as for the orthodox house.

279.

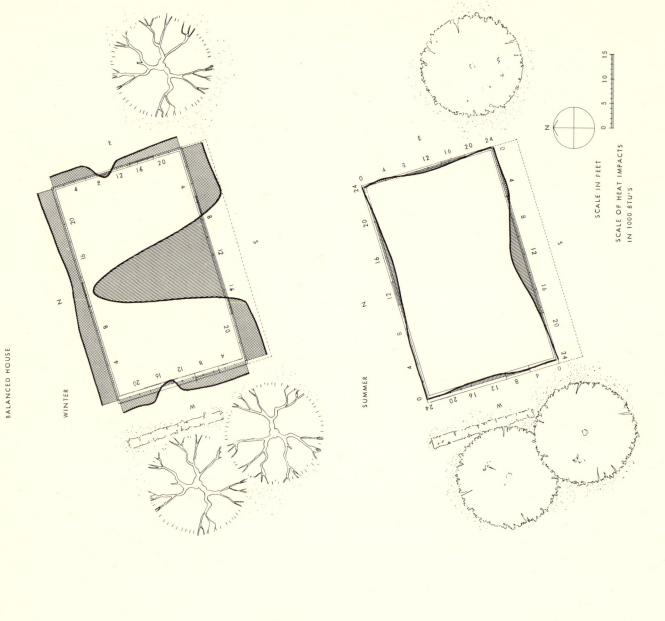

BALANCED HOUSE

WINTER

SUMMER

SCALE OF HEAT IMPACTS
IN 1000 BTU'S

SCALE IN FEET

NEW YORK

ORTHODOX HOUSE

WINTER

SUMMER

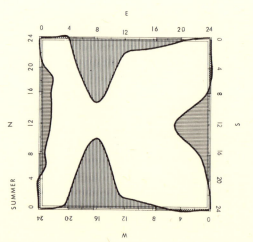

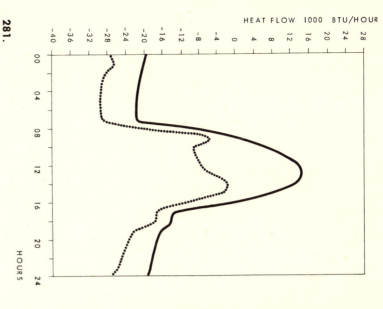

**281.**

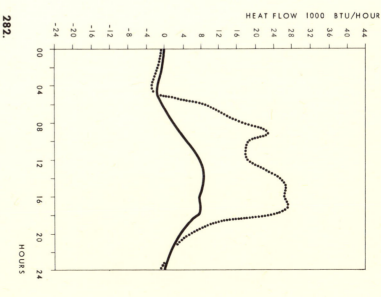

**282.**

CONCLUSIONS FOR NEW YORK AREA. A comparison of heat behavior between the orthodox and balanced structures is illustrated graphically in the accompanying plans for both winter and summer. On each side of the structures the hours of the day are indicated clockwise. The hourly heat amount transmitted by the surfaces is charted from the center of the wall, the heat gains toward the interior of the house, the heat losses toward the exterior. For any given time, the summation of the heat impacts at the four orientations will result in the total heat transmission of the building sides.

The daily total heat flow curves in winter of the orthodox and balanced houses are shown. Note that the orthodox house has negative heat flow throughout the day, whereas the balanced house gains heat for about seven hours. The losses of the balanced house are smaller too, making its performance throughout the day better than the orthodox structure. Shown also are the daily total heat flow behavior of the same houses in summertime. The balanced house reduces the heat peak of the orthodox house from 26,587 to 8,456 Btu.

The improvements in the seasons are the products of the following measures: in winter: orientation, house shape, and rearrangement of openings ($+86,429$ Btu gain) 19%; reduction of infiltration ($+87,319$ Btu) 19%, drop in convection through double-glass window ($+67,306$ Btu) 15%. The applied stone wall because of lower insulation value results in a loss of 2%. The ventilation of appliances works negatively also by 2%. The total reduction of heat loss is 49%.

The breakdown of the applied measures improves the conditions in summer as follows: orientation, shape, and rearrangement of openings ($-21,938$ Btu) 8%; shading of glass surfaces ($-132,408$ Btu) 48%; partial shading of walls ($-12,468$ Btu) 4%; double-pane south window ($-4,200$ Btu) 2%; roof alteration with light color and ventilation ($-15,780$ Btu) 6%; ventilation effect for heat created indoors ($-10,900$ Btu) 4%. The stone wall applied to the west shows a loss of 1% as a daily total, however its balancing effect works favorably. The total improvement over the orthodox house amounts to 71%.

From the seasonal data a yearly importance index can be compiled for the applied measures. As a criterion for such an index the transmitted-heat-flow sums were multiplied by the duration of the season (72% for underheated period, 28% for overheated), and since the final yardstick for evaluation is human stress, the summer heat impacts were again multiplied by two. Accordingly the yearly evaluation results show the following order. (1) Orientation has importance in both periods, but mainly during underheated times, with a yearly importance of 27%. (2) Shading of glass surfaces is equal to it in magnitude (27%), but only in one season. (3) Reduction in infiltration is a close third with 23%. (4) Lower heat transmission in glass surface (double pane) accounts for 18%. (5) Roof ventilation is 3%. (6) Shading of walls is 2%. (7) Ventilation of appliances and stone wall both work in such a summation negatively with a total of $-3\%$.

**MINNEAPOLIS ORTHODOX HOUSE — JAN 21**

Heat flow data (1000 BTU/HOUR vs HOURS: 00–24; Y-axis 10 to −24).  283.

**MINNEAPOLIS ORTHODOX HOUSE — JULY 21**

Heat flow data (1000 BTU/HOUR vs HOURS: 00–24; Y-axis 20 to −6).  284.

**Table (left) — JAN 21**  (ROOF column top annotation: 1,225)

| HRS | WOOD FRAME E 220 | S 220 | W 220 | N 220 | SINGLE GLASS E 60 | S 60 | W 60 | N 60 | DOOR N 60 | ROOF | HEAT CRT INDOORS | INFILTRATION | HOURLY TOTALS |
|---|---|---|---|---|---|---|---|---|---|---|---|---|---|
| 0 | -1,590 | -1,570 | -1,570 | -1,590 | -3,960 | -3,960 | -3,960 | -3,960 | -16 | -3,956 | 585 | -10,231 | -35,778 |
| 1 | -1,620 | -1,601 | -1,612 | -1,620 | -4,080 | -4,080 | -4,080 | -4,080 | -17 | -4,018 | 585 | -10,584 | -36,807 |
| 2 | -1,651 | -1,632 | -1,642 | -1,651 | -4,200 | -4,200 | -4,200 | -4,200 | -17 | -4,104 | 585 | -10,866 | -37,778 |
| 3 | -1,701 | -1,682 | -1,695 | -1,701 | -4,260 | -4,320 | -4,260 | -4,260 | -17 | -4,875 | 585 | -11,113 | -39,240 |
| 4 | -1,700 | -1,722 | -1,785 | -1,700 | -4,320 | -4,320 | -4,320 | -4,320 | -18 | -5,010 | 585 | -11,290 | -39,920 |
| 5 | -1,781 | -1,760 | -1,770 | -1,781 | -4,380 | -4,380 | -4,380 | -4,380 | -18 | -5,120 | 585 | -11,395 | -40,560 |
| 6 | -1,810 | -1,785 | -1,795 | -1,810 | -4,320 | -4,320 | -4,320 | -4,320 | -18 | -5,218 | 1,585 | -11,360 | -39,491 |
| 7 | -1,820 | -1,800 | -1,810 | -1,820 | -4,260 | -4,260 | -4,260 | -4,260 | -18 | -5,292 | 1,585 | -11,184 | -39,199 |
| 8 | -1,821 | -1,798 | -1,800 | -1,821 | -840 | -3,960 | -3,960 | -3,960 | -18 | -5,389 | 2,585 | -10,866 | -31,848 |
| 9 | -1,790 | -1,770 | -1,778 | -1,790 | 2,400 | 2,580 | -3,480 | -3,480 | -18 | -5,316 | 6,195 | -10,443 | -18,690 |
| 10 | -1,616 | -1,600 | -1,727 | -1,699 | 1,980 | 6,000 | -3,120 | -3,120 | -17 | -5,243 | 195 | -10,060 | -20,027 |
| 11 | -1,389 | -1,350 | -1,650 | -1,688 | -480 | 7,860 | -2,820 | -2,940 | -16 | -5,035 | 195 | -9,561 | -18,874 |
| 12 | -1,345 | -1,155 | -1,585 | -1,599 | -2,580 | 8,880 | -2,580 | -2,820 | -15 | -4,386 | 195 | -9,173 | -18,163 |
| 13 | -1,360 | -990 | -1,490 | -1,521 | -2,460 | 8,100 | -120 | -2,580 | -14 | -3,099 | 195 | -8,714 | -14,053 |
| 14 | -1,449 | -907 | -1,496 | -1,466 | -2,520 | 6,720 | 2,400 | -2,520 | -14 | -2,609 | 195 | -8,502 | -12,168 |
| 15 | -1,389 | -869 | -1,250 | -1,399 | -2,700 | 3,360 | 3,180 | -2,700 | -13 | -2,401 | 195 | -8,967 | -14,993 |
| 16 | -1,360 | -934 | -1,132 | -1,370 | -3,060 | -1,320 | 60 | -3,060 | -13 | -2,278 | 195 | -8,644 | -22,916 |
| 17 | -1,370 | -1,068 | -1,115 | -1,375 | -3,420 | -3,420 | -3,420 | -3,480 | -13 | -2,499 | 195 | -8,820 | -27,246 |
| 18 | -1,410 | -1,260 | -1,300 | -1,409 | -3,480 | -3,480 | -3,480 | -3,540 | -14 | -2,928 | 4,085 | -8,996 | -27,152 |
| 19 | -1,449 | -1,430 | -1,447 | -1,449 | -3,540 | -3,540 | -3,540 | -3,600 | -15 | -3,479 | 1,585 | -9,280 | -31,124 |
| 20 | -1,470 | -1,455 | -1,695 | -1,470 | -3,600 | -3,600 | -3,600 | -3,720 | -15 | -3,638 | 1,585 | -9,420 | -31,978 |
| 21 | -1,500 | -1,488 | -1,500 | -1,500 | -3,720 | -3,720 | -3,720 | -3,720 | -15 | -3,712 | 1,585 | -9,631 | -32,641 |
| 22 | -1,535 | -1,519 | -1,488 | -1,535 | -3,720 | -3,720 | -3,720 | -3,840 | -16 | -3,797 | 1,585 | -9,772 | -32,957 |
| 23 | -1,564 | -1,550 | -1,560 | -1,564 | -3,840 | -3,840 | -3,840 | -3,840 | -16 | -3,871 | 1,585 | -10,020 | -33,920 |
| DAILY TOTAL | -37,490 | -34,695 | -37,692 | -38,328 | -69,360 | -19,140 | -69,540 | -86,280 | -383 | 97,213 | 31,530 | -238,892 | -697,483 |

**Table (right) — JULY 21**  (ROOF column top annotation: 1,225)

| HRS | WOOD FRAME E 220 | S 220 | W 220 | N 220 | SINGLE GLASS E 60 | S 60 | W 60 | N 60 | DOOR N | ROOF | HEAT CRT INDOORS | INFILTRATION | HOURLY TOTALS |
|---|---|---|---|---|---|---|---|---|---|---|---|---|---|
| 0 | -24 | -39 | -30 | -48 | -420 | -420 | -360 | -420 | -1 | 294 | 585 | -1,058 | -1,941 |
| 1 | -73 | -90 | -79 | -101 | -540 | -540 | -480 | -540 | -1 | 159 | 585 | -1,411 | -3,111 |
| 2 | -121 | -141 | -127 | -152 | -660 | -660 | -600 | -660 | -2 | 24 | 585 | -1,764 | -4,278 |
| 3 | -167 | -191 | -178 | -202 | -660 | -660 | -600 | -660 | -2 | -122 | 585 | -1,835 | -4,692 |
| 4 | -216 | -240 | -227 | -255 | -720 | -720 | -660 | -720 | -2 | -257 | 585 | -1,870 | -5,302 |
| 5 | -224 | -251 | -238 | -264 | -720 | -540 | -480 | -480 | -2 | -392 | 585 | -1,835 | -2,081 |
| 6 | -229 | -255 | -242 | -271 | 2,040 | -60 | -120 | 1,320 | -2 | -416 | 1,585 | -1,693 | 7,597 |
| 7 | -92 | -244 | -229 | -200 | 7,980 | 300 | 240 | 540 | -2 | -428 | 1,585 | -1,411 | 11,639 |
| 8 | 222 | -200 | -194 | -117 | 11,580 | 900 | 600 | 720 | -2 | -318 | 2,585 | -822 | 15,614 |
| 9 | 367 | -147 | -143 | -121 | 12,240 | 3,000 | 900 | 1,080 | -1 | 208 | 6,195 | -318 | 22,000 |
| 10 | 462 | -13 | -59 | -70 | 10,980 | 5,040 | 1,260 | 1,320 | 0 | 1,004 | 195 | 176 | 17,235 |
| 11 | 486 | 180 | 26 | 15 | 7,920 | 6,600 | 1,560 | 1,620 | 1 | 1,935 | 195 | 706 | 17,524 |
| 12 | 438 | 339 | 101 | 92 | 4,200 | 7,080 | 1,740 | 1,740 | 1 | 2,817 | 195 | 1,129 | 17,472 |
| 13 | 354 | 464 | 182 | 172 | 1,800 | 6,960 | 1,860 | 1,860 | 2 | 3,515 | 195 | 1,411 | 21,355 |
| 14 | 246 | 537 | 251 | 235 | 1,860 | 5,520 | 4,380 | 1,800 | 2 | 3,993 | 195 | 1,588 | 24,627 |
| 15 | 277 | 565 | 462 | 275 | 1,800 | 3,600 | 8,400 | 1,680 | 2 | 4,275 | 195 | 1,588 | 26,299 |
| 16 | 293 | 539 | 647 | 299 | 1,620 | 1,920 | 11,640 | 1,560 | 2 | 4,263 | 195 | 1,517 | 25,995 |
| 17 | 288 | 451 | 763 | 299 | 1,500 | 1,320 | 13,140 | 1,680 | 2 | 4,067 | 2,695 | 1,235 | 26,420 |
| 18 | 268 | 325 | 807 | 282 | 1,200 | 1,020 | 12,540 | 1,560 | 2 | 3,552 | 4,085 | 988 | 23,629 |
| 19 | 222 | 229 | 744 | 266 | 900 | 420 | 9,000 | 2,400 | 1 | 2,866 | 1,585 | 706 | 11,839 |
| 20 | 178 | 183 | 598 | 275 | 420 | 120 | 2,940 | 1,440 | 1 | 2,033 | 1,585 | 353 | 5,686 |
| 21 | 125 | 119 | 235 | 169 | 120 | 0 | 120 | 120 | 0 | 1,261 | 1,585 | 0 | 3,494 |
| 22 | 70 | 61 | 81 | 55 | 0 | -120 | -120 | 0 | 0 | 661 | 1,585 | -353 | 1,680 |
| 23 | 22 | 11 | 18 | 2 | -120 | -300 | -300 | -120 | -1 | 428 | 1,585 | -706 | 219 |
| DAILY TOTAL | 3,172 | 2,192 | 3,169 | 615 | 64,740 | 39,780 | 64,800 | 17,160 | -2 | 35,422 | 31,530 | -3,679 | 258,919 |

BTU / DAY

## MINNEAPOLIS BALANCED HOUSE — JAN 21

Table (hourly heat flow, BTU)

| HRS | WOOD FRAME E 234 | S 146 | W 234 | N 266 | SINGLE GLASS E 30 | W 30 | N 30 | DOUBLE GLASS S 150 | DOOR | ROOF | HEAT GET INDOORS | INFIL-TRATION | HOURLY TOTALS | BTU DAY |
|---|---|---|---|---|---|---|---|---|---|---|---|---|---|---|
| 0 | -1,687 | -1,040 | -1,682 | -1,918 | -1,980 | -1,980 | -1,980 | -4,650 | -1 | -3,956 | 585 | -5,116 | -25,570 | |
| 1 | -1,724 | -1,064 | -1,717 | -1,960 | -1,980 | -1,920 | -1,980 | -4,800 | -1 | -4,018 | 585 | -5,292 | -26,277 | |
| 2 | -1,757 | -1,083 | -1,750 | -1,998 | -2,040 | -1,860 | -1,980 | -5,100 | -2 | -4,103 | 585 | -5,433 | -26,956 | |
| 3 | -1,813 | -1,116 | -1,802 | -2,100 | -2,100 | -2,130 | -2,160 | -5,250 | -2 | -4,875 | 585 | -5,557 | -28,298 | |
| 4 | -1,855 | -1,145 | -1,844 | -2,109 | -2,130 | -2,160 | -2,160 | -5,250 | -2 | -5,557 | 585 | -5,645 | -28,771 | |
| 5 | -1,895 | -1,168 | -1,881 | -2,155 | -2,160 | -2,190 | -2,199 | -5,400 | -2 | -5,645 | 585 | -5,696 | -29,318 | |
| 6 | -1,923 | -1,184 | -1,907 | -2,187 | -2,190 | -2,160 | -2,160 | -5,250 | -2 | -5,696 | 1,445 | -5,645 | -28,462 | |
| 7 | -1,939 | -1,194 | -1,926 | -2,197 | -2,160 | -2,130 | -2,160 | -5,250 | -2 | -5,645 | 1,445 | -5,696 | -28,471 | |
| 8 | -1,932 | -1,191 | -1,926 | -2,165 | -2,130 | -2,100 | -2,130 | -4,950 | -2 | -5,180 | 2,585 | -4,410 | -28,410 | |
| 9 | -1,904 | -1,174 | -1,891 | -2,104 | -1,980 | -2,040 | -1,980 | -600 | -2 | -5,218 | 2,585 | -4,498 | -21,410 | |
| 10 | -1,719 | -1,059 | -1,833 | -2,011 | -1,560 | -1,740 | -1,740 | 18,000 | -1 | -5,243 | 1,585 | -4,604 | -8,974 | |
| 11 | -1,476 | -894 | -1,755 | -1,931 | -1,410 | -1,290 | -1,470 | 21,450 | -16 | -5,034 | 195 | -4,710 | -939 | |
| 12 | -1,429 | -766 | -1,685 | -1,841 | -1,290 | -1,230 | -1,410 | 23,850 | -15 | -4,385 | 195 | -4,357 | 2,559 | |
| 13 | -1,648 | -657 | -1,605 | -1,772 | -1,230 | -1,200 | -1,290 | 21,900 | -14 | -3,299 | 195 | -4,587 | 5,257 | |
| 14 | -1,539 | -602 | -1,540 | -1,689 | -1,260 | -1,590 | -1,470 | 18,790 | -14 | -2,609 | 195 | -5,298 | 6,494 | |
| 15 | -1,476 | -577 | -1,389 | -1,530 | -1,350 | -1,350 | -1,330 | 11,100 | -13 | -2,401 | 195 | -5,780 | 5,298 | |
| 16 | -1,448 | -619 | -1,205 | -1,330 | 30 | 30 | 450 | 450 | -13 | -2,278 | 195 | -5,027 | -1,531 | |
| 17 | -1,457 | -708 | -1,186 | -1,663 | -1,710 | -1,710 | -1,200 | -4,200 | -14 | -2,499 | 1,445 | -4,322 | -13,927 | |
| 18 | -1,499 | -850 | -1,383 | -1,713 | -1,740 | -1,740 | -1,710 | -4,350 | -15 | -2,927 | 2,585 | -4,816 | -19,882 | |
| 19 | -1,539 | -949 | -1,540 | -1,780 | -1,770 | -1,770 | -1,770 | -4,200 | -15 | -3,479 | 2,585 | -4,604 | -19,719 | |
| 20 | -1,565 | -967 | -1,565 | -1,817 | -1,800 | -1,800 | -1,800 | -4,350 | -15 | -3,638 | 1,335 | -4,710 | -22,201 | |
| 21 | -1,598 | -987 | -1,598 | -1,854 | -1,860 | -1,860 | -1,860 | -4,500 | -16 | -3,711 | 1,335 | -4,816 | -22,892 | |
| 22 | -1,630 | -1,007 | -1,628 | -1,860 | -1,860 | -1,860 | -1,860 | -4,500 | -16 | -3,797 | 1,335 | -4,886 | -23,563 | |
| 23 | -1,666 | -1,028 | -1,854 | -1,894 | -1,920 | -1,920 | -1,920 | -1,650 | -16 | -3,871 | 1,335 | -5,010 | -24,219 | |
| DAILY TOTAL | -39,918 | -23,029 | -40,066 | -46,432 | -34,680 | -34,770 | -43,140 | 53,100 | -383 | -97,207 | 20,630 | -119,104 | -404,999 | |

## MINNEAPOLIS BALANCED HOUSE — JULY 21

| HRS | WOOD FRAME E 234 | S 146 | W 234 | N 266 | SINGLE GLASS E 30 | W 30 | N 30 | DOUBLE GLASS S 150 | DOOR | ROOF | HEAT GET INDOORS | INFIL-TRATION HOURLY | TOTAL | BTU DAY |
|---|---|---|---|---|---|---|---|---|---|---|---|---|---|---|
| 0 | -52 | -34 | -53 | -63 | -210 | -180 | -210 | -450 | -1 | 176 | 585 | -529 | -1,021 | |
| 1 | -103 | -67 | -105 | -125 | -270 | -240 | -270 | -600 | -1 | 95 | 585 | -706 | -1,807 | |
| 2 | -154 | -100 | -158 | -187 | -330 | -300 | -330 | -900 | -2 | 14 | 585 | -882 | -2,744 | |
| 3 | -204 | -134 | -210 | -250 | -380 | -330 | -330 | -900 | -2 | -73 | 585 | -918 | -3,116 | |
| 4 | -252 | -167 | -261 | -312 | -360 | -330 | -360 | -750 | -2 | -154 | 585 | -935 | -3,448 | |
| 5 | -264 | -174 | -278 | -324 | -60 | -150 | -270 | -750 | -2 | -235 | 585 | -918 | -3,170 | |
| 6 | -269 | -177 | -278 | -330 | -270 | -180 | -150 | -450 | -2 | -250 | 585 | -847 | -1,358 | |
| 7 | -255 | -170 | -315 | -277 | -60 | 90 | -30 | -150 | -2 | -191 | 795 | -706 | -160 | |
| 8 | -217 | -150 | -241 | -218 | 180 | 60 | 90 | 450 | -1 | -257 | 1,585 | -441 | 1,206 | |
| 9 | -164 | -119 | -192 | -277 | 360 | 180 | 240 | 750 | -1 | 125 | 795 | -159 | 2,197 | |
| 10 | -85 | -64 | -107 | -121 | 420 | 330 | 360 | 1,350 | 0 | 622 | 195 | 88 | 3,418 | |
| 11 | -4 | -9 | -18 | -19 | 450 | 450 | 480 | 1,800 | -1 | 1,161 | 195 | 353 | 5,200 | |
| 12 | 64 | 41 | 57 | 71 | 570 | 540 | 540 | 2,100 | 1 | 1,690 | 195 | 565 | 6,584 | |
| 13 | 137 | 93 | 139 | 164 | 600 | 600 | 630 | 2,400 | 2 | 2,109 | 195 | 706 | 7,745 | |
| 14 | 195 | 133 | 204 | 239 | 600 | 660 | 600 | 2,400 | 2 | 2,396 | 195 | 794 | 8,448 | |
| 15 | 233 | 151 | 248 | 289 | 570 | 690 | 570 | 2,250 | 2 | 2,565 | 195 | 794 | 8,587 | |
| 16 | 256 | 174 | 277 | 320 | 540 | 690 | 570 | 1,950 | 2 | 2,558 | 195 | 759 | 8,291 | |
| 17 | 253 | 171 | 280 | 317 | 420 | 570 | 480 | 1,650 | 2 | 2,440 | 1,445 | 667 | 8,695 | |
| 18 | 238 | 162 | 269 | 301 | 330 | 420 | 390 | 1,200 | 2 | 2,131 | 2,585 | 494 | 8,522 | |
| 19 | 193 | 131 | 224 | 248 | 180 | 180 | 210 | 450 | 1 | 1,720 | 1,335 | 176 | 5,225 | |
| 20 | 150 | 103 | 175 | 187 | 60 | 60 | 60 | 150 | 1 | 1,220 | 1,335 | 0 | 3,677 | |
| 21 | 102 | 69 | 115 | 134 | 0 | 60 | 0 | 0 | 1 | 757 | 1,335 | 0 | 2,512 | |
| 22 | 49 | 33 | 52 | 62 | -60 | -60 | -60 | -150 | 0 | 397 | 1,335 | 0 | 1,422 | |
| 23 | -2 | -6 | -5 | -1 | -300 | -120 | -150 | -300 | -1 | 257 | 1,335 | -176 | 363 | |
| DAILY TOTAL | -155 | -105 | -132 | -210 | 3,280 | 3,390 | 3,090 | 16,050 | -2 | 21,953 | 20,630 | -1,881 | 65,269 | |

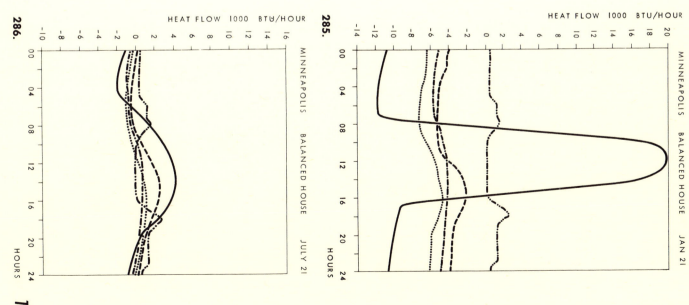

285. MINNEAPOLIS BALANCED HOUSE JAN 21 — HEAT FLOW 1000 BTU/HOUR vs HOURS

286. MINNEAPOLIS BALANCED HOUSE JULY 21 — HEAT FLOW 1000 BTU/HOUR vs HOURS

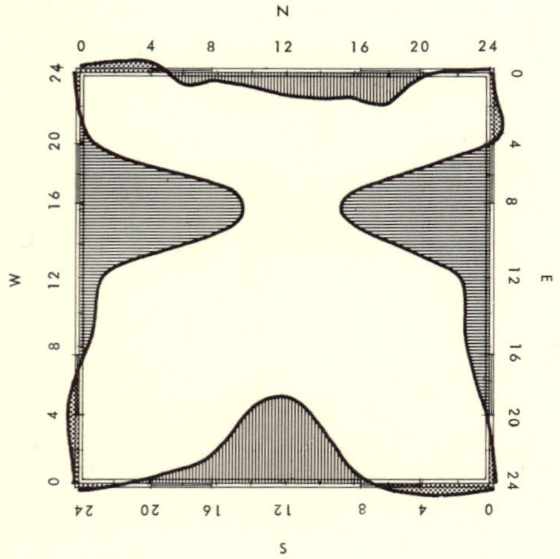

BALANCED HOUSE

WINTER

SUMMER

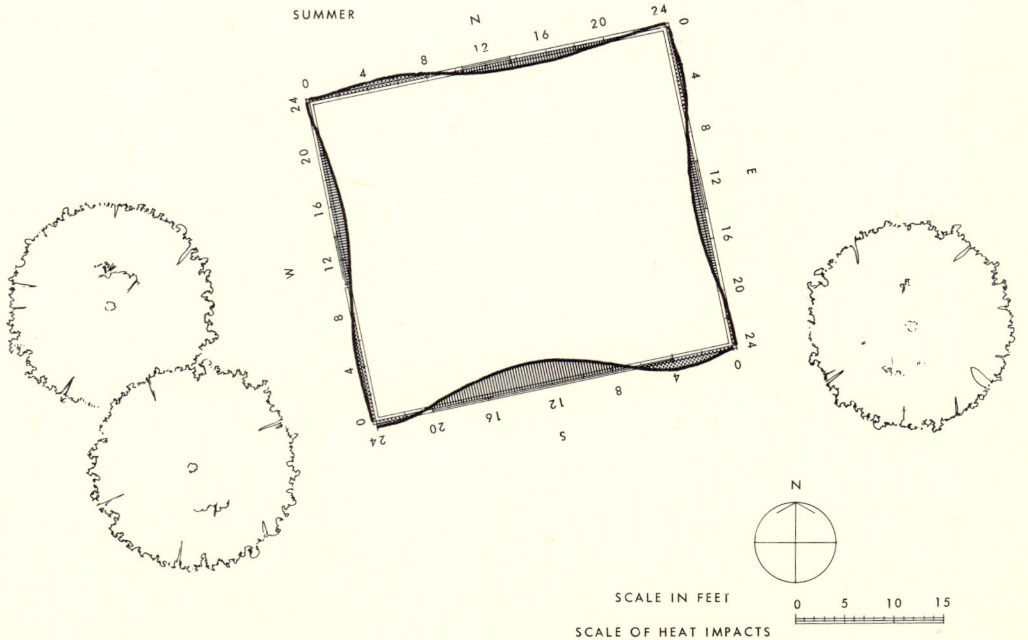

MINNEAPOLIS

ORTHODOX HOUSE

WINTER

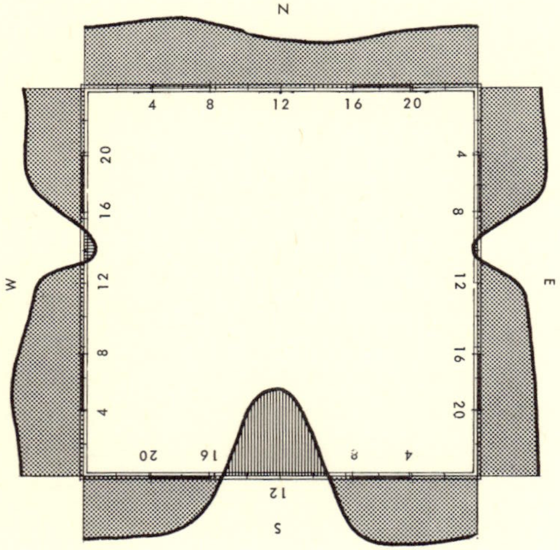

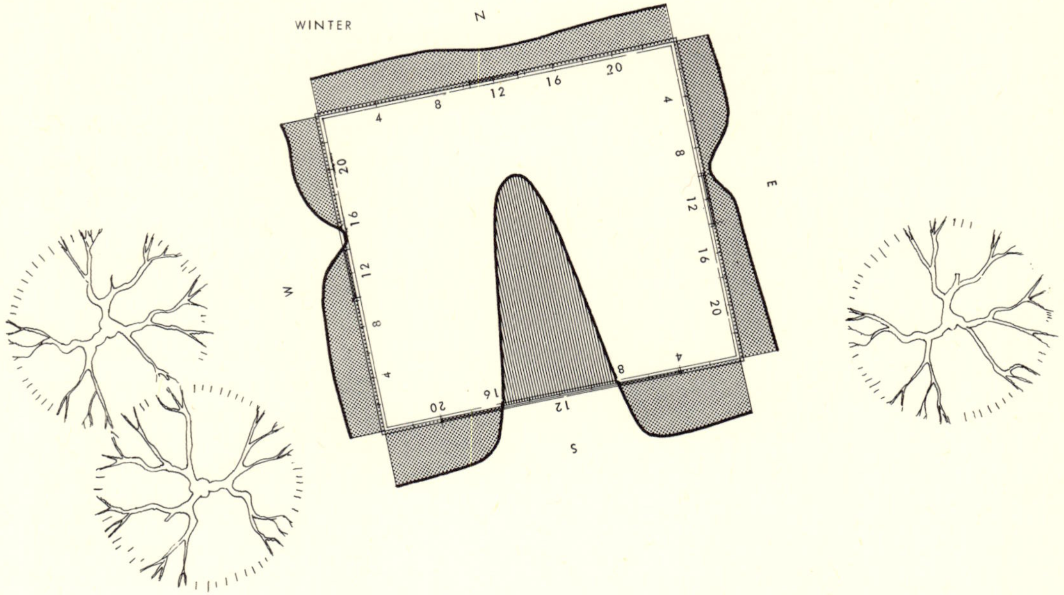

SUMMER

SCALE IN FEET

SCALE OF HEAT IMPACTS
IN 1000 BTU'S

N

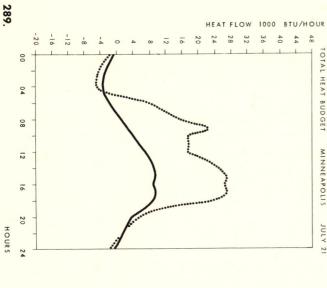

HEAT FLOW 1000 BTU/HOUR

TOTAL HEAT BUDGET     MINNEAPOLIS     JULY 21

HOURS

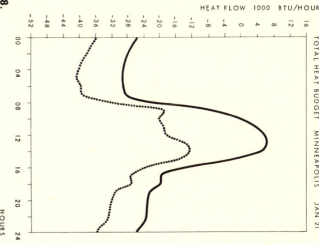

HEAT FLOW 1000 BTU/HOUR

TOTAL HEAT BUDGET     MINNEAPOLIS     JAN 21

HOURS

# HEAT ANALYSIS OF STRUCTURES IN COOL AREA

The heat budget of the orthodox house in Minneapolis, during winter indicates that the heat losses arise from the following sources: woodframe construction, east 5%, south 5%, west 5%, and north 5%; window areas, east 10%, south 2%, west 10%, north 12%; heat-loss through the roof 13%, through infiltration 33%. There is a 4% gain through the heat created indoors. In summertime the heat gain of the orthodox house results in terms of percentage from the following sources: wood-frame wall, east 1%, south 1%, west 1%; window area, east 25%, south 15%, west 25%, north 7%. The roof contributes 14% to heat gain; the heat created indoors amounts to 12%. There is a small loss of 1% through infiltration.

The arrangement of the balanced house was changed by orientation, overhangs and shading, ventilated roof construction, double-glazed south window, weather stripping, and ventilated appliances. The winter heat-loss breakdown in percentages is as follows: wood-frame wall, east 8%, south 5%, west 7%, north 10%; window areas, east 7%, west 7%, north 9%. Heat loss through the roof amounts to 21%, through infiltration 25%. An 11% heat gain comes through the 150 sq ft double-glazed south window, and the heat created indoors amounts to a 4% rise. In summertime the heat behavior of the wall surfaces is negligible. Window area at east supplies 5%, south 24%, west 5%, and north 5% of the total heat gain. The roof contributes 31%, and heat created indoors amounts to 30%. The daily infiltration total brings a loss of 3%.

A daily heat behavior comparison in Minneapolis between the orthodox and balanced structures is illustrated graphically both for winter and summer. The indications are the same as described for the New York example. Note the effect of solar impact in winter on the south side of the balanced house. In summer the reduction of heat load by the balanced house, as compared to the orthodox, is apparent.

On the daily total heatflow curves between the orthodox and balanced houses in wintertime, note that the balanced house has less heat loss throughout the day, and by solar energy utilization positive flow occurs in some daytime hours. The summer behavior of the same houses shows the peak heatload value of 26.420 Btu of the orthodox house reduced to 8.695 Btu peak impact by the arrangements of the balanced structure.

The improvements on a seasonal basis are the products of the following measures. In winter: orientation, and rearrangement of openings (+82.631 Btu gain) 12%; reduction in infiltration (+119.788 Btu) 17%; cut in convection through the glass area by using double glass (+100.950 Btu) 15%. The applied ventilation of appliances works negatively by 2%. Summed up, the total reduction of heat-loss by a balanced house is 42%.

In summer the applied measures improve the conditions of the orthodox house as follows: orientation, shape, and rearrangements of openings (−19.650 Btu) 8%; shading of glass surfaces (−141.330 Btu) 54%; roof alteration by light color and ventilation (−14.169 Btu) 5%; shading of wall surfaces (−9.573 Btu) 3%; ventilation of appliances (−10.900 Btu) 4%. The application of a double-pane south window and the reduction of infiltration do not amount to a practicable difference in the heat effects. The total reduction of heat gain is 75% as compared to the orthodox house.

On the basis of the seasonal data the yearly importance index is evaluated according to the heat-flow sums, duration of season (here for

## PHOENIX ORTHODOX HOUSE — JAN 21

| HRS | WOOD FRAME | | | | SINGLE GLASS | | | | ROOF | HEAT CPT INDOORS | INFILTRATION | HOURLY TOTALS |
|---|---|---|---|---|---|---|---|---|---|---|---|---|
| | E 220 | S 220 | W 220 | N 220 | E 60 | S 60 | W 60 | N 60 | 1,225 | | | |
| 0 | -528 | -506 | -528 | -550 | -1,500 | -1,500 | -1,500 | -1,500 | -1,470 | 585 | -3,972 | -12,969 |
| 1 | -572 | -550 | -572 | -594 | -1,620 | -1,620 | -1,620 | -1,620 | -1,470 | 585 | -4,234 | -13,887 |
| 2 | -594 | -594 | -594 | -638 | -1,680 | -1,680 | -1,680 | -1,680 | -1,593 | 585 | -4,410 | -14,558 |
| 3 | -638 | -616 | -638 | -660 | -1,740 | -1,740 | -1,740 | -1,740 | -1,715 | 585 | -4,604 | -15,246 |
| 4 | -660 | -660 | -660 | -682 | -1,860 | -1,860 | -1,860 | -1,860 | -1,838 | 585 | -4,762 | -16,117 |
| 5 | -682 | -682 | -704 | -726 | -1,920 | -1,920 | -1,920 | -1,920 | -1,838 | 585 | -4,904 | -16,631 |
| 6 | -704 | -704 | -726 | -748 | -1,920 | -1,920 | -1,920 | -1,960 | -1,960 | 1,585 | -5,010 | -15,947 |
| 7 | -726 | -726 | -748 | -770 | -780 | -1,440 | -1,920 | -1,860 | -1,838 | 1,585 | -5,116 | -14,584 |
| 8 | -748 | -748 | -748 | -770 | 5,280 | 2,520 | -1,560 | -1,440 | -2,083 | 2,585 | -5,010 | -2,722 |
| 9 | -682 | -682 | -770 | -792 | 6,480 | 6,420 | -960 | -960 | -2,083 | 6,195 | -4,358 | 7,808 |
| 10 | -220 | -330 | -704 | -726 | 5,100 | 5,100 | -420 | -600 | -2,083 | 195 | -3,492 | 5,840 |
| 11 | 22 | 44 | -594 | -616 | 360 | 9,120 | 360 | -180 | -1,593 | 195 | -2,576 | 8,142 |
| 12 | 22 | 352 | -462 | -484 | 420 | 11,280 | 2,580 | 180 | -735 | 195 | -1,976 | 9,632 |
| 13 | -44 | 616 | -330 | -352 | 360 | 11,820 | 6,000 | 240 | 245 | 195 | -1,534 | 13,436 |
| 14 | -220 | 726 | -220 | -264 | 360 | 11,400 | 7,800 | 300 | 980 | 195 | -1,182 | 16,695 |
| 15 | -176 | 770 | 110 | -198 | 60 | 10,020 | 6,780 | 360 | 1,348 | 195 | -952 | 17,357 |
| 16 | -154 | 682 | 352 | -154 | 60 | 4,020 | 6,780 | 60 | 1,348 | 195 | -1,006 | 12,183 |
| 17 | -132 | 528 | 506 | -132 | -420 | 4,440 | 720 | -360 | 1,225 | 2,695 | -1,218 | 7,852 |
| 18 | -154 | 242 | 352 | -154 | -660 | -660 | -660 | -660 | 490 | 4,085 | -1,782 | 439 |
| 19 | -220 | -132 | -132 | -220 | -960 | -960 | -960 | -960 | 0 | 1,585 | -2,416 | -5,375 |
| 20 | -308 | -286 | -308 | -396 | -1,080 | -1,080 | -1,080 | -1,080 | -613 | 1,585 | -2,822 | -7,380 |
| 21 | -396 | -374 | -396 | -396 | -1,200 | -1,200 | -1,200 | -1,200 | -858 | 1,585 | -3,210 | -8,845 |
| 22 | -440 | -418 | -440 | -462 | -1,380 | -1,380 | -1,380 | -1,380 | -1,103 | 1,585 | -3,458 | -10,256 |
| 23 | -506 | -484 | -506 | -528 | -1,440 | -1,440 | -1,440 | -1,440 | -1,225 | 1,585 | -3,722 | -11,146 |
| DAILY TOTAL | -9,460 | -4,532 | -9,460 | -11,924 | 420 | 58,380 | 420 | -23,220 | -20,707 | 31,530 | -77,726 | BTU DAY -66,279 |

## PHOENIX ORTHODOX HOUSE — JULY 21

| HRS | WOOD FRAME | | | | SINGLE GLASS | | | | ROOF | HEAT CPT INDOORS | INFILTRATION | HOURLY TOTALS |
|---|---|---|---|---|---|---|---|---|---|---|---|---|
| | E 220 | S 220 | W 220 | N 220 | E 60 | S 60 | W 60 | N 60 | 1,225 | | | |
| 0 | 528 | 506 | 528 | 484 | 900 | 900 | 900 | 900 | 1,960 | 585 | 2,310 | 10,501 |
| 1 | 484 | 440 | 462 | 440 | 720 | 720 | 720 | 720 | 1,837 | 585 | 2,000 | 9,728 |
| 2 | 440 | 396 | 440 | 396 | 600 | 600 | 600 | 600 | 1,715 | 585 | 1,745 | 8,117 |
| 3 | 396 | 352 | 396 | 352 | 540 | 540 | 540 | 540 | 1,592 | 585 | 1,552 | 7,385 |
| 4 | 374 | 330 | 352 | 308 | 540 | 540 | 540 | 540 | 1,470 | 585 | 1,321 | 6,900 |
| 5 | 352 | 286 | 330 | 286 | 480 | 480 | 480 | 480 | 1,347 | 585 | 1,145 | 6,251 |
| 6 | 308 | 264 | 286 | 242 | 7,740 | 840 | 780 | 2,340 | 1,225 | 1,585 | 1,004 | 16,614 |
| 7 | 286 | 242 | 264 | 220 | 12,120 | 1,980 | 1,260 | 2,340 | 1,102 | 1,585 | 1,535 | 22,394 |
| 8 | 594 | 242 | 286 | 418 | 13,500 | 1,980 | 1,800 | 2,400 | 1,102 | 2,585 | 2,327 | 26,994 |
| 9 | 1,254 | 352 | 352 | 506 | 12,420 | 2,580 | 2,220 | 2,400 | 1,347 | 6,195 | 3,000 | 35,648 |
| 10 | 1,408 | 506 | 506 | 528 | 9,420 | 3,540 | 2,640 | 2,700 | 2,450 | 195 | 3,525 | 27,418 |
| 11 | 1,430 | 682 | 616 | 594 | 5,880 | 3,000 | 3,060 | 3,060 | 3,675 | 195 | 4,060 | 27,872 |
| 12 | 1,298 | 880 | 704 | 682 | 3,300 | 5,340 | 3,180 | 3,120 | 5,390 | 195 | 4,495 | 27,909 |
| 13 | 1,100 | 1,012 | 792 | 770 | 3,300 | 4,860 | 6,120 | 3,300 | 5,390 | 195 | 4,830 | 31,669 |
| 14 | 858 | 1,078 | 858 | 836 | 3,300 | 4,200 | 10,080 | 3,360 | 6,002 | 195 | 5,115 | 35,882 |
| 15 | 902 | 1,122 | 1,210 | 880 | 3,180 | 3,540 | 13,380 | 3,360 | 6,247 | 195 | 5,340 | 39,356 |
| 16 | 924 | 1,100 | 1,540 | 924 | 2,940 | 3,180 | 14,640 | 3,120 | 6,247 | 195 | 5,355 | 40,105 |
| 17 | 946 | 1,012 | 1,782 | 946 | 2,820 | 2,820 | 13,500 | 2,880 | 6,002 | 2,695 | 5,290 | 40,513 |
| 18 | 946 | 946 | 1,848 | 990 | 2,280 | 2,340 | 9,240 | 2,460 | 5,512 | 4,085 | 5,040 | 35,687 |
| 19 | 902 | 902 | 1,804 | 1,056 | 1,800 | 1,800 | 1,800 | 1,800 | 4,777 | 1,585 | 4,600 | 22,826 |
| 20 | 836 | 814 | 1,386 | 1,012 | 1,500 | 1,500 | 1,500 | 1,500 | 3,920 | 1,585 | 3,918 | 19,171 |
| 21 | 748 | 726 | 748 | 726 | 1,260 | 1,260 | 1,260 | 1,260 | 2,695 | 1,585 | 3,403 | 15,671 |
| 22 | 660 | 638 | 660 | 616 | 1,140 | 1,140 | 1,140 | 1,140 | 2,450 | 1,585 | 3,018 | 14,187 |
| 23 | 594 | 550 | 594 | 550 | 1,020 | 1,020 | 1,020 | 1,020 | 2,205 | 1,585 | 2,259 | 12,417 |
| DAILY TOTAL | 18,568 | 15,378 | 18,766 | 14,762 | 51,720 | 92,460 | 92,460 | 47,160 | 76,924 | 31,530 | 78,787 | BTU DAY 538,515 |

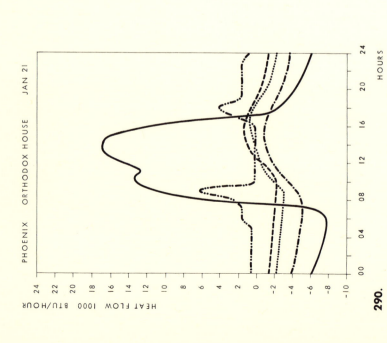

PHOENIX ORTHODOX HOUSE JAN 21

HEAT FLOW 1000 BTU/HOUR — HOURS

290.

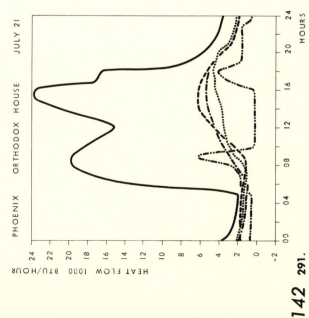

PHOENIX ORTHODOX HOUSE JULY 21

HEAT FLOW 1000 BTU/HOUR — HOURS

291.

## STONE MASONRY · SINGLE GLASS (Phoenix Balanced House — Jan 21)

| HRS | E 260 | S 218.4 | W 320 | N 297.4 | E 80 | S 120 | W 20 | N 21 | DOOR 21 | ROOF | HEAT INDOORS | INFILTRATION | HOURLY TOTALS | BTU DAY |
|---|---|---|---|---|---|---|---|---|---|---|---|---|---|---|
| 0 | -546 | -284 | -735 | -684 | -2,000 | -3,000 | -500 | -132 | -116 | -1,470 | 585 | -1,986 | -11,252 | 10,283 |
| 1 | -546 | -284 | -735 | -684 | -2,160 | -3,240 | -540 | -141 | -88 | -1,593 | 585 | -2,117 | -11,842 | 9,152 |
| 2 | -546 | -284 | -735 | -654 | -2,240 | -3,360 | -560 | -147 | -65 | -1,715 | 585 | -2,205 | -12,331 | 8,689 |
| 3 | -546 | -305 | -735 | -684 | -2,320 | -3,480 | -580 | -149 | -46 | -1,838 | 585 | -2,302 | -12,817 | 8,220 |
| 4 | -546 | -327 | -735 | -684 | -2,400 | -3,600 | -600 | -155 | -36 | -1,838 | 585 | -2,381 | -13,528 | 7,702 |
| 5 | -572 | -349 | -735 | -684 | -2,480 | -3,720 | -620 | -162 | -27 | -1,838 | 585 | -2,432 | -13,919 | 7,241 |
| 6 | -572 | -371 | -735 | -714 | -2,560 | -3,840 | -640 | -164 | -34 | -1,838 | 585 | -2,505 | -13,407 | 8,353 |
| 7 | -572 | -371 | -768 | -714 | -2,560 | -3,840 | -640 | -176 | -72 | -1,960 | 795 | -2,558 | -11,117 | 10,415 |
| 8 | -572 | -371 | -768 | -744 | -2,040 | -2,880 | -620 | -172 | -88 | -2,083 | 1,585 | -2,505 | -5,452 | 12,476 |
| 9 | -598 | -371 | -768 | -744 | -1,040 | -2,049 | -480 | -146 | -145 | -2,083 | 2,585 | -2,179 | 5,452 | 13,277 |
| 10 | -598 | -393 | -800 | -773 | 480 | 12,830 | 80 | -116 | -170 | -2,083 | 2,585 | -767 | 14,680 | 13,953 |
| 11 | -598 | -393 | -800 | -773 | 480 | 18,300 | 100 | -59 | -179 | -2,083 | 1,585 | 0 | 18,377 | 15,402 |
| 12 | -598 | -393 | -800 | -773 | 560 | 20,030 | 860 | -36 | -176 | -1,960 | 245 | 940 | 20,054 | 16,523 |
| 13 | -598 | -393 | -800 | -773 | 2,880 | 22,840 | 2,000 | -46 | -172 | -2,083 | 195 | 1,225 | 20,136 | 17,127 |
| 14 | -598 | -415 | -832 | -803 | 6,800 | 23,650 | 2,600 | 80 | -146 | -2,083 | 195 | 1,348 | 21,390 | 17,635 |
| 15 | -598 | -415 | -832 | -803 | 8,640 | 2,040 | 2,260 | 120 | -116 | -988 | 195 | 1,348 | 20,584 | 17,816 |
| 16 | -598 | -415 | -832 | -803 | 7,040 | -880 | -560 | 20 | -145 | -735 | 195 | 980 | 17,073 | 17,553 |
| 17 | -598 | -415 | -832 | -803 | -560 | -1,322 | -480 | -27 | -82 | 0 | 195 | 585 | 8,825 | 18,403 |
| 18 | -598 | -415 | -832 | -803 | -1,280 | -1,920 | -620 | -36 | -46 | 1,335 | 195 | 585 | 979 | 18,717 |
| 19 | -572 | -415 | -800 | -773 | -1,440 | -2,160 | -560 | -46 | -34 | 1,335 | 195 | 585 | -3,172 | 15,966 |
| 20 | -572 | -371 | -800 | -773 | -1,600 | -2,400 | -360 | -59 | -88 | 1,335 | 195 | 585 | -6,325 | 14,755 |
| 21 | -546 | -305 | -768 | -684 | -1,840 | -2,760 | -400 | -101 | -103 | -858 | 195 | 585 | -8,380 | 13,717 |
| 22 | -546 | -327 | -768 | -684 | 80 | 2,260 | -460 | -116 | -124 | -1,605 | 195 | 585 | -8,436 | 12,659 |
| 23 | -546 | -284 | -735 | -684 | -2,000 | -2,880 | -480 | -124 | -103 | -1,729 | 1,335 | 585 | -9,436 | 11,577 |
| **DAILY TOTAL** | -13,806 | -8,577 | -18,745 | -17,726 | 560 | 110,127 | -7,740 | -2,685 | -20,727 | -20,727 | 20,630 | -38,863 | 2,548 | |

## STONE WALL · STONE WALL IN GARDEN · SINGLE GLASS IN GARDEN · SINGLE GLASS (Phoenix Balanced House — July 21)

| HRS | E 260 | S 218.4 | W 260 | N 297.4 | W 60 | E 80 | W 120 | S 80 | W 20 | W 20 | N 20 | DOOR 21 | ROOF | HEAT OFF INDOORS | INFILTRATION | HOURLY TOTALS | BTU DAY |
|---|---|---|---|---|---|---|---|---|---|---|---|---|---|---|---|---|---|
| 0 | 728 | 633 | 754 | 862 | 156 | 156 | 1,200 | 1,800 | 300 | 300 | 21 | 1,225 | 1,225 | 585 | 1,155 | 10,283 | |
| 1 | 728 | 633 | 754 | 862 | 156 | 156 | 960 | 1,440 | 240 | 240 | 21 | 1,470 | 1,470 | 585 | 1,000 | 9,152 | |
| 2 | 728 | 633 | 754 | 892 | 156 | 156 | 880 | 1,320 | 220 | 200 | 74 | 1,348 | 1,348 | 585 | 873 | 8,689 | |
| 3 | 754 | 633 | 754 | 892 | 156 | 156 | 800 | 1,200 | 200 | 180 | 65 | 1,225 | 1,225 | 585 | 776 | 8,220 | |
| 4 | 754 | 633 | 754 | 862 | 156 | 156 | 720 | 1,080 | 180 | 160 | 59 | 1,103 | 1,103 | 585 | 662 | 7,702 | |
| 5 | 728 | 612 | 754 | 862 | 156 | 156 | 640 | 960 | 160 | 160 | 50 | 585 | 585 | 585 | 573 | 7,241 | |
| 6 | 728 | 612 | 728 | 833 | 150 | 150 | 960 | 1,080 | 300 | 240 | 44 | 1,335 | 1,335 | 585 | 503 | 8,353 | |
| 7 | 728 | 612 | 728 | 833 | 150 | 150 | 1,680 | 1,920 | 480 | 360 | 44 | 958 | 958 | 1,335 | 767 | 10,415 | |
| 8 | 702 | 590 | 702 | 803 | 150 | 150 | 2,240 | 2,760 | 520 | 480 | 65 | 735 | 735 | 1,585 | 1,164 | 12,476 | |
| 9 | 702 | 590 | 702 | 803 | 150 | 150 | 2,480 | 3,360 | 620 | 600 | 95 | 799 | 799 | 1,585 | 1,500 | 13,277 | |
| 10 | 702 | 568 | 702 | 773 | 144 | 144 | 2,720 | 3,840 | 680 | 680 | 120 | 1,103 | 1,103 | 195 | 1,764 | 13,953 | |
| 11 | 702 | 568 | 773 | 773 | 144 | 144 | 3,040 | 4,320 | 760 | 800 | 139 | 1,470 | 1,470 | 195 | 2,029 | 15,402 | |
| 12 | 702 | 568 | 773 | 892 | 144 | 144 | 3,040 | 4,680 | 800 | 840 | 155 | 1,715 | 1,715 | 195 | 2,249 | 16,523 | |
| 13 | 702 | 568 | 773 | 862 | 144 | 144 | 3,040 | 4,800 | 800 | 880 | 172 | 1,960 | 1,960 | 195 | 2,417 | 17,127 | |
| 14 | 702 | 568 | 676 | 862 | 144 | 144 | 3,120 | 4,800 | 840 | 900 | 183 | 2,205 | 2,205 | 195 | 2,558 | 17,635 | |
| 15 | 676 | 568 | 676 | 833 | 156 | 150 | 960 | 4,800 | 860 | 920 | 193 | 2,328 | 2,328 | 195 | 2,672 | 17,816 | |
| 16 | 676 | 546 | 676 | 833 | 156 | 150 | 640 | 4,560 | 860 | 860 | 193 | 2,450 | 2,450 | 195 | 2,672 | 17,553 | |
| 17 | 676 | 546 | 676 | 744 | 144 | 144 | 1,080 | 4,320 | 820 | 820 | 199 | 2,573 | 2,573 | 197 | 2,681 | 18,403 | |
| 18 | 676 | 546 | 744 | 744 | 138 | 144 | 2,800 | 3,960 | 740 | 740 | 199 | 2,573 | 2,573 | 1,445 | 2,646 | 18,717 | |
| 19 | 702 | 568 | 702 | 773 | 144 | 144 | 2,960 | 3,240 | 540 | 540 | 193 | 2,695 | 2,695 | 1,335 | 2,302 | 15,966 | |
| 20 | 702 | 590 | 702 | 803 | 150 | 144 | 2,560 | 2,880 | 480 | 500 | 162 | 2,573 | 2,573 | 1,335 | 1,958 | 14,755 | |
| 21 | 728 | 612 | 702 | 833 | 150 | 156 | 2,160 | 2,520 | 420 | 420 | 139 | 2,450 | 2,450 | 1,335 | 1,702 | 13,717 | |
| 22 | 728 | 612 | 728 | 862 | 156 | 150 | 1,920 | 2,280 | 380 | 380 | 122 | 2,083 | 2,083 | 1,335 | 1,508 | 12,659 | |
| 23 | 728 | 612 | 728 | 862 | 156 | 156 | 1,360 | 2,040 | 340 | 340 | 109 | 1,838 | 1,838 | 1,335 | 1,129 | 11,577 | |
| **DAILY TOTAL** | 17,108 | 14,308 | 17,134 | 19,449 | 3,576 | 150 | 47,360 | 69,960 | 11,840 | 12,620 | 2,943 | 41,510 | 20,632 | 39,111 | | 317,551 |

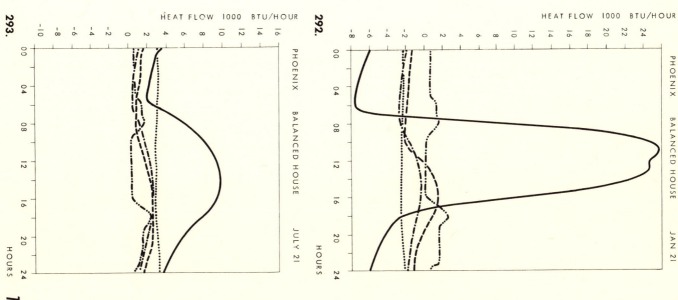

**292.**
HEAT FLOW 1000 BTU/HOUR
PHOENIX BALANCED HOUSE JAN 21
HOURS

**293.**
HEAT FLOW 1000 BTU/HOUR
PHOENIX BALANCED HOUSE JULY 21
HOURS

143

PHOENIX

ORTHODOX HOUSE

WINTER

SUMMER

BALANCED HOUSE

WINTER

SUMMER

SCALE IN FEET

SCALE OF HEAT IMPACTS
IN 1000 BTU'S

294.

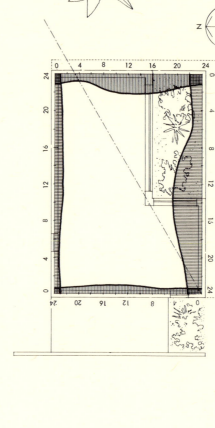

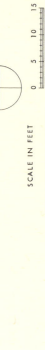

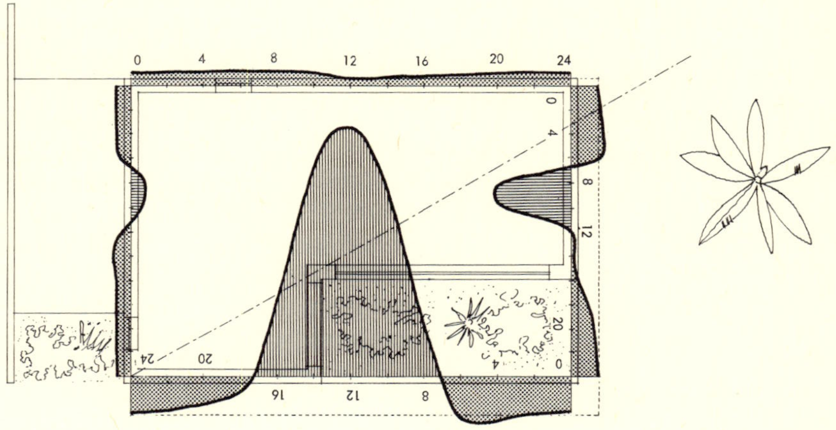

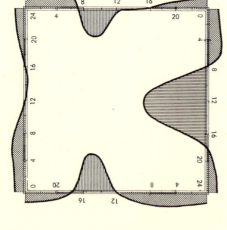

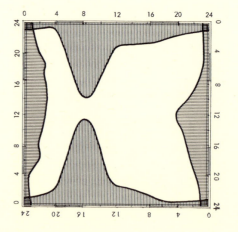

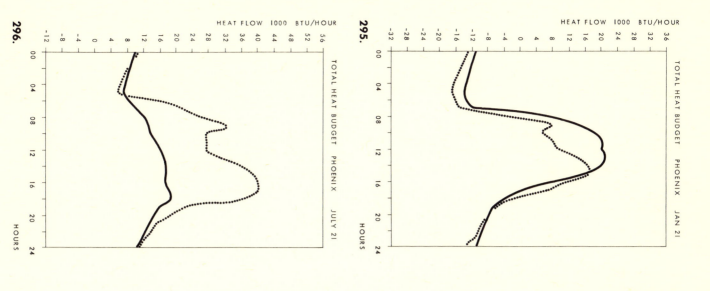

## HEAT ANALYSIS OF STRUCTURES IN HOT-ARID AREA

In Phoenix, Arizona the heat losses for the orthodox house arise in winter from the following sources in terms of percentage: woodframe wall, east 6%, south 3%, west 6%, north 8%. Window areas at east and west bring negligible amounts of heat gain, south counteracts the total loss with a 37% positive gain; north loses 15%. Heat loss through the roof is 13%, through infiltration 49%. The heat created indoors amounts to 20%. In summertime the heat gains of the orthodox house result from the following sources: woodframe construction, east 3%, south 3%, west 4%, north 3%; window area, east 17%, south 10%, west 17%, and north 9%. Transmission through roof contributes 14%, infiltration amounts to 14%, and heat created indoors adds 6% to the total.

The arrangement of the balanced house was changed by orientation, overhangs and shading, masonry walls, ventilated roof construction, weather stripping, ventilated appliances, and by surrounding some of the house with cooling garden plants. The winter heat-loss breakdown in percentages is as follows: woodframe walls, east 11%, south 7%, west 14%, north 14%. Window areas east and west bring small, negligible gain, north loses 6%. Heat loss through the roof amounts to 16%, through infiltration 30%, through the door 2%. A heat gain of 86% of the total loss is supplied by the south window, and the heat created indoors adds 16%. In summer the east wall brings 5%, south 5%, west 6%, and north 6% heat gain. Window areas on the east account for: 15%, south 22%, west 4%, north 4%, of the total incoming heat. Heat gain through the roof amounts to 13%, through infiltration 12%, through door 1%, heat created indoors 7%.

The daily heat behavior comparison between orthodox and balanced structures in Phoenix is illustrated in plan view for winter and summertime. Note that on the plan of the balanced house the arrangement of openings (east 80, south 120, west 20, and north 20 sq ft area) takes care of sol-air orientation. The schematically indicated gardens lower temperature loads (here conservatively taken as −5° F at peak values). A carport shades the west wall. Note solar heat gain in wintertime, and the amount of heat load in summer reduced by the balanced house.

In the comparison of the daily total heat-flow curves between the orthodox and balanced houses in wintertime, note that the balanced house has less loss through most of the day, and that the solar gain is balanced around the noon axis. Peak heat gain is 20.584 Btu, while the peak gain of the orthodox house is 17.357 Btu. The summer behavior of the orthodox house is 17.357 Btu. The summer behavior of the orthodox house (40.513 Btu) reduced to 17.794 Btu by the arrangements of the balanced structure.

On a seasonal basis the improvements in underheated period 75%, for overheated season 25% of the year), and stress coefficient. Accordingly the yearly importance for the applied measures show the following order: (1) reduction in infiltration 28%; (2) cut of heat loss by glass surfaces 24%, here applied in the double-window effect (note that the first two factors relate to the adverse cool temperature conditions; (3) orientation 22%; (4) shading of glass surfaces 22%; (5) alteration of roof accounts only for a small value of 2%; (6) similarly wall shade is of only 2% importance; (7) ventilation of appliances on a yearly basis show a negative value of 1%.

winter are the products of the following measures: orientation, shape, and rearrangement of openings (+58.951 Btu) brings a gain of 89% of the total loss. The applied masonry walls, because of larger surface and somewhat lower insulation value, shows a loss (−15.304 Btu) of 23%. However, the calculation method does not register its advantageous quality of internal heat absorbtion. A cut in infiltration conserves (+38.864 Btu) 58%. Ventilation of appliances causes a loss (−10.880 Btu) of 16%. Some of the above percentage figures may look high, as the original winter budget amount is quite low in this region, and the heat loss can be balanced in full under the given conditions.

In summer the measures applied to the balanced house improve on the conditions of the orthodox house as follows: Orientation (−9.820 Btu) shows little, 2%, reduction—however, this figure is somewhat misleading, as with other arrangement the effect could rise to (−85.000 Btu) 16%—shading of glass surfaces (−118.454 Btu) cuts the load by 22%. As wall surfaces became larger the heat transmission grew also (+12.760 Btu) to +2%, but this is counterbalanced by the applied masonry material (−4.172 Btu) and the microclimatic effects of the garden and wall shade (−15.310 Btu), totaling a 4% reduction. Reduction of infiltration amounts to (−39.393 Btu) 7%, alteration of the roof to (−35.514 Btu) 6%, ventilation of appliances (−10.880) to 2%. The total reduction of heat gain as compared to the orthodox house is 42%.

On the basis of the seasonal data the yearly importance index can be evaluated according to the heat-flow sums, stress coefficient, and duration of seasons (here taken as 37% for underheated, 63% for overheated period). Accordingly the applied measures show the following order: (1) shading of glass surfaces 46%, (2) reduction in infiltration 19%, (3) altered and ventilated roof construction 14%, (4) orientation 11% (however, this effect could account for 14%, with compensating discount from shading to 43%), (5) garden effect and wall shade 7%, (6) ventilation of appliances 6%, (7) masonry walls −6% (but the summation does not show the advantage gained by daily balance).

## HEAT ANALYSIS OF STRUCTURES IN HOT-HUMID AREA

In Miami, Florida, the percentage heat gains for the orthodox house arise in summer from the following sources: woodframe wall, east 3%, south 2%, west 3%, north 2%; window areas, east 20%, south 8%, west 20%, and north 9%. Heat gain through the roof amounts to 15%, through infiltration 9%, and by heat created indoors to 9%. In winter under the given conditions heat loss occurs only by infiltration.

The arrangement of the balanced house was changed by orientation, rearrangement of openings, building shape, ventilated roof construction, weather stripping, ventilated appliances, overhangs, and shading. In summer the heat gain breakdown is as follows: woodframe construction at each orientation accounts for 4%, for a total of 16%; glass areas at south gain 25%, at north 25%. The roof brings 10%, infiltration 11%, and heat created indoors amounts to 13% of the total. Winter heat loss is negligible, and is caused by infiltration.

Plan

East view

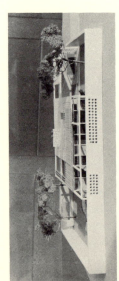

South view

**297.** Adaptation of principles in Phoenix area.

## WOOD FRAME / SINGLE GLASS / ROOF / HEAT GET INDOORS / INFILTRATION — JAN 21 (MIAMI ORTHODOX HOUSE)

| HRS | WOOD FRAME E 220 | S 220 | W 220 | N 220 | SINGLE GLASS E 60 | S 60 | W 60 | N 60 | ROOF | HEAT GET INDOORS | INFILTRATION | HOURLY TOTALS |
|---|---|---|---|---|---|---|---|---|---|---|---|---|
| 0 | -53 | -46 | -57 | -68 | -300 | -300 | -300 | -300 | 49 | 585 | -706 | -1,496 |
| 1 | -70 | -64 | -73 | -86 | -360 | -360 | -360 | -360 | -24 | 585 | -882 | -2,054 |
| 2 | -88 | -84 | -92 | -106 | -420 | -420 | -420 | -420 | -74 | 585 | -1,058 | -2,597 |
| 3 | -112 | -108 | -118 | -132 | -480 | -480 | -480 | -480 | -122 | 585 | -1,234 | -3,161 |
| 4 | -136 | -134 | -143 | -160 | -540 | -540 | -540 | -540 | -196 | 585 | -1,324 | -3,668 |
| 5 | -161 | -158 | -167 | -185 | -540 | -540 | -540 | -540 | -257 | 585 | -1,446 | -3,949 |
| 6 | -172 | -147 | -178 | -196 | -600 | -540 | -600 | -600 | -331 | 585 | -1,500 | -3,339 |
| 7 | -189 | -189 | -195 | -185 | -540 | -840 | -540 | -540 | -367 | 585 | -1,412 | -3,668 |
| 8 | -196 | -196 | -205 | -216 | -600 | 840 | -600 | -600 | -416 | 585 | -1,597 | -3,949 |
| 9 | -64 | -121 | -185 | -222 | -180 | 4,740 | -180 | -240 | -429 | 585 | -670 | 1,597 |
| 10 | 220 | 118 | -125 | -205 | 600 | 10,620 | 600 | 360 | -270 | 195 | -176 | 3,709 |
| 11 | 343 | 323 | -46 | -143 | 960 | 11,700 | 960 | 960 | 551 | 195 | 246 | 8,063 |
| 12 | 338 | 482 | 18 | -59 | 1,560 | 12,000 | 1,380 | 1,380 | 1,458 | 195 | 706 | 12,818 |
| 13 | 275 | 596 | 97 | 18 | 1,560 | 11,700 | 3,900 | 2,766 | 2,766 | 195 | 846 | 19,073 |
| 14 | 160 | 671 | 165 | 84 | 1,500 | 10,620 | 7,500 | 2,878 | 2,878 | 195 | 934 | 19,730 |
| 15 | 187 | 690 | 370 | 127 | 1,380 | 8,460 | 9,540 | 3,148 | 3,148 | 195 | 934 | 22,927 |
| 16 | 182 | 642 | 500 | 160 | 1,140 | 5,460 | 8,460 | 3,136 | 3,136 | 195 | 846 | 26,035 |
| 17 | 160 | 541 | 642 | 178 | 900 | 3,180 | 5,460 | 2,707 | 2,707 | 195 | 706 | 25,899 |
| 18 | 129 | 382 | 565 | 185 | 360 | 1,560 | 3,180 | 2,045 | 2,045 | 4,085 | 530 | 21,859 |
| 19 | 85 | 156 | 497 | 180 | 120 | 120 | 1,620 | 1,274 | 1,274 | 2,695 | 318 | 17,859 |
| 20 | 48 | 97 | 382 | 185 | 60 | 120 | 840 | 478 | 478 | 195 | 88 | 12,818 |
| 21 | 18 | 33 | 202 | 189 | 60 | 60 | 660 | 270 | 270 | 1,585 | -88 | 8,063 |
| 22 | -4 | -46 | 84 | 198 | -120 | -120 | -120 | 184 | 184 | 1,585 | -264 | 3,709 |
| 23 | -29 | -125 | 33 | 211 | -180 | -180 | -180 | 123 | 123 | 1,585 | -442 | 1,597 |
| DAILY TOTAL | 871 | 3,431 | 875 | -804 | 33,660 | 80,700 | 33,300 | 5,040 | 18,081 | 31,530 | -7,604 | 199,080 BTU DAY |

## WOOD FRAME / SINGLE GLASS / ROOF / HEAT GET INDOORS / INFILTRATION — JULY 21 (MIAMI ORTHODOX HOUSE)

| HRS | WOOD FRAME E 220 | S 220 | W 220 | N 220 | SINGLE GLASS E 60 | S 60 | W 60 | N 60 | ROOF | HEAT GET INDOORS | INFILTRATION | HOURLY TOTALS |
|---|---|---|---|---|---|---|---|---|---|---|---|---|
| 0 | 216 | 196 | 211 | 198 | 480 | 480 | 480 | 480 | 1,225 | 1,585 | 1,146 | 5,489 |
| 1 | 209 | 189 | 205 | 189 | 420 | 420 | 420 | 420 | 1,017 | 1,585 | 1,094 | 5,119 |
| 2 | 205 | 185 | 198 | 185 | 420 | 420 | 420 | 420 | 968 | 1,585 | 1,058 | 5,039 |
| 3 | 200 | 178 | 194 | 180 | 420 | 420 | 420 | 420 | 943 | 1,585 | 1,058 | 4,842 |
| 4 | 178 | 194 | 194 | 185 | 480 | 420 | 480 | 420 | 907 | 1,585 | 918 | 4,879 |
| 5 | 185 | 185 | 198 | 185 | 360 | 420 | 420 | 480 | 894 | 585 | 918 | 4,978 |
| 6 | 185 | 185 | 198 | 180 | 360 | 900 | 660 | 2,160 | 882 | 585 | 1,058 | 4,978 |
| 7 | 180 | 178 | 194 | 185 | 1,320 | 1,440 | 840 | 2,940 | 858 | 585 | 1,094 | 15,500 |
| 8 | 185 | 185 | 198 | 180 | 1,560 | 1,740 | 1,440 | 2,160 | 858 | 585 | 1,058 | 22,151 |
| 9 | 189 | 189 | 205 | 185 | 1,680 | 1,920 | 1,620 | 2,160 | 943 | 918 | 1,058 | 24,977 |
| 10 | 198 | 198 | 306 | 185 | 1,920 | 1,980 | 1,910 | 1,980 | 968 | 918 | 918 | 27,713 |
| 11 | 207 | 220 | 326 | 180 | 1,920 | 1,980 | 1,980 | 1,980 | 1,017 | 1,058 | 918 | 19,745 |
| 12 | 244 | 244 | 306 | 185 | 2,040 | 2,220 | 2,040 | 2,040 | 1,151 | 1,058 | 1,446 | 17,402 |
| 13 | 275 | 275 | 334 | 189 | 2,040 | 2,160 | 2,040 | 1,980 | 2,070 | 1,694 | 1,200 | 15,684 |
| 14 | 279 | 279 | 350 | 196 | 2,040 | 2,220 | 2,040 | 1,990 | 3,025 | 1,764 | 1,094 | 19,086 |
| 15 | 279 | 279 | 334 | 211 | 2,740 | 2,160 | 4,740 | 2,340 | 3,871 | 1,798 | 1,058 | 23,760 |
| 16 | 301 | 301 | 337 | 220 | 4,740 | 1,800 | 11,700 | 2,760 | 4,544 | 1,834 | 918 | 25,556 |
| 17 | 334 | 319 | 378 | 235 | 8,520 | 1,620 | 13,140 | 2,100 | 4,949 | 1,798 | 918 | 27,880 |
| 18 | 396 | 337 | 493 | 246 | 11,820 | 1,440 | 11,910 | 1,980 | 5,120 | 1,834 | 1,306 | 28,606 |
| 19 | 409 | 352 | 862 | 257 | 1,560 | 1,740 | 11,880 | 1,980 | 4,986 | 1,798 | 1,412 | 28,386 |
| 20 | 372 | 370 | 832 | 257 | 1,680 | 1,920 | 660 | 1,980 | 4,630 | 1,738 | 1,552 | 22,586 |
| 21 | 367 | 365 | 713 | 268 | 1,920 | 1,980 | 660 | 540 | 3,197 | 1,622 | 1,482 | 9,785 |
| 22 | 528 | 548 | 372 | 255 | 1,980 | 540 | 540 | 540 | 2,278 | 1,585 | 1,552 | 8,514 |
| 23 | 667 | 396 | 334 | 246 | 540 | 540 | 540 | 540 | 1,360 | 1,585 | 1,412 | 7,487 |
| DAILY TOTAL | 8,910 | 6,505 | 8,912 | 7,267 | 73,620 | 27,060 | 73,620 | 33,900 | 55,503 | 31,530 | 33,840 | 360,667 BTU DAY |

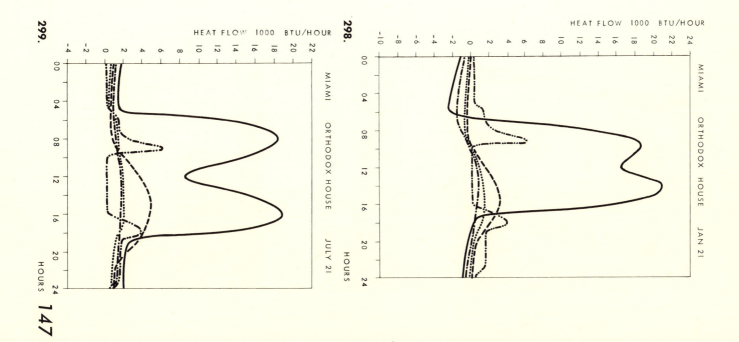

HEAT FLOW 1000 BTU/HOUR — MIAMI ORTHODOX HOUSE JAN 21

HEAT FLOW 1000 BTU/HOUR — MIAMI ORTHODOX HOUSE JULY 21

HOURS

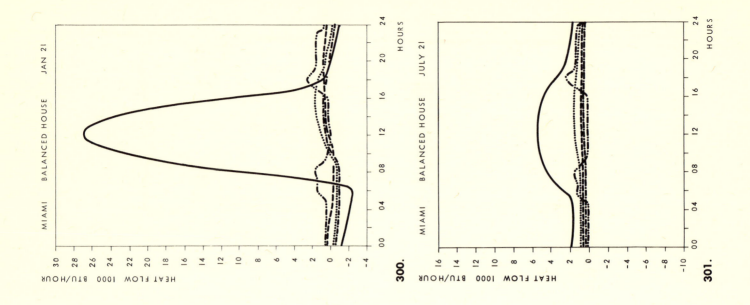

**300.** MIAMI BALANCED HOUSE JAN 21 — HEAT FLOW 1000 BTU/HOUR vs HOURS

**301.** MIAMI BALANCED HOUSE JULY 21 — HEAT FLOW 1000 BTU/HOUR vs HOURS

### JAN 21

| HRS | WOOD FRAME E 208 | S 257 | W 208 | N 257 | SINGLE GLASS E 0 | S 120 | W 0 | N 120 | ROOF 1,225 | HEAT GRT INDOORS | INFILTRATION | HOURLY TOTALS |
|---|---|---|---|---|---|---|---|---|---|---|---|---|
| 0 | -50 | -54 | -54 | -79 | | -600 | | -600 | 184 | 585 | -353 | -1,021 |
| 1 | -67 | -74 | -69 | -100 | | -720 | | -720 | 110 | 585 | -441 | -1,496 |
| 2 | -83 | -98 | -87 | -123 | | -840 | | -840 | 61 | 585 | -529 | -1,954 |
| 3 | -106 | -126 | -112 | -154 | | -960 | | -960 | 12 | 585 | -617 | -2,438 |
| 4 | -129 | -157 | -135 | -188 | | -1,080 | | -1,080 | -61 | 585 | -662 | -2,907 |
| 5 | -152 | -185 | -158 | -216 | | -1,080 | | -1,080 | -123 | 585 | -723 | -3,132 |
| 6 | -162 | -172 | -168 | -229 | | -1,200 | | -1,200 | -196 | 1,335 | -750 | -2,742 |
| 7 | -178 | -221 | -185 | -252 | | 1,680 | | -720 | -233 | 1,335 | -706 | 580 |
| 8 | -185 | -229 | -193 | -259 | | 9,480 | | -480 | -282 | 1,585 | -573 | 8,864 |
| 9 | -60 | -141 | -175 | -239 | | 15,840 | | 1,200 | -306 | 795 | -335 | 16,579 |
| 10 | 208 | 139 | -118 | -167 | | 19,200 | | 1,920 | -270 | 195 | -88 | 21,019 |
| 11 | 324 | 378 | -44 | -69 | | 22,920 | | 2,280 | -159 | 195 | 132 | 25,957 |
| 12 | 320 | 563 | 31 | 20 | | 24,000 | | 2,760 | 25 | 195 | 353 | 28,267 |
| 13 | 259 | 696 | 92 | 97 | | 23,400 | | 2,760 | 208 | 195 | 467 | 28,174 |
| 14 | 152 | 784 | 156 | 177 | | 21,240 | | 2,760 | 380 | 195 | 467 | 26,311 |
| 15 | 177 | 807 | 350 | 215 | | 16,920 | | 2,280 | 551 | 195 | 423 | 21,918 |
| 16 | 173 | 750 | 479 | 208 | | 10,920 | | 1,920 | 649 | 195 | 353 | 15,647 |
| 17 | 152 | 632 | 535 | 187 | | 3,120 | | 720 | 649 | 1,445 | 265 | 7,705 |
| 18 | 123 | 447 | 470 | 149 | | 240 | | 240 | 612 | 2,585 | 159 | 5,025 |
| 19 | 81 | 182 | 191 | 92 | | 120 | | 120 | 551 | 1,585 | 44 | 2,716 |
| 20 | 46 | 72 | 48 | 49 | | -120 | | -120 | 490 | 1,335 | -44 | 1,756 |
| 21 | 16 | 36 | 17 | 10 | | -240 | | -240 | 404 | 1,335 | -132 | 1,206 |
| 22 | -4 | 5 | -6 | -18 | | -360 | | -360 | 319 | 1,335 | -221 | 690 |
| 23 | -27 | -23 | -29 | -49 | | -480 | | -480 | 245 | 1,335 | -282 | 210 |
| DAILY TOTAL | 828 | 4,011 | 836 | -938 | | 161,400 | | 10,080 | 3,820 | 20,630 | -3,793 | 196,874 BTU/DAY |

### JULY 21

| HRS | WOOD FRAME E 208 | S 257 | W 208 | N 257 | SINGLE GLASS E 0 | S 120 | W 0 | N 120 | ROOF 1,225 | HEAT GRT INDOORS | INFILTRATION | HOURLY TOTALS |
|---|---|---|---|---|---|---|---|---|---|---|---|---|
| 0 | 208 | 254 | 204 | 267 | | 960 | | 960 | 686 | 585 | 573 | 4,697 |
| 1 | 200 | 242 | 196 | 257 | | 840 | | 840 | 649 | 585 | 547 | 4,356 |
| 2 | 187 | 229 | 183 | 242 | | 840 | | 840 | 625 | 585 | 529 | 4,260 |
| 3 | 181 | 218 | 177 | 231 | | 840 | | 840 | 588 | 585 | 459 | 4,119 |
| 4 | 177 | 213 | 173 | 226 | | 840 | | 840 | 563 | 585 | 459 | 4,076 |
| 5 | 173 | 208 | 168 | 221 | | 840 | | 840 | 551 | 585 | 529 | 4,115 |
| 6 | 173 | 208 | 164 | 221 | | 1,200 | | 1,320 | 539 | 1,335 | 547 | 5,711 |
| 7 | 177 | 213 | 173 | 226 | | 1,800 | | 1,920 | 539 | 1,335 | 600 | 6,983 |
| 8 | 196 | 229 | 185 | 244 | | 2,160 | | 2,280 | 551 | 1,585 | 661 | 8,089 |
| 9 | 227 | 260 | 208 | 275 | | 2,400 | | 2,400 | 564 | 795 | 723 | 7,852 |
| 10 | 245 | 290 | 227 | 306 | | 2,520 | | 2,520 | 600 | 195 | 794 | 7,697 |
| 11 | 266 | 314 | 248 | 332 | | 2,760 | | 2,640 | 649 | 195 | 847 | 8,251 |
| 12 | 283 | 342 | 268 | 357 | | 2,760 | | 2,760 | 698 | 195 | 882 | 8,545 |
| 13 | 291 | 360 | 285 | 378 | | 2,760 | | 2,760 | 759 | 195 | 899 | 8,567 |
| 14 | 297 | 375 | 295 | 388 | | 2,640 | | 2,640 | 797 | 195 | 917 | 8,544 |
| 15 | 299 | 378 | 304 | 396 | | 2,640 | | 2,640 | 880 | 195 | 899 | 8,571 |
| 16 | 302 | 383 | 310 | 401 | | 2,400 | | 2,520 | 845 | 195 | 882 | 8,238 |
| 17 | 295 | 373 | 310 | 391 | | 2,160 | | 2,280 | 857 | 1,445 | 864 | 8,975 |
| 18 | 287 | 362 | 302 | 365 | | 1,920 | | 1,680 | 845 | 2,585 | 811 | 9,175 |
| 19 | 279 | 347 | 291 | 365 | | 1,200 | | 1,200 | 845 | 1,335 | 776 | 6,638 |
| 20 | 254 | 316 | 260 | 334 | | 1,080 | | 1,080 | 809 | 1,335 | 741 | 6,209 |
| 21 | 239 | 296 | 237 | 311 | | 1,080 | | 1,080 | 772 | 1,335 | 706 | 6,056 |
| 22 | 231 | 283 | 227 | 298 | | 960 | | 960 | 747 | 1,335 | 653 | 5,694 |
| 23 | 223 | 272 | 218 | 285 | | 960 | | 960 | 711 | 1,335 | 617 | 5,581 |
| DAILY TOTAL | 5,689 | 6,965 | 5,617 | 7,335 | | 40,560 | | 40,680 | 16,603 | 20,630 | 16,920 | 160,999 BTU/DAY |

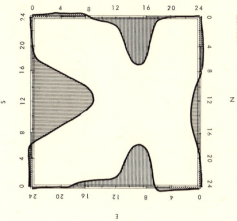

MIAMI

ORTHODOX HOUSE

SUMMER

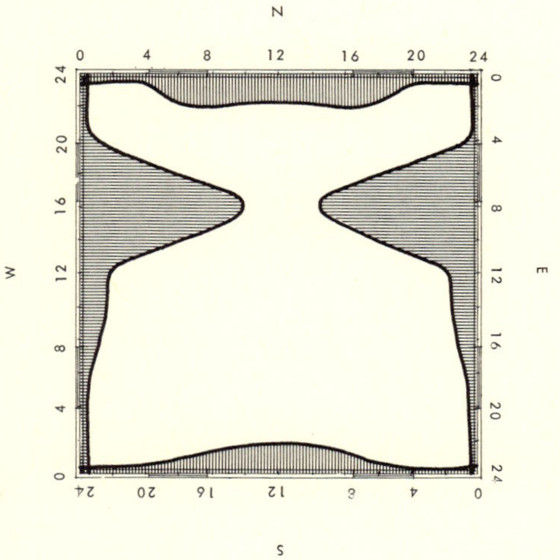

WINTER

BALANCED HOUSE

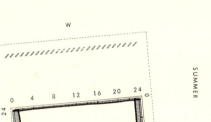
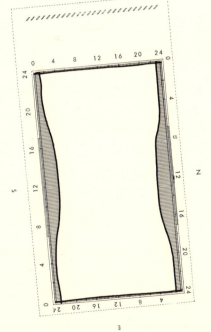
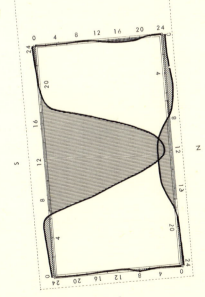

SUMMER

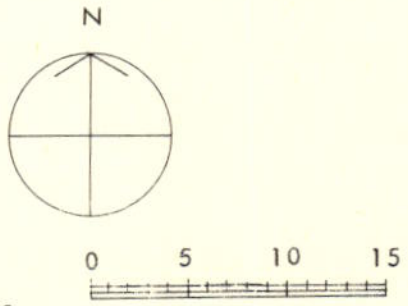

WINTER

SCALE OF HEAT IMPACTS
IN 1000 BTU'S

SCALE IN FEET

149

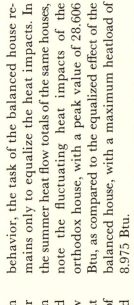

TOTAL HEAT BUDGET    MIAMI    JULY 21

HEAT FLOW 1000 BTU/HOUR

HOURS

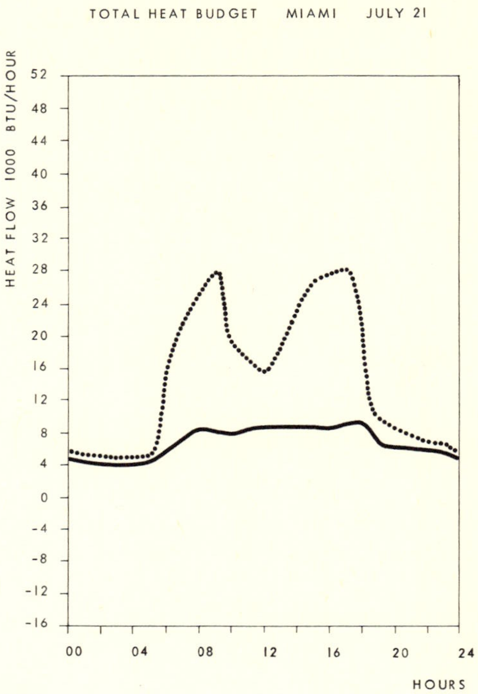

**304.**

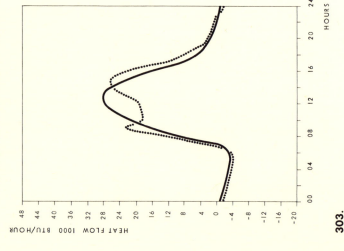

TOTAL HEAT BUDGET    MIAMI    JAN 21

HEAT FLOW 1000 BTU/HOUR

HOURS

**303.**

The daily heat behavior comparison between orthodox and balanced structures at winter and summer in Miami is illustrated in plan view with the method of indication described on page 119. Note the rearranged window openings (120 sq ft at south, 120 sq ft at north side) in the balanced house, the use of overhangs, and the shading effects of trees and carport. The reduced heat load in summer is apparent in the graph of the balanced house.

The daily total heat-flow curves between the orthodox and balanced houses in winter are shown. As under the given conditions the orthodox structure registers positive thermal behavior, the task of the balanced house remains only to equalize the heat impacts. In the summer heat flow totals of the same houses, note the fluctuating heat impacts of the orthodox house, with a peak value of 28.606 Btu, as compared to the equalized effect of the balanced house, with a maximum heatload of 8.975 Btu.

Since the underheated period prevails only 12% of the year in this region the winter conditions have relatively small importance for the evaluation. In addition structures under average sunlit conditions will keep the thermal level near comfort conditions. All walls,

except north, behave positively with a small amount of heat gain (2%). The roof supplies from 2% to 9% heat gain depending on the construction. Glass areas capture the most heat energy, over 80% of the total. Of this, the south side provides more than the sum of all other exposures; the second largest amount comes from east and west, and even the north orientation works positively.

The improvement of the balanced structure over the orthodox house in summertime is the product of the following measures: orientation, shape, and rearrangement of openings (−84.913 Btu) 24%; shading of glass sur-

150

Plan

305. Adaptation of principles in Miami area.

faces (−40.680 Btu) cuts the load by 11%. Note that here where orientation was fully exploited the usual predominance of shading effect is lessened. However, because of their interrelatedness both aspects may be considered in conjunction as creating 35%. The applied "shaded" roof construction (−38.900 Btu) accounts for 11%. Reduced infiltration (−16.920 Btu) brings a reduction of 4%. Wall

shading (−7.355 Btu) amounts to 2%, ventilation of appliances (−10.900 Btu) to 3%. Total reduction of heat gain as compared to the orthodox house is 55%.

The yearly importance index for climate balancing is evaluated here on summer criteria, because of the duration of the overheated period (88%) and the negligible stresses

of the underheated season. Accordingly, the order of the applied measures is as follows: (1) orientation and shading of glass surfaces 64% (both solar aspects may be considered jointly because of their interdependence here); (2) horizontal exposure gains in importance, with roof construction at 20%; (3) reduction in infiltration lessens 7%; (4) ventilation of appliances 5%; (5) shading of wall surfaces 4%.

South view

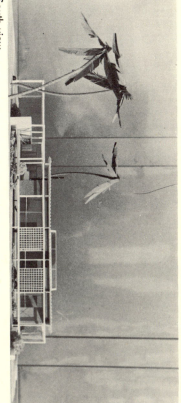

North view

East view

151

## SUMMATION OF REGIONAL CONCLUSIONS

As was pointed out at the beginning of the chapter, the adopted calculation method has its limitations, and therefore permits only an abstracted picture of the thermal behavior of structures. Further, for the sake of unified conclusions, a standard structure, the "orthodox" house, was analysed in the various climatic settings as was the "balanced" house (which derived mainly from architectural modifications of the orthodox house). Such a method does not allow adequate handling of certain important aspects, such as insulation effects, which can make a marked change. Detailed balancings such as microclimatic alterations were not applied, or in some cases only approximated. The yearly importance indexes of the applied measures were evaluated according to stresses on human sensations, with heat loads considered twice as important as temperature losses. Such a ratio would naturally be much higher if taken from the standpoint of air-conditioning costs.

Therefore, the previously described findings are valid directly to the specific houses designated, and under the defined circumstances stated. Other houses with different proportions or with dissimilar material characteristics may differ in their quantitative analyses.

However, from these findings the following conclusions can be drawn:

*On thermal loads in the four regions,*

(1) Underheated conditions are the main determinant of thermal design requirements in the cool (Minneapolis −697.000 Btu, 75% duration) and temperate (New York −454.000 Btu, 72% duration) regions. At lower latitudes the winter stresses decrease rapidly (Phoenix −66.000 Btu, 37%; Miami 0.0 Btu, 12%).

(2) The summer stresses are more equally divided among the regions (with the largest load occurring in the hot-arid zone) but the duration swiftly diminishes toward north. (Minneapolis +260.000 Btu, 25%; New York +276.000 Btu, 28%; Phoenix +539.000 Btu, 63%; Miami +361.000 Btu, 88%). Both in hot-arid and hot-humid regions the thermal design specifications are based mainly on overheated conditions.

(3) The total yearly range of stresses (the combined amounts of winter and summer loads) rises toward the higher latitudes (Minneapolis 975.000, New York 730.000, Phoenix 605.000, Miami 361.000).

(4) The relation of the seasonal load amplitudes indicates that a structure in the hot-humid zone should be constructed for the single purpose of reducing heat loads. The shelters in the temperate and hot-arid zones have the dual role of conserving or decreasing thermal impacts in the appropriate seasons. The structure of the cool zone tends to have the single function of avoiding heat loss, and this unilateral function will be even more prominent at higher latitudes.

*On the importance of climatic elements,*

(5) In high latitudes the temperature effects (infiltration, convection) have a major role in the thermal load. For lower latitudes the solar aspects overrule. In southern zones the radiation effects dominate the climatic situation.

*On the importance of structural elements,*

(6) The wall surfaces of a structure receive the greatest load in the high latitudes; their role becomes less important toward the southerly regions.

(7) The role of the roof has reverse characteristics; its heat load and also its importance rises toward the low latitudes. In southern regions its design requires specific attention.

(8) The most sensitive single element of the structure is the window area. Its positioning for winter and solar control during summer produce the largest effect on heat-flow balance.

*On the importance of livability,*

(9) A house of neutral design with regard to the climatic environment (here called the "orthodox" house) can be improved for wintertime more effectively in the lower latitudes than in northerly zones (at Minneapolis 42%, at New York 49%; in Phoenix it can be relieved of full load under average clear conditions). The average regional magnitude of the heat-loss reduction that can be achieved by the architectural use of natural possibilities (here called a "climate-balanced" house) can be taken to be 64%.

(10) Structures in the northern latitudes can be relieved of thermal loads during the overheated period more efficiently than those in the southern zones (at Minneapolis 75%, in New York 71%, in Phoenix 42%, and in Miami 55%). The average heat-load reduction of a balanced house over a neutral house can be taken to be 61%.

## THE THERMOHELIODON

The major shortcoming of calculation methods as a means of clarifying the principles of heliothermic planning is that they produce results measured in terms of abstracted measures of heating which, unlike temperature, are not easily relatable to human physical sensations.

To avoid this difficulty several attempts have been made to develop an empirical method which would make actual measurements of the temperatures obtained in diverse structures under varying climatic conditions (see Appendix B).

# XII. EXAMPLES IN FOUR REGIONS

## ARCHITECTURAL APPLICATION TO COMMUNITY LAYOUTS

THE foregoing chapters are concerned with investigations of the effects of climatic influences on buildings. Studies treating exact and factual approaches usually halt at the boundary line of abstract analysis, and this is correct and commendable for most theoretical fields. However, architecture is primarily practical in its nature; the value of principles lies largely in their applicability to present and future problems.

First, tabulations were prepared to summarize the findings and data in a synoptic form. At each of the four regions discussed, first a climatic analysis indicates the general conditions of the prevailing weather elements, their relative importance, and directional effects; then categorizations with reference to housing layout, building design, and building elements indicate recommendations or specify data of direct applicability. These interpretations refer in abbreviated form to the material discussed in the previous chapters. The cited climatic data are all based on the A.I.A. Regional Climate Analyses,[1] as the additional interpretations are compiled with reference to it and to other pertinent sources.[2] In sun-angle computations the data of the next rounded latitude degree was used in the specific locales.

The second part of the summaries contain architectural interpretations of housing layouts in the different regions, to illustrate the analytical data in examples of synthesized solutions. Visual expression can convey more easily the architectural differences occurring in the different regions.

In the examples, all factors—such as site,

housing organization, building types and their quantities—were held constant (with only unavoidable slight modifications) in order that the effect of the climatic impacts should be the only motivating force in the variations. Naturally such an approach, however valid in its intentions, has certain restricting limits. The plans could have had more liberty if we had chosen a rugged terrain for the cool region in contrast to a water-rich flat area for the hot-humid area. Similarly, sharper expression could have been achieved with the use of cold and tropical zones instead of cool and hot-humid locations; however, the program was confined to applications within the boundaries of the United States and to restricted building types. Finally, the emotional values arising from the nature of the site and the color of local traditions had to be suppressed for sake of clarity.

Each site given for the examples covers an area of four square miles. The locations of the housing layouts were selected within this territory. The topography consists of an upper and lower plateau divided by a south-east sloping ridge. A stream is located at the lower plain, where the main access highway runs in an east-west direction.

The general organization of the housing layouts are based on the principles of a neighborhood unit. The total population of each neighborhood consists of about 4,800 inhabitants of middle and upper-middle income groups. The family size averages 3.5 persons. The neighborhood is composed of four residential colonies of about 1,200 inhabitants each, and of a central core.

The dwellings consist of two, three, and four bedroom units; and are divided into

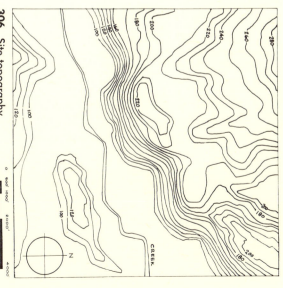

306. Site topography.

307. Organization scheme.

153

throughout the year. Short heavy rains in the summer; long, fine misty rains or snow in winter.

DETAILED ANALYSIS:

1. *Temperature*: Maximum temperature rises above 90° on about 15 days; June through September. Minimum temperature falls below 30°, or is at freezing point, 147 days from October through May.

*Total annual hours:*

| | |
|---|---|
| over 85° F | 4% |
| 65–85° | 23% |
| 45–65° | 25% |
| 25–45° | 26% |
| 0–25° | 18% |
| Under 0° | 4% |

2. *Sun:* Weather is sunny 58% of possible hours but has poor yearly distribution. 74% of possible hours—too much during summer; 40% of hours—too little in winter. Throughout the year, 147 days are cloudy and 105 are clear, the remainder being partly cloudy. In December, half of the days are completely overcast, seven days completely clear. In all months from October through June, cloudy days are more frequent than clear days.

3. *Wind:* For nearly $\frac{3}{4}$ of the year wind causes considerable heat loss from buildings. Prevailing wind comes from NW, with SE next in importance throughout the year. SE wind is sometimes split, veering to East; but NW wind is persistent in direction. On hot summer afternoons the wind is sometimes from the S-SW direction.

4. *Precipitation:* Average rainfall is about 27". Maximum record exceeded 40", minimum 11.5". Four to five times more precipitation in the summer than in the winter.

5. *Snow:* Average snowfall is about 40.5". Maximum up to 85", minimum about 14".

---

A  Detached houses  60%  870 units
A1  Row houses  20%  280 units
A2  Apartments  20%  280 units

Each colony has a central day nursery with play area; adjoining colonies are provided with branch library, drug store, and place of worship. The neighborhood center consists of:

C. Commercial area: shopping center, supermarket, stores, offices.

D. Administration area: post office, administration facilities, offices.

E. Cultural and recreational area: elementary school and kindergarten, theatre-auditorium, club and restaurant.

F. Sports and recreational area: arena for football and track, tennis courts, and picnic grounds with open green area.

The communication system consists of a circumferential road connected to the highway; and of residential roads branching off and serving the residential sections in a manner that pedestrian walks toward the center sections should have the minimum possible traffic interference.

In the following applications four localities are used as examples. The climatic environments of Minneapolis, New York, Phoenix, and Miami are selected as representatives for cool, temperate, hot-arid, and hot-humid climatic zones.

## COOL REGION

### SPECIFIC CLIMATIC INTERPRETATION IN MINNEAPOLIS

IN GENERAL:

Recorded temperatures range from −34° to 108° F. Too much sun in summer and not enough in the winter. Cold winds during a long winter. Persistent NW-SE wind pattern

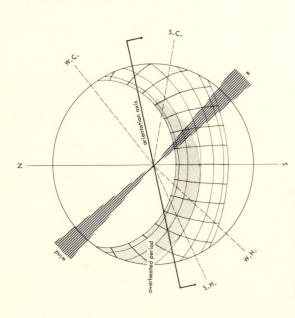

**308.** Directional analyses.

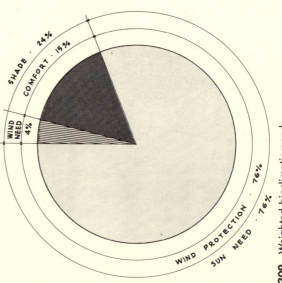

**309.** Weighted bioclimatic needs.

detached houses, row houses, and apartment house types. The approximate ratio of dwelling units are proportioned as:

**1. SITE SELECTION**
SSE slope for sun gain is desirable. Middle or lower middle of slope is preferable to prevent excessive wind effects and to avoid cool air pools.

**2. TOWN STRUCTURE**
The layout shall provide sheltering effect against winds. Larger building units may be grouped close together but spaced to utilize sun heat effects. The houses tend to join to expose less surface to heat loss. The town structure is an insolated dense layout.

**3. PUBLIC SPACES**
Wind sheltered, open, with periodically shaded areas.

**4. LANDSCAPE**
The generally varying topography shapes street layouts and space utilization into an irregular character.

**5. VEGETATION**
Evergreen windbreaks in NE-SW direction at a distance of 20 times the tree height are desirable. Deciduous shade trees near house. Avoid dense planting too close to structure because of dampness effect.

**GENERAL OBJECTIVES IN THE COOL REGION:** Increase heat production. Increase radiation absorption, and decrease radiation loss. Reduce conduction and evaporation loss.

6. *Relative Humidity and Vapor Pressure:* Relative humidity is higher outdoors in the winter than in the summer—70 to 100% compared with 45 to 80%. Vapor pressure (absolute humidity) is much higher in the summer than in the winter. It frequently becomes oppressive in June, July and August for a total of about 27 days.

**1. HOUSE TYPES**
In residential structures, two-story houses or arrangements under one roof are preferable for compactness. Row houses or adjoining buildings have the advantage of lesser heat loss. In larger volumed apartment house types, compact arrangements such as "point houses" are advantageous.

**2. GENERAL ARRANGEMENT**
Conservation and economy of heating is about three times as important as provision for summer comfort. The extreme conditions both in winter and summer suggest solutions of separated zones for this dual role of the structure. Entrance spaces with storage of clothing is desirable. Avoid exterior steps and steep drives.

**3. PLAN**
Design mainly determined by conditions prevailing in cool and cold months. Indoor living period represents 70% of annual hours. As plan aims to satisfy those conditions through compactness, provision for summer comfort with additional living areas and/or utilization of outdoor spaces is essential.

**4. FORM, VOLUME**
Structures shall be compact with minimum exterior surface. Volume effect is highly desirable. Proportion 1:1.1-1.3 elongated on E-W axis gives optimum effects.

**5. ORIENTATION**
Optimum sun orientation lies 12° E of South. The prevailing wind pattern (NW-SE) may influence the orientation of free standing buildings.

**6. COLOR**
Sun exposed surfaces in medium colors; recessed surfaces can be of dark absorbent colors if shade in summer can be provided.

310. Organization and site selection.

## APPLICATION

The site was selected for habitation purposes mainly because of sun exposure and wind protection. The SSE slopes receive favorable distribution of the seasonal insolation, and also balance the daily sun heat. This exposure also gives protection from the prevailing NW wind effects; however, the veering SE winds can be deflected by vegetation. In the layout organization the detached houses (A) follow in a belt-like fashion the lower middle part of the preferable slopes, with treebelt protection at the windward ridges. Group housing (A1) establishes a connection between the residential colonies, where courtyard formations secure wind-protected areas. At the lower plateau are grouped the high apartment house units (A2); the centrally located commercial (C) and administration buildings (D). School (E), sports and recreational facilities (F) are situated in the public green area.

## BUILDING ELEMENTS

### 1. OPENINGS AND WINDOWS

Sun windows will provide good auxiliary heat sources. Except on the South side and partly East, the windows should be small. Windows should be shade-protected during overheated times. Heavy draperies or shutters are desirable to reduce heat loss during cool periods. Double glazing is essential. Controlled ventilation is a primary requirement (max. 20 fpm air movement); weather-stripping. At overheated times, cross ventilation is desirable.

### 2. WALLS

Exterior surfaces of smooth non-absorbent materials are preferable. Low thermal capacity insulation.

### 3. ROOF

A sloping roof is desirable to encourage snow removal by wind action. Flat roofs without parapet walls clear themselves more rapidly. Snow load is unlikely to exceed 15 psf. Simple roof formation is desirable to prevent moisture penetration and ice-filled gutters.

### 4. MATERIALS

a. Low thermal capacity insulation should be designed to resist a winter thermal gradient of 88° F; required insulation value relative to S is: E—1.2; W—1.2; N—1.3; roof—1.4.

b. High heat capacity mass in the interior to balance extreme heat variations is desirable; west wall material with 6 hr time lag balances internal heat distribution.

c. Vapor seal on warm (interior) side of outer walls is important.

d. Avoid exterior materials that are absorptive and subject to freeze-thaw damage. Extreme temperature ranges create necessity for avoiding materials subject to stress from expansion, contraction, and excessive dryness.

### 5. SHADING DEVICES

Shading in summer is desirable, but should not interfere with solar impact during underheated times. Toward S, horizontal shading devices (66° profile angle) may be used. Near SE corner one deciduous tree, and at W side two deciduous trees, can provide adequate shade for smaller residential structures. External operating devices in multi-story buildings are impractical because of icing problems.

### 6. FOUNDATION, BASEMENT

Basement should receive sunlight in summer or have artificial dehumidification to prevent condensation resulting from earth temperatures.

### 7. MECHANICAL EQUIPMENT

Water and sewer pipes should be kept out of exterior walls, particularly NW and SE walls. Yearly heating requirements are: 2130 hours of low heat output (10 degree-day conditions), 2000 hrs medium heat (30 degree-day cond.), 1500 hrs high heat (50 degree-day cond.), and 300 hrs at maximum heat output (70-75 degree-day cond.).

311.

The southeast view of the housing layout illustrates the relatively dense arrangement of the habitation area compared to the openness of the public spaces. Note the pattern of the treebelt which becomes denser at the ends to offset veering winds. The layout of the build-

ing units is marked by close grouping. The over-all orientation is somewhat more than 10° east of south.

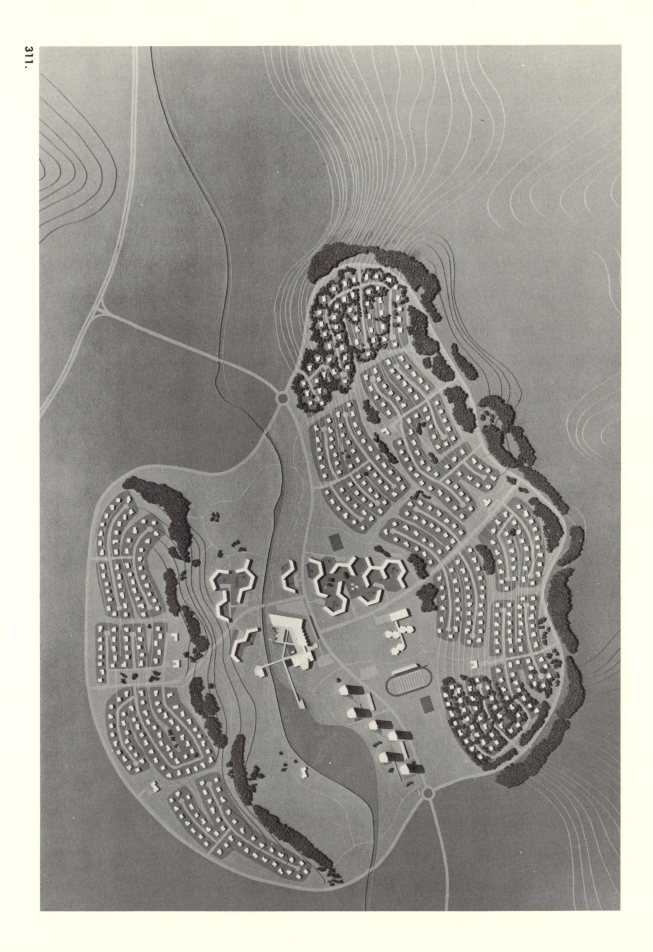

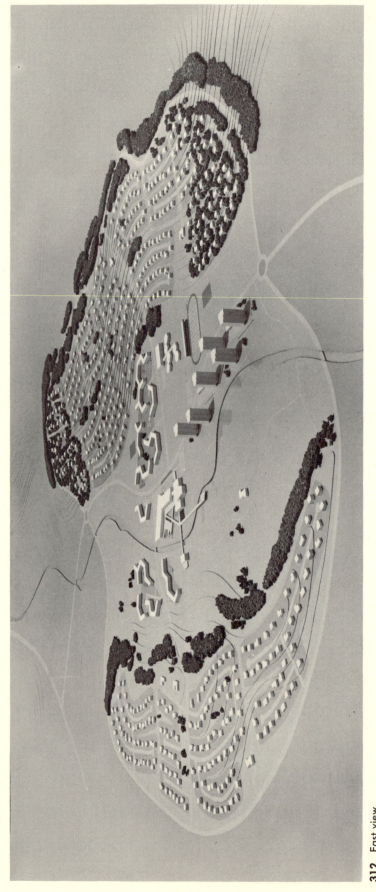

312. East view.

The general character of a town structure in the cool environment can be characterized as a wind-protected, insolated, dense layout.

The two views illustrate the neighborhood unit from the west and northwest side, the detached houses are formed for compactness with squarish design to expose relatively small surface areas to the weather elements.

This enables the use of smaller lot divisions, and hence a more intense land utilization of the preferable site exposures. With dense arrangements the wind impacts can be lessened; however, care should be exercised not to interfere with the beneficial insolation. At the upper end of the housing layout an alternate scheme is illustrated, where the house units are placed in clearings of wooded areas. However, this efficient arrangement needs larger lot divisions. In general, in the cool zone the houses tend to huddle together for mutual protection and even to join, thus reducing heat loss.

In the lower plain, where the cool-air drainage might have effect, multi-story dwelling units are preferable. In the plan, group houses are indicated with a broken honeycomb pattern. The wings with southeast, south, and southwest exposures have unilateral, and those with north-south axis bilateral, arrangements. The resulting courtyards reduce the wind impacts and allow the establishment of sun nooks. The apartment houses utilize the volume effect: cubical design with large content but small perimeter. Here the "point-house" arrangement is adapted, with closed north side and staggered south exposure. The public buildings are in compact formations, with closed surfaces toward the north and the windward side, but opened up to the south.

The residential road system branches from the circumferential road in finger pattern. The free network of walkways, in this climate zone allowing larger walking distances, connects the habitation areas to the central facilities.

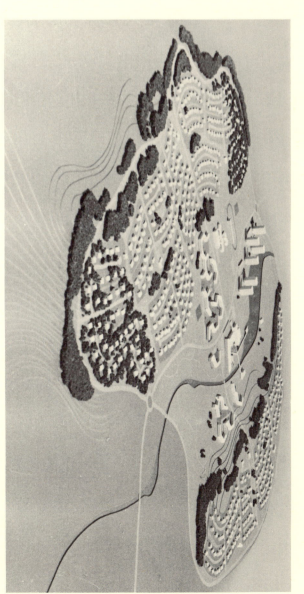

313. View from northwest.

314. View from southwest.

159

## INTERPRETATION IN NEW YORK–NEW JERSEY AREA

### DETAILED ANALYSIS

*1. Temperature:* Highest recorded temperature is 102°; lowest −14° F. However, recommended summer design temperature is 88° based on conditions occurring on exceptionally hot afternoons from May through September. Winter design temperature might be taken as 8° F, a condition which is exceeded only 1% hours yearly.

*Temperature distribution in annual hours,*

| | | |
|---|---|---|
| over 85° F | 3% | occurring sometimes in July and August |
| 65° to 85° | 28% | major summer climate |
| 45° to 65° | 32% | spring and fall weather conditions |
| 25° to 45° | 31% | major winter climate |
| 0° to 25° | 6% | occurs in Dec., Jan., and Feb. |

*2. Sun:* The distribution of clear and cloudy days is fairly uniform throughout the year. Maximum amount of possible sunshine occurs in September (68%), minimum in January (53%). Solar heat can be a valuable contribution during underheated times. Shading is necessary at the hot periods. Careful balance should be established.

*3. Wind:* Wind velocities are generally stable throughout the year, with 10 mph summer and 12 mph winter average speeds. Prevailing winds during underheated periods (October–April) come from NW direction, during overheated season they are variable from S to SW. During the hottest part of summer months the prevailing direction is south. High velocity winds (over 15 mph) are infrequent. However, in January and February NW, W, and SW strong winds occur. 40 mph wind velocities are probable in any month; velocities over 60 mph are seldom measured.

*4. Precipitation:* Monthly averages are fairly uniform throughout the year; varying from 3.0″ in November to 4.3″ in August. Greatest precipitation of 14.5″ was recorded in September. Heavy cloudbursts in summer might bring 1″ rain in fifteen minutes, or 4″ to 5″ in a single day.

*5. Snow:* Design for snowfall up to 3′. Amount of snowfall varies considerably. Snow cover lasts normally only a couple of days.

*6. Relative Humidity and Vapor Pressure:* Yearly average of relative humidity lies between 56–76%. It is lower in winter than in summer, where it rises to 80% or more through four months. Vapor pressure is highest in July and August averaging 24 mm Hg, but in extreme situations it rises to 24 mm during the three summer months.

### APPLICATION

In the temperate zone the selection of the site has to be based mainly on the prevailing requirements of the underheated period; however, conditions occurring at overheated times must be considered also. Both from the point of view of radiation and wind effects the SSE slopes are preferable. However, the land use of the horizontal sites allows a ring arrangement, with a centrally located public core. The tree belts secure wind shadow from the persistent NW winds, but without blocking the cooling S and SE breezes from the habitation area. Near the peripheral residential colonies (A) are located the row house units (A1), and the group of apartment houses (A2). In the central green area are placed the commercial (C) and administrative (D) buildings, and the school (E) with sports and recreational facilities (F).

In the view of the central green area of the temperate zone housing layout, the tree belts secure wind protection, the pattern of the resi-

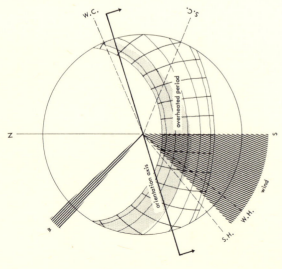

**315.** Directional analyses.

**316.** Weighted bioclimatic needs.

**1. SITE SELECTION**
Slopes East of South are preferable, similar to orientation requirements. "Warm slope" area is best, but lower and upper inclined portions are also advantageous if wind sheltering is provided. Breeze utilization in warm periods is important.

**2. TOWN STRUCTURE**
An open and free layout of buildings which tends to merge with nature is preferred. Town pattern utilizes the possibilities of free arrangement.

**3. PUBLIC SPACES**
Open lawns with grouped shade trees are desirable. Roads are best planned in SW direction to avoid winter winds and channel summer breezes. Walking distances can be arranged freely.

**4. LANDSCAPE**
Indoor and outdoor relationships in house design should be considered. Use of outdoor living areas can be extended for several months as adjuncts to interior areas, if properly designed.

**5. VEGETATION**
Windbreaks are desirable against winter NW wind direction. Tree layouts, however, should not block prevailing S-SW summer breezes. Evergreen trees are best for wind protection, deciduous for shading purposes. Lawns near structure are useful for radiation absorption. Shade trees are preferred on E and W sides of residences.

**1. HOUSE TYPES**
This region permits the most flexible arrangements. A close relationship between house and nature is desirable and possible. Unilateral buildings can be developed with relatively free formations.

**2. GENERAL ARRANGEMENT**
The large range of thermal conditions requires the utilization of radiation and wind effects, as well as protection from them. Hence, a dual role is required of the structure.

**3. PLAN**
Freedom in plan design is characterized by spatial connections of outdoor and indoor areas. Buildings should open to S-SE and be closed on westerly sides. Bedrooms should be located on easterly sides, open porch on S-SE side (useful 31% of year, or if glass enclosed, 61% of the year).

**4. FORM, VOLUME**
Wings protruding along the N-S axis receive less "penalty," than in other zones. Therefore cross-shaped or free building formations are possible; however, elongation in E-W axis is preferable, with the optimum shape being 1:1.6. Volume effect is not too important.

**5. ORIENTATION**
Sol-air orientation of 17½° E of S secures balanced heat distribution. The orientation of high buildings should be correlated with wind exposure.

**6. INTERIOR**
Provision for adequate cross ventilation is necessary. Humidity-producing areas should be separated from rest of building. Sun penetration is desirable; therefore depths of interiors should not be excessive.

**7. COLOR**
Medium colors are advantageous: dark colors only in recessed places protected from summer sun; light colors on roof surfaces.

GENERAL OBJECTIVES IN THE TEMPERATE REGION: As both underheated and overheated periods are represented in substantial part during the year a balance should be established by reducing or promoting on a seasonal basis the heat production, radiation, and convection effects.

**318.** Organization and site selection.

dential streets allow the summer breezes to penetrate into the housing section. The overall orientation of the buildings is turned 18 degrees east of south. The formation and the layout of the buildings have freedom in this zone.

The temperate region is characterized by relatively moderate climate stresses throughout the year, therefore this zone permits quite flexible building plans. Even protruding wings on the north-south axis receive less penalty than in other regions, consequently cross shaped, or free-form buildings may be used. However, structures elongated on the east-west axis are definitely preferable. This relative freedom is indicated in the

## BUILDING ELEMENTS

### 1. OPENINGS AND WINDOWS

Arrangements of window areas are of utmost importance for internal heat balance. South exposed glass areas work well on seasonal bases. Protection is needed from summer radiation. Openings should be screened. Location of openings should allow cross ventilation. Reduced openings on westerly side is desirable. Single glass surfaces transmit, on the average, 10 times (but at certain exposures, 30 times) as much as the amount of heat exchange transmitted by uninsulated wall surfaces.

### 2. WALLS

Avoid absorptive materials, or those which are affected by freeze-thaw action: rain and moisture penetration is mostly on NW exposures.

### 3. ROOF

Eave and gable ventilation is needed: this might be closed in winter. Attic fan is also effective. Gutters should be able to carry 1″ of rain off total roof area in 15 minutes. Snow and rain pockets must be avoided.

### 4. MATERIALS

a. Insulation index is 70; required insulation value relative to S is: E—1.3; W—1.3; N—1.4; roof—1.5.

b. West wall material with 6 hour time lag balances internal heat distribution.

c. Vapor barrier on warm side prevents condensation.

### 5. SHADING DEVICES

Deciduous trees on East and West sides, 68° overhang on South exposure, protects low structures. Eggcrate type of sunshade on E and W; vertical fins on N side protects higher buildings.

### 6. FOUNDATION AND BASEMENT

Summer basement temperatures will remain approximately midway between deep ground temperatures (53) and average diurnal temperature (73), at about 63. Dehumidification is desirable for about 30-40% of the year.

### 7. MECHANICAL EQUIPMENT

Yearly heating requirements are: 2830 hours of low heat output (10 degree-day conditions), 2690 hours medium heat (30 degree-day cond.), 508 hours high heat (50 degree-day cond.), and a few additional hours of maximum heat.

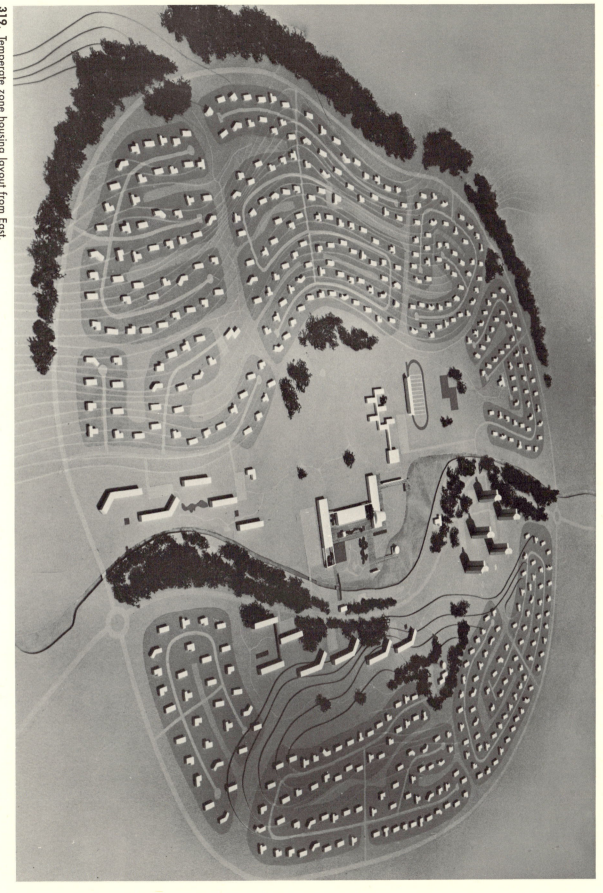

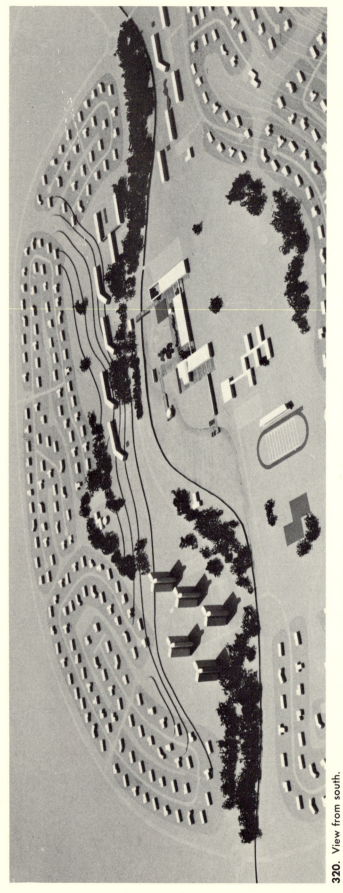

320. View from south.

321. High rise zone.

layout of the detached house units. Between these, the simple oblongs and the L-shaped units facing SE are the advantageous formations. The row-housing units have unilateral plan arrangements facing SSE, with closed surfaces and buffer rooms placed at the weather side. Such a scheme is equally adaptable to tall housing units. However, to emphasize the possibilities of freedom, shamrock-formed apartment houses are shown here, with livable areas grouped toward the SE, SW, and E orientations, closed at windward directions, and with solar-control balcony arrangements on the sunny exposures. The public buildings are loosely composed, with wind-shaded sunny exterior spaces. In the commercial and administrative center the protected southerly side allows outdoor activities.

The concentric layout of the habitation area is served by a circumferential road, from which leads the residential road pattern. In the green areas adjoining the private lots lies the network of walkways channeling the pedestrian traffic into the centrally located commercial, educational, and recreational facilities.

The general character of a town structure in the temperate environment is characterized by open and free arrangement, where houses and nature merge.

**322.** Western view.

sunshine hours compared to the possible hours. Maximum occurs in June with 93%, minimum in January with 75%. Solar heat, with adequate arrangements, may be sufficient for heating requirements during underheated period. High value of nocturnal outgoing radiation could be major source of natural cooling arrangements.

3. *Wind:* Prevailing wind axis lies in E-W direction. Highest wind velocities, which can be utilized in spring and fall, occur at afternoons. Exceptionally strong winds are not to be expected. Winds over 20 mph might be dust laden. Night winds follow topography, with cool air drainage from the mountains. Day winds come from S, SE and SW; westerly directions prevail at afternoons, and are more pronounced in summer.

4. *Precipitation:* Average yearly rainfall to about 8 inches, but at least to 3 inches. Usually there is a trace of rain every month. Driest months are May and June; July, August, September are relatively the wettest. Water conservation, and saving rainfall becomes important.

5. *Relative Humidity and Vapor Pressure:* Air is dry during all periods of the year. In June the relative humidity ranges between 10 and 40%. In January varies from 34 to 70% during the day. Vapor pressure occurs only in August, about 17 mm Hg. Low humidity conditions open up possibility for evaporative cooling arrangements.

APPLICATION

The climatic environment of the hot-arid region is marked by clear sky, relatively long overheated period, dry atmosphere, and large diurnal temperature range. Sites at low levels, but still above valley floor, can benefit from cool air flow. Water bodies moderate the extreme temperatures and by evaporation

## INTERPRETATION IN PHOENIX

DETAILED ANALYSIS

1. *Temperature:* Highest recorded temperature is 118°; lowest 16° F. As only 1% (about 88 hours per year) rises above 106°, this is recommended as design temperature value for summer conditions. For winter design temperature 32° F can be taken, as only 1% hours per year go lower. The region is characterized by large (about 30° F) daily temperature variation. The use of these differences can lead to interior temperature balance.

*Temperature distribution in annual hours:*

| | | |
|---|---|---|
| over 105° | 2% | occurs sometimes in June, July, August afternoons |
| 85° to 105° | 23% | normal afternoon temperatures from May to October |
| 65° to 85° | 33% | general April and May, September and October temperatures |
| 45° to 65° | 32% | major winter climate |
| 25° to 45° | 10% | December, January, February usual nocturnal temperatures |
| under 25° | under 1% | occurs only at exceptional cases |

2. *Sun:* Sun intensity values are the highest of all regions. Average solar heat in June received on a horizontal plane ranges from 2100 to 2800 Btu/sq ft/day; with hourly maximum of around 350 Btu/sq ft. Minimum horizontal solar radiation in January varies between 511 and 1200 Btu/sq ft/day. Throughout the year there are 84% actual

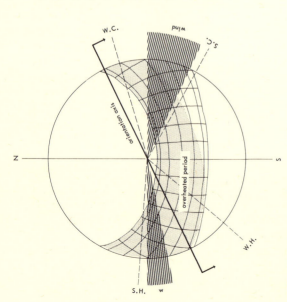

**323.** Directional analyses.

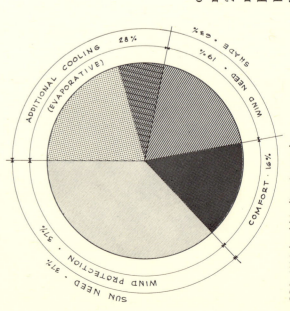

**324.** Weighted bioclimatic needs.

# HOUSING LAYOUT

**1. SITE SELECTION**
On SE-E slope exposures, lower portions are preferred, where cool air flow effect can be utilized and controlled. High altitudes, and locations with evaporative possibilities, are advantageous.

**2. TOWN STRUCTURE**
The walls of houses and gardens should provide shade to outdoor living areas, similar to the effect of horizontal "eggcrate" devices. Unit dwellings or groups should create patio-like areas: concentration is desirable. The town structure should thus react against heat with a shaded and dense layout.

**3. PUBLIC SPACES**
There should be a close connection between public spaces and residential areas. Half and full shade protection is desirable; paved surfaces should be avoided; pools of water are beneficial.

**4. LANDSCAPE**
As vegetation is generally sparse, concentration of plant- and grass-covered areas in the manner of an "oasis" is desirable.

**5. VEGETATION**
Vegetation is desirable both as a radiation absorbent surface and for its evaporative and shade giving properties.

# SHELTER DESIGN

**1. HOUSE TYPES**
Compact "patio" house type is preferred; adjoining houses, row houses, and group arrangements (all continuous on E-W axis), which tend to create a volume effect, are advantageous. High massive buildings are preferable.

**2. GENERAL ARRANGEMENT**
Heat loss, rather than gain, is the objective. Therefore, closed building arrangements around green areas are preferable: utilizing evaporative cooling effects and night out-going radiation losses. Lythosphere arrangements are here applicable: i.e., subterranean utilization. High ceilings are not necessary. Outdoor or roof sleeping possibilities should be considered.

**3. PLAN**
Inward looking layout can benefit from microclimatic advantages. Walled-in house arrangement can benefit from cool air pool effects. Single floor and a convenient plan with economy of movements avoids heat gain. Evaporative possibilities should be utilized. Heat-producing areas should be separated from other areas of the house. Non-inhabited spaces should be placed on west side to baffle sun impact.

**4. FORM, VOLUME**
Compact shapes are preferable, yet somewhat elongated on E-W axis; the optimum shape is 1:1.3. Volume effect is important. Building forms should have minimum solar projection.

**5. ORIENTATION**
Exposures 25° E of S secure balanced orientation, but all exposures are good from S to 35° E of S. For bilateral buildings with cross ventilation, 12° S of W axis is preferred.

**6. INTERIOR**
Deep room arrangements can be used as a cooling contrast to intense outdoor heat. Use of low emissivity, "cool" colors reduces heat reflection on interior surfaces. Connection with patio areas has cooling effect on adjacent spaces.

**7. COLOR**
White paint has high reflection ratio on sun exposed surfaces. Dark absorptive colors are adaptable where reflections toward interior are expected (such as under eaves). Deep-set surfaces can be dark colored for winter radiation absorption. Bright color contrasts are in agreement with the general character of the region.

GENERAL OBJECTIVES IN THE HOT-ARID REGION: Reduce heat production. Reduce and promote loss of radiation. Reduce conduction gain. Promote evaporation.

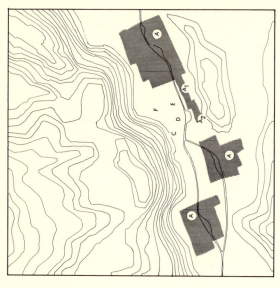

**325.** Organization and site selection.

secure desirable microclimatic effects. (Here the paths of the waterways were chosen with some liberty.) The cool morning conditions regulate the orientation axis of the layout for early heat intake, with provision for shade in the later hours. High temperatures beg utilization of the volume effect in the town structure by concentration. Accordingly the residential colonies (A) are in closed grouping. The row house units (A1), the apartment buildings (A2), the centrally located shopping (C), administrative (D), school (E), and recreational (F) facilities reflect the same compact character.

The western view illustrates the cohesive tendency of the housing layout grouped around the desirable locations, and dense in mutual protection. The closeness within the residential colonies reduces the walking distances. Communication to the center facilities

## BUILDING ELEMENTS

### 1. OPENINGS AND WINDOWS

Relatively small openings reduce intense radiation. Windows should be shielded from direct radiation, and set high to protect from ground radiation. Openings should be tight-closing as protection against high diurnal heat. External shades are preferred. Openings should be located on S, N, and, to a lesser degree, on E sides.

### 2. WALLS

Walls of daytime living areas should be of heat-storing materials; walls of night-use rooms of materials with light heat capacity. E and W walls should preferably be shaded. High reflective qualities are desirable for both thermal and solar radiation.

### 3. ROOF

Generally, heat storage insulation is best, which uses the flywheel effect of outgoing radiation for daily heat balance. However a shaded, ventilated roof is also applicable, primarily over night-use rooms. Water spray or pool on roof is effective. High solar reflectivity is a basic requirement; emissivity is essential for long-wave radiation.

### 4. MATERIALS

1. Insulation index is 45°; required insulation value relative to S is: E—1.1; W—1.2; N—1.0; roof—1.6.
2. High heat capacity walls are essential. Necessary time lags for internal heat balance are: E—0 hours; S—10 hrs.; W—10 hrs.; N—10 hrs., or no lag; roof—12 hrs.

### 5. SHADING DEVICES

Devices should be separate from structure, and exposed to wind convection.

### 6. FOUNDATION, BASEMENT

Lythosphere type of houses are possible in this zone.

### 7. MECHANICAL EQUIPMENT

Equipment should have high operating efficiency in heat producing devices, such as those for cooking.

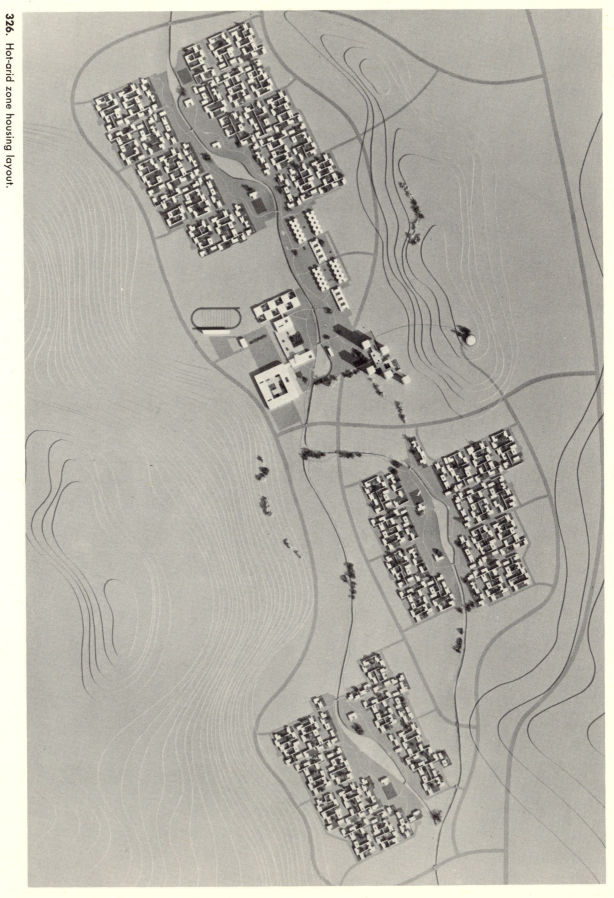

is presumed to be by car, although pedestrian paths are provided. In other hot-arid areas where vehicles are scarce, the colonies would adjoin. The layout of the housing areas forms a pattern, similar to an eggcrate shading device, maintaining coolness in the courtyards. The over-all orientation axis lies 25° east of south.

The house units of the hot-arid region tend to be cubical in shape as a reaction to the recurring high temperatures. Desired large time-lags call for heavy construction materials. Adjoining houses benefit by volume effect. Courtyard arrangements, where the house lies on the east-west axis and the garden walls in north-south direction, balance the solar and shade effects. Shaded grass surfaces cooled by nightly outgoing radiation and by evaporation moderate daily temperatures. This holds true for the buildings themselves also; patios with pools, or sprinkled lawns change the environment for the better. All this suggests inward-looking house schemes, which at the same time achieve privacy.

The multiple dwelling units are placed in walking distance of the center. The row houses (A1) consist of closely massed units on the east-west axis. Close to the community buildings (C) are located the multi-story apartment houses (A2). The east and west sides should be unpierced. Apertures on north and south could be combined with protruding, staggered balconies serving the double purpose of day shading and of releasing night outgoing radiation. In the court of the formed square commercial area shops are located. The classrooms in the school building (E) are adjacent to courtyards.

The traffic arteries feed the residential sections with short cul-de-sac roads; the separate green ways mark the walks to the communal lawn areas.

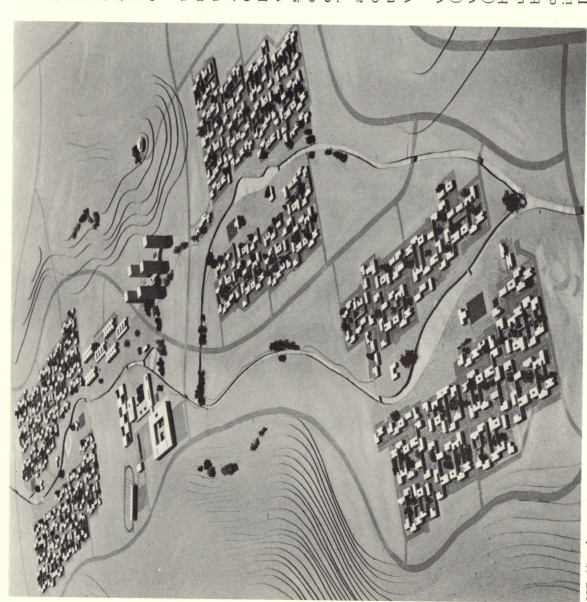

**327.** View from east.

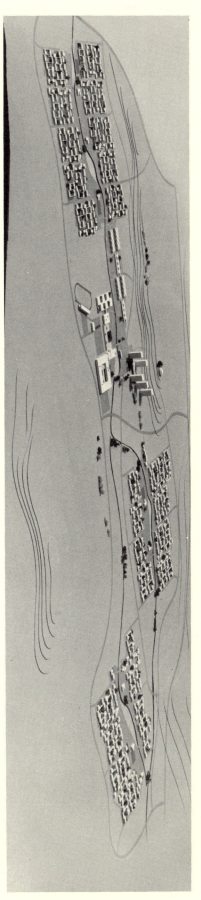

The overall layout of the town structure in a hot-arid region reflects a closed, dense character.

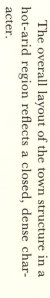

# HOT-HUMID REGION

## INTERPRETATION IN MIAMI

### DETAILED ANALYSIS

1. *Temperature:* Highest recorded temperature is 96° F; winter temperatures never remain below freezing point throughout a day. Summer design temperature can be taken as 90°; in winter as 47° F (discounting the 1% of coldest temperature). The region is characterized by small temperature variation; the monthly temperature range is 22° F through the year. The daily temperature variation is only about 6° in summer, about 13° F in winter.

*Temperature distribution in annual hours:*

| | | |
|---|---|---|
| over 85° | 11% | typical for June, July, September afternoons; less frequently for March, April, May, October afternoons |
| 65° to 85° | 75% | major climate zone. All average monthly temperatures lie in this range |
| 45° to 65° | 14% | primarily a nocturnal range from December till March. Occasionally a daytime range during cold spells in winter |
| under 45° | 0% | negligible |

2. *Sun:* Actual sunshine hours account for 66% of the possible hours in the yearly average. Maximum in March and April with 72%; minimum in June with 61%. Summer cloudiness cuts the intensity of solar radiation; it builds up during the hot part of the day, reducing solar input. Large proportion of diffuse radiation. Shaded conditions are required nearly throughout the year.

3. *Wind:* Average wind velocity of 10 mph comes from easterly direction both in mornings and afternoons. The large part of the night hours and evenings are mostly calm, or bring only light breezes. Winter night winds are stronger and come from north as well as from east. Northerly winds are common from October through March. Sea-breeze and trade-wind combination may reach 20–30 mph velocities on summer afternoons, with stronger winds on hottest days. Strongest winds are generally under 50 mph; however, 123 mph maximum wind velocity was recorded from NE direction. Hurricanes can be expected from E and SE directions, mainly from September through November.

4. *Precipitation:* The average yearly rainfall of about 60 inches comes principally in the summer months. September is generally the rainiest month, with average precipitation of 18 days. Rain in at least every second day can be expected from June till September. Winter average is one rainy day out of four. Maximum rainfall can amount to 24 inches per day in November. In March, April, May, and in August 8″ to 10″ rainfalls may occur during a 24 hour period. Rain can fall up to 2″ in half an hour; but rarely above $\frac{1}{2}$″ in a five minute period.

5. *Relative Humidity and Vapor Pressure:* The average yearly vapor pressure is nearly 18 mm Hg. From July to October the daily conditions rise over 20 mm Hg; a situation where conditions are hardly bearable without a breeze. 25% of the year is in such an extremely uncomfortable range. A further 50% is still in vapor pressure areas where air movements are required to restore the feeling of comfort.

### APPLICATION

In the hot-humid zone high temperature conditions prevail which remain quite consistently in the vapor-pressure area. The

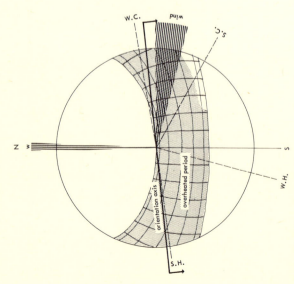

**330.** Directional analyses.

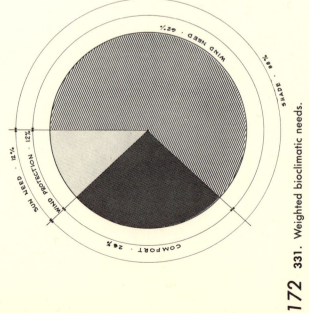

**331.** Weighted bioclimatic needs.

# HOUSING LAYOUT

**1. SITE SELECTION**

High elevations on windward side are desirable; specifically, locations near crest slightly offset from prevailing wind direction receive most air movement. Souther and northern slope directions rather than E and W sides are preferred because of less radiation.

**2. TOWN STRUCTURE**

Accent should be on separated houses to utilize air movements. A shaded environment becomes an important consideration. The character of the town fabric should be loose and scattered.

**3. PUBLIC SPACES**

Minimum walking distances and shaded areas are preferred.

**4. LANDSCAPE**

In the generally flat areas, the integrated use of water is both possible and desirable. Water drainage must be provided away from house; grading, also, must be provided for run-off of intensive rainstorms.

**VEGETATION**

Shade trees should be high-branching so that they do not interfere with breezes. Low vegetation must be kept away from houses so as not to block air movement. Air coming into a structure from across a shaded lawn is desirable.

---

# SHELTER DESIGN

**1. HOUSE TYPES**

Individual, preferably somewhat elevated, house types are advantageous. Freely elongated, high buildings are preferred, with a loose density.

**2. GENERAL ARRANGEMENT**

Buildings should be shaded structures which encourage cooling air movements; shade protection should be on all sun-exposed sides, mainly on roof and E and W exposures.

**3. PLAN**

As temperatures are not too excessive, free plans can be evolved as long as the house is under protective shade; a free air path through interior is important. Plan might be organized into separate elements, since 75% of the time outdoor conditions are near comfort, if shaded. Paving should be avoided. Screened areas are necessary to keep out insects. Roll-back walls are useful. Heat- and moisture-producing areas should be ventilated and separated from the rest of the structure. Vapor, insect, and humidity control is necessary in storage spaces.

**4. FORM, VOLUME**

Strong radiation effects on the E and W sides should dictate the shape of buildings to a slender elongation. The optimum shape is 1:1.7, but up to 1:3.0 on the E-W axis is also acceptable. A volume effect is undersirable.

**5. ORIENTATION**

Sol-air orientation is balanced at 5° E of South, with relatively small deviation from it (10°) to remain desirable. Orientation with long side toward differing wind directions acceptable only under shaded conditions.

**6. INTERIOR**

Interior spaces must be shaded and well ventilated. Flexible spaces, by the use of screened, movable, or low partitions, are desirable. Floor materials must be impervious to moisture. Daytime living areas should allow the flow of E to W winds. An area of safe retreat is necessary during hurricane periods.

**7. COLOR**

Reflective light colors in the pastel range are best, in order to avoid glare both inside and outside.

---

GENERAL OBJECTIVES IN THE HOT-HUMID REGION: Reduce heat production. Reduce radiation gain. Promote evaporation loss.

**332.** Organization and site selection.

natural remedy for such a situation lies in increased air movement; therefore here the utilization of wind effects is the primary consideration in site selection. In the example the higher plateau was chosen for the housing layout for its undisturbed wind exposure, including the ridge sides where speedier flow can be expected. For sun orientation here, where overheated conditions prevail practically all year long, exposures with minimum solar heat intake are advantageous. A position very near to the east-west axis does not correspond to the demand of easterly wind exposure. Therefore, adjustment has to be made to satisfy both requirements. In the plan the sun orientation was accepted as the dominant factor (somewhat unjustly to the Miami requirements) as this is more typical to the general hot-humid situations. In the layout organization there is a parallel tendency. In the central bend between the detached houses (A) are the communal facilities

# BUILDING ELEMENTS

## 1. OPENINGS AND WINDOWS

Customary distinction between walls and openings disappears. Ventilation is needed 85% of the year; E-W cross ventilation is essential. Roll-back opening walls are practical. Elements such as screening, louvres, jalousies, and grills are useful to admit air flow and to protect from sun. Structure must be sheltered from sun and rain; it must be shielded from sky radiation and glare. Removable shutters are desirable for hurricane protection.

## 2. WALLS

Walls have less importance here than in any other region. They are used primarily for screening from insects and for their flexible wind penetration qualities, rather than as thermal barriers. Folding window-wall solutions are possible.

## 3. ROOF

Strongest thermal impacts occur here: the design emphasis changes from walls to roof. A ventilated double roof is desirable, the upper roof functioning as sun protection. It must be watertight, insulated, and reflect solar rays. A wide overhang is necessary for rain protection and for reduction of sky glare (the rain often comes at a 45° angle).

## 4. MATERIALS

a. Insulation index is 35°; required insulation value relative to S is: E—1.4; W—1.5; N—1.1; roof—2.3.

b. Light heat capacity walls are best, for thermal lag may cause night re-radiation of heat and morning condensation.

c. Prevention of deterioration of materials by moisture and animate sources is necessary.

## 5. SHADING DEVICES

Sunbreakers are important because of powerful radiation mainly on E and W sides; note also that the N wall gets more radiation impact in summer than S wall.

## 6. FOUNDATION, BASEMENT

Basement is impractical because of constant high humidity. Foundations must be protected from moisture, mold, fungus, termites, and other gnawing insects and animals. Building on high stilts provides better ventilation in living areas, and can create a sheltered area below as well.

## 7. MECHANICAL EQUIPMENT

40 hours of the year need moderate heating, with approximate thermal differential between indoors and outdoors of 25-30 F; 1250 hours require low heating (average daily differential of 5°-10°); and 940 hours need no special requirements. During 6650 hours of the year, cooling would be desirable; however, such installation with its high cost is in sharp contrast to normal outdoor conditions. Mechanical ventilation with fans, would be effective. Domestic solar water heater is here a possibility.

## 8. OTHERS

The structure must be protected against fungus, mold, and dampness effects. A flow of breeze is necessary to compensate for this. Structures must be designed to withstand hurricane velocity winds.

333. Hot-humid zone housing layout.

334. View from south.

335. East view.

of shopping (C), administrative (D), sport (F), and school buildings (E). Nearby lie the groups of row (A1) and apartment houses (A2).

To benefit from air flow, the hot-humid housing layout tends to spread, resulting in low density and low land utilization. At the same time a relative closeness to the communal facilities is required to shorten the walking distances. To strike a balance between those diverse demands, in the layout example the usually centered public open area was divided into two green belts to offer shaded pedestrian walks.

As buildings located on a north-south axis in the hot-humid zone receive more undesirable radiation than in any other climatic zone, the over-all orientation lies consistently near to the east-west axis. However, as the temperature impacts are not too excessive, freely elongated building shapes are not only allowable, but advantageous. This also corresponds to the air-flow requirements. The residential section, theoretically placed in shade protection of high-branching trees (omitted in the plans for clarity), has a staggered arrangement of detached houses. The longish houses should be closed, or protected by shading walls at the east and west sides with parasol roof construction. Under sun shelter the plans can have freedom, as convection heat has only secondary importance. Elevated structures benefit from stronger air flow. The row houses (A1) consist essentially of staggered individual dwelling units in a multi-story pattern separated by terraces, allowing the penetration of the surrounding air flow. The apartment houses (A2) are slim and high. The elongated slab form intercepts little radiation; the heights obstruct the air flow and build useful high pressure areas before the building. The elevations should consist of a wind-permeable shaded pattern.

Open, loosely connected buildings compose the community center (C); leaving free way for air currents as well as for shaded pedestrian walks.

The general character of a town structure in the hot-humid environment is a low density layout with consistent sun-wind orientation, and with a freedom in plans under protective shade.

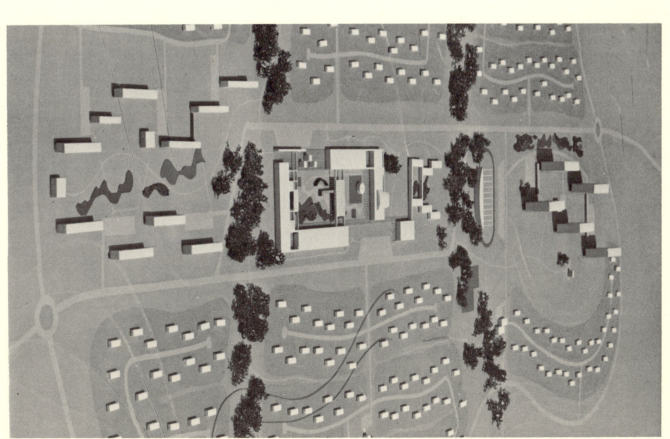

**336.** Community center from west.

# APPENDIX A

## APPENDIX A-1

Winslow, Herrington, and Gagge combined air temperature, radiation, and air movement into a single value, defined by the following expression:

$$T_o = t_s - \frac{M - E \pm S}{K_R + K_C} = \frac{K_R}{K_R + K_C}\, mrt + \frac{K_C}{K_R + K_C}\left[\sqrt{\frac{V}{V_o}}\, t_a - \left(\sqrt{\frac{V}{V_o}} - 1.0\right) t_s\right]$$

where

$t_s$ = mean skin temperature in degrees centigrade.
M = metabolic rate, Cal./m²/hr.
E = evaporative heat loss, Cal./m²/hr.
S = body heat debt or gain (storage), Cal.²/m²/hr.
$K_R$ = total radiation constant = $4.92 \times 10^{-8} \times$ effective radiating surface of the body in m², determined experimentally.
$K_C$ = convection constant, depending on size and posture of subjects, and determined experimentally.
mrt = mean radiant temperature in degrees centigrade.
V = velocity of air, cm/sec.
$V_o$ = standard velocity at which $K_C$ has been determined, 7.6 cm/sec.

The above equation explains how the human body receives certain climatic elements. The body wants to maintain its thermal stability—primarily a matter of regulating heat gain or loss to bring its metabolism into equilibrium:

$$M - E \pm C \pm R = 0$$

or it can be expressed:

$$M - E \pm A_R K(\Delta T_w) \pm A_C(\Delta T_A) \sqrt{V} = \Delta H$$

where:

M = observed rate of metabolism
E = rate of cooling due to perspiration actually evaporated.
C = rate of cooling due to convection.
R = radiation.
$A_n$ = the effective radiation area for a given subject in a given position.
K = radiation constant.

$\Delta T_w$ = difference between skin temperature and mean radiant temperature.
$A_c$ = the convection constant for a given subject in a given position.
$\Delta T_A$ = difference between skin temperature and air temperature.
V = velocity of air movement.
$\Delta H$ = change in mean body temperature.

## APPENDIX A-2

To determine the effect of the sun's radiation, the following equation (Prof. Yaglou's formulation) was used.

Heat loss by $R + C = S \times S_c \dfrac{(t_s - t_a)}{\dfrac{Clo}{c} + \dfrac{V.Clo}{c}}$

Heat loss by $E = E_c$

where:

E = heat loss by evaporation.
R = heat loss by radiation.
C = heat loss by convection.
S = mean body surface area of clothed man (average of clothed and unclothed area, 23 sq ft).
$S_c$ = fraction of surface areas exposed to radiation and convection (0.9).
$t_s$ = comfortable skin temperature (93° F).
$t_a$ = dry-bulb temperature.
Clo = one unit insulation of clothing.
V.Clo = air effect on clothing at 1 to 2 mph wind (0.4).
c = coefficient of 1 Clo unit − 0.88 F (Btu, sq ft).
$E_c$ = latent heat loss at low temperatures by evaporation (130 Btu per hour).

All the above values were adapted to conditions for man standing outdoors, with 1 Clo unit, at 1-2 mph wind velocity, with a metabolic rate of 430 Btu per hour.

## APPENDIX A-3

Solar energy may be divided into two types; direct, and diffuse radiation. Diffuse radiation is the sum of scattered sky radiation and reflected direct radiation and is less important as a source of heat than the direct radiation.

Total solar radiation ($I_t$) can be defined as the sum of direction radiation ($I_D$) and diffuse radiation ($I_d$) where

$I_t$ = total incident solar radiation in Btu/hr/sq ft.
$I_D = K \times I_{Dn}$, where $I_{Dn}$ designates the direct solar radiation to a receiving surface normal to the sun's rays expressed in Btu/hr/sq ft and where K = cosine of the angle of incidence Θ. Since the angle of incidence is a spatial angle Fig. A-1 it is difficult to define in some cases. Therefore, for vertical walls it is usual to substitute K as a function of the solar altitude and the surface solar azimuth, thus

$$K = \cos \beta \cos \gamma.$$

For horizontal surfaces the cosine K equals the sine of the solar altitude.

$I_d$ = the diffuse sky radiation. As was described before, this is principally a consequence of "scattering" caused by the atmosphere. A lesser part is composed of reflections from the ground and other objects. Diffuse radiation does not have directional beaming, although its intensity is different for various orientations, it strikes at all angles.

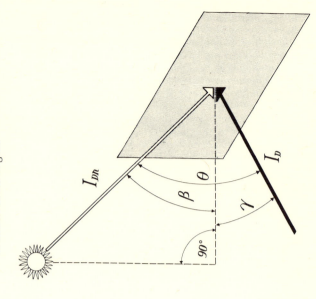

A-1. The angle of incidence for direct radiation.

Under warm and sunlit conditions heat input will take place; and during cold periods, at night, or on surfaces surrounded by low temperature objects, the heat exchange will work in reverse, resulting in heat loss from the exposed surface rather than heat gain. The basic heat-balance equation gives the rate of heat entry $(Q/A)_L$ into the outer side of the building surface. This equation can be written as

$$\left(\frac{Q}{A}\right)_L = \alpha_D I_D + \alpha_d I_d + f_{co}(t_o - t_L) + E_L R_s - E_L R_s, \text{ Btu/hr/sq ft}$$

where

α = absorbtivity (dimensionless) of weather side for incident solar radiation. Subscripts D and d refer respectively to direct and diffuse.

I = incident solar radiation, Btu/hr/sq ft. Subscripts D and d refer respectively to direct and diffuse.

$t_o$ = outside air temperature, °F.

$t_L$ = temperature of weather side of surface, °F.

$f_{co}$ = unit convective conductance of weather surface, Btu/hr/sq ft, °F.

in the computations compensation was made for it by replacing $f_{co}$ with $f_{cro}^3$, the surface conductance for radiation and convection combined, equal to 4.0.

The instantaneous rate of heat gain within the enclosure, when the interior temperature is held constant, is approximately:[4]

$$(2) \quad \frac{q}{A} = U(t_m - t_i) + \lambda U(t_e^* - t_m)$$

where

q = instantaneous rate of heat gain within the enclosure, Btu/hr/sq ft

A = area of weather surface, sq ft

U = overall coefficient of heat transfer, Btu/hr/sq ft

$t_m$ = 24-hr average sol-air temperature

$t_i$ = indoor temperature (in calculations for winter assumed to be constant at 70°, for summer at 74°F)

λ = amplitude decrement factor

$t_e^*$ = sol-air temperature at a time earlier than that for which the heat flow is being computed; where the time differential equals the time lag of the wall or roof.

The heat balance for glass surfaces may be expressed as follows:[5]

$$(3) \quad \frac{q}{A} = [\tau_D I_D + \tau_d I_d] + [\alpha_D I_D + \alpha_d I_d +$$
$$\qquad (1) \qquad\qquad\quad (2)$$
$$\epsilon_{go} R_s - \epsilon_{go} R_{go} - f_{co}(t_{go} - t_o) - S]$$
$$\quad (3) \qquad (4) \qquad\qquad (5)$$

where

$\frac{q}{A}$ = instantaneous rate of heat flow, Btu/hr/sq ft

$\tau_D, \tau_d$ = transmittance of glass for direct and diffuse solar radiation, respectively

$I_D, I_d$ = incident direct and diffuse radiation, respectively, Btu/hr/sq ft

$\alpha_D, \alpha_d$ = absorbtance of glass for direct and diffuse solar radiation, respectively

$\epsilon_{go}$ = emissivity of glass at temperature $t_{go}$

$R_s$ = low temperature radiant energy falling on glass from outdoor surroundings, Btu/hr/sq ft

$R_{go}$ = low temperature radiant energy emitted by a surface with emissivity equal to 1.0 at temperature $t_{go}$

$f_{co}$ = outdoor convective conductance, Btu/hr/sq ft, °F

$t_{go}$ = temperature of outdoor surface of glass, °F

$t_o$ = temperature of outdoor air, °F

S = rate at which glass stores energy, Btu/hr/sq ft.

In the applied computations $I_D$ and $I_d$ were calculated with the Radiation Calculator (see page 36). Values for $(\tau_D + \alpha_D)$ and $(\tau_d + \alpha_d)$ were taken from the table of the Sun Angle Calculator.[6] Equation (4) has been used in place of an evaluation of the last three terms of equation (3).

$$(4) \quad \frac{q}{A}c = U(t_o - t_i)$$

where

$\frac{q}{A}c$ = heat flow due to conduction and convection

$t_o$ = outside air temperature

$t_i$ = indoor air temperature

U = 1.13, single-glazed window

U = 0.55, double-pane window glass.

The sensible heat load due to infiltration was computed according to the following equation:

$$H_s = 0.018Q(t_o - t_i)$$

where

$H_s$ = sensible heat gain, Btu/hr

Q = volume change of air, cubic ft/hr

$t_o$ = outside temperature

$t_i$ = inside temperature.

$$(1) \quad t_e = t_o + \frac{\alpha_D I_D + \alpha_d I_d + \epsilon L(R_s - R_L)}{f_{co}}$$

where

t = sol-air temperature

α = absorbtivity (dimensionless) of weather side of wall or roof for incident solar radiation. Subscripts D and d refer respectively to direct and diffuse.

I = incident solar radiation, Btu/hr/sq ft. Subscripts refer to direct and diffuse radiation.

εL = emissivity of surface at temperature $t_L$ (also equals absorbtivity for $R_s$), dimensionless.

$R_s$ = low temperature radiant energy falling on surface from outdoor surroundings, Btu/hr/sq ft.

$R_L$ = low temperature radiant energy emitted by black body at temperature $t_L$, Btu/hr/sq ft.

$f_{co}$ = unit convective conductance of weather surface, Btu/hr/sq ft (Fahrenheit degree).

As the term $\epsilon L(R_s - R_L)$ is difficult to evaluate,

# APPENDIX B

**B-1.** Holzkirchen experiment.

**B-2.** Australian timber frame house and models of it.

**B-3.** Test model structure.

**B-4.** Test model under construction.

## APPENDIX B
## THE THERMOHELIODON

One of the attempts to develop an empirical method of measuring the temperatures in diverse structures under varying climatic conditions was the Holzkirchen experiment in Germany, where a whole group of test structures were erected. These buildings, which were alike in overall design but constructed of different materials, were "mechanically lived in" with automatic devices varying the thermostats, operating the ventilation systems and generally simulating the conditions of daily use. The thermal performance of these test units was carefully recorded by automatic devices and the results compared, so as to indicate the relative efficiency of diverse materials and construction methods.

However, the erection of groups of test houses involves a considerable amount of time and expenditure and results in a relatively inflexible arrangement. The test facilities, and thus the results, are pertinent only to the area in which they are constructed, and without extensive rebuilding can investigate only one type of design or orientation at a time.

A more flexible and less expensive method was developed at the Australian Commonwealth Experimental Building Station involving the use of model structures. The Australian researchers confirmed, after many tests comparing models with a prototype structure, that models built of the same material as their prototypes could be used to investigate thermal stresses. The models illustrated (Fig. B-2) were one-ninth scale; others were constructed at one-fourth scale. The variation between models and prototype was found to be generally not more than ∓1° F.

Although the Australian models are relatively economical and allow a considerable degree of design flexibility, they still are limited in that they are dependent upon the local climate and subject to daily and seasonal variations which impede research.

To overcome such limitations a laboratory machine, the Thermoheliodon, has been sponsored by the National Science Foundation and has been developed at the Princeton University Architectural Laboratory. This creates a simulated environment in which model buildings may be tested for thermal performance. The construction of this machine, is under the direction of the author in collaboration with Professors Alfred E. Sorenson and Dr. Robert M. Drake Jr. of Princeton University's Department of Mechanical Engineering, conducting the thermal scaling criteria.

This machine combines the flexibility of models with the ability to simulate almost any climatic conditions. At the same time the Thermoheliodon, operating under laboratory conditions, can divorce itself from the natural time cycle and accelerate the test "day," increasing the rate of experimentation. The aim of this testing is to investigate, in terms of temperature, the integrated effects of the thermal environment and to investigate the application of thermal balance principles to building design and construction.

# DESCRIPTION OF THE THERMOHELIODON

The laboratory machine consists of two major elements, the testing apparatus and the instrument panel. Its components can be described as follows (numbers refer to the illustration, Fig. B-6):

1. Experimental model constructed according to thermal scaling requirements, provided with thermistors for interior heat measurements and thermocouples to measure exterior temperatures.

2. Experimental area four feet in diameter consisting of a sunken pan filled with soil native to the locale being tested, thus insuring proper thermal relations between the model and the ground. The pan rotates to give the model any desired wind orientation.

3. Plexiglas dome which covers the experimental area to allow recirculation of the air for heating and cooling purposes.

4. Air inlet designed to direct air over the experimental area and constructed from strips of corrugated plexiglas.

5. Outlet to receive air for recirculation. Within it ten heating coils, operated in groups of two, simulate temperature fluctuations during the test "day."

6. Grills over four 300 watt incandescent lamps which simulate diffuse sky radiation by reflection from the dome's inner surface. The outer ring of the experimental surface is covered by neutral gray linoleum.

7. Latitude ring forming a track for the sun's path which may be adjusted to the desired latitude.

8. Protractor for positioning latitude.

9. Crank for tilting latitude ring.

10. Counterweight.

11. Month-bridge allowing compensation in the sun's path for seasonal variation. Adjustments are calibrated for 10 day intervals.

12. $\frac{1}{75}$ HP geared motor to drive the sun around the latitude ring. A 180° run takes 20 minutes (12 hours scaled to $\frac{1}{36}$).

13. Polished aluminum parabolic reflector four feet in diameter designed to produce parallel rays from the radiation source.

14. Incandescent 5000 watt bulb for simulating the sun's radiation.

15. Small hemispherical aluminum reflector to intercept non-parallel direct radiation and redirect energies to the parabolic reflector. An equalizing grill placed in front of the large reflector is not shown in the drawing.

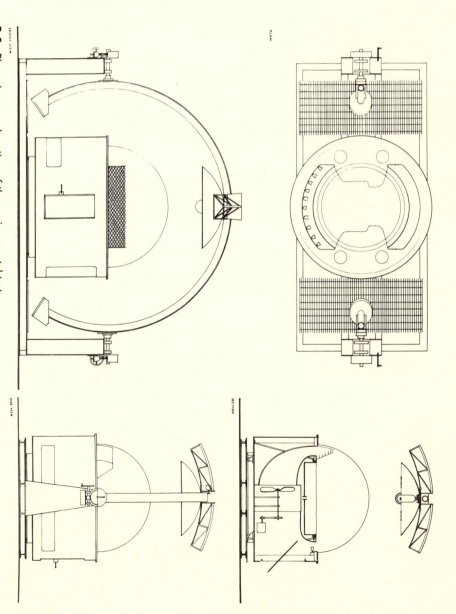

**B-5.** Plan, views, and section of the environmental testing apparatus.

16. Understructure of the testing apparatus built of steel H sections.

17. Iron cat walk.

18. Cylindrical base of the experimental area which rotates on cast iron rollers to allow for any desired sun orientation.

19. Grill to allow access to a 1 HP motor equipped with variable pulleys operating a 24 inch fan which recirculates the air through a wire-lath and asbestos-plaster throat leading to the inlet.

20. $\frac{3}{4}$ HP air-conditioning unit for temperature reduction.

21. Temperature-measuring wires enter from the cold junction and terminal strips (not shown in the drawings as they are on the other side of the base) into flexible plastic tubes which allow rotation of the base. The wiring is carried from the tubes to the instrument panel through a conduit under the floor.

22. Chalk board.

23. Compartment for instruments.

24. Ambient temperature and relative humidity recorder.

25. Clock geared to run at scaled time (one hour equals 100 seconds).

26. Two 8-point switches to control the thermo-couples.

27. Potentiometer to measure the emf developed by the thermocouples.

28. Main switch for the artificial sun's 50 amp current supply.

29. Main switch for low current supply.

30. Control switches for heaters, indirect radiation, fan, sun-motor, and for instrumentation.

31. Powerstat for varying the voltage and conse-quent intensities of the sun's radiation.

32. Variac for controlling the intensity of diffuse radiation.

33. Galvanometer to register air temperatures under the dome.

34. Automatic recording instrument adjusted to read the thermistor-relayed interior temperatures at two-second intervals.

35. Balancing panel for thermistors.

## MODEL SCALING CRITERIA

Models have been used extensively in other fields of investigation such as aerodynamics and fluid mechanics. Recently the model technique has been extended to include some architectural problems.

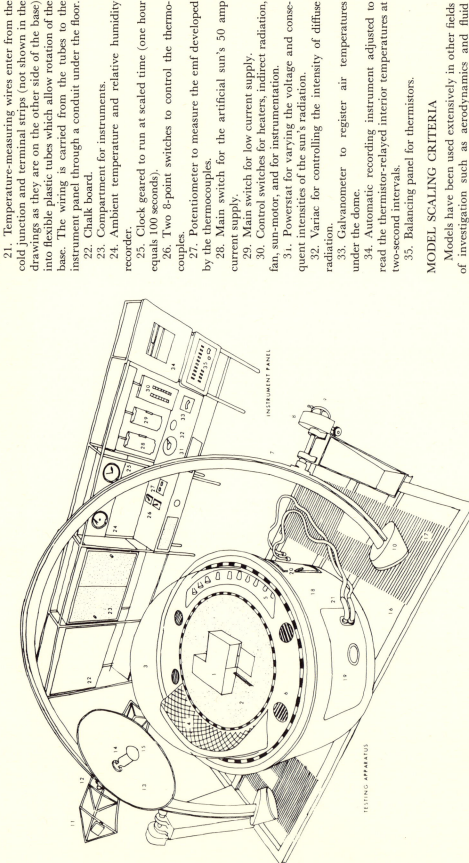

INSTRUMENT PANEL

TESTING APPARATUS

182   B-6. Explanatory drawing of the Thermoheliodon.

B-7. Plexiglass air inlet.

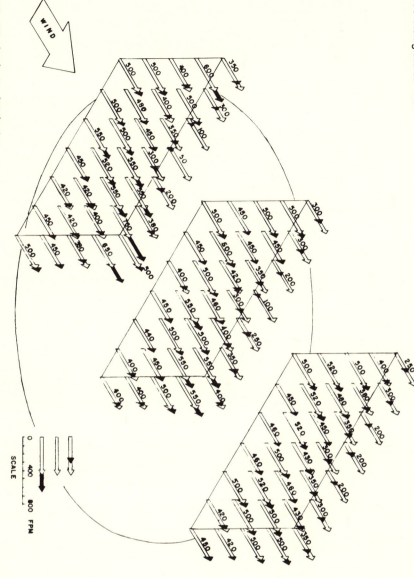

WIND

SCALE
0    400    800  FPM

B-8. Wind velocity distribution.

Air flow patterns, illumination, and structural forms have all been investigated in model form.

Model scaling for climatic conditions, however, is somewhat more complex. In order to study successfully the diurnal and annual thermal behavior of structures it is necessary to establish model systems which are geometrically, dynamically and thermally similar to their prototypes. Some problems encountered in the scaling method are presently under testing and investigation.

Geometrical similarity is the easiest task to accomplish, since complications occur only with extreme reduction in scale and these can be avoided by working with models of a reasonable size.

Dynamic similarity presents some difficulties, as in order to establish a direct correspondence between heat convection on the exposed surfaces of the model and the prototype it would be required that the Reynolds number should be the same for both. As high velocities are undesirable because of the fragility of the models, and a change of density by pressurization is impractical in the present system, it has been accepted, as a compromise, to reproduce Reynolds numbers large enough so that the same bluff-body pattern is achieved in the model and prototype without full similarity in the boundary layer thickness distribution.

The similarity conditions for the conduction of heat in solids are known for various convection and radiation boundary conditions and can be described for simple systems in terms of the dimensionless parameters, the Fourier and Biot modulus, in conjunction with a geometrical length ratio. In general the thermal property values and the heat transfer coefficients are considered to be constants. In the present case the effective heat-transfer coefficient comprises parallel effects of radiation and convection and furthermore its magnitude changes with time because of the variation in the radiant energy component. There is also some dependence of the heat-transfer coefficient on temperature because of the radiation effect. In addition to the changes in the transfer coefficient, the thermal properties of the model and prototype materials vary with temperature. Adjustments have to be made for the above to satisfy similarity requirements.

Thermal similarity presents in itself the most involved problem as it depends on the previous similarities; any deviation from geometrical or dy-

183

**B-9.** View of the Thermoheliodon and instrument panel.

**B-10.** Latitude adjuster, month bridge, and motor for daily "sun" movement.

namical similarity will be felt in the thermal case. In addition it is dependent on the grain width and on the unequal heat flow in non-isotropic materials, as in the case of wood and most fabricated and laminated building materials.

The similarity conditions are approached analytically and studied experimentally by comparing materials and construction elements exposed to atmospheric convection and solar radiation to scaled model samples in the Thermoheliodon. Likewise data from full-scale structures are compared with scaled model building experiments.

## THE SIMULATION OF CLIMATIC ELEMENTS

To simulate natural air movement in the Thermoheliodon a laminar air flow was desired, covering the four-foot-wide experimental area to a height of 12 inches. Such a flow pattern is not a natural condition since air speeds are slightly higher away from the ground surface. It is however a convenient abstraction for controlling the factors involved in this experimentation. The machine is capable of operating at air speeds ranging from 150 fpm to 1000 fpm, although most tests will be run at 440 fpm (5 mph) for ease in calculations.

Certain other prior considerations affected the achievement of this condition. The necessity for heating the air decreed that it must be recirculated through a short path for the most efficient use of the heating coils. Such recirculation involves a number of sharp turns in the airflow, as opposed to the long, straight path necessary to attain ideal wind patterns. It also was necessary to construct a low and transparent air inlet so as to block out a minimum of radiation. As a result certain distortions were introduced into the system which have been reduced to an acceptable variation by placing balancing layers of screening in the throat of the air inlet. The final overall distribution pattern is illustrated in Fig. B-8.

The air temperature levels within the Thermoheliodon generally range from room temperature to 150° F. These levels are desirable because temperatures above room temperature force the model to release outgoing radiation to the cooler dome surface in simulation of the radiation flow from actual buildings to the cooler sky above them, while 150° is the maximum safe temperature for the plexiglas dome. The recirculating air is heated by a bank of 10 heating coils operated in pairs and cooled by a small refrigeration unit.

In these experiments absolute humidity levels are disregarded as having a relatively small role in thermal interaction. However, relative humidity fluctuation occurs automatically with temperature variations.

To simulate radiation conditions is was first necessary to reconstruct the movements of the sun path, since the sun's radiation is directional. The "latitude ring," suspended on horizontal axes can be adjusted to any desired geographical location. Compensation for seasonal variation can be made by positioning the lamp on a "month bridge" which is constructed to allow the necessary 46° 54" variation between winter and summer solstice, and is calibrated by 10 day intervals. The bridge and lamp are driven around the circular latitude ring by means of a $\frac{7}{5}$ HP motor, to reproduce daily sun movement.

The actual radiation source for the artificial sun is a 5000W General Electric bulb backed by a chemically brightened aluminum parabolic reflector four feet in diameter. A second, smaller reflector redirects the non-parallel direct rays from the lamp, to the reflector, while a semi-transparent metal grill has been placed over the reflector to equalize the distribution of energy (Fig. B-9). This arrangement produces a maximum of 340 Btu/hr/ft² with distribution over the surface deviating $\mp15\%$. Since the filament is not a point source and the relatively rough reflector produces some diffusion, the direct-radiation rays are not quite parallel; however, they can be considered so for experimental purposes.

The spectral distribution of the lamp's energy is concentrated in somewhat longer wave lengths than the sun's, but tests have shown that the minor deviations involved will not be significant in these experiments. Variations in the sun's intensity are produced by using a Powerstat to control the current reaching the lamp.

The less important factors of diffuse radiation and long-wave radiation exchange have also been taken into account. The former is produced by four 300 watt bulbs reflected and diffused by the dome surface. The latter exchange between buildings and their surroundings is induced by keeping a temperature differential between the model and the surrounding dome surface.

## INSTRUMENTATION

Exterior temperature measurements are taken by thermocouples, interior measurements by thermistors. The thermocouples are 26 ga. copper constantan accurate to $\mp1\frac{1}{4}°$ F from 75° to 200° and are read manually on a Potentiometer. Thermistors have been selected to measure the inside temperatures because of the smaller differentials. The reactions of these thermistors, which are accurate to more than $\frac{1}{100}$ of a degree, are registered on an automatic recording machine which measures 16 points at a rate of one every two seconds.

A clock registering the accelerated, scaled time is coordinated with the movements of the artificial sun to facilitate regular manual measurements and to dictate the variations in radiation intensity controlled by the powerstat.

The Thermoheliodon research project is currently under development. Presently its degree of accuracy is being tested by two complementary methods: (a) comparison of material samples and construction units observed under natural conditions with similar samples at model scale; (b) measurements of existing whole-building prototypes with scaled model structures under simulated conditions.

# BIBLIOGRAPHY AND REFERENCES

## PREFACE

1. Olgyay, Victor, "The Temperate House," *Architectural Forum*, Vol. 94, March 1951, pp. 179–94.
2. Olgyay, Victor, "Bioclimatic Approach to Architecture," *BRAB Conference Report No. 5*, National Research Council, Washington, D.C., 1953, pp. 13–23.
3. Olgyay, Aladar, "Solar Control and Orientation to Meet Bioclimatic Requirements," *ibid*, pp. 38–46.
4. Olgyay, Victor and Olgyay, Aladar and Associates, "Application of Climatic Data to House Design," U.S. Housing and Home Finance Agency, Washington, D.C., 1953.
5. Olgyay, Victor and Olgyay, Aladar, "The Theory of Sol-Air Orientation," *Architectural Forum*, March 1954, pp. 133–137.
6. Olgyay, Victor and Olgyay, Aladar, "Environment and Building Shape," *Architectural Forum*, August 1954, pp. 104–108.
7. Olgyay, and Olgyay, Aladar, *Solar Control and Shading Devices*, Princeton University Press, Princeton, N.J., 1957.
8. Fitch, James M., *American Building: The Forces That Shape It*, Houghton-Mifflin Company, Boston, 1948.
9. Egli, Ernst, *Climate and Town Districts. Consequences and Demands*, Verlag Fur Architectur-Erlenbach, Zurich, 1951.

## CHAPTER I

1. Huntington, Ellsworth, *The Human Habitat*, D. Van Nostrand Company, Princeton, N.J., 1927, Chapter I.
2. Markham, S. F., *Climate and the Energy of Nations*, Oxford University Press, London, 1947.
3. Santos, Eurico, *Passaros do Brasil*, F. Brigiet and Cia., Rio de Janeiro, 1940.
4. Steiner, A., Neuere Ergebn. U.D. Sozialen Wärmehaushalt D. Einheim. Hautflügler. Die Naturwissenschaften, 1930.
5. Hesse, R., Tiergeographie Auf Okolog, Grundlage, G. Fischer, Jena, 1924.
6. Huntington, Ellsworth, *Principles of Human Geography*, 6th edition, John Wiley and Sons, New York, 1951, pp. 404–408.
7. Huxley, Julian, *Man in the Modern World*, Mentor Books, The New American Library, New York, pp. 61–73.
8. Thorndike, Lynn, *The Sphere of Sacrobosco and its Commentators*, The University of Chicago Press, Chicago, 1949, Chapter 11, pp. 233–234.
9. *ibid.* p. 129.
10. Vitruvius, *De Architectura*, Book VI, Chapter 1, Translated by Frank Granger (Ariba). 1934.
11. Köppen-Geiger, *Handbuch der Klimatologie*, Volume I, Gebruder Borntraeger, Berlin, 1936.

12. Trewartha, Glenn T., *An Introduction to Weather and Climate*, McGraw-Hill Book Company, New York, 1943.
13. Dollfus, Jean, *Les Aspects de L'architecture Populaire dans le Monde*, Albert Morancé, Paris, 1954.
14. *ibid.*
15. Smith, E. Baldwin, *The Dome*, Princeton University Press, Princeton, 1950.
16. Gropius, Walter, *Scope of Total Architecture*, Harper and Brothers, New York, 1955.
17. Neutra, Richard, *Survival Through Design*, Oxford University Press, New York, 1954.
18. "Building an Entire New City in India, Chandigarh," *Architectural Forum*, September 1953, pp. 142–149.

## CHAPTER II

1. Huntington, Ellsworth, *Principles of Human Geography*, 6th edition, John Wiley and Sons, New York, 1951, pp. 399–404.
2. *ibid.*
3. Fitch, James M., *American Building, The Forces That Shape It*, Houghton Mifflin Company, Boston, 1948.
4. Winslow, C. E. A. and Herrington, L. P., *Temperature and Human Life*, Princeton University Press, Princeton, N.J., 1949.
5. Bedford, T., *Environmental Warmth and Human Comfort*, British Journal of Applied Physics, February 1950, pp. 33–38.
6. Lee, Douglas H. K., *Physiological Objectives in Hot Weather Housing*, U.S. Housing and Home Finance Agency, Washington, D.C., 1953, p. 2.
7. Markham, S. F., *Climate and the Energy of Nations*, Oxford University Press, London, 1947.
8. Herrington, L. P., *Human Factors in Planning for Climate Control*, Building Research Advisory Board, Washington, D.C., 1950, pp. 85–91 (Research Conference Report No. 1).
9. Bedford, T., *op. cit.*
10. Klima, Wetter, *Mensch Symposium*, Quelle and Meyer, Leipzig, 1938.
11. Markham, S. F., *op. cit.*
12. Brooks, Charles Ernest P., *Climate in Everyday Life*, Ernest Bemm, London, 1950.
13. Drysdale, J. W., *Climate and House Design; Physiological Considerations*, Sydney, Australia Commonwealth Experimental Building Station, 1948, 15 pp. (Duplicated Document No. 25).
    Drysdale, J. W., *Climate and Design of Buildings; Physiological Study No. 2*, Sydney, Australia, Commonwealth Experimental Building Station, 1950, 21 pp. (Duplicated Document No. 32).

14. Houghton, F. C. and Yaglou, C. P., "Cooling Effect on Human Beings Produced by Various Air Velocities," American Society of Heating and Ventilation Engineers, *Transactions*, Vol. 30, 1924, p. 193 (ASHVE Research Report No. 691).

Houghton, F. C. and Yaglou, C. P., "Determination of the Comfort Zone," American Society of Heating and Ventilation Engineers, *Transactions*, Vol. 29, 1923, p. 361 (ASHVE Research Report No. 673).

Yaglou, C. P. and Miller, W. E., "Effective Temperature with Clothing," American Society of Heating and Ventilation Engineers, *Transactions*, Vol. 31, 1925, p. 89 (ASHVE Research Report No. 717).

15. Rowley, Jordan, and Snyder, *Comfort Reactions of Workers*, Heating, Piping and Air Conditioning, ASHVE Journal Section p. 113, June 1947.

16. Yaglou, C. P., "Method for Improving the Effective Temperature Index, *Heating Piping and Air Conditioning*, ASHVE Journal Section, p. 131, September 1947.

17. Brooks, C. E. P., *op. cit.*

18. Brunt, Dr. David, Professor of Meterology, Imperial College of Science and Technology, London.

19. Committee on Atmospheric Comfort, *Thermal Standards in Industry*, American Journal of Public Health Yearbook II, Vol. 40, May 1950.

20. *ibid.*

21. *Heating, Ventilating, Air Conditioning Guide*, 29th edition, New York, American Society of Heating and Ventilation Engineers, 1951, pp. 117–316.

22. Emerick, R. H., "Comfort Factors Affecting Cooling Design," *Progressive Architecture*, December 1951, pp. 97–99.

23. Siple, Paul, Climatologist and Military Geographer, General Staff, Department of the Army.

24. Carrier Psychrometric Chart, American Society of Heating and Ventilating Engineers Guide, New York, 1946.

25. Yaglou, C. P., "Radiant Cooling—Investigated in Texts at Harvard and Discussed at New York Meeting by Dr. Yaglou." *Heating and Ventilating*, pp. 102, 104, May 1947.

CHAPTER III

1. *House Beautiful*, monthly articles, October 1949 through January 1951.

2. *Regional Climate Analysis and Design Data*, Bulletin of the American Institute of Architects, edited from November 1949 on.

3. Scaëtta, M. H., "Terminologique, Biclimatique, et Microclimatique," *Meteorologie*, July 1935, pp. 342–347.

CHAPTER IV

* For a fuller explanation of the first two factors, see *Solar Control and Shading Devices*, Chap. XI.

1. Geiger, Rudolph, *The Climate Near the Ground*, Harvard University Press, Cambridge, 1950.

2. *ibid.*, pp. 2–4.

3. Data principally from *Handbook of Chemistry and Physics*, Chemical Rubber Publishing Company, Cleveland, 1949; and *Smithsonian Meteorological Tables*, Smithsonian Institution, 1951, pp. 442–443.

4. Data from U.S. Quartermaster Corps observations.

5. Geiger, *op. cit.*

6. Geiger, *op. cit.*

7. Lauscher, F., *Bericht ü. Mess. d. nächtl. Ausstrahlung auf d. Stolzalpe*, Meteorologische Zeitschrift 45, 1928, pp. 371–375.

8. Data from U.S. Quartermaster Corps observations.

9. Moon, P., "Proposed Standard Solar Radiation Curves for Engineering Use," *Journal of the Franklin Institute*, Vol. 230, No. 5, November 1940, pp. 4–7.

10. Malone, Thomas and Friedman, D., *Solar Radiation and Heat Transmission in Dwellings*, Research Report, Massachusetts Institute of Technology, Cambridge, 1952.

11. *ibid.*

12. American Society of Heating and Ventilating Engineers, *Heating, Ventilating, Air Conditioning Guide*, Vol. 29, 1951, p. 267.

13. "Orientation of Buildings," *Journal of the R.I.B.A.*, Vol. 40, 1933.

14. Neubauer, Dr. L. W., *The Solaranger*, University of California, Davis, California, 1949.

15. Phillips, R. O., "Sunshine and Shade in Australia," Sydney, Australia Commonwealth Experimental Building Station, 1948 (Duplicated Document No. 23).

16. Libby-Owens-Ford Glass Company, "Solarometer," Toledo, Ohio.

17. Lee, D. H. K., *Physiological Objectives in Hot Weather Housing*, U.S. Housing and Home Finance Agency, Washington, D.C., 1953, pp. 71–72.

18. Kutner, L., *Zentralblatt der Bauverwaltung*, 1930, Vol. 50, p. 281.

19. Grobler, J., *Die Wohnung*, Vol. 6, 1931, p. 95.

20. Beckett, H. E., "Orientation of Buildings," *Journal of the R.I.B.A.*, Vol. 40, 1933, p. 62.

21. Pleijel, Gunnar, "The Little Sundial," Orengrundsgatan 10, VI, Stockholm, Sweden.

22. Olgyay, Aladar, *Shading and Insolation Measurement of Models*, University of Texas Press, Austin, 1953.

23. Hand, Irving F., "Charts to Obtain Solar Altitudes and Azimuths," *Heating and Ventilating*, October 1948, pp. 86–88.

24. Libby-Owens-Ford Glass Company, "Sun Angle Calculator," Toledo, Ohio.

25. Moon, *op. cit.*

26. American Society of Heating and Ventilating Engineers, *op. cit.*

27. Yaglou, C. P., "Radiant Cooling, Investigated at Harvard," *Heating and Ventilating*, May 1947, pp. 102–104.

28. Geiger, R., *op. cit.*

29. United States Quartermaster Corps, *The Climate of the Soldier*, Part IV, Washington, D.C., January 1949 (Environmental Protection Series No. 124).

30. Mackey, C. O. and Watson, E. B., "Summer Weather Data and Sol-Air Temperature," *ASHVE Transactions*, Vol. 51, 1945, p. 75.

CHAPTER V

1. Landsberg, Helmut, "Microclimatic Research in Relation to Building Construction," *Architectural Forum*, March 1947, pp. 114–119.

2. Geiger, Rudolph, *The Climate Near the Ground*, Harvard University Press, Cambridge, 1950.

3. Landsberg, Helmut, "Climate and Planning of Settlements," Convention Symposium I, *Urban and Regional Planning*, The American Institute of Architects, Washington, D.C., May 1950; Landsberg, Helmut, "Microclimatic Research in Relation to Building Construction," *BRAB Conference Report No. 1, Weather and the Building Industry*, Washington, D.C., January 1950.

4. Geiger *op. cit.*, p. 195.

5. Landsberg, *op. cit.* (3).

6. Malone, Thomas and Friedman, D., "Solar Radiation and Heat Transmission in Dwellings," Research Report, Massachusetts Institute of Technology, Cambridge, 1952.

7. Geiger, *op. cit.*

8. Landsberg, *op. cit.* (3):

9. *ibid.*

10. *ibid.*

11. *ibid.*

CHAPTER VI

1. Vitruvius, *On Architecture*, translated by Frank Granger, William Heineman, London, 1931.

2. Schanderl, H. D., *D. derzeitig Stand d. Kopasspflanzenprobleme*, Bioklimatische Beiblätter der Meteorologischen, Zeitschrift 4, 1937, pp. 49–54.

3. Scanmoni, A., "Ü Eintritt und Verlauf d. männlichen Kieternblüte," *Zeitschrift für Forst-und Jagdwesen*, 70, 1938, pp. 289–315.

4. Bardet, Gaston, "Le Factor Soleil en Urbanisme," *Techniques et Architecture*, No. 7–8, July-August 1945, pp. 202–206.

5. Rey, A. Pidoux, J., and Bardet, G., "La Ville Salubre de L'avenir: Principes scientifiques d'Orientation des Voies Publiques et des Habitations," in *Congrès International et Exposition Comparée Des Villes*, 1st edition, Rapport, Ghent, 1913, pp. 217–224.

6. Marboutin, Felix, "L'Actionometre et l'Orientation des Rues et des Façades," *La Technique Sanitaire et Municipale*, March, pp. 60–67; April, pp. 83–90; May, pp. 98–105; June, pp. 126–131, 1931.

7. Bardet, *op cit.*

8. Lebreton, Jean, *La Cité Naturelle*, P. Dupont, Paris, 1945, p. 50.

9. Vinaccia, Gaetano, *Per la Citta di Domani*, Fratelli Palombi, Rome, 1943.
10. Hilberseimer, Ludwig, *The New City: Principles of Planning*, P. Theobald, Chicago, 1944.
11. Wright, Henry N., *Solar Radiation as Related to Summer Cooling and Winter Heating in Residences*, John B. Pierce Foundation Report, New York, 1936.
12. Aronin, Jeffreye, *Climate and Architecture*, Reinhold, New York, 1953, pp. 94–99.
13. The American Public Health Association, Committee on the Hygiene of Housing, "Planning the Neighborhood," Public Administration Clearing House, Chicago, 1948 (*Standards for Healthful Housing, Vol. I*).

## CHAPTER VII

1. Libbey-Owens-Ford Glass Company, "Sun Angle Calculator," Toledo, Ohio.
2. "Shade Factors," American Society of Heating, Refrigerating and Air-Conditioning Engineers, *Heating Ventilating Air Conditioning Guide*, 1960
3. G. V. Parmelee and D. J. Vild: ASHVE Research Report No. 1485, Design data for slat type sun shades for use in load estimating, *ASHVE Transactions*, Vol. 59.
4. C. Strock: *Handbook of Air Conditioning, Heating and Ventilating*, 1959.
5. Ossisic and Schutrum, "Solar Heat Gain Factors for Windows and Draperies," *ASHRAE Journal*, Vol. 1. 1959.
6. Tonne, Friedrich, "Besonnung und Tageslicht," *Gesundheits-Ingenieur*, 1951.
7. Pleijel, Gunnar, Royal Institute of Technology, Stockholm, Sweden.

## CHAPTER VIII

1. Thompson, D'arcy W., *On Growth and Form*, Cambridge University Press, Cambridge, England, 1952.
2. American Society of Heating and Ventilating Engineers, *Heating, Ventilating, Air Conditioning Guide*, New York, 1951, p. 275.
3. Everetts, John, Jr., "Analysis and Influence of Climatology Upon Air Conditioning Design," BRAB Conference Report No. 1, Washington, D.C., 1950, pp. 123–131.

## CHAPTER IX

1. De La Rue, E. Aubert, *Man and the Winds*, Philosophical Library, New York, 1955, Chapter I.

2. N. de G. Davies, *The Town House in Ancient Egypt*, Metropolitan Museum, Series I (1928–29), p. 10.
3. Wiener, S. Imanuel, "Solar Orientation: Application of Local Wind Factors," *Progressive Architecture*, February 1955, pp. 114–118.
4. Bates, Carlos G., "The Windbreak as a Farm Asset," *Farmers' Bulletin* No. 1405, U.S. Department of Agriculture, Washington, D.C., 1944.
5. Woodruff, N. P. and Zingg, A. W., *Wind-Tunnel Studies of Fundamental Problems Related to Windbreaks*, U.S. Department of Agriculture, Washington, D.C., 1952.
6. Woodruff, N. P., "Shelterbelt and Surface Barrier Effects," Agricultural Experiment Station, Manhattan, Kansas, Technical Bulletin 77, December 1954.
7. *ibid*, p. 22.
8. Stoeckeler, Joseph H., and Williams, A. Ross, "Windbreaks and Shelterbelts," *Yearbook of Agriculture, 1949*, Washington, D.C., pp. 191–199.
9. Munns, E. N. and Stoeckeler, J. H., "How Are the Great Plains Shelterbelts?" *Journal of Forestry*, April 1946, Vol. 44, No. 4.
10. Bates, *op. cit.*
11. Stoeckeler and Williams, *op. cit.*
12. White, Robert F., "Effects of Landscape Development on the Natural Ventilation of Buildings and Their Adjacent Area," Texas Engineering Experiment Station, *Research Report 45*, March 1945.
13. British Building Research Station Data.
14. Holleman, T. R., "Air Flow Through Conventional Window Openings," Texas Engineering Experiment Station, *Research Report 45*, March 1954.
15. British Building Research Station Data.
16. Rogers, S. Tyler, "Design of Insulated Buildings for Various Climates," *Architectural Record Book*, 1951.
17. Caudill, W. W., Crites, S. E., and Smith, E. G., "Some General Considerations in Natural Ventilation of Buildings," *Research Report 22*, 1951.
   Smith, E. G., Reed, B. H., and Hodges, H. D., "The Measurement of Low Air Speeds by the Use of Titanium Tetrachloride," *Research Report 25*, 1951.
   Smith, E. G., "The Feasibility of Using Models for Predetermining Natural Ventilation," *Research Report 26*, 1951.
   McCutchan, G. and Caudill, W. W., "An Experiment in Architectural Education Through Research," *Research Report 32*, 1952.
   Caudill, W. W. and Reed, B. H., "Geometry of Classrooms as Related to Natural Lighting and Natural Ventilation," *Research Report 36*, 1952.
   All reports in the series of the Texas Engineering Experiment Station, College Station, Texas.

* The material in this chapter was developed in cooperation with Aladar Olgyay, and is condensed from *Solar Control and Shading Devices*, Princeton University Press, 1957.

## CHAPTER X

1. American Society of Heating and Ventilating Engineers, *Heating, Ventilating, Air Conditioning Guide 1951*, Vol. 29, New York, p. 272.
2. Nathan, H. A. G., "Moisture Content and Heat Insulating Properties of Building Materials," (Translation of Swedish article by G. Hobohm), National Research Council of Canada, TT1–95, 1949.
3. Rogers, S. Tyler, "Design of Insulated Buildings for Various Climates," *Architectural Record Book*, New York, 1951, p. 42.
4. Lobry de Bruyn, C. A., "Weathering and Durability of Building Materials," Building Research Congress, London, 1951, Division 2, p. 22.
5. Holmes, B. M., "Deterioration Problems of Materials and Structures in Hot Climates," *BRAB Conference Report No. 5*, Building Research Advisory Board, Washington, D.C., 1952, pp. 96–107.
6. *ibid.*
7. Leroux, M. Robert, *La Climatologie de l'Habitation*, Institut Technique de Batiment et des Travaux publics, Circulaire Serie B, No. 7, 1946.
8. Drysdale, J. W., "Heat Capacity and the Distribution of Mass in the Design of Buildings for Hot Climates," *BRAB Conference Report No. 5*, Building Research Advisory Board, Washington, D.C., 1952, pp. 121–125.
9. Lee, H. K, *Physiological Objectives in Hot Weather Housing*, U.S. Housing and Home Finance Agency, Washington, D.C. 1953, p. 62.
10. *Heating, Ventilating, Air Conditioning Guide 1951.*
11. *ibid.*

## CHAPTER XI

1. American Society of Heating and Ventilating Engineers, New York, *Heating, Ventilating, Air Conditioning Guide 1951*, Vol. 29, p. 272.
2. *ibid*, p. 272.
3. *ibid*, p. 275.
4. *ibid*, p. 275.
5. *ibid*, p. 287.
6. Libbey-Owens-Ford Glass Company, "Sun Angle Calculator," Toledo, Ohio.

## CHAPTER XII

1. "Regional Climate Analysis and Design Data," *Bulletin of the American Institute of Architects*, Edited from November 1949 on.
2. Lee, Douglas H. K., *Physiological Objectives in Hot Weather Housing*, U.S. Housing and Home Finance Agency, Washington, D.C., 1953, p. 2.

# INDEX

## PICTURE CREDITS

I.  1. "Switzerland Builds," G. E. Kidder Smith.
2. After S. Eurico, "Passaros do Brasil."
3. Gerard F. Hill, "Termites from the Australian Region." 6. and 7. Courtesy of the Pierpont Morgan Library. 12, 13, 14, and 15. Courtesy of the American Museum of Natural History. 17. After J. Dollfus. 18. L'Architecture d'Aourdhui. 19. E. A. Gutkind, "Our World from the Air." 20. and 21. Architectural Forum. 22, 23, and 24. E. A. Gutkind, "Our World from the Air." 25. Architectural Review. 26. House and Home. 27. After M. Milankovitch, "Matematische Kilmalehre." 28. After B. Haurwitz and J. M. Austin, "Climatology."

II.  33. E. Huntington, "The Human Habitat." 39. Courtesy of "Heating, Ventilating, Airconditioning Guide."

III.  47. and 48. Courtesy of the American Institute of Architects, Bulletin, Nov. 1949.

IV.  60., 61., and 62. Courtesy of R. Geiger, "The Climate near the Ground." 63. U. S. Quartermaster Corp. 64. and 65. Courtesy of the Libbey-Owens-Ford Glass Co. 76. After "The Climate and the Soldier," U. S. Quartermaster Corp.

V.  82, 83., and 84. R. Geiger, "The Climate near the Ground." 85. and 101. After H. Landsberg. 97., 98., and 99. R. Geiger, in Köppen-Geiger "Handbuch der Klimatologie."

VI.  104. After A. Scamoni. 105. S. A. Stubbs, "Bird's-Eye View of the Pueblos."

VII.  150., 151., and 152. By permission, Educational Facilities Laboratories. 160. Ralph Steiner. 161. F. Tonne, "Besonnungs-Schreiber." 162. G. Pleijel. 167, 168., and 169. From Curtain Wall Research Project, Study No. 6, School of Architecture, Princeton University.

VIII.  171. From D. W. Thomson, "On Growth and Form." 172. After W. Troll, "Vergleichende Morphologie der hoherer Pflanzen."

IX.  180., 181., and 182. E. Egli, "Climate and Town Districts," B. Smith, "The Egyptian House," and T. Rogers, "Design of Insulated Buildings." 185.-189. I. S. Wiener, "Solar Orientation," in Progressive Architecture. 190. N. P. Woodruff and A. W. Zingg, "Wind-Tunnel Studies of Windbreakers." 191. C. G. Bates, "The Windbreak as a Farm Asset." 192. J. H. Stoeckeler and R. A. Williams, "Windbreaks and Shelterbelts." 200. R. F. White, "Effects of Landscape Development on Natural Ventilation of Buildings."

X.  230. After: D. H. K. Lee, "Physiological Objectives in Hot Weather Housing."

XII.  311., 312., 313., 319., 320., 322., 326., 327., 328., 329., 333., 334., 335., and 336. Elizabeth Menzies.
B-2. Australian Commonwealth Experimental Building Station.